DATE DUE

Presidential Upsets

Presidential Upsets

Dark Horses, Underdogs, and Corrupt Bargains

Douglas Clouatre

 PRAEGER

AN IMPRINT OF ABC-CLIO, LLC
Santa Barbara, California • Denver, Colorado • Oxford, England

Library of Congress Cataloging-in-Publication Data

Clouatre, Doug.
    Presidential upsets : dark horses, underdogs, and corrupt bargains / Douglas Clouatre.
        p. cm.
    Includes bibliographical references and index.
    ISBN 978-1-4408-2866-9 (hardcopy : alk. paper) — ISBN 978-1-4408-2867-6 (ebook)   1. Presidents—United States—Election—History.   I. Title.
    JK524.C55   2012
    324.973—dc23   2012038152

ISBN: 978-1-4408-2866-9
EISBN: 978-1-4408-2867-6

17   16   15   14   13   1   2   3   4   5

This book is also available on the World Wide Web as an eBook.
Visit www.abc-clio.com for details.

Praeger
An Imprint of ABC-CLIO, LLC

ABC-CLIO, LLC
130 Cremona Drive, P.O. Box 1911
Santa Barbara, California 93116-1911

This book is printed on acid-free paper ∞

Manufactured in the United States of America

Contents

Preface

In the midst of a presidential election, hopes and reality tend to clash. Supporters of the major party candidates enter the election completely convinced of their candidate's ultimate victory. Reality has the effect of destroying those hopes in the worst possible terms either through a crushing loss that was apparent to all but those most dreamy-eyed or in a sudden and unexpected defeat that leaves supporters wondering how their candidate lost.

A presidential upset is the latter of these. In a presidential upset, a candidate's supporters believe with good cause that their candidate will win with opinion polls and campaign events appearing to show that victory in November is certain. When Election Day comes those beliefs are shattered as the candidate sees his inevitable victory become a historic defeat. The result is such a surprise that the election becomes part of popular lore whether it is Harry Truman's stunning victory in 1948 or John Kennedy's tainted victory in 1960 with subsequent elections compared with these.

Supporters of the defeated candidate search for an explanation, attributing the loss to the candidate's personality, the candidate's campaign, to events beyond the candidate's control, or even to corruption in the election process. Frequently upsets are misinterpreted by the candidates and their supporters who then focus on the next presidential election to prove their analysis is correct only to see their party lose once again.

This book will examine 11 presidential elections generally recognized as upsets. In addition to describing the upsets the book will explain why the upset occurred and rank it among the other presidential upsets. There will be a focus on the issues, the candidates, the political era, the mistakes made by the expected winner, and the critical decisions made by the winner which led to the upset.

Constructing a book requires more than one hand or mind. Among those who helped by reading, editing, and suggesting improvements are Nicholas Thayer and Joshua Carson who provided important comments and guidance in improvement. A special thanks to Misty McClain who provided essential help in editing and suggesting improvements. Finally, there are Grogo and Alfreida Leedham whose antics always help in regaining perspective.

1

Anatomy of a Presidential Upset

Presidential election upsets are the stuff of American lore when a hard-scrabble underdog battles the favored candidate and sweeps to victory on the votes of ordinary people who admire his feistiness. There are scenes of triumph, Truman holding above his head a copy of the Chicago Tribune prematurely announcing his defeat, and stories of overconfident candidates such as Charles Evans Hughes going to bed on election night in 1916 certain of victory only to awake the next morning to unexpected defeat. Controversies also cloud upsets: the corrupt bargain of 1824 denying Andrew Jackson the presidency, southern carpetbaggers rejecting Democrat votes during the 1876 election, or the open corruption of the dead voting for John Kennedy in Chicago in 1960. The 2000 election offered its own infuriating and humorous debate over dimpled, pregnant, and swinging chads as 1940s technology was used to determine the first 21st-century president. There were also Aaron Burr's treachery, Henry Clay's tragedy, and Richard Nixon's sweaty upper lip—all part of presidential upsets.

Separating presidential election upsets from other presidential elections offers certain challenges as does ranking the upsets. An upset election is by definition an unexpected event in which a candidate who was expected to win loses instead. That expectation is based on predictions by both political professionals and laymen. Understanding the art and science of presidential election predictions allows one to rank presidential upsets and to know which election would be considered the greatest upset.

Professional election predictions may have begun with Louis Bean, an obscure economist at the U.S. Department of Agriculture, who used his statistical knowledge to create a political measure known as the

Bean Poll. Using his data, Bean predicted Truman would win in 1948—his prediction earning him fame as few political observers expected the president to be reelected.[1] Bean authored subsequent books on his 1948 prediction and predictions about other elections.[2]

Bean's basic measures were expanded as political scientists developed new and more complex measures of political behavior while integrating economic data that might have an effect on presidential voting. Some were basic measures, integrating fewer than a dozen economic and political variables into a formula that would predict electoral vote counts based on past elections.[3] Other measures integrated dozens of economic statistics, weighting each according to their influence on voter behavior.[4]

By the early 1990s, several models had been developed for predicting presidential election outcomes. These models reflected the emphasis on statistics among political scientists as they struggled to reduce campaign rhetoric, partisanship, and voter decision making into numerical measures. Combined with these were more solid economic measures of inflation, unemployment, GDP growth, and public approval ratings. The calculations and formulas are impressive and at times incomprehensible with economic statistics regressed against past total electoral votes to arrive at a prediction.

The first real test of the models came in 1992, and political scientists were soon embarrassed after they predicted a fairly easy reelection victory for George H. W. Bush. The election of Bill Clinton sent analysts back to the drawing board as they searched for variables not in their model but relevant to Bush's defeat. Looking back on 1992, they found two important differences, the primary challenge of Bush by Pat Buchanan and the third-party candidacy of Ross Perot, both of which were not included in the models but had a negative impact on Bush's electoral chances.[5]

With mathematical models limited to factors that were statistically measurable, other models have been developed, moving beyond complex equations to include broader measures of political trends. Allen Lichtman, a professor at American University, offered 13 keys to predicting a presidential election. Lichtman utilized not only quantitative data including long-term and short-term economic growth along with losses for the party in power during midterm election but also more qualitative measures that could not be broken down into statistics. Lichtman integrated factors from the 1992 election including an independent candidacy and a primary challenge to an incumbent.

Other factors ranged from international policies—an unusual variable as few presidential elections are decided on the basis of foreign policy—dramatic changes in social policy, social unrest, and the charisma displayed by each candidate.[6]

According to Lichtman, each of these factors played an equal role in predicting a winner. Yet, Lichtman's 13 variables can be repetitive and at times irrelevant for some elections, while other factors are relevant to only one or two elections. Election upset analysis is also affected by modern memory, as the most recent elections are deemed upsets because of the observers' proximity to the event.

The best example of this is Harry Truman's unexpected 1948 victory over Thomas Dewey, considered the modern template for presidential upsets. Yet, the reelection rate of modern presidents casts doubt on the conventional wisdom that Truman's victory was the greatest upset in history. Truman was an incumbent president running for reelection in a Democrat-majority country and defeating a previously beaten candidate leading a divided minority party. These facts are usually not associated with election upsets. Instead by examining the 1948 and other presidential upsets through the prism of six electoral factors, Truman's election was an upset but not the greatest upset.

Polls: The 1948 election was the first to widely use public opinion surveys to predict the election and with disastrous results. Three of the eleven elections ranked as upsets utilized polling—the elections in 1948, 1960, and 2000. The absence of polling, though, does not foreclose the use of public opinion measures that were cruder than modern measures. Prior to the development of public opinion surveys, politicians relied on state and local elections in pivotal states to predict presidential outcomes. Unlike the 20th-century election model of a single day for national voting, 19th-century elections were conducted over a two-month period during the fall of election year. States such as Indiana, Ohio, South Carolina, and Maine held elections for state legislature, governor, and Congress. One popularly repeated phrase, "As goes Maine, so goes the country," was based on the observation that the party that won Maine's gubernatorial and state legislative races frequently won the presidency. Political candidates and their parties used election results much like 21st-century polls, pouring money into states considered close or winnable and pulling money out of states considered lost or states considered easily won based on state results. Upset elections are those that produce results different than suggested by state results or opinion polls in election years.

Midterm elections: An even earlier indicator of presidential popularity is midterm elections. Because midterms occur two years prior to a presidential election, their predictive force is more diluted but still important as they reveal the public's view of a president in the middle of his term. In a midterm, the ruling party is expected to lose seats based on voter turnout and general dissatisfaction with the party controlling the White House. Such dissatisfaction may be temporary as was true in 1982 and 1994, when large midterm losses may have predicted a presidential loss but instead were a mere speed bump in the reelection campaigns of Ronald Reagan and Bill Clinton. Midterm losses may force or convince a president to change his policies, but the general rule is that large midterm losses including loss of one or both houses of Congress is a predictor of presidential defeat, and a candidate or party that can shake off such losses to win the presidency could be considered an upset.

The political cycle: It is a cliché to say that the American political system is marked by constant change, but even clichés offer important truths. Disaffection, anger, and boredom with the party in power can bring change in the presidency regardless of public opinion, economic factors, or midterm losses. Twelve or more years of same-party control of the White House has occurred only five times since the 1830s—the advent of the two-party system. Some decades have witnessed continuous change, the 1840s and the 1880s sporting five presidential administrations. Whether through electoral defeat, denial of party renomination, or unexpected death, the presidency is a remarkably unstable office when compared to Congress with its 80 and 90 percent reelection rates and political careers spanning decades.

Only once since the 1830s has a two-term president been followed by another two-term president with George W. Bush following Bill Clinton—the only time in American history that the parties exchanged two-term presidencies. With two-term presidencies rare and consecutive two-term presidencies even rarer, the American electoral system is biased against a single party controlling the White House over several decades. Any candidate following a sitting president of the same party suffers a severe handicap with electoral victory by that candidate considered an upset.

The political era: Historians and political scientists divide American political history into eras, sometimes naming them for presidents, other times for their policies, and on occasion for the results of those policies. The Jacksonian and Reagan eras were named for iconic figures whose ideology dominated the political debate long after their presidencies ended. The Gilded Era, the result of industrial policy and subsidies of the 1860s and 1870s, was followed by the progressive era at the start of the 20th century: a reaction to those policies. The New Deal Era, named after the federal government's accession of responsibility for the economy, lasted for four decades and was marked by collectivistic policies that relied on bureaucratic regimentation that soon soured the American taste for big government. Each of the eras was dominated by a political party that succeeded at electing presidents and maintaining majorities in Congress, sometimes for decades at a time. With the dominant party enjoying a large plurality of the voting public, any presidential candidate able to defeat the dominant party's candidate would be considered an upset. This occurred in 1800, 1848, 1916, and 2000.

Electoral chaos: Disputed elections are a constant feature of democracies. After the 2000 disputed presidential election, democracies around the world suffered from close results that threatened their stability. Disputed elections tend to be close elections, sometimes producing undemocratic results as winners of the popular vote lose the election based on the electoral count or a political compromise. A candidate losing the popular vote but winning the presidency would be considered an upset victor and includes J. Q. Adams, Rutherford Hayes, Benjamin Harrison, and George W. Bush.

The economy: The central measures in statistical models of presidential elections are gross domestic product growth and the unemployment rate, both of which serve as signs of the economy's health and the public's perception of the president's economic policies. Americans have come to expect continuous prosperity, ignoring the fact that bad economic times in their country rarely resemble the economic shambles that mark other countries. Woe to any party unable to provide prosperity as American voters are remarkably fickle, blaming presidents for bad times but not always giving them credit for economic growth. Any incumbent president or party that presided over prosperous times would be expected to win the election; defeat of the president or party would be considered an upset and occurred in 1800, 1844, 1888, 1960, and 2000.

Other factors contributing to upsets include voting corruption (a factor in 1876 and 1960), unequal candidates (a factor in 1844 and 1960), and unusual or extraordinary voting patterns in states (a factor in 1844, 1848, and 1960). These factors affect the perception of an election and of the voters who believe a candidate is favored only to discover some untoward or unexpected event led to a surprising result. The more factors that are relevant to a presidential campaign the greater the presidential upset.

BEYOND PREDICTIONS

Modern American voters are frequently puzzled by the electoral system used to choose a president. Many voters study the popular vote, the measure of the people's views of the president, but the constitution says little about the popular vote because it is the electoral vote that determines the next president. The original constitution, completed in 1787 and ratified the next year, utilized indirect methods of choosing both senators and presidents. Prior to the passage of the 17th Amendment, state legislatures had the authority to choose senators, while the presidential electoral system was even more indirect.

The framers of the constitution debated several methods of selecting presidents. Tired and frustrated after months of debate and compromise, the framers created an ad hoc method of electing presidents known as the Electoral College. Found in Article II, Section I of the constitution, the first Electoral College ignored the development of parties and instead made the two top electoral vote getters in the election the president and vice president. The Electoral College created the temporary position of presidential elector, usually prominent state leaders, and granted state legislatures authority to determine the identity of electors who would cast the official ballots for president.

Prior to the Civil War, states used three methods of choosing electors. The first was direct selection by the state legislature. In other states, voters chose the electors using one of two methods. The winner-take-all system used statewide elections, with the candidate who won the most votes in a state winning all of that state's electoral votes. The second method was election by House district. Presidential candidates could win a single electoral vote if they won the most votes in a congressional district.

The two systems tended to produce varied results. The winner-take-all system produced larger electoral majorities, whereas the district system tended to divide a state's electoral votes and produce narrow electoral victories. By the 20th century, states had adopted the winner-take-all system, but by the turn of the 21st century, two states—Nebraska and Maine—had returned to a form of the district system.

The second Electoral College system, created by the 12th Amendment, was a reaction to the 1800 disputed election. The amendment teamed the president and vice president, strengthening the two-party system while eliminating the importance of electors who became mere vote casters—their decisions predetermined at the ballot box.

The Electoral College remains one of the few elements of federalism—the division of power between the states and national government—that dates back to the original constitution. Presidential elections stretching back to 1796 have been decided by a few men or voters in a key state. During the 19th century, New York was a critical swing state with several upsets decided by its electoral votes. Other states including South Carolina in 1800, Pennsylvania in 1844 and 1848, Indiana in the 1880s, California in 1916, Illinois and Texas in 1960, and Florida in 2000 enjoyed outsized influence in choosing a president. The actions of local officials including Aaron Burr, Martin Van Buren, Hiram Johnson, William Daley, and Jeb Bush proved more important to the outcome than the candidates, the issues, or the campaign. Small events ranging from a ballot at the feet of a confused House member, a missed meeting at a hotel, and rearranged names on a ballot also contributed to presidential upsets. In all of these instances, a simple mistake caused a front-running candidate to stumble to defeat.

2

The Catholic President

NIXON VERSUS KENNEDY, 1960

In 1960 many Republicans rued their decision to pass the 22nd Amendment. The Republican-dominated 80th Congress ratified the amendment as a response to Franklin Roosevelt's refusal to abide by George Washington's two-term tradition. Roosevelt's successor Harry Truman was not covered by the amendment, but did not run for reelection after two difficult terms. His successor Dwight Eisenhower was the first Republican president elected since 1928 and the first to come against the two-term limit.

Eisenhower was a popular president leading an unpopular party and was the best chance Republicans had for retaining the White House in 1960. The man who would try to replace him, Richard Nixon, was well known as Eisenhower's vice president but despised by broad swathes of the electorate including Democrats and independent voters. Unfortunately for Nixon he could not follow Eisenhower's blueprint for success in 1952 and 1956. In both elections the World War II hero ran practically nonpartisan presidential campaigns, using his personal popularity rather than that of the Republican Party to win two landslides. The partisan Nixon, known for attacking Democrats as traitors and socialists, was dependent upon his party to bring out the vote. Lacking the personal appeal of his predecessor, Nixon ran as a continuation of the Eisenhower administration and promised to build upon the president's success.

EISENHOWER ADMINISTRATION

Eisenhower entered office as a foreign policy president having declared during the 1952 election that he would go to Korea and end the stalemated war. He did and then spent eight years trying to prevent a nuclear war with the Soviet Union. During his presidency the man who planned and executed the Normandy landings resisted an expansion of military spending. Eisenhower offered a series of arms control proposals including Atoms for Peace and Open Skies intended to relieve tensions with the Soviet Union. His Secretary of State, John Foster Dulles, practiced a more hardline diplomacy, though his brinkmanship strategy enjoyed little success.[1]

Eisenhower deferred to Congress on most domestic issues. Having witnessed the Republican 80th Congress nearly destroy itself trying to repeal the New Deal, Eisenhower rejected wholesale social and economic changes. His signal domestic achievement—the start of the interstate highway system—was a holdover from his experience during military maneuvers trying to negotiate the country's poor road system. The old general struggled with Republican leaders Robert Taft and William Knowland, who expected a Republican president to lead the charge to unwind the New Deal. Eisenhower enjoyed a better relationship with Democrat Senator Lyndon Johnson and House Speaker Sam Rayburn, who shared his caution in making domestic policy. Eisenhower's moderation kept his approval ratings above 60 percent, but his inaction left issues such as civil rights to fester.

The Supreme Court's 1954 decision in *Brown v. Board of Education* mandated school integration, but Eisenhower, wanting to maintain political viability in states like Florida and Texas, did little to enforce it. His order in 1957 sending federal troops to integrate schools in Little Rock, Arkansas, was his one act of leadership on the issue. Even as Congress debated the 1957 Civil Rights Act, Eisenhower left the lobbying and compromising on the bill to Nixon and Lyndon Johnson. Eisenhower was most animated in holding the line on government spending, fighting off calls for greater defense expenditures in the face of the Soviet launching of Sputnik. His successor John Kennedy exploited Sputnik during the 1960 campaign, claiming the Soviets enjoyed a numerical and technological superiority or "missile gap" when in reality the Soviets were far behind the United States in both.

However, Eisenhower's greatest achievement in eight years was returning the Republican Party to political relevance. The old general's managerial skill and political moderation created economic prosperity that erased the memories of the Hoover administration. The next Republican presidential candidate could run on extending these successes while expanding on Eisenhower's appeal to southern Democrats on economic issues. Campaigning for a third Eisenhower term would not be an innovative strategy for Nixon, but many campaigns had been won on the promise to continue peace and prosperity. Nixon was an established figure who boasted of foreign policy experience, having debated Soviet premier Nikita Khrushchev and battled communists in South America. Going into the 1960 campaign the vice president was the front-runner for a third consecutive Republican term.

The Democrats enjoyed advantages. In the 1958 midterm elections 13 new Democrat senators were elected, expanding the party majority to 15. These senators would become part of the Great Society's 87th Congress with liberals Edmund Muskie, Eugene McCarthy, and Philip Hart representing the far left of the party. Voters in 1958 also rejected the right-to-work referendums in California and Ohio which contributed to the defeat of Republican leaders John Bricker and William Knowland.

Eight years of Eisenhower offered the Democrats an opportunity to exploit public exhaustion with the president and his party. As the majority party, Democrats needed only to nominate a candidate who could appeal to independents and southern Democrats—the two groups that voted for Eisenhower.

THE REPUBLICAN NOMINATION

Prior to the disastrous 1958 midterms, the Republican field was filled with potential. Senator William Knowland, successor to Robert Taft as the party leader, shared his California political base with Nixon, and many conservatives saw him as a successor to the moderate Eisenhower. Knowland was born of wealth; his family owned the Oakland Tribune, a premier Republican newspaper. After his appointment to fill Hiram Johnson's seat in 1945, he won reelection in 1946 and 1952 and would have won a third term, but became bored as part of the senate minority. Feeling ready for the presidency, he maneuvered to win the Republican nomination for governor, convincing the incumbent, Goodwin Knight, not to seek reelection but rather to run for the empty Senate seat. The switch proved a political millstone as the Democrat candidate, Pat Brown, accusing the senator of using the governor's chair as a springboard to the presidency. Knowland's support for an unpopular right-to-work referendum energized union and liberal voters who voted against the referendum and the senator. Knowland

and Knight were defeated for governor and senator respectively, ending their political careers and leaving Nixon as the most powerful California Republican.[2]

The losses gave Nixon maneuvering room to appeal to Democrats and independents who treated Nixon with suspicion. His bipartisan appeal was a dramatic turn from his early political career in which he treated Democrats as an existential threat to the country.[3]

Nixon proved a superior politician during this period as he maneuvered between extremes. His anticommunism disarmed the Republican right, whereas his liberal views on civil rights and public spending placed him in the ideological middle, separated from both Republican and Democrat conservatives who wanted the federal government to do nothing about segregation. The balancing of the party's wings reinforced suspicions Nixon was willing to say anything to get elected and discarded principles with ease.

After graduating from Whittier College, Nixon served in the Office of Price Control, a World War II agency that enforced wartime rationing of consumer goods in order to limit inflation. Nixon's disgust with agency cronyism turned him to the Republicans. In his first congressional campaign in 1946 Nixon earned the reputation as a tough anticommunist. Trying to unseat Congressman Jerry Voorhis, Nixon tied him to the Congress of Industrial Organizations-Political Action Committee (CIO-PAC), a left-wing interest group, and Brooklyn Congressman Vito Marcantonio, an avowed socialist. Voorhis had no answer to Nixon, and a political career was born.[4]

Sitting on the House Un-American Activities Committee (HUAC), Nixon led the investigation to uncover communist infiltration of the Truman administration. A break came with the testimony of Whittaker Chambers, Time magazine editor and former federal bureaucrat, who revealed that the former number two State Department official, Alger Hiss, was a communist. The Truman administration sneered at HUAC and Nixon, but in 1950 Hiss was convicted of perjury, proving he had been a communist spy at the highest reaches of the American government during the war.

Nixon's triumph over Hiss launched him into the 1950 California Senate race. During the campaign Nixon labeled his opponent Helen Gahagan Douglas the "pink lady," a sly implication to her gender and alleged leftist sympathies. Douglas's response was to label Nixon as "Tricky Dick," a name that would follow him to the grave. In 1952 he was picked by Eisenhower to run as vice president and barely survived a scandal involving a political slush fund. He defused the scandal with his televised Checkers's speech where he spoke of his daughter's dog. His election made him the second youngest vice president in history.[5]

Nixon's climb from naval officer to vice president included stepping on other politicians ranging from Earl Warren to Harry Truman, all of whom developed a lifetime animus against him. Democrats identified him as enemy number one with his attacks on the party in 1954 and 1958 singeing the ears of politicians. In 1960 Nixon struggled to change his image as "Tricky Dick," the politician who would say or do anything to get elected, and promote a new Nixon, one more mature and capable of handling high office rather than acting as the party hatchet man. Yet, it was Nixon's reputation as a relentless campaigner that convinced nonpolitical Eisenhower to select him for vice president, thus creating one of the country's most unusual political alliances.[6]

Eisenhower and Nixon were the most diverse president and vice-presidential team since Lincoln and Andrew Johnson. A career military man, Eisenhower understood the petty politics of the American army, but had only limited experience with the broad ideological divisions of national politics. Distrustful of the New Deal and the Roosevelt administration, Eisenhower kept his own counsel during the war and postwar reconstruction. His views were so hidden that in 1948 disgruntled Democrats considered him a dark-horse candidate to run against Truman. A beneficiary of a bipartisan image, Ike was one of the least partisan 20th-century presidents. His vice president was the polar opposite.

Richard Nixon was a dyed-in-the-wool Republican who struggled to advance in an era of Democrat dominance. Eisenhower recoiled at Nixon's raw partisanship while his rhetorical excesses raised doubts in the old general that Nixon had the temperament for the presidency. Eisenhower had the gift of separating the political from the personal and used his personal popularity to win reelection. Nixon was more of a traditional politician, a juxtaposition of the two men's personalities and experiences as the younger Nixon was forced to rely on a weak party and strong policies to win votes. The media would make an unfavorable comparison between the grinning Ike and the snarling Nixon while a more apt comparison was the passive Eisenhower ignoring domestic issues while the activist Nixon rallied congressional Republicans to defeat the Bricker Amendment on foreign policy and build Republican support for civil rights.

Eisenhower's treatment of Nixon was the worst of any president toward a vice president who harbored political ambition. In 1956 Republican gadfly Harold Stassen mounted a campaign to remove Nixon from the national ticket. Stassen was serving in the Eisenhower administration when he launched his campaign, but the president did little to dissuade him. Instead the president suggested Nixon expand his executive experience by accepting a cabinet post. Although such a move might prove beneficial in a corporate setting, it would have been disastrous in the political world, ending Nixon's presidential hopes. The vice president rejected the offer, but Eisenhower refused to endorse Nixon, instead deferring to the Republican convention to choose the vice president, much as it had in 1952. This left Nixon to battle for delegates even as members of the administration, including Stassen, campaigned to remove him.[7]

By 1960 Eisenhower was maneuvering to find an alternative to Nixon, his favorite candidate being Treasury Secretary Robert Anderson, or his own brother, Milton; however, neither man enjoyed a political following or exhibited a predisposition toward politics. Nixon, the faithful vice president, was shown the back of Eisenhower's hand when the president campaigned in defense of his own record rather than for Nixon's election.[8] Eisenhower's disdain for his vice president showed through during a 1960 press conference when reporters badgered him for examples of policies advanced by the vice president. Ike responded with a curt "If you give me a week, I might think of one," which only undermined Nixon's attempts to tie himself to the administration.[9]

However, even without Eisenhower's direct support, Nixon rolled up endorsements and support of both state and national Republicans and was headed for an uncontested nomination. Unlike the sharp Democrat primary season where the candidates faced hard campaigning and difficult questions, Nixon glided, dulling his political edge while his easy victories affected the Democrat race. During the Wisconsin primary, many Catholic Republicans crossed party lines to vote for Kennedy and expanded his margin of victory.[10]

When a Republican challenger did not appear by summer 1959, New York governor Nelson Rockefeller made rumblings about a presidential run. Elected in 1958 when few Republicans won, Rockefeller used his name and personal fortune to create the image of a modern Republican, closer to a Democrat than any other major Republican figure. The original Republican in Name Only (RINO), Rockefeller

infuriated conservatives for nearly 16 years as governor and then as
Gerald Ford's vice president.

Rockefeller campaigned in three Republican primary seasons, 1960,
1964—where he would come closest to winning—and 1968. His Hamlet-
like performance at the conventions infuriated supporters and opponents alike. In 1959 Rockefeller commissioned a series of polls to measure
his viability and then collected scores of experts to produce policies he
could use for a presidential campaign. The effort presented an image of a
serious candidate whose staff grew to such a size he was forced to house
it in two New York buildings.[11] The planning constituted the first presidential exploratory committee though unlike modern campaigns most of
Rockefeller's efforts were at policy development rather than fund-raising
because he could use his family fortune to outspend any candidate—
even the Kennedys.

However, Rockefeller's path remained blocked by Nixon who was
endorsed by Republican financial donors after years of outreach.
Rockefeller generated little interest from state party machines; their
delegations pledged to the vice president who had campaigned for
them in tough elections. After several months of consideration and
work, Rockefeller announced in late 1959 he was not going to challenge Nixon.[12]

However, the governor remained restless. In April 1960 he traveled
cross-country, making speeches in Pennsylvania, Illinois, and North
Dakota and picked up the endorsement of the *Denver Post* for a draft-
Rockefeller movement. During the trip a Gallup poll showed Kennedy
beating Nixon 53–45, an unsurprising result considering the positive
coverage garnered by Kennedy during the primaries.[13] With public
opinion on his side Rockefeller seized on the Eisenhower administration's bungling of the U-2 crisis and on June 6 announced he was again
a candidate, speaking vaguely of a convention draft without offering
a clear plan for defeating Nixon. Few Republican insiders believed
Rockefeller could win as Nixon had swept the primaries and locked
up most state delegations. The governor's only victory was to convince New York Republicans to go to the convention uncommitted—
a weak symbolism that protected Rockefeller from losing his state's
votes.[14]

Rockefeller's challenge appeared to be a ploy for the governor to influence the platform or even an attempt to undermine Nixon and hobble
him in the general election so as to prepare the path for Rockefeller's
1964 nomination.[15] During his brief campaign, Rockefeller produced

a flurry of proposals, making good use of his experts to distance his candidacy from the Eisenhower administration by demanding more spending on foreign and domestic programs. Attacking the popular president earned the governor little support at the convention but publicized his views and established him as the leader of the liberal eastern wing of the party. Nixon decided to accommodate Rockefeller and unify the party.[16]

Initially, Nixon tried to silence the governor by offering him the vice presidency, but discovered Rockefeller lacked a desire for titles while sporting an ego that would not allow him to serve under Nixon. A meeting was arranged between the governor and vice president; Nixon visited Rockefeller at his Park Avenue apartment on July 22 only days before the Republican convention. Rockefeller sought a more liberal Republican Party that would escape its balanced budget obsession and reinstate east coast dominance, whereas Nixon sought the governor's acquiescence if not his endorsement. After several hours of negotiation both men appeared to meet their goals. Rockefeller convinced the vice president to strengthen the party's position on civil rights and propose increases in domestic and defense spending beyond the Eisenhower budget. After working into the early morning hours, Rockefeller and Nixon fashioned an agreement that allowed the governor to support the vice president.[17]

The so-called Treaty of Fifth Avenue was not well received at the convention. Nixon's negotiations with Rockefeller had ignored party conservatives who viewed the governor as a hindrance rather than a help to the party. The platform's call for stronger civil rights protection undermined the conservative southern strategy intended to build on Eisenhower's penetration of the solid Democrat south. In 1956 Eisenhower won Tennessee, Florida, Texas, and Virginia, mainly on economic issues such as Tidelands drilling though his passive approach to the Brown desegregation decision pleased southern Democrats. The Republican southern strategy was bearing fruit as some southern states approved unpledged electors rather than Kennedy electors, thus splitting the party base and offering Republicans a toehold in the region; however, the Nixon–Rockefeller pact drove southerners from the party while convincing conservatives to challenge Nixon at the convention.[18]

Their choice was the most conservative member of the Senate, Barry Goldwater. First elected as senator in 1952 by defeating the Democrat majority leader Ernest McFarland, Goldwater replaced the deceased

Robert Taft as Mr. Republican. Reelected in 1958, Goldwater was recognized by activists as the conservative alternative to Eisenhower and Nixon.[19] The two- term senator was not known for his diplomacy but rather his penchant for "Ready, Fire, Aim" shooting from the lip.[20] Goldwater resisted the big government impulses of the Fifth Avenue Treaty and was determined to move the party's center of gravity to the Mountain West. At a press conference Goldwater denounced the agreement as "immoral" and the "Munich of the Republican Party." The senator's anger focused on the civil rights plank demanded by Rockefeller and his proposal for stronger civil rights laws along with verbal support for the sit-in protesters who challenged segregation laws.

As the conservative revolt gathered steam with Goldwater's home state of Arizona joining South Carolina in endorsing him, the senator was granted a prime-time convention speech. However, instead of launching a full-fledged assault on Nixon's nomination and splitting the convention, Goldwater demanded that conservatives "grow up" and retake control of their party, which they had not led since Alf Landon's disastrous 1936 presidential campaign. The speech ended the conservative challenge, but kicked off the battle for the 1964 nomination as Goldwater offered a conservative vision much different than the proposals from Rockefeller and Nixon.[21]

Even with the Goldwater challenge, Nixon was nominated on the first ballot and faced his first decision when choosing a vice president. Unbeknownst to Nixon this would be the first of his three vice-presidential choices including Henry Cabot Lodge in 1960, Spiro Agnew in 1968, and Gerald Ford in 1973. Nixon never selected a candidate who could immediately fill the role as president, though Agnew's hard-charging campaigning resembled the Nixon of 1952 and 1956. The Agnew choice was likely influenced by his first selection, Cabot Lodge, who offered little help during the campaign.

The final representative in the Cabot Lodge political dynasty, Henry Cabot Lodge, had a thin record of achievement after winning his Senate seat in 1946 from the scandal-tarred Democrat David Walsh.[22] After a bland six years in office, Lodge was defeated by John Kennedy in 1952. Lodge's selection to the Republican ticket went against the tradition of 20th-century vice presidents who were selected for geographic balance or their prowess in campaigning. Cabot Lodge offered neither. As part of the Republican northeastern wing his place on the ticket further alienated conservatives though less so than if Nixon had chosen Rockefeller. Nixon had no chance to win Massachusetts from

Kennedy, and with Lodge running a diffident campaign, his presence hurt the ticket in other regions. During the campaign Lodge took midday naps as if he were a doddering British aristocrat standing for election in a rotten borough.[23] With Lodge on the ticket much of the campaigning fell on Nixon who quickly exhausted himself scurrying across the country.

DEMOCRAT CANDIDATES

The Democrat primaries proved more dramatic. An eight-year absence from the White House and the perceived weaknesses of the Eisenhower administration drew out several regional candidates. First among these was Lyndon Johnson. Born in the Texas hill country between Austin and San Antonio, Johnson was a rabid New Dealer whose oily personality included hyperbolic compliments to his seniors such as Speaker Sam Rayburn and Georgia Senator Richard Russell.[24] A Senate defeat in 1941 hardened Johnson and drove him to use the same dirty tricks when running seven years later. In a close 1948 Senate election Johnson prevailed with his 87-vote victory earning him the moniker "Landslide Lyndon." Johnson's demonstrated skill in manipulating the notoriously corrupt Texas election proved the deciding factor in John Kennedy selecting him as vice president because the senator was expected to keep his home state in the Democrat column.[25]

Joining Johnson from the Senate was Hubert Humphrey, a liberal ideologue known more for his speeches than his legislative achievements. As the mayor of Minneapolis and senatorial candidate in 1948, Humphrey used his convention speech to challenge the party on civil rights and declaring it was time to fulfill the American promise of equality. Humphrey's speech convinced a majority of the delegates to vote for a strong civil rights plank in the party platform and caused southern delegates to walk out of the convention and create their own southern Democrat party. After 1948 Democrats began abandoning their tradition of segregation and racism and become the party of civil rights in the north.

Humphrey and his liberal Senate allies chafed under Lyndon Johnson's leadership as the Texan and his southern allies outmaneuvered the outmatched liberals and prevented passage of their proposed civil rights legislation.[26] Humphrey's eloquence would prove no match for the manipulative Johnson and the well-financed Kennedy.

Another candidate was Missouri Senator Stuart Symington, another indifferent and colorless campaigner, who needed a deadlocked convention and Harry Truman's influence to win him the nomination. The former president had yet to regain his luster, whereas his support of Symington revived memories of what Democrats believed was a failed presidency. Truman had endorsed Alben Barkley's 1952 campaign and Averell Harriman's 1956 campaign, neither man gaining traction and diluted Truman's influence. Symington ran on competence and ethics — noting the scandals that plagued Lyndon Johnson and the Kennedy family—and on defense expertise, making pointed criticisms of Eisenhower's refusal to spend more money on defense.[27]

John Kennedy was the least prominent of the Democrats, his public persona little known outside of the northeast. A two-term senator from a controversial family, Kennedy had left little imprint on the Senate. Known by his colleagues as a lightweight and womanizer—sometimes sharing mistresses with his father and younger brother—Kennedy benefitted from a physical attractiveness enhanced by drugs and an unlimited campaign budget. Working with ghostwriters, Kennedy saw his *Profiles in Courage* win the Pulitzer Prize for history—his father's influence gathering the votes for the award—while a massive public relations campaign portrayed Kennedy as an athlete, family man, and intellectual.[28]

Kennedy's wealth and his connections gave many liberal Democrats heartburn, their New Deal philosophy targeting the malefactors of great wealth and their undue influence over the political process. The Kennedy fortune was based on the stock speculation that Joseph Kennedy had been chosen to regulate as the first head of the newly created Securities and Exchange Commission. For middle-class Americans who were less obsessed with a candidate's wealth, Kennedy's Catholicism was an issue. The hierarchical and at times authoritarian nature of the Roman Catholic Church excited fear in many Protestants about foreign influence over American government.

The Kennedy presidential campaign began in 1956 when he was proposed as a vice-presidential candidate for Democrat nominee Adlai Stevenson. Kennedy's competition was limited to Tennessee Senator Estes Kefauver, famous for his hearings on the mob and his alcoholism. The Kennedys tried to use his Catholic beliefs to their advantage, commissioning a survey by the chair of the Connecticut Democrat Party showing that Kennedy could attract Catholics who had voted for Eisenhower in 1952. Kennedy was the front-runner for the nomination until Speaker Sam Rayburn intervened, convincing enough delegates to choose Kefauver. When Stevenson–Kefauver went down to defeat, Kennedy escaped certain political doom because Democrats would have blamed his Catholicism for Stevenson's loss.[29]

After easy reelection in 1958, Kennedy geared up for his presidential run, fixing on national security and a "missile gap," which allowed him to argue the Soviet Union had a larger arsenal than the United States. He faced a hybrid nomination system with a few states such as New Hampshire, Wisconsin, West Virginia, Oregon, and Nebraska holding primaries while most states chose delegates in state party conventions. With a minimal number of primaries the national conventions were still influential in selecting delegates. In 1952 Kefauver had swept the primaries seemingly on his way to the nomination, but his foibles caught up with him, and the Democrats selected Adlai Stevenson. In 1960 the formidable but tainted Johnson and the dull Symington sat out the primaries hoping to repeat 1952 while Humphrey and Kennedy bloodied each other in a nationwide campaign.

Neither man had a clear advantage in the primaries. Humphrey was a Midwestern candidate, despised in the south and little known on the coasts. Kennedy was a playboy whose Catholicism was controversial in the protestant south while his family name and northeastern roots generated suspicion in Middle America. Yet, Kennedy effectively framed the debate by focusing on two primary states, Wisconsin and West Virginia, and lowering expectations by suggesting a Catholic candidate could not win in either. Thereafter, the Kennedys combined tough campaigning and a flood of money to exceed those expectations.

In Wisconsin, Humphrey enjoyed a regional advantage: his 12 years as Minnesota senator was much reported in the neighboring state. With high expectations set for his opponent, anything but a smashing victory could be sold by Kennedy as a Humphrey defeat. However, the Kennedys were not interested in moral victories or doing better than expected. Instead they utilized their hired professionals who enjoyed local knowledge and political connections while dispersing the Kennedy clan around the state. Meeting Kennedy's mother, brothers, or sisters was treated as a candidate visit, and the personal touch immunized Kennedy from charges of being a wealthy aristocrat floating to victory on his family's money. While Kennedy and his family jetted around the state, Humphrey was left to bounce along back roads in his campaign bus.[30]

Humphrey depended on the support of the state's sizable labor population who backed his positions on civil rights, income redistribution, and high taxes. However, Humphrey lacked the organization, much less the money to build one, and Kennedy easily outspent him while using the religion issue to smack at the senator. Kennedy played up his Catholicism, dragging out the Bailey poll from 1956 to demonstrate he would win if only Protestants did not vote purely on religion. A double standard was born in Wisconsin as Catholic voters were free to vote for Kennedy based on his religion while Protestants were accused of bigotry if they dared mention religion as an issue.[31]

The religion issue worked for Kennedy as he attracted Catholic Democrats and Republicans—the latter uninterested in their party primary as Nixon lacked opposition in Wisconsin. The result was a crushing victory for Kennedy as he won 479,000 votes to Humphrey's 372,000 votes and won 21 of 31 delegates. He also undermined Humphrey's argument the senator could defeat Nixon in the Midwest.[32]

Humphrey limped into the heavily Protestant West Virginia, which would test Kennedy's Catholic strategy. The state was a trap for Humphrey as a victory would be spun by the Kennedy campaign as another example of vicious Protestant bigotry. Contrarily, a Kennedy victory would end the Humphrey campaign as it would prove he could not win a state so hostile to Kennedy.[33]

West Virginia was dotted with rural political machines operated by sheriffs and county officials who sought money from candidates to draw out their voters. Desperately poor, many West Virginians saw the election as an opportunity for picking up pocket money, which Kennedy had in abundance. The campaign spread money through the various county seats and relegated religion to a minor issue as local Democrat bosses focused on money and political power. Total spending for the West Virginia campaign exceeded $200,000 when a budget of $50,000 was considered large for a state campaign. During the campaign Kennedy was forced to change the rhetoric he used in prosperous Wisconsin by quieting talk of a New Frontier which sounded out of touch with a population that had not "eaten since the day before yesterday." The confident Kennedy team predicted a second-place showing, lowering expectations even as they bought a sweeping victory.[34]

Behind the scenes some West Virginia Democrats maneuvered to defeat Kennedy on behalf of Lyndon Johnson. The leader of the stop-Kennedy movement was former KKK member Senator Robert Byrd, who threw his resources behind Humphrey. Byrd saw the

Minnesota senator as the only means to halt the Kennedy bandwagon. However, Byrd's efforts could not match the Kennedy campaign as Humphrey bumped along in his bus, stopping at mountain hamlets while skimming from his daughter's wedding fund to pay for radio advertisements.[35]

With Humphrey stumbling toward defeat, the Kennedy brothers drove the knife in deeper: compliments of Franklin Roosevelt Jr. The dead president's son spread the story that Humphrey evaded the World War II draft, drawing an unfavorable comparison with Kennedy the war hero. The charge was false as Humphrey had reported for the draft, but was rejected for medical reasons. The attack alienated the Minnesota senator from Kennedy but made Humphrey an attractive vice-presidential candidate for Lyndon Johnson in 1964. Johnson was familiar with Bobby Kennedy's dirty tricks and understood Roosevelt would not have attacked Humphrey without the younger Kennedy's approval.[36]

West Virginia ended Humphrey's 1960 campaign as Kennedy won 50 of 55 counties and earned 61 percent of the vote. Suddenly, Kennedy was the front-runner, sweeping to victories in the remaining primaries and heading to the Los Angeles convention with a seemingly insurmountable lead. By the time Kennedy's main opponent Lyndon Johnson had regrouped and mounted a stop-Kennedy movement, he could not overcome the Massachusetts' senator's well-funded campaign.[37]

The Kennedy machine swept into Los Angeles and offered sit-downs with delegations and jobs to challengers in order to smooth the nomination. Stuart Symington drew a deal to be appointed Secretary of the Air Force. Johnson proved more difficult. As the southern candidate he controlled the votes and the hearts of southern Democrats. Kennedy needed a solid south and could not afford to alienate Johnson or southern stalwarts such as Sam Rayburn and Richard Russell. Johnson was unimpressed with the Kennedy campaign and confident in his own abilities, but committed the cardinal sin of politics—underestimating his opponents while overestimating his own political standing.

Dismissing Kennedy as "that boy," Johnson strutted about the convention as if his wheeler-dealer ways would work on delegates much as it did on weak and sodden senators. Johnson forgot that state parties were controlled by governors or urban mayors who could dispense jobs and rally voters, rather than senators who spent much of their time in Washington. Johnson predicted he would win the nomination on the third ballot while his ally, Georgia Senator Richard Russell predicted he would carry 500 delegates on the first ballot. Even Eisenhower privately expressed support for Johnson, expressing disbelief that the Democrats would nominate the inexperienced Kennedy over Johnson.[38]

While Kennedy and Johnson maneuvered for delegates, a third candidate rose, Adlai Stevenson—the darling of the New Deal left. Stevenson's two presidential campaigns against Eisenhower had earned him a martyr status and a belief he deserved a regular rather than a sacrificial campaign. Many liberals distrusted the Kennedys, recalling Joseph Kennedy's isolationism and ties to big business, and latched onto Stevenson. The former Illinois governor had wisely remained outside the scrum, disdainful of an electoral system that had twice rejected him and waited for a draft. His silence also registered his unwillingness to join Henry Clay and William Jennings Bryan as a three-time loser, the same feeling shared by Democrats who never made the call to Illinois. Instead, the Kennedy campaign ignored much of the daily crises associated with conventions and the overheated rhetoric that surrounded the nomination process.[39]

Yet, they would have to withstand several tidal waves. One was begun by Harry Truman: the ex-president's propensity for sewing discord was suddenly directed at his own party. Truman publicly doubted Kennedy's "maturity and experience" to be president and latched onto Kennedy's weak response to the shooting down of the U-2 spy plane and capture of American Gary Francis Powers. Truman warned the young nominee lacked the gravitas and international respect of an Eisenhower or even a Nixon. Truman further raised the issue of Joseph Kennedy's influence over his son and therefore replaced the pope with a more ominous figure.[40]

Lyndon Johnson struck a nerve with insinuations that Kennedy suffered from Addison's disease—a debilitating kidney condition. Observers only had to compare Congressman Kennedy in 1946, hollow-eyed, wraithlike figure propped up on crutches with the tanned and steroid-enhanced presidential candidate and wonder what caused the dramatic recovery. As with previous presidential candidates suffering from medical conditions, the Kennedys trotted out a pair of doctors to lie and offer a claim of perfect health for Kennedy, pointing to his vitality and declaiming he was suffering from a potentially deadly illness.[41]

As charges and denials flew around the convention, keeping newspaper reporters happy with stories, Bobby Kennedy cultivated big city bosses, including Chicago's William Daley who could deliver his state delegation and his state for Kennedy. Daley's defection halted the draft-Stevenson campaign.[42]

The Stevenson movement reached its height during Eleanor Roosevelt's speech on the convention's third day. The former first lady appealed for Stevenson's nomination, but rhetoric could not match the cold hard fact Kennedy had the delegates. Kennedy won on the first ballot with 806 votes to Johnson's 409, just 45 more than he needed for a majority. The win exhibited the strength of the well-financed and organized Massachusetts campaign.[43]

Filling the vice-presidential slot proved more delicate than winning the convention. John Kennedy preferred Lyndon Johnson even as Bobby Kennedy dismissed him as an uncouth and a corrupt southern yokel.[44] However, Johnson filled a need as Texas had voted Republican in 1956 over the Tidelands issue and appeared vulnerable to Nixon's economic arguments. If Texas fell to the Republicans and took other moderate states with it, then Kennedy was doomed. Johnson's knowledge of Texas politics and his influence in the South would allow Kennedy to ignore the region and focus on the Midwest and far west. Yet, Johnson was a poor public campaigner, his drawl and poor speaking skills making him a burden in a television campaign. The same folksy personality allowed Johnson to convince white Democrats that a Massachusetts liberal would not challenge the segregationist status quo. Although Johnson might make promises on civil rights that Kennedy could not keep, the problems could be deflected until the 1964 election.

After a bitter debate within his campaign Kennedy offered Johnson the vice presidency. Some claim the offer was made with the expectation it would be rejected as the vice presidency was considered a backwater—the final office for a politician rather than a stepping stone to the presidency. Johnson's outsized personality would have to be placed in a blind trust, forcing him to leave his beloved Senate which he had fought so hard to reach just as a Democrat president would push legislation that he wanted passed. The majority leader made a quick calculus about his chances to become president, realizing that three 20th-century vice presidents—Theodore Roosevelt, Calvin Coolidge, and Harry Truman—had succeeded a deceased president. Having made the calculations, Johnson accepted the job that would be the most frustrating political position he would ever hold.[45]

The Johnson choice drew scorn from liberals who were shocked by the selection of a segregationist to a liberal ticket while unions were angry with Johnson's support of the anti-union Landrum–Griffith Act. Southern senators were upset by the loss of one of their own from the majority leader's position. They wanted a southerner running the Senate schedule, having accepted Johnson's argument the 1957 Civil Rights Act could have been worse without his intervention. Even Bobby Kennedy remained unconvinced with the choice, the two men fighting an eight-year battle for control of the Democrat party.[46]

After Johnson accepted the offer, Kennedy gave his acceptance speech in the Los Angeles Coliseum. Unlike most Kennedy campaign events, this one suffered from poor planning, poor visuals, and an unruly bug that made its way into Kennedy's mouth during the speech. It proved the campaign's low point for the Democrats.[47]

Some southerners rebelled at the inclusion of a strong civil rights plank in the platform. The same issue threatened to split southern Democrats much as it had in 1948. However, Nixon was a less palatable choice for president than the popular Eisenhower and only made worse after Henry Cabot Lodge's promise to appoint a black cabinet member. Kennedy's Catholicism made him a controversial choice as his religion struck at the basic prejudices of the region.[48] If a second generation of Dixiecrats peeled away enough electoral votes from Kennedy, House Democrats might choose the next president. Even Johnson was not convinced of victory and he had Texas state law changed to allow him to run for reelection to the Senate and for vice president on the Kennedy ticket.

After the Los Angeles convention, southern governors sprang into action, convincing their state conventions to choose unpledged presidential electors. Mississippi and Alabama were the first to act, removing the state electors from the Kennedy column. The movement was slowed in Louisiana, where the state convention chose Kennedy-pledged delegates and in Georgia where Richard Russell kept the state for the regular democrats. Russell was among a group of southern senators who feared the consequences of southerners defeating Kennedy. A Nixon victory would put Johnson back into the Senate, angry at his defeat and likely working with liberal senators to remove opponents from prime committee chairmanships. Russell and others realized that even with Kennedy in the White House, southern control of the prime committees would prevent movement on civil rights legislation.[49]

Their path blocked, segregationists sought their own candidate and asked Barry Goldwater to accept the nomination to a new conservative party. Goldwater had no desire to leave the Republican Party on a fool's errand and declined.[50]

THE CAMPAIGN

With both conventions over, the general election began. The Democrat campaign did not start out well. Kennedy was hit by a Gallup poll that showed Nixon leading by six points and at the magic 50 percent level. Efforts to trim that deficit were slowed by the need for Kennedy and Johnson to be in the Senate and finish the 1960 congressional session. Dwight Eisenhower appeared to take a page from his predecessor's campaign book. In a press conference he demanded that Congress pass bills during the summer session and focused on a civil rights bill that Johnson had delayed so as not to irritate southerners.[51]

Kennedy proposed two bills: an increase in the minimum wage, which had a chance at passage, and a second bill establishing a Medicare health insurance program for the elderly. The leader of Republican opposition was Barry Goldwater, who joined with southern Democrats to attach multiple amendments onto the minimum wage and defeat it. The Medicare bill produced more sound than action with the media taking its cue from the Democrats and publishing horror stories about retirees decimated by $700 medical bills. The Medicare argument, which would continue until creation of the program in 1965, would focus on cutting skyrocketing medical costs by creating a government insurance program. Medicare was sold during the 1960 campaign as a means to reduce health costs, a promise that continues into the 21st century as health care costs continue to rise.[52]

The Nixon campaign also started badly. After banging his knee on a car door in North Carolina he suffered an infection and required hospitalization from August 29 to September 9. In that two weeks he saw his early lead in the polls evaporate as Kennedy campaigned alone. The two-week hiatus also created chaos as Nixon struggled for the remainder of the campaign to keep his 50-state promise. Nixon had promised in his convention speech to campaign in all 50 states, and at times Nixon's schedule appeared more tied to keeping the promise than focusing on the large states with heavy electoral votes. Three days after leaving the hospital, Nixon nearly collapsed in St. Louis, suffering from a constant fever and pain in his knee that prevented him from standing for long periods of time.[53]

The 50-state promise demonstrated Nixon's ignorance of the critical role of television in the campaign. Nixon was lost in the barnstorming efforts of the 1930s and 1940s when candidates swept across the country trying to contact as many voters as possible. The television era discounted retail politics and direct contact for slickly produced 30-second and one-minute commercials that could reach more voters in a day than a month of personal campaigning by a candidate. However, television advertisements in 1960 would be unrecognizable to modern voters with candidates relying on 30-minute broadcasts and five-minute infomercials to spread their message.[54] Personal appearance also became more important than policy positions. Good hair, good teeth, and a light tan projected an image of leadership. Nixon may have been the last "ugly president," sporting a widow's peak with deep-set eyes and a continuous flop sweat that would have gone unnoticed before the advent of television but in 1960 swung some voters to Kennedy.

His leadership style of tight control of his surroundings was the opposite of Eisenhower's propensity for delegation. Nixon was his own campaign manager, not trusting others to make decisions while manipulating his aides and creating a constant state of conflict, a style he repeated in his administration a decade later. As the incumbent vice president, Nixon was on the defensive—an uncomfortable position for him. His early campaigns had been attack-oriented, with Jerry Voorhis, Helen Douglas, Harry Truman, and Adlai Stevenson suffering the sting of Nixon's words. As part of the Eisenhower administration he was forced to defend a record and his midterm campaigns in 1954 and 1958 fell flat, as Democrats deflected his attacks and instead made Eisenhower's record an issue. The same would be true in 1960 as Republicans defended a record while Democrats were free to attack and make promises.

The Kennedy campaign was very different from that of Nixon, the senator not engaging in the same type of frenetic campaigning that exhausted the vice president. Herein, Lyndon Johnson offered some aid as he split the burden of campaigning by focusing on the south. At his oiliest he remained in the background, focusing on the south while dropping his best drawls and stories about long-dead family who fought for the Confederate cause: his campaign sometimes resembled a race for recording secretary of the Daughters of the Confederacy rather than for vice president. His speechwriters were given specific instructions: no words longer than seven letters;

no sentences longer than six words; and no paragraphs longer than three sentences—all intended to limit the confusion of his simple-minded constituents.[55]

Johnson's strongest opponent in Texas was not Nixon but former governor Allen Shiver and his Shivercrats. Shiver had broken from the regular Democrat party in 1956, helping Eisenhower win the state, and in 1960 he unsuccessfully tried to convince Texas Democrats to join the unpledged delegate movement and deny Kennedy the state's electoral votes. Johnson kept Texas in the Kennedy column, infuriating the Shivercrats who responded in 1962 by electing Republican John Tower to Johnson's vacant Senate seat.

NIXON–KENNEDY DEBATES

A television campaign demanded a televised debate, the first of its kind and the start of the farcical joint press conferences that modern presidential debates have become. While the first presidential debate took place in 1960, congressional and state debates had been a constant in American politics since the 19th century. The best known was the Lincoln–Douglas Senate debates of 1858 though other states used personal appearances by candidates to test their mettle. In South Carolina, Senate and gubernatorial candidates had debated each other from the 1890s, the debates moving from county to county like a summer carnival. The appearances of the candidates, putting forth their views, while withstanding arguments, heckling, and fistfights in the crowd, were a form of entertainment to the crowd. The 1924 South Carolina Senate debate saw the incumbent senator break a chair over the back of his opponent, much to the delight of the crowd, though the senator was defeated in the primary election. While the debates may not have resembled the Roman Senate, it offered voters the opportunity to see their candidates operate under the pressure of time and dissent—a rare occurrence in modern campaigns.[56]

Before 1960 two presidential candidates had never met on the same stage. It was not until the 1920s that candidates campaigned throughout the country though Stephen Douglas, William Jennings Bryan, and Theodore Roosevelt broke that precedent. Unfortunately, the new debate format emphasized appearance over policy and confused rather than enlightened the audience. With the glare of television lights on them, candidates became more cautious, dependent upon image coordinators and advisors who counseled repeating bland answers that said little and elicited little media interest the next day. Unlike in 1858 when Stephen Douglas postulated his Freeport Doctrine which set restrictions on slavery and challenged Lincoln on the seminal issue of the day, televised debates became a form of gotcha journalism, used to create stories for the benefit of the media rather than the education of the voters.

Conducted in four parts, the Nixon–Kennedy debates scored high on ratings as people tuned into the major networks to watch their next president. The results were decided by makeup, suntan, and creative editing. Nixon entered the debate confident he could defeat the lightweight Kennedy after having faced down the more dangerous Khrushchev. However, his hospital stay had left him pale, thinner, and stiff from a painful knee that made him look nervous. Throughout his career, Nixon suffered from flop sweat whenever he faced the television cameras, a result of his general discomfort with people.

Kennedy, tanned and pumped up with steroids as part of his treatment for Addison's disease, resembled a movie star candidate who appeared much younger than Nixon though the vice president was only five years older. Throughout the debate each candidate's reaction to the other was carefully edited. Cameras focused on Nixon as his eyes shifted, sweat forming on his upper lip as his pale skin became nearly transparent. Kennedy was always shown as confident, staring hard at his opponent. The television producer for the debate was Don Hewitt, who would use similar camera techniques a decade later in the "investigative journalism" show *Sixty Minutes*.[57]

Beside the cameras and personal appearance, Nixon faced a more formidable opponent than during his early debates with Jerry Voorhis. In 1946 Nixon had confronted Voorhis with written proof of the congressman's CIO connections and strode across the stage to show him the papers. Voorhis never recovered, and Nixonian intimidation was born. Kennedy was a different breed, and the presidential debate precluded such stunts, even as the lame and sweating Nixon lacked the energy to make the attempt. The first debate saw Kennedy on the attack and forced Nixon to parry and defend the Eisenhower administration. Nixon was an effective debater, but his forensic skills were overwhelmed by the television images of a sweating, shifty-eyed politician which marked the return of the original Tricky Dick.

The first debate was on September 26, and the two candidates made different preparations. Nixon continued campaigning, making a speech before the carpenters' union in Chicago, thereafter spending the afternoon of the debate boning up on issues as if cramming for a college exam. Nixon made the mistake of thinking issues and arguments were more important than appearance and presence. Kennedy was more relaxed, spending the afternoon tanning and performing an informal run through with his advisors. He topped off the day with a call girl, which he would make part of his pre-debate routine.[58]

The Kennedy campaign had won the debate negotiation, convincing Nixon to debate two weeks after leaving the hospital. The Kennedy campaign also forced Nixon to stand during much of the debate, his bent leg becoming more painful. The television studio was also overheated with the debate producers convinced by the Kennedy campaign to focus on Nixon as he sloughed sweat from his face.[59] Nixon refused makeup and did not color-test his suit for the television cameras. His only effort at modifying his appearance was using the drugstore facial applicant—lazy shave—which only made him appear paler. This drew a general conclusion that the television camera made Kennedy look forceful and Nixon look guilty.[60]

The first debate was the most watched and established Kennedy as presidential material, widening his lead over the vice president. Nixon was thrust into the more comfortable position as underdog though his attacks fell flat because Kennedy lacked a record, and the vice president was dogged by his past. The British embassy offered a postmortem on the debate: its dispatch to London described Nixon as aged and shriveled and his habit of running his tongue in and out of his mouth making him appear reptilian.[61]

Nixon was further hobbled by his refusal to take the advice of his top media aide Ted Rogers, who had worked with the vice president during the 1956 election. In that campaign Nixon had become upset after facing unfriendly questions in front of a televised audience, blaming Rogers for the incident. After the debate Nixon followed Rogers's directions as the aide limited his travels and focused on letting the candidate rest more frequently and fattening him up to improve his television image.[62]

Three more contests followed, offering Nixon ample opportunity to recover as the candidates focused on foreign policy, but the scheduling of the debates hindered Nixon's comeback attempt. The second debate was held in Washington DC at 7:30 P.M. or 4:30 P.M. on the west coast, limiting the size of the audience. The third debate on October 13 had Nixon in Los Angeles in a studio with the panel of questioners whereas Kennedy was in New York, again limiting the face-to-face contact between the men. The final debate was in New York but held at ten at night, limiting the east coast audience. Beside the unusual times and formats, the content of the debates revealed the dangers of televised contests as each candidate tried to outduel the other in their bellicose rhetoric.[63]

Two issues, Taiwan and Cuba, dominated the last three debates and pushed both men into extreme positions. The establishment of a nationalist Chinese state on Taiwan was considered a humiliation by the Chinese communist regime. Recapturing Taiwan by force was beyond the capabilities of the Peoples' Army and could have led to another war with the United States. The communist response was the bombardment of two nationalist Chinese islands—Quemoy and Matsu. Not even specks on the map, the two islands were little more than military garrisons and lacked any strategic value.

The defense of the two islands became an issue during the second Eisenhower term, and when pressed on the matter the president offered his usual convoluted answer intended to confuse his opponents. Eisenhower refused to explicitly promise to defend the islands, but said he would do so if an invasion of the islands was considered a Chinese move on Taiwan. Such nuance was unacceptable in a hotly contested presidential race, and Nixon made Quemoy and Matsu's defense a test of who was toughest on communism. In the second and third debates, the old Nixon returned as he hectored Kennedy for not agreeing to defend the islands. Kennedy's weak but accurate response that the islands represented no strategic value was swept away by Nixon's charge the two islands were the first line of defense for the free world.[64]

Nixon's hammering of Quemoy and Matsu forced the Kennedy campaign to surrender. The campaign agreed to endorse Eisenhower's policy on Quemoy and Matsu if it was removed as an issue in the debates. Not sensing a trap in the Kennedy surrender, Nixon agreed only to be blindsided on another foreign policy issue: Cuba.

The fall of Batista in 1959 elevated a former baseball pitcher–turned–bloodthirsty tyrant to the Cuban presidency. For half a century Fidel Castro kept his country in a Marxist Leninist time warp, brutalizing and murdering his people while keeping every citizen in a state of medieval penury. The existence of a communist state only 90 miles from the United States alarmed Eisenhower, and he assigned his CIA director, Allen Dulles, to make plans for mounting an overthrow of the Castro regime. By October 1960 a Cuban exile army had been built to mount a counterrevolution. As the Democrat presidential nominee, Kennedy was briefed by Dulles on these plans, but this did not prevent him from challenging Nixon in the fourth debate. Kennedy demanded to know why the administration was doing nothing to overthrow Castro. His question allowed the Democrat to claim the anticommunist high ground while placing Nixon in a quandary. If Nixon defended inaction while the administration was planning an invasion, he would look foolish and out of touch when it came. Revealing that the invasion was imminent would humiliate Kennedy but damage national security to attain political advantage. In the debate Nixon refused to support the military overthrow of Castro, ensuring Democrats would use Cuba against the Republicans.[65]

Observers of the 1960 election argue the Kennedy–Nixon debates were the decisive factor in the election. With his successful performance, Kennedy raised his status from playboy senator to potential president. As polls turned toward the Democrats, it appeared Nixon made a fatal mistake in accepting the debate. However, these conclusions ignore Nixon's deliberate strategy of raising his campaign during the last weeks of the election. The vice president believed that the real campaigning began in the last two weeks and was unconcerned with poor polling numbers during the late summer and early fall. His calculus was based on Truman's stunning 1948 comeback and Eisenhower's surge in the last weeks of the 1956 campaign. The debates also helped Nixon in fleshing out issues with the vice president performing well in the last three debates. Besides the debate, other factors contributed to Nixon's defeat including his failure to appeal to southerners and the religion issue.

SOUTHERN STRATEGY

Many conservatives lobbied Nixon to appeal to the southern vote. After the Rockefeller debacle, Nixon appeared to give up on detaching the most Democrat region from Kennedy even as the vice president had some advantages in the region. His support of the 1957 Civil Rights Act angered the most racist of Democrats, but their jumping from the Kennedy campaign eliminated those electoral votes for either party. Moderate southerners who were attracted by Republican economic arguments had been voting with the GOP in Congress since 1938. The conservative coalition slowed the Roosevelt administration during the war period and halted many of Truman's initiatives on nationalized health care, labor unions, and integration. The Little Rock crisis had sent some southerners scurrying back to the Democrat Party on the issue of race, but many remained open to voting for Nixon if given the right reason.

Nixon initially tried to exploit the growing divide between southern Democrats and the national Democrat party. During an early September visit to Atlanta, Nixon was greeted by an estimated 200,000 people—many of them curious to see a Republican candidate as few national Republicans visited the state. The overwhelming greeting in a southern city reflected growing Republican support in the urban and suburban south with northern transplants and educated southerners moving away from the rural Democrat party and its fierce defense of segregation.[66]

The southern Republican movement had begun before Nixon's nomination when Barry Goldwater made the rounds speaking before the growing state parties. By 1960 he had become a favorite among conservative audiences, speaking in such unlikely forums as the South Carolina Republican Party. On March 26, South Carolina Republicans nominated Goldwater for president: the first sign Nixon faced dissent from his right flank.[67]

The 1960 election initiated the rise of South Carolina Republicans, led by two Democrats—Senator Strom Thurmond and former governor James Byrnes. Thurmond's 1948 Dixiecrat campaign signaled southern displeasure with the Democrat party's civil rights agenda. He was joined by Governor Jimmy Byrnes, a former member of the Roosevelt and Truman administrations. In the 1950s he mounted challenges to the *Brown v. Board of Education* decision and began to separate himself from the national Democrat party, which was becoming more unpopular in the state.

Byrnes and Thurmond's turn away from the national Democrat Party produced a revitalized South Carolina Republican Party as Eisenhower came within 10,000 votes of winning the state in 1952 and 1956. With Byrnes and Thurmond supporting Nixon over Kennedy, the Republican had a chance to win the state for the first time since 1876, but Nixon ignored signs the solid south was slipping from the Democrats.[68]

South Carolina received only a glancing visit from Nixon on November 3, and Governor Byrnes issued a less-than-full endorsement as he told South Carolinians to vote for the man and not the label. Nixon made unfavorable comparisons between southern heroes Andrew Jackson and Thomas Jefferson on the one hand and New Deal liberals such as labor leader Walter Reuther and Harry Truman on the other. Thurmond endorsed Nixon though the senator's endorsement was racially tinged and directed against the Democrat party rather than for the Republican Party.[69] The 1960 election would mark the next-to-last time that South Carolina voted Democrat for president with Kennedy winning just 51 percent of the vote and joining Illinois and Texas in giving Democrats their narrowest margin of victory.

Nixon's avoidance of a southern strategy may have reflected concern that southern support of the Republican ticket was based on opposition to Kennedy's religion and the civil rights proposals of Democrats rather than acceptance of Republican policy. Religion was a wedge issue in the south. With the Protestant church dominant in the region, southern Democrats faced the twin bigotries of race and religion. Fear that Nixon would attack segregation was matched by concerns that a Catholic president would follow orders from Rome rather than the American electorate. Egged on by Protestant ministers, southern voters faced a quandary over which group they hated more—blacks or Catholics. Some Democrats chose both and settled on Virginia's Harry Bird, but most southerners followed the party of their grandfathers and stayed loyal to Kennedy, preferring a Catholic to a Republican.

Racism jolted the campaign in the fall when Martin Luther King was arrested in Georgia on a traffic violation and shipped off to a state prison. While there were concerns about his treatment, his prominence likely precluded violence, but with tensions rising, both candidates faced a choice. Nixon could intervene with the full force of the federal government behind him, but Republicans enjoyed little influence over a political system dominated by Democrats. Kennedy had influence over southern officials, but intervening for King would alienate white Democrats he had picked Lyndon Johnson to cultivate. The Kennedy campaign reached out to the Georgia governor who agreed to release King. The move galvanized the black vote and helped Kennedy carry northern states with large black populations while Martin Luther King, whose name suggested strong Protestant roots that could have been exploited by the Republicans, turned toward Kennedy. This change in attitude was made clearer when Martin Luther King Sr. confessed his earlier opposition to Kennedy was based on the candidate's Catholicism.[70]

THE CATHOLIC PRESIDENT

The religion issue was the most overstated and understated issue of the campaign. The overstatement fell on the Democrat side as the

Democrat campaign highlighted the religion issue by choosing Protestant states where Kennedy could make his Catholicism and challenge Protestant voters to ignore their bigotry and vote for a Catholic. The Catholic issue was also understated in that the Kennedy campaign never admitted the worst anti-Catholic bias was in the party's base region—the south. The campaign's aggressive focus on stamping out bigotry targeted southern Protestants who had grown up on warnings about Papish plots against the country. The Kennedy campaign realized that if religion became the main issue in the region, Nixon could pick off key southern states including Texas and win in November.

Acceptance of Catholics in government was a slow grinding process. The first major Catholic appointment was that of Chief Justice Roger Taney to the Supreme Court in 1836—the institution more accepting of religious minorities than any other branch of government. Within Congress, Catholic representation increased as cities became urban enclaves for ethnic groups including Irish and Italians; however, it was not until 1928 that a Catholic, New York Governor Al Smith, was nominated for president on a major party ticket. Part of the Tammany Hall organization known for its electoral corruption and machine politics, Smith was distrusted by rural voters. Smith had little knowledge of the world outside the confines of New York City, his urban insularity hurting him on the national stage. Smith's Catholicism combined with his urban background and strong opposition to prohibition confirmed the worst fears of most Protestants that the Democrat party did not represent their values.

In 1928 the solid south split, dooming Smith's candidacy because Herbert Hoover won North Carolina, Texas, Tennessee, Kentucky, and Virginia and swept to victory with 58 percent of the vote. Smith competed for the party nomination in 1932 when it appeared that Hoover was doomed; however, the Democrats did not want to take a chance and nominated Franklin Roosevelt instead; the Smith candidacy appeared to end the quest for a Catholic president.

Prejudice against a Catholic president extended even to those who were formerly Catholic. While Franklin Roosevelt toyed with not seeking a third term in 1940, he considered potential replacements. One of those was Jimmy Byrnes, but the future South Carolina governor had been baptized a Catholic before later converting to the Episcopalian church—the taint of the church preventing his nomination.[71]

Twenty years would elapse before John Kennedy entered the public eye. His father, Joseph Kennedy, had hoped to be the first Catholic president; however, his disastrous tenure as American ambassador to Great Britain revealed his Irish bias against the English, and his isolationism became a burden when war was declared. Kennedy then focused his ambitions on his sons. His eldest, Joseph Jr., appeared poised for a political career, but his death during World War II turned the old man's attention to his second eldest son.

John Kennedy's quick rise from congressman to senator to presidential candidate was fueled by his family's money and his father's ruthlessness. The machine politics of the time required large cash sums distributed to local and state leaders in return for turning out the vote. The same type of politics would be less successful on a national stage as American pluralism produced so many different power centers and points of view, paying off or silencing each went far beyond even the resources of Joseph Kennedy.

Kennedy faced considerable opposition from mainline Protestant leaders; chief among these was the prominent clergyman Norman Vincent Peale. Author of the best-selling book *The Power of Positive Thinking*, Peale enjoyed a massive public following and influence over religion and politics. Peale reasoned that the framers had intended to include Catholics in the governmental system because they had not participated in the formation of government.[72] The Republican Peale refused to accept the possibility of a Catholic president and worked hard for Hubert Humphrey in the West Virginia primary.[73]

Another protestant leader, Billy Graham, joined Peale in opposing Kennedy. He warned a Kennedy victory would place a Catholic in the White House, one in the Speaker's chair, and one as Senate majority leader.[74] Graham later wrote an article for *Life Magazine* praising Nixon with his words serving as a non-endorsing endorsement. Though Graham would not specifically endorse Nixon, his name on the article praising the candidate made clear his support. The Kennedy campaign complained and quashed the article.[75] Graham carefully chose his word when asked about an endorsement, refusing to mention names, but noted it was "no time to experiment with a novice," a clear indication of support for Nixon. He also warned that the "Roman Catholic Church is not only a religious institution but also a secular institution."[76] Graham was an informal Nixon advisor and warned the Republican against appointing a Catholic vice president, noting that Catholic voters would choose a president sharing their faith more likely than a vice president of their faith; he then warned Nixon against running on the Catholic issue as it would repel voters.[77]

   Graham's instincts were correct as 1960 America was much different than 1928 America and less accepting of a purely anti-Catholic
campaign. Peale and Graham relied on constitutional arguments of
preserving a separation of church and state and the possibility of a
Catholic president supporting state funding of parochial schools and
promoting Vatican teachings on marriage and procreation. Many critics warned the church's hierarchical organization and its teaching
of papal infallibility challenged democratic accountability and the
framers' desire to keep religious authority separate from government
authority.[78]

   In August 1960, Peale joined a group of Protestant clergy in Switzerland at the National Conference of Citizens for Religious Freedom
(NCCRF) which used the rhetoric of separation of church and state to
mask its anti-Catholic theme. Another group, the National Association
of Evangelicals (NAE), publicly opposed a Catholic president and supported Nixon as part of an explicit strategy of maintaining Protestant
domination of politics. Peale's efforts created a backlash; his newspaper columns were pulled, and he was forced to publicly denounce the
idea that people should vote based on religion.[79]

   Some in the Democrat party had their own doubts about a Catholic president. Liberals were suspicious of the Church's strong anticommunism and opposition to revolutionary politics. Among those
criticizing the church was Eleanor Roosevelt whose ire was raised by
the church's support of General Franco in Spain and their silence in the
face of European fascism during World War II.[80] The ghost of Senator
Joseph McCarthy hovered over the Kennedy campaign because of the
family's close connections to the senator. Robert Kennedy had been
one of McCarthy's close aides during his early investigations; he then
attended his funeral while John Kennedy was conveniently absent
during the vote on McCarthy's censure.[81]

   Many prominent liberals were hostile to the church including Justice
Hugo Black, who made separation of church and state a constitutional
doctrine in the 1940s. In his opinions in the Court, Black crusaded
against church-sponsored censorship of books and movies which
challenged his absolutist views on free speech and free press. Outside
official Washington, the American Civil Liberties Union (ACLU) and
Protestants and other Americans United for Separation of Church and State
(POAU) opposed the accommodation of church and state.[82]

   Much like Peale, Graham, and other Protestants, the POAU questioned Kennedy's loyalty to the constitution. They feared a Catholic

president would follow papal commands rather than his own conscience. The POAU chairman, Paul Blanshard, offered a rejoinder to William F. Buckley's *God and Man at Yale* with his own *God and Man in Washington*, in which he questioned the ability of a Catholic president to separate the spiritual from the temporal.[83]

The POAU criticized Catholic social teaching on censorship, birth control, interfaith marriage, and public money for parochial schools, issues where the church was opposed by Protestant liberals. The difference between the POAU and Peale and Graham was that liberals lacked a choice as their hatred of Nixon precluded voting Republican, and they were forced to accept at face value Kennedy's promise to maintain a separation of church and state.

The Nixon campaign and Republicans were quick to exploit the religion issue while loudly and frequently denouncing bigotry. Their point man was former Missouri congressman Orland Armstrong who prodded Protestant leaders to formally endorse Nixon and condemn Kennedy.[84] At the May 1960 Baptist convention a Christian Citizenship Resolution questioned whether members of certain churches could oppose a freedom of conscience on procreation and the banning of public money for religious issues. Though the resolution did not mention Kennedy, few doubted it targeted his campaign.[85] In the south, Protestant ministers instructed their congregations to vote Nixon. In Texas these instructions were fought hard by Sam Rayburn and Lyndon Johnson, who feared religion would overwhelm race as the key issue for Democrat voters.[86]

The Kennedy campaign tried to exploit the backlash vote as it emphasized the candidate's religion while condemning those who made Catholicism an issue for voting against Kennedy. On September 12, Kennedy spoke to the Protestant clergy in Houston, turning the focus on bigotry and hypocrisy and arguing that religion should never determine someone's vote. The speech was celebrated as a defense of religious liberty, but it was also a blatantly hypocritical argument as Kennedy openly appealed to Catholics for their vote based on religion. The political aspects of the speech became more apparent when the campaign used a tape of Kennedy's words for campaign commercials.[87] Kennedy also moved to shore up the Democrat left, promising to maintain a near absolute separation of government from his Catholic beliefs while warning that limits placed on Catholic politicians would eventually lead to Protestant politicians suffering the same discrimination.[88]

Besides arguments on a constitutional plane, some anti-Catholic rhetoric ranged from the conspiratorial to the bizarre. One screed that was distributed in swing states claimed that Catholics were responsible for the assassination of three presidents—Lincoln, Garfield, and McKinley—and the attempted assassination of Theodore and Franklin Roosevelt. According to the same source Woodrow Wilson's illness was caused by his Catholic nurse was well as Warren Harding's death.[89]

Another attack linked the Catholic Church and communism, a bizarre argument considering the Catholic Church's unyielding opposition to the Soviet Union.[90] Another topic was the sexual transgressions of the church with insinuation of sexual abuse of nuns found in books such as *The Priest, the Women and the Confessional,* and the *Convent Horror.* The Church denied that women were being sexually abused.[91]

With religion and race dividing the country, Nixon and Kennedy entered the last weeks of the campaign nearly tied in public opinion polls. In the last weeks before the election, Nixon brought in Eisenhower to campaign, hoping the president's popularity would rub off on him. The Republican continued his frenzied campaigning around the country—part of his strategy of attracting undecided voters that he was certain would decide the election. The Republican's energetic campaign had logged over 65,000 miles; he had spoken in 188 cities to potentially 10 million voters.[92]

The Kennedy campaign could be more sedate with the candidate better rested and confident. While Nixon counted up swing states he hoped he could take, the Kennedy campaign relied on Democrat political machines in Illinois, Pennsylvania, Texas, and New Jersey to deliver those states with little effort by the candidate.

ELECTION NIGHT

For the first time the electoral votes of 50 states were up for grabs. However, unlike in 1876, which saw the newly minted state of Colorado provide the decisive electoral votes, neither Hawaii nor Alaska proved important to the election. The 1960 election did resemble 1948 in the threat of southern Democrats splitting from the regular party, but like in 1948 the breakaway southern states did not affect the final result. The southern Democrat candidate, Virginia's Harry Byrd, was able to snatch 15 electoral votes from Kennedy though the region remained strongly Democrat. It would be the last time a solid south would vote for a Democrat even with Jimmy Carter and Bill Clinton at the top of the ticket.

Kennedy's southern coalition was an odd mix of the few black voters allowed to cast a ballot in the region and the white Democrats who opposed any black voting. The two group's vision of Kennedy was diametrically opposed with black southerners interpreting Kennedy's intercession on Martin Luther King's behalf as a sign of his support for civil rights. White Democrats, soothed by the words of Lyndon' Johnson and the fact that southern Democrats controlled congressional committees, chose to believe Kennedy was less of a threat to segregation than Nixon. Their assumption proved correct as President Kennedy's fumbling halted the civil rights momentum generated during the Eisenhower administration.

With the Democrats' southern base secure, the two campaigns focused on the Midwest for votes. Kennedy was certain to sweep the northeast with Massachusetts and New York as the biggest prizes while Nixon enjoyed an advantage in the intermountain and Pacific West with California as the biggest prize. Democrats enjoyed a sizable advantage in the industrial states of Michigan, Pennsylvania, Ohio, Indiana, and Illinois, where unionized labor forces and urban bosses turned out massive votes, real and otherwise, and swamped rural and suburban counties. Kennedy would sweep Michigan and its 20 electoral votes by 67,000 votes. He won Pennsylvania's 32 electoral votes by 116,000 ballots. Nixon won Ohio's 25 electoral votes by 273,000 votes and Indiana's 13 votes by 220,000 votes.[93]

Kennedy tended to win the closest states: Hawaii by just over 100 votes; New Mexico by 2,300. He won Minnesota by 22,000 out of one and half million votes and Missouri by 10,000 out of nearly two million votes. Nixon's closest victory came in his home state: the Republicans won by 37,000 out of more than 6.5 million votes cast. Overall, Kennedy rolled up a vote plurality of 119,000 over Nixon out of 68 million votes cast and a majority of 303–219 in the Electoral College—the closest vote since 1916. Kennedy's margin of victory came in four states: Massachusetts provided a half million Democrat vote plurality; New York provided over 380,000; and Georgia and Louisiana provided vote margins of 184,000 and 176,000, respectively, confirming the wisdom of the Austin to Boston Axis as the Democrats combined major northeastern states with the major southern states.[94]

Nixon held onto two southern states won by Eisenhower in 1952 and 1956 as he won Florida by 47,000 votes and Tennessee by 75,000 votes. Nixon also came close in South Carolina, losing by fewer than 10,000 votes in that predictably Democrat state. In addition Democrats lost Virginia to Harry Byrd and split the Alabama electoral votes six to five while losing one electoral vote in Oklahoma. Nixon took much of the intermountain west, losing only New Mexico and Nevada.[95]

However, the electoral map by the early morning of November 8 was reduced to two states: Texas and Illinois. Both states suffered under powerful Democrat machines with Texas dispersed among rural and urban counties, particularly along the Rio Grande, while Illinois' machine was concentrated in Cook County. The 1960 election in Texas was the opposite of the 2000 election in Florida. In Florida the punch card ballots proved unreliable, and the critics of the process promoted paper ballots. In Texas, Republicans criticized the use of paper ballots in rural counties, where Nixon performed poorly, versus the punch card and machine balloting in large cities such as Dallas and Houston where Nixon rolled up large majorities. The 1960 election was one of the last presidential contests before the 1965 Civil Rights Act gave the Justice Department authority to oversee elections in states such as Texas. States were still free to manipulate vote counts on a racial or partisan basis by using the vestiges of discriminatory voting laws.

Texas state law required voters to cross off the names of candidates they did not vote for while marking for their preferred candidate. Failure to mark off names was grounds for election officials to toss out a ballot. The complicated requirement became a means of fraud when combined with the use of numbered ballots that could be matched with sign in sheets. This was used to ensure that bribed voters supported the Democrat ticket; however, it also allowed the easy rejection of ballots. Republican discovered tens of thousands of rejected ballots; not so coincidentally, most were for Nixon. The discarded votes exceed the Democrat margin of victory.[96] The key counties were found in the Rio Grande Valley, sporting large Mexican populations. Many of the rural counties were controlled by local party machines—the most prominent being run by Sheriff George Parr of Jim Wells County. The thuggish Parr, whose demeanor and appearance symbolized every northerner's image of a hostile red neck, had helped Johnson win his 1948 senatorial race. His vote stealing skills were undiminished by time and age, and Parr-controlled counties gave the Democrat ticket an advantage of four to one.[97]

If contesting the Texas results was a difficult proposition, challenging the Chicago vote proved an impossibility. Chicago Democrats had run the city for nearly 30 years with Mayor Richard Daley and his Democrat machine having mastered maximizing the party vote through legal and illegal means. Daley's ward system was based on pure ethnic politics with Irish, Italian, black, Polish, and Mexican wards run by local Democrat leaders. These leaders were chosen because of their ability to run up large Democrat majorities that could be used to win local and state races and overwhelm Republican vote totals in the suburbs and central Illinois. With nearly every local and state election official elected or appointed with the approval of the Daley machine, few government officials would ensure a fair count much less a recount.[98]

Nixon had little chance of overturning the Kennedy victory. In addition to Texas and Illinois, the Republican would have to seek, receive, and win recounts in South Carolina and New Jersey, two states also controlled by a Democrat apparatus hostile to Nixon. Within a week Nixon had decided not to contest the election, deciding a disputed election would only harm the American election system and harm the country's overseas reputation.[99]

AFTERMATH

Richard Nixon's narrow and controversial loss would haunt his political career. John Kennedy, likely dragged into office by a tainted vote in Texas and Illinois, entered the White House at full speed and immediately stumbled. Two foreign policy crises involving Cuba and the building of the Berlin Wall nearly provoked a nuclear holocaust and produced a Soviet state determined to compete with and defeat the United States. Kennedy's assassination created a mythical figure which ignored his stalled domestic agenda and a deepening military commitment in Vietnam.

It would be Lyndon Johnson, the unwanted and disdained vice president, who would galvanize and pass the Kennedy agenda, seizing the opportunity of national grief to jam through major civil rights and social programs and also a military buildup in Vietnam. Johnson would take the blame for continuing Kennedy's aggressively anticommunist foreign policy, and his presidency ended with a whimper at the end of March, 1968 when he announced his decision not to run for reelection.

Richard Nixon never fully recovered from his 1960 defeat. After losing the 1962 California gubernatorial election he revived his career and won the presidency in 1968. Running for reelection in 1972, Nixon was determined not to face an uncertain outcome, and using political espionage techniques developed by Kennedy and Johnson in the 1960s, he was soon embroiled in the Watergate scandal. His attempts to cover up the break-in combined with the Vietnam War destroyed his presidency.

The Kennedy family would not escape the bad omen of the 1960 election. Joseph Kennedy, having driven his son into the White House, suffered a debilitating stroke in 1961 and lived as an invalid throughout the decade. Robert Kennedy won election as New York senator in 1964 and then challenged Johnson and Hubert Humphrey for the 1968 Democrat nomination. His death after the California primary threw the nomination fight to the convention and placed the burden of the family legacy on the youngest brother, Edward. The death of a campaign aide under suspicious circumstances and stories of frat boy antics including a naked late night stroll on a Florida beach undermined Edward's legacy as he was remembered by many in the public as a puffy, red-faced politician—a poor comparison to his older brother who never aged.

3

The Narrowest of Margins

GARFIELD VERSUS HANCOCK, 1880

The 1880 election followed on the heels of the 1876 election which left bitterly disappointed Democrats wondering how they had lost an election they were certain they would win. However, if 1876 raised expectations among Democrats, the 1880 election would see the party confident they could end the Republican domination of the presidency. The campaign began nearly the moment of Rutherford Hayes's inauguration, a continuation of the country's longest and most contentious campaign. While partisans of the 1876 loser, Samuel Tilden, blamed Republicans for their loss, they would have been more accurate at pointing a finger at southern Democrats including South Carolina governor Wade Hampton III, who had ended the debate over Hayes's election. In return for guaranteeing a Republican victory, Hampton and other southern Democrats had regained power in the three states, South Carolina, Louisiana, and Florida, which had helped Hayes win in 1876. The loss of the three states to the Democrats hurt Republicans in 1880 as they would have to replace the southern electoral votes with northern votes.

Tilden had won 184 undisputed electoral votes in 1876—one short of the presidency. With the Solid South providing 138 guaranteed electoral votes, the Democrat nominee could concentrate on a few northern states. Chief among these was New York with 35 electoral votes and Indiana with 15 electoral votes which would send the Democrats into the White House. Tilden had won both states in 1876, and Democrats were confident they could repeat the New Yorker's success. Democrats were aided in 1880 by a divided Republican Party.

The party lost House seats in three consecutive elections—1874, 1876, and 1878—the latter election producing the first Democrat Congress since 1858. The slow decline in Republican congressional strength was the starkest sign of voters turning against the party. Democrats were more enthused and united, their fury over the 1876 loss deepening their determination to replace Hayes. However, Democrats in 1880 suffered from the same handicap as in the previous years: a weak field of candidates who struggled to overcome a stronger Republican candidate.

Republicans could campaign on the relative success of the Hayes administration. In 1876 the party struggled under the record of the scandal-ridden Grant administration and the 1873 Depression. By 1880 Grant's dismal was a distant memory, and the Republicans could run on Hayes's record of correcting the worst abuses of the spoils system while improving the economy to such a level that many Americans experienced growing prosperity.

HAYES ADMINISTRATION

Rutherford Hayes entered the White House in 1876 as one of the weakest presidents to date. Having dedicated his presidential campaign to reform, Hayes's path to the White House was paved with the very patronage and party politics he had renounced. A four-month election controversy saw three southern states run by carpetbag Republican governments exclude enough Democrat votes to tilt their states to Hayes. The electoral commission's eight Republican members outvoted seven Democrats in granting disputed electoral votes to Hayes.

Elected by the barest margin—a single vote on the commission and a single electoral vote in the Electoral College—President Hayes faced an embittered Democrat Party, a divided Republican Party, and a public clamoring for government reform and an end to a four-year economic depression. However, Hayes's four years in the White House defied expectations, and by 1880 he had revived the Republican brand. His first effort to revive public faith in his party was directed toward the Republican Party bosses. During the Grant administration state leaders such as New York's Roscoe Conkling and Pennsylvania's Don Cameron had seized control of government patronage in their states. The result was disastrous as party loyalty replaced competence in choosing government officials. A cascade of scandals nearly destroyed the Republican Party as Grantism was added to the political lexicon.

Hayes could only defeat the bosses by regaining control over presidential appointment power. The New York Customs House was the center of the struggle because it employed hundreds and was used by Conkling to fund the New York Republican Party with employees providing voluntary political contributions for the party. During the Grant administration, Conkling kept tight control of the customs house as his close ally Chester Arthur ran it as a party fiefdom. Hayes regained control by firing Arthur and replaced him with his own appointee, angering Conkling and the Stalwart wing of the Republican Party.

In 1876 the Hayes campaign had also been hamstrung by a four-year depression triggered by excessive speculation in railroads and an attempt to corner the gold market. As prices collapsed and deflation made debts harder to repay, business and farming sank in a wave of foreclosures; unemployment soared in an era without national welfare programs. Hayes offered economic management, appointing the most effective treasury secretary since Salmon Chase. John Sherman skillfully built up federal gold reserves to ease the transition from a greenback currency to one using gold and silver. By 1878 the currency system had stabilized, and the economy was recovering. Sherman's effectiveness revived Republican prospects for 1880 though it did undermine Hayes's arguments against patronage appointment as the former senator was chosen for his political connections and Ohio origins.

Hayes's effectiveness made it impossible for Democrats in 1880 to campaign against his administration as they had campaigned against Grant in 1876. Having promised to run for only a single term and keeping his promise, Hayes was one of the more effective one-term presidents. However, the president made his share of enemies within the party establishment. His decision to turn over the South to Democrats would create the Solid South voting bloc and anger many Republicans. Hayes's attempt to rebuild the Republican Party in a coalition with former southern Whigs failed badly, and the last southern Republicans in Congress were defeated as the Solid Democrat South took hold.

The Republicans could use the Democrat-controlled Congress as a campaign issue. The 45th Congress, the first of the Hayes administration, began dismantling the legal framework used during Reconstruction. The Posse Comitatus Act forbade the use of army troops within the United States, a deliberate rejection of congressional Reconstruction. The Bland Allison Act revived the silver debate, requiring the national government to monetize silver, a dream of many soft-money Democrats. Both bills signaled how the party would rule if a Democrat won the White House in 1880.

The 46th Congress sported the first Democrat majority in both chambers in 20 years, but the Democrats struggled to pass currency laws as the party was divided between the soft and hard money factions. In the House, Democrats narrowly elected a hard money speaker. The Senate was narrowly divided: the Democrat majority created by the loss of four southern Republican senators. Democrats regained their political rights in the south, associating the party with former confederates who tried to destroy the union—an image that could be best fought by nominating a Union war hero.

Even with Hayes not running for reelection, Republicans did not lack for qualified candidates with the administration offering its own candidate in Treasury Secretary John Sherman. Responsible for stabilization of the currency with implementation of the 1875 Specie Resumption Act, Sherman would have been a front-running candidate in any other election year. With Ulysses Grant's return and the continued presence of former speaker James Blaine, Sherman was relegated to the role of spoiler. The third-term movement and the candidacies of Sherman and Blaine marked one of the strongest Republican fields in its history.[1] However, a strong field sometimes produced deadlocked conventions, and 1880 produced the longest convention in the party's history—a sign of potential division and trouble for the general election.

DEMOCRAT CANDIDATES

While the Republicans enjoyed an experienced field, Democrats struggled to find a candidate who could finally defeat the Republicans. The Democrat nomination for 1880 was less valuable than the 1876 nomination and would depend entirely on the decision of that year's nominee: former New York Governor Samuel Tilden.

The second governor from that state to be nominated by the Democrats after the Civil War, Tilden built his presidential candidacy on his reputation as a reformer. Having defeated the Tammany Hall political machine in New York City, Tilden was nominated in a rush of excitement by the Democrats in 1876 who then bungled the campaign.

Outmaneuvered by the Republicans in Florida, Louisiana, and South Carolina, Tilden offered no direction to congressional Democrats when the electoral vote controversy reached Washington. The resulting electoral commission doomed Tilden whereas his perceived mistreatment of southern leaders such as Wade Hampton III drove them into a compromise with the hated Republicans.

After Hayes's inauguration, angry Democrats blamed Tilden for being inactive and Republicans for stealing the election. In 1878 a House Committee set out to prove the latter only to have the corruption charges against Republicans backfire on them. During the hearings Republicans uncovered scores of coded messages, the cipher telegrams, between Tilden's nephew, William Pelton, and state officials in Florida, Louisiana, Oregon, and South Carolina. According to the telegrams, Pelton offered the officials money for their support on the states' canvassing boards which counted votes and assigned electoral votes to candidates. The cipher telegrams showed the Tilden campaign was more active in winning the election than then believed, but the stories of attempted bribery hobbled his 1880 campaign for nomination.

Five consecutive presidential defeats had coarsened Democrats against Republican attacks on the party's alliance with Confederates—the strategy known as the bloody shirt campaigns that yielded victory after victory even as the economy declined and public corruption dominated the news. However, 15 years after the end of the war Democrats were heartened even as they sought a candidate who could survive the Republican attacks.

Chief among these was the Union General Winfield Scott Hancock. Bearing the name of the Mexican War hero and the 1852 Whig presidential candidate, Winfield Scott Hancock had served in the Army of the Potomac and had been wounded at Gettysburg and in the Bloody Angle battle at Spotsylvania. The end of the war took Hancock to unfamiliar duties for a military officer as he became responsible for implementing Reconstruction in the southwest.

President Andrew Johnson, determined to enforce his form of presidential Reconstruction, removed Lincoln appointee General Phil Sheridan from the Fifth Military District encompassing Louisiana and Texas. The former Democrat Johnson replaced Sheridan with the Democrat Hancock, hoping he would enact a speedier and less onerous Reconstruction on southerners and return state government to local Democrat control.

During his five-month tenure as commander of the district, Hancock overrode Sheridan's order allowing blacks to vote in open elections. Hancock issued General Order 40 which criticized Sheridan for involving the military in civil affairs. Instead, Hancock singlehandedly overturned congressional intent by ruling that federal power could be

overridden by state officials. Congressional Republicans and supporters of strict Reconstruction were dismayed to hear stories of Louisi-
anans cheering Hancock and former Confederate President Jefferson
Davis in the same breath and quickly realized that Reconstruction in
the fifth district had been diverted by the general.[2]

In Louisiana, Hancock forced out the Sheridan-appointed Governor Flanders, replacing him with the Unionist Democrat, Joshua Baker,
who disapproved of black suffrage and civil rights. In New Orleans,
Hancock scrubbed the city council clean of black representatives; he
then tried to replace the black militia with white troops. Ulysses Grant
rejected the request and ordered his subordinate to return the elected
officials to their positions.[3]

Hancock also undermined Reconstruction efforts in Texas. During
a state referendum in February 1867 he forbade soldiers from patrol-
ling polling places. Hancock expressed concern that those same troops
intimidated white voters—a clear rejection of the federal mandate for
troops to prevent white Democrat intimidation of black voters. The
Republican governor denied Hancock's claims that federal troops exacerbated rather than prevented voter harassment.[4]

Having taken Johnson's side on the Reconstruction debate, Hancock
became a target after congressional Republicans seized control of
southern policy and subsequently impeached Johnson, thus ending
presidential Reconstruction. Hancock was removed in March 1868,
but his exploits in battling for southern Democrats and former Confederates earned the respect of the national Democrat party. As a
military hero Hancock had the advantage over other Democrat candidates when facing the war hero Ulysses Grant who was the certain Republican nominee in 1868. The two Democrat front-runners,
New York governor Horatio Seymour and United States Chief Justice
Salmon Chase, were expected to deadlock the convention. Another
candidate, Ohio's Thomas Hendricks, would soon earn the title of
perennial also-ran, but offered himself as a compromise candidate
during the deadlock.

The 1868 Democrat convention was more chaotic than previous conventions as candidates battled for a nomination that promised a slim
chance of victory against the popular Grant. Democrats faced an uphill battle as northern voters equated the party with the Confederacy
whereas the southern party base was under the control of congressional Republicans who imposed military governments on the southern
states. The devalued nomination opened opportunities for second-tier

candidates, including Hancock, even though his campaign was run by amateurs who understood little of the nomination process.

On the first ballot, Hancock's haphazard campaign managed him a second place finish behind Ohio Congressman and 1864 vice-presidential candidate George Pendleton. At that point the Hancock campaign collapsed, its managers having made no contingency for gaining votes on the second ballot to exhibit momentum. On the second ballot Hancock fell below 50 votes, and his candidacy appeared dead; however, no candidate could reach the necessary two-thirds vote as Seymour climbed into the top position then fell back.

Party leaders then began a process of rotating front-runners, shifting delegates to different candidates to see if the convention broke in the candidate's favor. On the 18th ballot Hancock claimed the lead with 137 delegates, which was well short of the nomination. When the jump in Hancock's delegates failed to produce a rush toward him, his numbers declined starting with the 21st ballot. The next name among the rotating front-runners was Indiana's Thomas Hendricks, who took the lead but also could not reach a two-thirds majority. The delegates then returned to Governor Seymour whose criticism of the war was critical to Democrats who planned to campaign on antiwar and anti-Reconstruction policies. Seymour won the nomination, a pyrrhic victory as he was crushed by Grant in the fall, whereas a disappointed Hancock learned lessons from his 1868 defeat and applied them to his campaign for the 1880 Democrat nomination.[5]

Grant's election cast Hancock into the wilderness as the president marginalized his old subordinate and political opponent. Hancock was transferred to Dakota Territory where Indian conflict was certain to mar his military record; he was later switched to the backwater of the Atlantic command, where he watched the parties nearly rip apart South Carolina over the 1876 election.[6] During his internal exile, Hancock was not mentioned as a candidate during 1872 and 1876, but the loss in 1876 deepened Democrat despair that they could ever find a winning candidate.

Having passed over Hancock in 1868 because of his inexperience and poorly managed campaigns, Democrats offered him a second chance, hoping his military heroism would catapult them to victory much as it had with Andrew Jackson in 1828. Military heroes as presidential candidates offer rewards and dangers. Voters find heroism appealing in a political leader, with generals serving as the ideal of a nonpartisan leader who worked for the public interest rather than a

narrow faction. The downside risk was the opposing party exploiting a general's lack of political experience and his unfamiliarity with
issues. In some cases the nomination of a military candidate signals a
desperate party seeking a popular rather than competent candidate.
The Whigs in 1840, 1848, and 1852 nominated military heroes because
their most prominent leader, Henry Clay, proved unable to win. The
party was successful in electing presidents, but the Harrison and Taylor
administrations were cut short by unexpected death; the party suffered through the Tyler and Fillmore presidencies; neither of which is
viewed favorably in history. The Republicans have chosen military heroes including Ulysses Grant and Dwight Eisenhower though Grant's
nomination was borne less of desperation than the 1952 nomination of
Eisenhower, which was the result of the party's 20-year absence from
the White House.

DEMOCRAT CONVENTION

The 1880 Democrat convention opened in Cincinnati on June 22, and
Hancock, learning from his 1868 defeat, arrived with a highly organized campaign. The general relied on a strategy of building delegate
support over several ballots and saving votes to the later ballots to
offer the appearance of momentum.

Hovering over the Democrat convention was the man many Democrats considered elected president in 1876, Samuel Tilden. Having won
the popular vote and come within one electoral vote of victory, Tilden
enjoyed considerable popularity among ordinary Democrats. He was
less popular among the professionals who blamed him for the 1876
loss and bungling the postelection crisis. Many powerful Democrats
saw a second Tilden nomination as guaranteeing defeat.

Tilden entertained his own doubts about another presidential run.
Having never recovered fully from a stroke suffered while being New
York governor, Tilden had retired to his New York farm after his 1876
loss in an effort to regain his health and possibly make another presidential run.[7] Many Tilden partisans wanted their candidate to mount a
revolutionary campaign, having the governor pose as president-elect
seeking a second term. However, continuing his pattern of isolation
that began during the election controversy, Tilden refused to publicly
announce whether he was going to attempt a second presidential
run, leaving many in his party uncertain of his intentions. The April

meeting of the New York State Democrat convention recognized Tilden as a candidate and front-runner, but refused to nominate him—a blow to the draft-Tilden movement. Tammany leader, John Kelly, led the charge against the man who had jailed his predecessor, but could not defeat the unit rule which forced all New York delegates, even those opposed to Tilden, to vote as commanded by the party convention.[8]

Privately, Tilden supported the long shot candidacy of Ohio Congressman Henry Payne. The 70-year-old had sat on the Electoral Commission and voted with the Democrat contingent to elect Tilden. The governor kept in close contact with his managers in Cincinnati though he had not learned from the cipher telegram debacle. The adolescent nature of coding Democrat candidates with names such as oyster, peas, cheese, milk, and squash displayed a lack of seriousness on Tilden's part.[9]

Unbeknownst to most of the Democrat delegates and many New York delegates, Tilden had composed a letter asking the party not to nominate him. In the letter he condemned the "Electoral Commission, the existence of which I have no responsibility," while complaining the commission's "false count was not overruled."[10] Tilden claimed health and personal reasons prevented him from running; however, when the letter was read to the delegates, many wondered if it was part of a ploy to get Tilden drafted. Other delegates expressed relief at being freed from choosing a candidate who could win the nomination but lacked the campaign skills to win.[11]

With Tilden removed from contention, the convention could settle into the dreary task of counting votes and nominating a president. While Winfield Scott Hancock appeared to head the field, he was challenged by an old and familiar name in Democrat politics, Senator Thomas Bayard of Delaware. The Bayard name had a long and rich tradition in the state's politics with the senator's grandfather James Bayard having participated in the 1800 disputed election and chosen Thomas Jefferson over Aaron Burr. Senator Bayard had been a member of the 1877 Electoral Commission and voted each time to assign electoral votes to Tilden. His loyalty was not rewarded by the New Yorker because Tilden blamed the senator for supporting the commission which he blamed for his defeat.

Bayard's rise to the top tier of Democrats was aided by Tilden's struggles in New York. After his defeat, Tilden tried to exert influence in his home state politics and in 1879 supported the incumbent Democrat governor Lucius Robinson. The governor, though, was opposed by John Kelly, the Tammany leader, who was trying to wrest control of the party from Tilden and his allies. At the state Democrat convention Robinson was denied renomination, and a Tammany candidate replaced him. Robinson's defeat was as a blow to Tilden's presidential chances, and Democrats recognized if he could not control his state party, he had no hope of winning the presidency.[12]

Bayard, though, was hobbled by his actions during the Civil War. Representing a border and slave state, Bayard earned the reputation as an antiwar zealot and perceived copperhead, his actions opening up opportunities for Republicans to use the bloody shirt issue against him even as it made him more popular among southern delegates. Bayard's anticorporate rhetoric made him unpopular with large donors, and his open support of the greenback movement which included voting against the Specie Resumption Act heightened doubts if, as president, Bayard would implement radical economic policies. His comparisons of corporations with the ancient monarchical traditions of primogeniture[ ] and mortmain and also denunciations of the aggregation of wealth enhanced his popularity in rural areas but not in the northeast, which controlled large numbers of delegates.[13]

A third candidate, Supreme Court Justice Stephen Field, was part of a well-financed campaign propped up by wealthy Californians desperate to defeat the greenback movement that was burrowing into the Democrat party. The justice had established a reputation as a railroad judge, supporting the industry in bond cases before the Supreme Court. His frenzied dissents in state regulation cases including the *Slaughterhouse cases* and *Munn v. Illinois* made him an attractive candidate for corporate leaders; yet, his tilt toward a social Darwinist reading of the constitution alienated both conservatives and liberals: Republicans and Democrats. His 17 years on the Court removed him from political affairs, and his history as a War Democrat was a positive; however, that isolation also limited his political influence. Field was one of two Democrat justices on the Electoral Commission, and his strong arguments in favor of Tilden had sparked the sudden interest in a Field candidacy though he struggled to excite delegate interest and posed little threat to Hancock.[14]

The nominating speeches for the major candidates excited little interest until Hancock's life story was offered to the delegates. Hancock's speaker promised the general would "crush the last embers of sectional strife and be hailed as the dawn of the longed for day of perpetual brotherhood."[15] The flowery rhetoric propelled Hancock into the lead on the first ballot with the general sporting 171 delegates and Bayard 154. During the second ballot the leader of the New York delegation, Rufus Peckham, threw the state's delegation behind Pennsylvania Congressman Samuel Randall, who gained 98 delegates and jumped from six to 104.[16] However, Randall represented the last gasp of the New York delegation to deny both Hancock and Bayard the nomination. As Bayard's northern support melted away, he was left with mainly delegates from the former Confederacy including South Carolina's Wade Hampton III, making him a purely southern candidate and a certain loser in November. Hancock was pushed over the top on the third ballot, the Democrats believing they selected a man who was safe from Republican accusations that he was a Confederate sympathizer.[17]

THE 300

The Republican convention opened on June 2 in Chicago and promised to be a hard-fought affair. Grant entered as the front-runner, supported by the Republican establishment as he tried to revive the public acclaim first experienced after leading the Army of the Potomac over Robert E. Lee. His two terms as president marked by scandal and economic depression had left Grant a spent and unpopular man; however, after four years out of the public spotlight, Grant's luster had returned.

After serving his country as a general, secretary of war, and president for 16 years, Grant seemed eager to depart Washington. Two months after leaving the White House Grant departed on a round-the-world journey that would last nearly 30 months—a victory tour of sorts that was a celebration of his life and military career. Stopping first in Europe, Grant was a typical tourist, enjoying the art and culture of the continent. Stopping in Berlin, he met with German Chancellor Bismarck in the midst of an international conference settling a dispute between the Russians and Ottomans. He continued on to Greece, Egypt, India, China, and Japan; his arrival in each country was greeted with pomp and circumstance.[18]

Sailing from Japan, he arrived in San Francisco to another wild celebration. Three years out of office, Grant's reputation had risen, his faults forgotten, his fame rekindled. His return on September 9, 1879, was deemed too early with observers believing Grant should have returned immediately prior to the convention and ridden his revived fame to a third nomination. Yet, it would have been impossible to run a presidential campaign with the candidate traveling about the world.

Grant's third-term campaign faltered on the tactics of New York Senator Roscoe Conkling and his congressional allies including Pennsylvania's Don Cameron and the Illinois political boss John "Blackjack" Logan. Senator Logan earned his position as a political general who served mainly in the west with Grant fighting in the Vicksburg and Atlanta campaigns. Logan's military experiences cast him as a strong Reconstructionist and natural ally of Conkling and wielded the Republican apparatus partly built by his friend and political ally, Abraham Lincoln to build support for a third term.

The third-term bandwagon was started early in 1880 with the Pennsylvania Republican convention meeting on February 5 and the New York convention three weeks later. In composing their delegations ahead of other states and candidates, both Conkling and Cameron created an image of the inevitable Grant nomination with a solid base of three states pledged to the former president.[19]

Grant's most formidable opponent was former House speaker James Blaine, known by Republicans as the "Plumed Knight". Denied the 1876 Republican nomination by fewer than 30 votes, Blaine had straddled the issue of running in 1880 until the third-term movement began. Certain he was the only candidate who could halt Grant and prevent the Republicans from losing the presidency, Blaine offered himself as a reform candidate opposed to the Stalwarts. Presenting himself as the leader of the half breed or reform faction, he snatched the very delegates who defeated him in 1876 campaign, but his clashes with Conkling and the Stalwart faction placed him at odds with nearly one-half of his party.

John Sherman was the third major candidate at the convention. A veteran Washington politician, Sherman's achievements were overshadowed by his more illustrious brother William Tecumseh. As Hayes's treasury secretary, Sherman presented himself as a competent leader who acted on rather than just promised reform. Responsible for firing Chester Arthur as head of the New York Customs house, Sherman had created a powerful enemy in Conkling, but enhanced his image within the party's reform wing that favored a continuation of Hayes's efforts to root out corruption in the federal government. However, with Grant and Blaine dividing up most of the delegates, Sherman's best chance at victory was stalemate, standing back and allowing the two Republican heavyweights to batter each other into submission. With Grant's delegates unlikely to switch from their candidate, only a Sherman–Blaine fusion could prevent a third term. Sherman depended upon the support of approximately 100 delegates focused mainly in Ohio and a few southern states where Sherman had appointed Republican office holders.

The first convention battle involved process—the eternal fight over the unit rule. Under convention rules, each state delegation was pledged to a candidate with earlier state conventions divvying up the delegates among candidates. State machine leaders like Conkling and Cameron wanted to control the delegations by mandating that all of the state's delegates vote as mandated by the state convention. Conkling realized victory was certain with the combined forces of the New York, Pennsylvania, and Illinois delegations; however, without the unit rule a significant proportion of the delegates from those three states would desert Grant for Blaine or favorite son candidates.

Senator Conkling was not the only one to recognize the importance of the unit rule fight with the Blaine and Sherman delegations teaming together to defeat the rule. The leader of the anti-unit rule faction was Sherman's campaign manager, Congressman James Garfield, whose influence with Congress and standing in the establishment extended to many of the delegates and made him one of the more powerful players at the convention.

Frustrated with his loss on the unit rule, Conkling then attempted to remove the West Virginia delegation when it refused to automatically support the Republican nominee. The expulsion of a state delegation was a serious decision, and once again it was Garfield who led the fight against Conkling's proposal, creating an enemy in the New York senator but impressing the delegates who would not forget his leadership when the convention deadlocked.[20]

When the convention began on June 2, it became clear that the Grant and Blaine delegations would not desert their candidates for the other. Blaine and Conkling despised each other, the candidate having ridiculed Conkling's clothes and turkey strut in a much reported speech in the House of Representatives. A giant rally for Grant was held in Chicago the day before the convention, but the public show of affection had little effect on the delegates as members of the national convention appointed Ebenezer Hoar, another leader of the anti-unit rule faction, as the convention chair. The combination of technical defeats stifled Grant's support at a little over 300 delegates. Some 60 stray delegates who might have been forced to vote for Grant under the unit rule instead split their votes among various candidates and denied Grant the very votes he needed for a third nomination.

With the rules set, the voting began. Grant's first ballot strength was focused in the south as he picked up a majority of votes in Alabama, Arkansas, Florida, Kentucky, South Carolina, Tennessee, Texas, and Virginia. The southern support was not surprising as most southern Republicans were Grant appointees. They could recall the halcyon days of the Grant administration when southern Republican governments were backed by army bayonets. The return of Grant to the White House would not return Republicans to power, but it might revitalize southern Republicanism in states like North Carolina, Tennessee, and Virginia which sported a sizable Republican vote. In addition to the southern states, Grant bagged three of the larger delegations—New York, Pennsylvania, and Illinois—all under the thumb of the party bosses.[21]

Blaine was only 20 delegates behind Grant though his support was more scattered as he took the western states of California, Oregon, and Nevada, some of the northeast including Maine, New Hampshire, and Rhode Island along with Midwestern states in Iowa, Nebraska, Indiana, Kansas, and Michigan. Blaine's hold on his delegates was weaker than the one enjoyed by Grant, but neither man's supporters were willing to switch to the other. A few states including Vermont, Minnesota, and Massachusetts constituted a bloc of uncommitted delegates or those pledged to third-tier candidates. Conkling struggled to pull in the scattered votes or convince delegates that Grant was the inevitable winner

The delegate count had Grant with 304 delegates, Blaine at 284 delegates, with Sherman at 93. The totals remain fixed through 33 ballots with Grant at 309 and Blaine at 275, the former president never falling from the lead with a high count of 313. As delegates sweltered in the summer heat, it seemed the convention would never end: neither of the leaders was willing to compromise. Sherman's best chance at breaking the deadlock came on the 29th ballot when the Massachusetts's delegation in whole and Minnesota's in part broke to him. However, the treasury secretary had irritated both the Blaine and Grant factions ensuring their votes would never go to Sherman.[22]

As stalemate settled in tired delegates and state party leaders searched for a solution. In past conventions a dark horse or unknown candidate was offered as a compromise acceptable to all factions. In 1844 Democrats rallied around former Tennessee governor James Polk. In 1852 the party rallied around Franklin Pierce, former

New Hampshire senator. During that time Republicans had chosen prominent candidates, men with recognizable names even if they were considered second-tier rather than top-tier candidates. In 1880 a true dark horse, Sherman's campaign manager, James Garfield, attracted the interest of exhausted delegates.

A resident of Mentor, Ohio in northeastern Ohio, James Garfield enjoyed a state legislative career before joining the Ohio volunteers and fighting in Tennessee. He served as a chief of staff under General Rosecrans and the Army of the Cumberland. Garfield pushed the slow-moving Rosecrans to drive from Nashville to Chattanooga. When Rosecrans made his move, he allowed the Confederate Commander Braxton Bragg to escape and prompted Garfield to send a letter to treasury secretary and fellow Ohioan Salmon Chase, complaining of Rosecrans's incompetence. The letter would later sour relations between the two men 17 years later as Garfield's complaint was blamed for Rosecrans's dismissal.[23]

Rosecrans's capture of Chattanooga was followed by the massive battle of Chickamauga. After a missed march by a Union division caused the blue line to break, the stunned Rosecrans joined his defeated troops in fleeing north to Chattanooga. Garfield struggled to rally the soldiers and instead of joining his commander joined General Thomas in his spirited defense to save the army. It would be Garfield's last great military engagement.[24]

In summer 1862 Garfield returned to Ohio on sick leave. While he was stationed there he was nominated for a congressional seat, winning in November. Under the rules of the time, his service in Congress would not begin until December 1863, allowing him to return to Tennessee and the war. Garfield's congressional career matched the shifts in power and opinion of the era. Having survived Chickamauga, Garfield was a radical in handling the south; however, after the war his radicalism cooled, and he tilted toward Andrew Johnson's presidential Reconstruction. Garfield's disagreements with the radical Republicans came to the fore as he argued on behalf of Lambdin Milligan—the Confederate sympathizer convicted by a military court during the Civil War. Garfield joined former attorney general Jeremiah Black in arguing the case before the Supreme Court, and the former southern sympathizer and the Union general convinced the justices that Milligan's military trial violated the constitution.[25]

Garfield's opposition to radical Reconstruction changed after Andrew Johnson vetoed the 1866 civil rights bills while his anti-Republican rhetoric sent the congressman back to the radicals. He voted for the 14th and 15th amendments and the impeachment of Andrew Johnson; he rejected the Lincoln policy of issuing greenbacks, but supported a protective tariff as a means to build American industry. During his 18 years, Garfield rose through the House ranks, chaired the Appropriations Committee, and then served as the House Republican leader during the Hayes administration.

Garfield was a loyal Republican soldier during the 1876 election as he convinced the Louisiana canvassing board to overturn Democrat votes and give the state to Hayes. Garfield was also selected as a member of the 1877 electoral commission which upheld the electoral votes of disputed states. He successfully escaped the animus and charges of corruption that dogged John Sherman who had worked with him in Louisiana. Garfield relations with Hayes were strained even as Sherman's appointment to the Treasury Department opened a Senate seat that Garfield wanted. Hayes convinced him to remain in the House by dangling the possibility of Garfield being elected Speaker of the House with the help of former southern Whigs. After the agreement collapsed and Republicans remained in the minority, Garfield continued as the Republican House leader where he earned the respect of his colleagues while maintaining a lower profile than former House speakers Schuyler Colfax and James Blaine, who had been tainted with scandal during their tenure. As the 1880 election approached, Garfield again agreed to limit his own ambitions for a fellow politician. He agreed to head John Sherman's presidential campaign—an offer made by Sherman to prevent Garfield from seeking the nomination. In return Sherman used his influence to have Garfield elected as senator by Ohio legislators.[26]

Having accepted the duty of collecting delegates for his Ohio colleague, Garfield was honor bound not to seek his own nomination, but it did not prevent others from mounting a draft campaign as the Blaine and Grant forces deadlocked. Spearheading the Garfield-for-president campaign was Philadelphia banker Wharton Barker, who used his personal wealth and connections to influence the Wisconsin and Indiana delegations. Barker had a plan to play the Grant and Blaine factions against each other with his initial goal of halting the Grant bandwagon by using dissident members of the Pennsylvania delegation. When the third-term movement was stymied, New England delegates would join the Grant forces to halt Blaine creating a Blaine–Grant deadlock which caused the convention to grind to a halt on the 23rd ballot.

At that point Senator Conkling would look elsewhere, and faced with a choice of the despised Sherman or the unknown Garfield, he would choose the dark horse.[27]

The 34th ballot finally saw a break as Barker's legwork began paying dividends. The Wisconsin delegation switched from Blaine to Garfield, and on the 35th ballot Indiana joined Wisconsin, doubling Garfield's delegate count. As Blaine's support crumbled, Grant remained fixed just above 300. Conkling struggled to keep his delegates in line, promising the next break would be for Grant. The New York senator was approached by Blaine's managers who asked the New Yorker to shift his state's votes to Blain to halt the Garfield movement, but not surprisingly Conkling rejected the suggestion because he was certain that the ex-president was too beloved to be shunted aside for the unknown Garfield.[28]

The final break came on the 36th ballot; however, instead of a stampede for Grant, the move was toward Garfield as Blaine and Sherman delegates along with second-tier candidates switched to the Ohioan as a means to end the stalemate. Garfield swept to victory, collecting 399 delegates. As Grant delegates wandered the hall, stunned at the sudden defeat, Garfield was forced to choose a vice president on the fly. His first choice, Black Jack Logan, refused while his second choice, Chester Arthur, was another dark horse, his only government position being head of the New York Customs House and fired by Hayes. Always the loyal subordinate, Arthur sought Conkling's advice, the senator advising Arthur to reject the offer; however, Arthur rejected the advice and accepted, the best decision of his life.[29]

THE CAMPAIGN

The Stalwart's bitter disappointment with Grant's defeat was partly allayed by the choice of Arthur as vice president. Though Garfield had no direct control over the vice-presidential choice, the delegates who nominated him saw Arthur as the best method of uniting the party. Arthur's nomination was also an implicit rejection of Hayes's civil service reform and a signal that unlike Hayes, Garfield would not deliberately antagonize the Stalwarts. However, Arthur's selection distressed the reformers and forced Garfield to reject the Stalwart candidate, William Chandler, for national committee chair. Chandler had been Hayes's manager and was responsible for slipping him into office. Because the chair position was the de facto campaign manager, Garfield's choice would determine campaign issues and strategies. Garfield chose the nondescript Marshall Jewell, which soothed reformers concerns that the candidate had sold his soul to the Stalwarts.[30]

Garfield's balancing act continued after the convention as he traveled east from Ohio to New York City and a meeting with Senator Tom Platt. The gathering did not include Roscoe Conkling, whose frustration with Grant's defeat boiled over during the train ride back to New York from the convention. Conkling described Garfield as an angle worm and an artful dodger, both praise and criticism from a politician who had been described in similar terms by his opponents. Conkling went further, declaring he would have preferred his old enemy Blaine to Garfield as the Republican nominee.[31] The senator avoided the candidate during his New York visit, leaving it to Platt to reach an agreement with the nominee that included assurances the New York Republican boss would have influence in selecting government officials in the state. The agreement brought Conkling and Grant back into the fold, both men aggressively campaigning for Garfield in Republican strongholds. Garfield's success at uniting his party differed considerably with the Democrat struggles after Hancock's nomination.[32]

Hancock stumbled at the start of his campaign. His first decision was to select the chairman of the Democrat national committee, his de facto campaign manager responsible for setting the campaign issues and raising money for the campaign. Hancock leaned on the Tilden wing of the party, choosing William Barnum, the choice proving a disaster as Barnum struggled to raise money and failed to organize the campaign.[33] Hancock refused to resign his military commission and spent several weeks of the campaign holed up at his headquarters on New York's Governor's Island. The decision left Hancock separated from the campaign but also the public. While Garfield conducted a front porch campaign that allowed him contact with voters, usually supporters, Hancock was limited to visits from campaign staff and high-level Democrats—all of whom rode a ferry to the headquarters. The slow start left Hancock and the Democrats behind the Republicans, who had ample experience at organizing and running national campaigns. Hancock remained the commander of the Atlantic military division throughout the entire 1880 campaign—a clear conflict of interest that would not have been tolerated in the modern military.

Hancock's retention of his military command was part of the Democrat strategy to foil another bloody shirt campaign. The uniformed candidate highlighted the general's military heroism at Gettysburg and Spotsylvania; yet, the advantage was misplayed with Republicans used his record to once again put the Democrats on the defensive.

The Garfield campaign focused on Hancock's role in the trial and execution of the accused Lincoln assassins. Hancock struggled to explain the hanging of Mary Surratt, whose boarding house had been ground central for the assassination planning. After Surratt's death doubts were raised about her guilt with the general accused of moving with unseemly dispatch and lack of due process to rush the execution. The Mary Surratt controversy was combined with the religion issue. Republicans tried to appeal to Catholics by noting Surratt was Catholic, and her death might have been an expression of anti-Catholic sentiment by the general. Republicans then appealed to Protestants by accusing Hancock of pro-Catholic biases and support of public funds for Catholic schools.[34]

Amidst this controversy, Hancock also fended off accusations from his old commanding officer as Ulysses Grant accused him of grasping for higher office. Grant denounced Hancock's decisions as commander of the fifth military district, accusing him of appealing to Democrats by undermining civil rights enforcement and Reconstruction policy.[35]

Republicans expanded on the bloody shirt campaign, accusing Hancock of attempting a military coup in 1876 to seat Tilden and noting the endorsement of former confederates including South Carolina Governor Wade Hampton III. A pamphlet entitled *Rebel Echoes* was distributed and composed of a litany of the war's economic and political consequences that continued to affect the country.[36]

The attacks continued on all fronts with the Republican Stalwarts tying Hancock to the south. On September 17, Constitution Day, Conkling began his campaign for Garfield with a slashing attack on Democrats, reviving the old claim that if elected Hancock would sign a bill for confederate war claims against the federal government.[37] The senator then denounced the south as an economic stepchild and accused the region of producing less than the north with its lower tariff revenues acting as a drag on the treasury. He warned that southerners could not be trusted with the government's finances.[38] Hancock dismissed Conkling's ranting about Confederate war debt though he responded flippantly about Union war claims. His denial only continued the war issue while ignoring the senator might have silenced them. In engaging Conkling, Hancock hand delivered a winning issue to the Republicans.[39]

The tussle over the war threatened to make the election a dismal repeat of the last two decades, but the Maine state election on September 13 forced the Republicans to reconsider their tactics. The state elected a Democrat governor as part of a fusion ticket with the Greenback Party, humiliating James Blaine on his home territory. The Plumed Knight, fearful of losing his political base for a presidential run in four years, offered Garfield advice on switching strategies from the Civil War to economic issues. Recognizing the importance of industrial states such as Pennsylvania and Ohio, Blaine convinced Garfield to focus on the tariff, proposing a higher protective tariff to build the country's industrial base while excluding imports that would compete with American products. The tariff would also protect American jobs and create an internal market to ensure those jobs remained in the country.[40]

The Republican campaign script changed in October and put the Democrats on the defensive. Hancock was unprepared for the shift in the political debate and struggled to meet Garfield's pro-tariff arguments. Republicans enjoyed two advantages in emphasizing the protective tariff. The arguments appealed to northern manufacturing interests in swing states like Indiana, New York, and Pennsylvania. Opposition to the tariff was centered in the Democrat south where Republicans had little chance of winning.

The shift in tactics caught Hancock flat-footed. The general had been nominated to alleviate the effect of bloody shirt strategy; however, when the Republicans changed strategies, the Democrats also had to change. Hancock and his partisans began to regurgitate talking points on the tariff with the general agreeing to an interview with the *Patterson (NJ) Daily Guardian*. The interview had Hancock expressing limited support for a form of protective tariff. Disaster came at the end of the interview when the general declared that the tariff was a local issue.[41]

While the Republicans shifted from past campaign strategies, Democrats continued to pound the issue that nearly won them the 1876 campaign: political corruption. Garfield's congressional career placed him on Capitol Hill in the midst of the worst corruption scandals in the country's history. When the federal government commissioned the building of the transcontinental railroad, the Union Pacific railway formed a construction company, Credit Mobilier to engineer and construct the railway from Chicago to San Francisco.

When questions were raised over about the use of government subsidies in construction, executives of Credit Mobilier enlisted Massachusetts' Republican Congressman Oakes Ames to distribute the company's stock to prominent congressional Republicans to cool the ardor for investigation. When the stock distribution scheme was revealed, several prominent congressmen were trapped, the most powerful being former House Speaker and Grant's vice president Schuyler Colfax, who was forced from the Republican ticket in 1872 for his involvement. Colfax's successor, James Blaine, was also caught in the railroad scandal, tainting his political career though the consequences would not catch up to the Maine Republican until his failed 1884 presidential campaign.[42]

During Congressional hearings on the scandal Oakes revealed he had offered stock to Garfield; the issue centered on a check for $329 which Garfield claimed was a loan but Ames claimed was dividend on Garfield's shares of Credit Mobilier. The number 329 became the favorite attack for many Democrats who scribbled the amount on walls and sidewalks to remind voters of Garfield's involvement in the Republican scandal. Though the Credit Mobilier scandal was a reminder of the close relationship between Republicans and the railway industry during the Grant administration, the small amount cast doubt on the depth of the charges with voters doubting a man like Garfield could be bought for a mere $300.[43]

With scandal dogging Garfield and inexperience tripping up Hancock, the election turned to voter turnout. The 1880 contest would see one of the highest voter turnouts in presidential history, some 80 percent of voters choosing between Republican and Democrat. The interest in what was an uninspiring campaign can be attributed to the pull of patronage and the threat to Republican officeholders of losing the White House and being replaced in their jobs by Democrats. With Conkling and Platt working hard in New York to maximize the party vote, it was inevitable that turnout would increase though it was masked by the rise of the Solid South.[44]

The 1880 election was the first presidential contest featuring Democrats in full control of the 11 states of the old Confederacy. Forty years would pass before a Republican presidential candidate won a former Confederate state, and 84 would pass before a majority of the states voted Republican. With the south no longer competitive, Republicans faced a more difficult climb to an electoral vote majority. In 1876 Tilden had taken the key states of New York, Pennsylvania, and Indiana; all three were considered the most competitive large states. Hancock and the Democrats did not have to win all three states as they began with 11 southern states along with the border states of Missouri, Kentucky, and West Virginia, allowing them to focus their money and efforts on the three large northern states. Garfield and the Republicans would have to sweep all three states to have a hope of victory.

Garfield did enjoy an advantage over Hayes, who had to run on Grant's record of corruption and economic depression. The relative competence of the Hayes's administration provided a positive record for the Republicans, but the greatest asset for the party was the candidate himself. Garfield's dark-horse status aided his efforts to unify the party. A Grant nomination in 1880 would have alienated the Blaine faction whereas a Blaine victory at the convention would have been followed by the Stalwart's sitting on their hands during the election. Not seen as favoring one faction or the other, Garfield appealed to both wings without making guarantees, but convinced the two wings of the party he was on their side. With the unlikely pair of Blaine and Conkling working on his behalf, Garfield enjoyed a better chance at winning in 1880 than Hayes had in 1876.

GARFIELD BY A NOSE

The 1880 election produced the closest popular vote of any election. Nearly 8.9 million votes were cast with Garfield managing a 9,500-vote plurality. The closeness of the election was the result of a dramatic rise in the southern Democrat vote. While southern Republicans remained a force, though weakened by limits on voting rights, they were overwhelmed by the new state Democrat governments. In Florida, Republicans came within 4,000 out of 50,000 votes of winning and 9,000 out of 140,000 votes in North Carolina. The remainder of the south rolled up large majorities for Hancock, distorting the popular vote. The large southern pluralities hid the fact that Hancock had won a significantly smaller percentage of the northern vote than Tilden won in 1876.[45]

The New York governor that year won his home state, the neighboring state of Pennsylvania, and the reliably Republican state of Indiana. Hancock lost all three states. His time spend in New York at his army headquarters only made it a closer defeat as Garfield won by 21,000 votes out of nearly 1.1 million votes cast. Garfield won Pennsylvania by 37,000 votes whereas Indiana was the closest of the swing states with Hancock losing by only 7,000 votes.[46]

The Democrat did win a few close states; his California victory of 78 votes out of 160,000 total votes, the closest result of any state in presidential history up to that time. Hancock won Delaware by 1,100 votes and Nevada by 900. Garfield enjoyed an Electoral College majority of 214 to 155 for Hancock. New York's 35 electoral votes provided the margin of victory though Indiana and a few other states including Maine, Indiana, and Connecticut could have swung the election to Hancock with only a 30,000-vote change.[47]

The congressional races produced similarly close results with Democrats losing their Senate majority and the House. The Senate elections produced a tie which would initially be broken by the president Chester Arthur; however, after Garfield's death the president pro tempore former justice David Davis cast the deciding vote to create a Republican Senate. Republicans won a larger House victory, winning 19 seats and for the first time since 1874 controlling Congress.[48]

AFTERMATH

James Garfield would enjoy his presidency for less than a year. Beset by patronage seekers, Garfield struggled to right his administration after his razor-thin victory. His major achievement—the appointment of Stanley Matthews to the Supreme Court—would be his one success before a deranged assassin shot him in the Washington train station. Garfield lingered for months, with wounds infected by incompetent doctors, and the infection rather than the bullets killing him in September, 1881. Garfield would join William Henry Harrison as one of two presidents whose administrations were so brief they are not ranked by presidential scholars. Chester Arthur, the ultimate in spoilsman and the creation of Roscoe Conkling found himself in the White House without an agenda or political base. Arthur began the civil service system by signing the Pendleton Act. His one misstep was the nomination of Conkling to the Supreme Court, the senator turning down the seat after the Senate confirmed him. Arthur would be rejected by the Republicans in 1884, Conkling's longtime rival, James Blaine, finally winning the nomination on his third try. Arthur would die of kidney disease in 1886, forgotten.

Winfield Scott Hancock receded into obscurity after his defeat: his brief, unsuccessful political career was forgotten in comparison to his actions at Gettysburg and Spotsylvania. After Hancock's narrow defeat, Democrats returned to New York for their nominee, and in 1884 they nominated Grover Cleveland, who became the first Democrat president in a quarter century.

The events surrounding the 1880 election was repeated once in presidential election history. In 1952, Adlai Stevenson ran for a sixth consecutive Democrat presidential term dating back to 1932. Much like in 1880 he faced a successful general, Dwight Eisenhower, and attempted to exploit his political inexperience. However, Eisenhower proved a better candidate than Hancock and won easily, becoming the only Republican president in the 36 years between the New Deal and the Great Society.

4

The Court Rules for . . .

BUSH VERSUS GORE, 2000

Few periods of American history compare to the political turmoil of 1998–1999: the latter years of President Bill Clinton's second term. The two-year period began with a White House intern's story of her affair with the president and ended with the second presidential impeachment in history. In the midst of the impeachment drama, congressional Republicans were shaken by unexpected midterm losses, the resignation of House speaker Newt Gingrich, then the resignation of his successor, Robert Livingston, after his admission of an affair. Clinton's acquittal in the Senate did not calm the general feeling of disgust which swept through the country as the media revealed the peccadilloes of top politicians. The image of a successful Clinton presidency, built on a skyrocketing stock market and a calm international scene, would be challenged in the 2000 election as the Democrats sought to win a third consecutive presidential election for the first time since the 1940s. Vice President Al Gore's campaign depended on the public view of the mixed Clinton record.[1]

CLINTON ADMINISTRATION

Amidst all the fury and scandal of the Clinton years, the American economy appeared on the verge of permanent prosperity. The new technological advance of the Internet drove stock market speculation to new highs, the NASDAQ climbing above 5,000, the Dow Jones Thirty Industrials above 13,000. The Chinese foray into capitalism created a new middle class in Asia while keeping a lid on American inflation and interest rates by drastically lowering wage rates and the cost of imports. The curious contradiction of a corrupt administration presiding over massive economic growth was made even stranger by Clinton's complicated relationship with his own party.

The two decades prior to Clinton were difficult times for the Democrat party at the presidential level. While dominating Congress during much of the 1970s and 1980s, the Democrats won only one presidential election between 1968 and 1988. The public perception of Democrats as the anti-American and pro-government party made them unacceptable on Election Day. Reviving the party required a transformation and move to the right as New Democrats came to the fore. Among the leaders was Arkansas four-term governor Bill Clinton, who sought a third way of governing that deemphasized government and placed more of the onus on the private sector to solve societal problems. During his 1992 campaign and presidency he sought to soften the edges of the liberal agenda with epigrams such as abortion would be safe, legal, and rare and that the era of big government was over. Thereby, he sought to exploit American's dislike of the rhetoric of big government while enjoying the benefits of those same policies.[2]

Clinton changed the rhetoric of government, designating public spending as investments while pledging to balance budgets and reinvent government. In this last promise, Clinton assigned Vice President Al Gore the task of changing how bureaucracy operated. Gore went to work trying to make the federal workforce more svelte and efficient, reducing its size by eliminating positions and reducing the number of federal employees. Chief among this was Gore's much discussed National Performance Review (NPR). The NPR was one in a long line of government reform proposals, but unlike those of the 1930s through the 1950s—the Hoover and Brownlow reports—the NPR disdained the bureaucratic system of organizing government. In his speeches Gore called for greater flexibility for government workers, the NPR intending to free those workers from excessive regulation while adopting the private sector's financial incentive system that rewarded hard work. The Inside-the-Beltway issue became a national issue with Al Gore's famous appearance on the David Letterman show where he denounced government's regulation of such mundane objects as glass ashtrays. Gore and Letterman ridiculed the requirement that an ashtray not break into more than four pieces if shattered; they then demonstrated on a government-issued ashtray.[3]

Clinton's successes would be limited to a four-year period immediately following his first midterm election in 1994 and his second midterm election in 1998. In that period Clinton faced the first Republican-controlled Congress since the Eisenhower administration. Its leader, the brilliant but tempestuous House speaker Newt Gingrich, pushed Clinton to the right and likely saved his presidency by becoming a ready-made foil for the president. During that four-year period a stagnant economy was revived, government spending reduced, and a small federal surplus produced.

The start of Clinton's second term began ominously. After thrashing Senator Robert Dole in the 1996 presidential election, Clinton was greeted by the Supreme Court decision in *Clinton v. Jones,* allowing a sexual harassment civil suit to proceed against the president. The unanimous decision was the first claim of executive immunity since the Court upheld Richard Nixon's claim in *Nixon v. Fitzgerald.* In the midst of discovery for the trial it was revealed Clinton had an affair with a White House intern, Monica Lewinsky, and tried to obstruct justice by convincing Lewinsky to lie under oath. For several months in 1998 Clinton denied wrongdoing while a special prosecutor collected evidence of perjury and obstruction. The prosecutor's report, filed in August, was used by Republicans to impeach Clinton in December 1998. The subsequent 1999 impeachment trial ended in Clinton's acquittal as Republicans were unable to garner a majority vote much less the two-thirds necessary to remove the president. However, the spectacle of a president engaged in frat boy antics in the oval office hurt the Democrat party and forced Al Gore to make a difficult decision on whether to continue the New Democrat policies tainted by Clinton or to strike on his own and distance his campaign from the administration.

Gore's flirtation with the New Democrats began in 1988 with his first presidential run and ended with his 2000 campaign as he appealed to the party's left wing. The Democrat base had grumbled about Clinton's moderation while basking in his success as the first Democrat president to serve two full terms since Franklin Roosevelt. The old Democrats who dominated Congress viewed the New Deal and Great Society as the template for success. A passive presidency was to be limited to kindly Republican presidents whereas Democrats were activists who expanded government. The loss of Congress to Republicans in 1994 soured the old Democrats to Clinton's politics which upended their majority while easing his reelection. The continuation of Clinton's policies for a third term was a compromise too far. Liberals searched for a challenger to Gore and Clinton from the left, but struggled to find a plausible candidate, a sign of Clinton's effectiveness at weakening the left wing of his party.

Gore's challenger came in the person of former New Jersey senator Bill Bradley. The Gore–Bradley contest pitted a former member of the New Democrat movement against the man representing the first New Democrat administration. After a successful pro basketball career, Bradley had won a seat in the Senate in 1978 and served three terms. In 1986 he helped pass major tax reform legislation, which represented the Reagan policy of flattening the tax code by creating two rates and eliminating tax deductions. Bradley's success cast him as a different Democrat: one who could operate outside the rigid New Deal dogma that dominated much of the party. Bradley was mentioned in 1988 as potential vice-presidential material, his Ivy League education and pro-athletic career making him an attractive candidate. However, 1986 proved to be the height of his political career. A near election defeat by an unknown in 1990 and the Republican takeover of the Senate in 1994 convinced Bradley to retire.

Out of office for three years, Bradley attracted disaffected liberals and some moderates who worried about Gore's judgment in backing Clinton during the impeachment process and in continuing the president's New Democrat policies. Gore's opponents made their presence known when they propelled Bradley into the lead in the all-important money primary as the senator outraised Gore by fall 1999. Independent and liberal Democrats drove up Bradley's numbers while the press aided his campaign with positive coverage, a sign of reporters' boredom with the lackluster Democrat race.

Even as Bradley became a viable challenger, he suffered from the handicaps that made him popular among policy wonks. During his appearances the senator focused excessively on policy details, boring his audience who preferred hearing broad themes from presidential candidates. Bradley's three-year hiatus separated him from the Clinton scandals but also made him vulnerable to accusations he had abandoned the party. Gore repeatedly attacked Bradley for throwing in the towel against the Republicans whereas he and Clinton fought the good fight to prevent Congress from shredding the safety net. Bradley responded with the typical challenger's attack that Gore was unelectable. Highlighting opinion polls that showed Gore trailing Republican front-runner George W. Bush by double digits, Bradley argued that voters were suffering from Clinton fatigue and with the endless drama and corruption surrounding the administration.

Only a candidate who was not part of the administration could defeat the Republicans.[4]

At times Gore appeared rattled by the Bradley challenge. A series of missteps by Gore reminded voters of Clinton's corruption and Gore's vague personality. The most serious was Gore's selection of former House Democrat whip Tony Coelho as his campaign manager. The choice of Coelho raised red flags among the Democrats and the media who were reminded of his forced resignation from Congress in 1989 after reports of unusual financial. The collapse of the junk bond market and the savings and loan industry cost American taxpayers hundreds of billions of dollars, and Coelho's involvement in both painted a picture of a politically connected politician bending the rules for private profit.

After his resignation Coelho maintained political and business connections and in 1998 was chosen to head the American pavilion at that year's world expo in Lisbon, Portugal. However, by spring 2000 he was snarled in another scandal as the state department investigated claims of extravagant expenses: the exploitation of his position to benefit family members and friends and his use of publicly funded cars and apartments for potential investors in his private venture capital firm. As the investigations made Coelho an issue, he was forced from the Gore campaign before the Democrat convention.[5]

Gore also hired feminist and image consultant Naomi Wolf to mold his media image. Wolf's advice became fodder for Republicans when she advised Gore to adopt the persona of an alpha male who would dominate and control every situation. Wolf's advice drew snickering from the media and the public and added to Gore's image of endless pliability as a politician willing to bend his principles and personality for political gain. Gore's dramatic kiss of his wife Tipper at the 2000 Democrat convention may have also been part of Wolf's plan to present the alpha male type to the voters.[6]

However, for all of his early stumbles, Gore benefitted from the Democrat primary schedule, established as part of a three-decade reform effort of how the party chose its presidential candidates. The poor showing of Democrats in presidential elections coincided with that reform effort. After the debacle of the 1968 Democrat convention, the party's left wing shouldered its way into the nominating process, establishing quotas and proportional representation to enhance racial, ethnic, and gender diversity among the delegates. The creator of this system was South Dakota Democrat Senator George McGovern who rode the rules to victory in the 1972 Democrat primaries, then to disaster in the general election.[7]

McGovern's system then came under attack and for nearly 30 years the right and left wings of the Democrat Party battled over obscure nominating rules. To weaken the effects of primaries, Democrats created super delegates, high-level appointed or elected Democrats who earned automatic votes in the convention and could swing a nomination battle toward their preferred candidate. The primary system was further reformed with the creation of Super Tuesday: a collection of mainly southern primaries intended to give the region and conservative Democrats a voice in the nomination. The primaries of larger states were moved closer to the start of the year to enhance their influence over the early, smaller states of Iowa and New Hampshire. Yet, amidst all of these changes, Democrats elected only two men president in 30 years. By 2000, a new set of reforms were in place and aided Al Gore as the front-runner.

The reforms enhanced the importance of the Iowa caucuses and New Hampshire primaries by not scheduling any elections between February 1 and March 7. The arrangement created a five-week vacuum allowing Republicans to dominate the media message with primaries in South Carolina, Michigan, Arizona, Virginia, and Washington State, while the Democrats did not hold a primary. The gap would help Gore recover in case of a Bradley upset because it allowed the better-funded, better-known vice president to set right his campaign. In addition, Bradley would lose any momentum gained with a victory.

A Gore victory in Iowa and New Hampshire would cripple Bradley as he would be unable to pick off a primary victory to stem the momentum against him. The media would turn against him or even forget him, allowing Gore to run as the inevitable nominee.

THE STRAIGHT TALK EXPRESS

The Republican nomination battle was also influenced by changes in the nominating process. Four years earlier the front-runner, Senator Bob Dole, fended off a right-wing challenge from magazine publisher Steve Forbes and conservative commentator Pat Buchanan. Both men lashed out at Dole, weakening him during the primaries and contributing to his defeat in the general election.[8] The Republican establishment acted quickly, changing the rules in many states and opening their primaries to independent voters in the hope of diluting the influence of conservative activists. The expected beneficiary of this expansion of the primary electorate was Texas governor George W. Bush. As governor, Bush alarmed conservatives with his talk of compassionate conservatism: the addition of "compassionate" sounded like an attack on conservative principles and suspiciously like a diluted conservatism prone to making concessions to Democrats. The name Bush reminded conservatives of his father, George H. W. Bush, who had also made concessions to a Democrat Congress in 1990, breaking his no-new-taxes pledge and losing the 1992 election.

As the eldest of George H. W. Bush's four sons, George W. Bush had lived an unsatisfying existence after graduating from Yale Business School. He served briefly in the Texas Air National Guard—a service that proved contentious during his reelection campaign—and wandered from business venture to business venture, usually in an alcoholic haze. His transformation from overgrown frat party boy to sober Christian came in 1986 after his 40th birthday, which he celebrated much like past birthdays with an excess of alcohol. Tired of his lifestyle, he renounced alcohol and straightened his life, diving into his father's 1988 presidential election campaign even as he maintained a low political profile. Bush enjoyed one successful business as part owner of the Texas Rangers baseball team.[9]

In 1994 Bush launched an unlikely campaign for Texas governor against popular incumbent Ann Richards. She had earned national name recognition during the 1988 Democrat national convention, bemoaning "poor George" who was born with a "silver foot in his mouth."[10] Running for a second term, Richards enjoyed an approval rating of 60 percent, but was hindered by a Republican year and her unabashed ties to the unpopular Bill Clinton. Texas Republicans were also eager for a measure of revenge after the elder Bush's 1992 defeat, and electing his namesake was a perfect balancing of that defeat.[11]

Bush won easily in 1994 as Republicans demolished the Democrats' permanent congressional majority. His younger brother, Jeb, fared less well, narrowly defeated in the Florida governor's race. Fortunately for "Dubya," Jeb was not one to quit after a defeat and won the election in 1998, placing him in perfect position for his brother two years later.

By 1999 Bush was considering a presidential run. Offering a new brand of compassionate conservatism that included a record of working with Texas Democrat legislators and willingness to spend money, Bush was considered more moderate than the conservative

Republican Congress. Bush's appeal to independents and moderate Democrats heightened conservative angst that his moderation would undermine their conservative agenda. However, Bush utilized social issues and his personal witness as a born-again Christian to quiet, if not completely silence, those concerns. More important to his efforts was his father's million dollar rolodex, complete with names of tens of thousands of large donors who could raise massive sums of money and charm the Republican establishment. The fund-raising advantage allowed Bush to outspend even Steve Forbes, who had his deceased father's billions to draw upon. The money also allowed Bush to escape the spending limits of the federal campaign as he refused federal matching funds. This saved him from Bob Dole's fate as the 1996 nominee was forced to spend most of his money during the primaries and then watch helplessly as Democrats spent millions running advertisements against him without a Republican response. By January 2000, Bush appeared to be a juggernaut, much like Al Gore, on the straight road to the nomination.

With Bush representing the party's moderate wing, the conservative activist portion was represented by publisher Steve Forbes, who was self-financing his second presidential run while expanding from his one-note 1996 campaign that ceaselessly plugged his flat-tax idea. Joining Forbes was Gary Bauer, leader of the Family Research Council, an influential interest group within the antiabortion movement. With his money and experience in one national campaign, Forbes seemed the more formidable candidate. Yet, 2000 would not be 1996 redux, the conservative revolution of 1994 having run its course. The American public was exhausted by the Clinton years marked by partisan bickering and capped off by a presidential impeachment. Most voters sought a lowering of voices and a pause in the ideological battles that had torn apart Washington.[12]

The Republican right wing had been partly discredited by the Clinton impeachment battle and could not mount a credible campaign against the well-funded Bush. Instead, it fractured as candidates and their campaigns squabbled over illusory scandals including two former Bauer staffers alleging infidelity by the candidate.[13] With conservatives split and relegated to the back of the pack, the party's declining liberal wing mounted a challenge to Bush and at times seemed on the cusp of unseating the front-runner.

Senator John McCain, navy flier and prisoner of war during the Vietnam War, had easily won the Arizona Senate seat vacated by Barry

Goldwater in 1986. His reelection campaign proved tougher after he was embroiled in a savings and loan scandal involving Charles Keating—a corrupt savings and loan operator. Keating used his connections with McCain and other senators to avoid government investigation. When Keating's business collapsed with thousands of investors reduced to penury, the federal government was left with the bill.

The scandal forced the retirements of Michigan senator Don Riegle and California senator Alan Cranston, both Democrats, and threatened McCain's reelection. In response McCain became a born-again reformer, separating from the Republican Party and attacking the corrupt campaign finance system he used so effectively in his first term. By 2000 McCain sported the reputation as a burr in the saddle of establishment Republicans and launched his presidential campaign as a maverick willing to challenge the corrupt Washington system.

McCain began his campaign "Playing the POW Card," by focusing on the stories told in his bestselling autobiography *Faith of my Fathers*. His book presented him as a heroic figure, being shot down over Vietnam, surviving six years as a Vietnamese prisoner, and then running for Congress. The book was a celebration of McCain's life, but also offered insights into his personality, his poor record at the naval academy, his independent and petulant streak, all of which followed him into his senatorial career. By 2000 McCain enjoyed little legislative achievement and an excess of moralistic rhetoric.[14]

In his 14-year Senate career McCain alienated many of his colleagues with a fierce temper and a good-versus-evil perception of politics. The senator's hometown newspaper, the *Arizona Republic*, editorialized on McCain's temperament with stories of battles with Republican colleagues and his launching into profane tirades when they dared question him. Whispers about mental instability and the effect of years as a prisoner of war dogged McCain in his Arizona campaigns. To answer critics McCain released his health records including psychological exams conducted after his captivity. The press examined the records and gave McCain a clean bill of mental health though questions on his temperament followed McCain through the 2000 and 2008 campaigns.[15]

With his mental stability vouched for by the press, the senator ran a populist campaign, confronting the special interests and lobbyists who feared a McCain presidency because of his strong ethics and disdain for Washington corruption. McCain's focus on his lengthy war record drew comparisons with Bush's sparse record and allowed the senator to equate military service with presidential leadership. Bush became an obsession with McCain, the senator attacking the governor's lack of knowledge on the issues. These charges were recycled by the Gore campaign during the general election campaign. McCain called for a muscular foreign policy that included rolling back outlaw regimes such as North Korea and Iraq. His foreign policy proposals earned McCain a partial endorsement from the doyen of realist Republicans and the bête noire of conservatives, Henry Kissinger.[16]

By December 1999 McCain's attacks on Bush were having their desired effect. The Texas governor was caught unawares by the challenge, his advisors still expecting a challenge from the party's squabbling right wing and unable to react from a left challenge. According to the polls, McCain's Straight Talk Express had driven him to a three-point lead, 37 to 34 percent, over Bush in New Hampshire. Yet, the same poll showed him leading Bush by only three points in his home state of Arizona. A month later at the end of January 2000, McCain led nationally as likely Republican voters gave him a lead, but the margin proved an illusion as McCain trailed Bush among key Republican constituencies. McCain led among men—aged 34–39—partly because of his military career and muscular foreign policy. The senator also led among those earning over $75000 and among moderates. Bush led among women by two points, but had a massive 18-point lead among those with a high school education and 22 points among conservatives—the two largest voting blocs in Republican primaries. Bush also led on the electability issue with 78 percent of Republicans believing he could win in November while 57 percent said the same of McCain. The polls showed a close race, but as the primary season progressed, Bush's inherent advantages took their toll on McCain.[17]

IOWA AND NEW HAMPSHIRE

As the first election in the primary season, the Iowa caucuses had attained an outsized importance in choosing a president. Republicans attached less significance to the Iowa caucuses than did Republicans as both Ronald Reagan and George H. W. Bush lost the state's caucus, but won the nomination and the presidency in 1980 and 1988. George W. Bush enjoyed a sizable lead in the caucuses, his well-oiled organization and plentiful campaign funds coupled with a deliberate appeal to

Iowa evangelicals all but ensured victory against the more secular and dour McCain.

For Al Gore, Iowa represented his first chance to halt Bradley's momentum. Bradley mistakenly believed his dramatic rise in the Democrat polls made him a viable national candidate. The senator made a costly mistake in dividing his attention and resources between Iowa and New Hampshire rather than focusing on the latter where he had a genuine chance of winning. Working hard in Iowa and earning a respectable second-place finish only slowed his momentum because in a two-man race, second place equated with last place.[18]

Bradley's late entry into Iowa doomed him. The caucus process rewarded organizational skill and an ability to bring voters to the scattered caucus sites on a cold Iowa night. Gore's influence among Iowa grassroots Democrats and his well-funded campaign provided an insurmountable advantage. New Hampshire's primary required a different strategy. The state had been unkind to Democrat front-runners with Lyndon Johnson in 1968 and Edmund Muskie in 1972 humbled, their campaigns ending shortly after a weak primary performance. Bill Clinton was the first presidential candidate of either party to lose New Hampshire and win the general election.

Bradley was helped in New Hampshire by his ties to the northeast and his running to the left of Gore. It was also a must-win for the senator but also key to Gore. Bradley was unlikely to defeat the sitting vice president; his aloof style and four-year hiatus from politics weakened his appeal among grassroots Democrats and politicians. However, a Bradley win in New Hampshire would extend the primary season and force Gore to focus money and time on the primaries whereas a New Hampshire victory would end the Bradley insurrection.

Gore swept Iowa with 63 percent of the vote to Bradley's 35 percent. McCain did not challenge Bush, leaving the governor a clear field to knock out the challengers to his right. Steve Forbes, once considered the greatest threat to Bush, came in second with 30 percent of the vote while Bush earned 40 percent. It would be Forbes's best finish and the end of the viability of his campaign while McCain could shrug off his four percent finish having refused to campaign in Iowa.[19]

New Hampshire followed eight days later, the primary ending the Democrat campaign while reinvigorating the Republican contest. Bradley pinned his hopes on the state, appealing to both the Democrat left and independents who could vote in either primary. Gore appealed to the Clinton Democrats who believed that another four years of a new Democrat administration was best for the party and the country.

Bradley lost valuable time campaigning in Iowa rather than New Hampshire, and the divided efforts hurt him among the Granite State's population which felt entitled to the complete attention of challengers such as Bradley. The results produced a hairsbreadth win for the vice president with Gore winning just under 52 percent of the vote. Though Bradley would continue, a series of defeats heading through Super Tuesday dried up his funding and ended his campaign.[20]

McCain rather than Gore may have precipitated Bradley's defeat. The Arizona senator had established a near permanent position in the state with his Straight Talk Express and challenged Bush and the Republican establishment on immigration, campaign reform, and tax cuts. McCain's deliberate appeal to cranky independents who sought significant change in Washington served him well in the state but alienated mainstream Republican voters. Bush's campaign was flat, his message uninspiring to independents and the more secular Republicans who populated the state. By the weekend before Election Day it was clear Bush was going to lose although few predicted the drubbing of 49 percent to 30 percent. With the Democrat campaign all but over and the front-runner Bush seemingly vulnerable, McCain became the flavor of the month as journalists focused on the senator as a compelling election story.[21]

THE DERAILED EXPRESS

Media attention exploded around McCain, making him an instant presidential contender while galvanizing conservatives. After the smoke settled and Bush won the nomination, analysis of the New Hampshire victory demonstrated how the victory reflected the state's oddities rather than measuring McCain's popularity. In 1980, Reagan had defeated the elder George Bush, halting Bush's big mo but earning him the vice presidency. Eight years later Bush halted Bob Dole's momentum with a crushing victory over the senator. Four year after that instance, Bush's narrow victory over Pat Buchanan revealed the cracks in the president's campaign. Buchanan's popularity in the state continued in 1996 when he defeated Bob Dole. Representing the paleo conservative wing of the Republican Party, Buchanan's views were nearly polar opposites of McCain's.

Buchanan opposed free trade, open immigration, and the first Iraq War while supporting conservative social policy on abortion and gay rights. McCain's New Hampshire victory, coming only four years after Buchanan's, either represented a dramatic shift in the views of the electorate or a change in the composition of that electorate. The latter possibility gained credence with Bill Bradley's narrow loss to Al Gore. McCain and Bradley represented their respective party's reform wings and appealed to upper income college-educated voters who under New Hampshire law could vote in either primary. McCain won these voters partly on the electability issue because voters rated him most likely to win the nomination and the general election. The media attention heaped on the McCain campaign further enhanced his challenger status.[22]

The New Hampshire results revealed the weaknesses of both campaigns with observers noting that McCain was "dodging tough questions by quoting his biography while Bush answered tough questions with clichés."[23] While the McCain victory excited the media and sent the Bush campaign into crisis mode, Bush's newfound popularity with conservatives gave him the inside track to the nomination.

The Bush campaign struggled to correct the media perception that the McCain campaign rode on candor while the governor hid from reporters in his motorcade. The media portrayed McCain as strong when he attacked Bush, but when the governor responded he appeared weak. However, Bush had thrown few punches in New Hampshire, rejecting a tough advertisement comparing McCain to Clinton. Bush seeming indifference to his election was reflected in his answer to a question about voters supporting his policies. "If they don't agree," Bush had responded to a reporter's question, "that's all right. We'll go fishing in Texas."[24]

However, the governor's supporters were less sanguine. In a series of meetings after the defeat, the campaign mobilized conservative groups to throw rhetorical punches at McCain while Bush took the high road. The campaign trotted out a new slogan "A reformer with results" which highlighted Bush's experience at working with Texas Democrats to reform education and liability law.[25]

While Bush took the high road, conservatives slashed at McCain in South Carolina—the next important primary. The National Right to Life Committee attacked McCain's uneven position on abortion, claiming he favored research on aborted babies. Americans for Tax Reform targeted McCain's opposition to Bush's tax cut plan. A regional group, the National Smokers' Alliance, charged McCain's antismoking bill would have harmed tobacco farmers in the Carolinas, the one region of the country where smoking retained a level of popularity.[26]

Riding high from his New Hampshire victory and the glowing stories from the national media, McCain was unprepared for the sheer quantity and viciousness of the attacks. An email campaign was launched intimating that McCain fathered an illegitimate child and focused on his adopted Bangladeshi daughter. There were charges of hypocrisy on campaign finance because of McCain's contacts with donors. McCain responded late, then overly aggressively, running advertisements comparing Bush with Bill Clinton, an attack that turned off many Republicans who considered Clinton a liar and a felon—neither term applicable to Bush. After his 11-point loss in South Carolina, McCain transformed his Straight Talk Express into a snarling attack machine.[27]

The nastiness began in earnest during the next big primary, Michigan, where the three-term Republican governor John Engler all but guaranteed a Bush victory. In response McCain adopted the tactics he believed had defeated him in South Carolina. Phone banks were used to target Catholic voters, charging that Bush's visit to South Carolina's Bob Jones University was a sign of anti-Catholic bias. The university was known for its strong religious views including a strain of anti-Catholic rhetoric. The charge was ignored by the Bush campaign but infuriated congressional Republicans, who were struggling to tamp down the furor over the House of Representatives choosing a Presbyterian minister over a Catholic priest as House chaplain. The charges of Catholic bias would hurt other Republican politicians and may have contributed to the loss of a Republican senate seat in the state.[28]

The McCain campaign's use of phone banks and anonymous charges was a change in tactics from his earlier moralizing against negative campaigning and signaled the eruption of the Arizona senator's famous temper. Even after winning Michigan McCain turned his anger on traditional Republican constituencies during a speech in Virginia Beach where McCain tackled the topic of religion and its mixing with politics. The senator lumped together religious leaders from the left and right, characterizing the antisemitic Louis Farrakhan and Reverend Al Sharpton with Pat Robertson and Jerry Falwell as agents of intolerance. He decried Republican clerics as evil, a term usually reserved for the old communist Soviet Union or terrorist states.[29]

McCain found himself on the defensive when the author of the speech, former candidate Gary Bauer, called it as unwarranted and ill-advised and demanded a retraction. McCain limply responded by declaring he was a uniter not a divider and tried to use his POW days as an example of his faith. Bush responded with silence; Falwell and Robertson did the same: the campaign was pleased to watch McCain implode with the aid of the once supportive media, as he burned bridges with the very people he would need for 2008. By April 2000 the McCain insurgency ended, and the Arizona senator endorsed Bush. With the Bush–Gore general election battle set, the two campaigns settled into developing their strategies for victory.[30]

GORE AND THE GENERAL ELECTION

Al Gore faced a difficult strategic decision for the fall campaign. As the incumbent vice president he could embrace the Clinton administration's positive economic record, but also answer questions about the administration's many scandals. Gore could also separate his campaign from Clinton and appeal to the Democrat left wing which saw Clinton's triangulation policies as Republican lite.

Gore also suffered from the vice-presidential syndrome. As the second highest executive officer, Gore had few responsibilities and was expected to lay aside his ambitions on behalf of the president. Gore's obsequiousness, though, hurt his candidacy and was on full display during the impeachment controversy. After the House impeachment vote, Gore publicly defended Clinton, declaring the impeached president was one of the great presidents in history while denying Clinton had obstructed justice or engaged in perjury.

Reasserting his political independence in 2000 reinforced Gore's image as a grasping politician which he earned during his first presidential run in 1988. Facing defeat in the New York primary, Gore allied with New York Mayor Ed Koch, who used a press conference to launch a broadside against the demagogic Jesse Jackson—an attack interpreted by many Democrats as racist. Gore was denounced for surrendering his principles and being transformed from southern moderate to New York bigot.[31]

Changing that image had been a slow process; his tenure as vice president reversed the hurt feelings created in his 1988 campaign.

However, as the 2000 election progressed, Gore's bad tendencies re-appeared. In an effort to appeal to a cross section of Democrat voters, Gore sought a new Al Gore and began to resemble another former vice president, Richard Nixon. During his 30-year political career, Nixon created several new personalities though the snarling, attack-oriented candidate of 1946 was never far from the surface. Gore's constant persona changes became an issue and were reinforced by the alpha male debacle before coming to a head during the three presidential debates with George W. Bush.

As spring bled into summer, the national conventions offered an opportunity to test out fall campaign strategies. Gore made the unusual choice of running a prospective rather than a retrospective campaign. Most prospective campaigns were run by challengers who lacked a record on which to run with candidates focusing on future policy, challenging past policy, and promising change. A retrospective campaign is associated with a successful president seeking reelection or a candidate representing that administration and focusing on past accomplishments and promises to retain successful policies. In 1988, with Vice President George H. W. Bush running for a third consecutive Republican presidential term, the party ran a retrospective campaign, celebrating the accomplishments of the Reagan administration in foreign and domestic policy and promising to build on those accomplishments. Gore represented a relatively successful administration, but instead of embracing the Clinton record, he turned away from the incumbent's policies.

Gore's acceptance speech at the convention sounded more like a challenger than a vice president. According to Gore "This election is not an award for past performance." The quick dismissal of eight years of Democrat success resembled the type of speech expected of challenger Bush. Gore went on to note "I am not asking you to vote for me on the basis of the economy we have." His glossing over of the perceived prosperity of the time became controversial after the election as Gore was criticized for distancing himself from the scandal-plagued Clinton. A more likely strategy would have compared the Clinton years to the troubled George H. W. Bush administration and then asked the country if it wanted to return to the past—a play on George W. Bush's familial connections.[32]

The vice president's decision to run a prospective campaign may have been more a personal than a political decision. Within the campaign Gore earned the reputation for arrogance and a disastrous overconfidence that had him regularly rejecting the counsel of his advisors to demonstrate he was in control. The decision to look ahead rather than run on the Clinton record appears to have been that of Gore alone.[33]

Bush predictably ran a prospective campaign, adopting the theme originating in the 1960 Kennedy–Johnson campaign against Richard Nixon. Bush criticized the inaction of the Clinton administration in solving problems and promised that a Bush administration would confront rather than ignore problems. The image of a tired administration being replaced by an active president willing to act resembled Kennedy's 1960 promise to move the country toward a New Frontier.

Bush was careful not to attack the perceived prosperity of the time but rather promising to put "Conservative values and conservative ideas into the thick of the fight for justice and opportunity." Part of this was to put a conservative gloss on big government reform proposals. His "No child left behind" proposal increased federal involvement in local education policy but with an emphasis on testing opposed by the educational establishment. Bush's Medicare prescription drug plan included an expansion of the Medicare program but using private insurance companies to provide coverage with government subsidies for the poor.[34]

The issues and strategies raised in the conventions were expanded during August and September 2000 as the two men traveled around the country, focusing on key swing states including Florida, Ohio, Virginia, and Pennsylvania. However, the policy debate was interrupted by the presidential debates, and the vice president saw his campaign derailed by his attempt to present a new Al Gore to voters.

DEBATES

For the first time since 1980, presidential debates turned an election. In 1980 the battle between Jimmy Carter and Ronald Reagan was tight through much of the summer and fall, the two men exchanging leads until the single presidential debate a week before the election. The 2000 debates lacked that defining moment such as Reagan's "There you go again" quip at Carter but would prove nearly as disastrous for Gore.

After 1980 both parties were careful in scheduling debates several weeks prior to Election Day, hoping to dilute any gaffes and allow for damage control. In 2000 the four debates followed the pattern as they were scheduled within a two-week window, October 3–14, allowing three weeks of spinning and comment before the election. There were three presidential debates with a single vice-presidential debate between Dick Cheney and Joe Lieberman sandwiched between them.

The debates also marked the rise of the cable news networks as NBC and FOX pushed debate coverage to their cable channels MSDNC and Fox news, in order for NBC to show the baseball playoffs while Fox maintained its regular programming.[35]

The trio of presidential debates utilized three formats that were first used in 1992. In one debate the candidates would be standing; the second debate would have the candidates seated at a table with a moderator while a town hall format was used for the final debate. The formats were intended to humanize the candidates as real people, but the demands of television created a faux realism. The misnamed town hall debate had audience participants chosen on the basis of polling results to root out partisans. The spontaneous questions were submitted in advance to the moderator, Jim Lehrer, who selected his preferences. Ensuring no direct contact between candidate and voters with actual opinions, the debates offered the two men as deities unable to respond to the unexpected or unrehearsed.[36]

The most contentious portion of the debates was the back-and-forth maneuvering of the two campaigns seeking advantage in timing and format. Resembling children on the playground, the two men who would be president offered proposals and then accused their opponents of trying to avoid the debates. On September 3, Bush offered to debate Gore on two daytime talk shows. Gore accepted the offer in addition to the three scheduled debates; he then accused Bush of trying to avoid a prime-time encounter. The Bush campaign hotly denied the contention, accusing Gore of avoidance of debates which the Democrat then rejected. The end result of the posturing was an apparent Gore win, the Democrats maneuvering Bush into debate formats he disliked. Gore's triumphalism, though, was a miscalculation as debate expectations for Bush plunged while expectations for Gore soared. Lacking a complete annihilation of Bush on national television, Gore would be considered a loser. The vice president's strutting and boasting about his debate prowess further reinforced his image as a serial exaggerator, highlighted by his odd claim to have passed legislation creating the Internet.[37]

The first debate proved a near disaster for Gore. Held on October 3 in Boston, the debate had Gore at his worst, adopting the persona of the smartest kid in the class who bullied the other kids with his intellectual abilities. During a segment on Bush's promised Medicare prescription drug plan, Gore attacked the Texas governor, rambling on about the inadequacy of the Bush plan and lobbing numbers at the audience. Bush deflected the attack, noting Gore's ridiculed suggestion he had created the Internet by suggesting the vice president may have also invented the calculator. Bush also coined the term "fuzzy math," which he repeated in responding to Gore's attacks on his tax and prescription drug plan.[38]

The first debate offered few memorable moments but one large imprint, that of a petulant Gore sighing with disgust at Bush's answers, treating his opponent as less than qualified to be standing on stage with the vice president. Commentators declared Bush the winner by exceeding expectations while Gore was faced with trying to improve on his second debate performance. The first debate also trapped the vice president, his reaction to and treatment of Bush unpresidential. Repeating his mistakes in the second debate could be disastrous. Changing his approach, though, would reinforce the building impression that Gore was an empty suit, a politician willing to change his positions and personality to win.[39] However, the talk of a Gore defeat was not supported by early polling of debate viewers. A CBS News poll had 56 percent saying Gore was the winner while only 42 percent said Bush had defeated the vice president.[40]

In the second presidential debate on October 11, viewers saw a different Gore, more subdued, more agreeable. The debate had the candidates seated at a table, possibly calming Gore though the sedate vice president offered a frightening comparison with his performance eight days earlier, his toned down personality making it seem Gore adjusted his behavior according to opinion polls. Instead of making voters forget about his earlier performance, Gore opened new questions about his candidacy.[41] By the end of the second debate another personality change had occurred, that of George W. Bush. The unserious frat boy running on his father's coattails and rolodex was transformed into presidential material. Viewers of the debate agreed that Bush had won with 51 percent saying he had bested the vice president whereas 48 percent said Gore was the winner.[42]

The October 17 "town hall" debate offered the most memorable moment of the three encounters. In the format candidates wandered the stage answering preselected questions from a poll-selected audience. While answering one question, Bush turned to find Al Gore standing uncomfortably close to him. Bush's startled reaction summed up the relationship between the candidates, the overbearing Gore crowding the easygoing Bush, who seemed amused rather than angered by the incident. The scene reminded many of the recent New York Senate debate when Republican Rick Lazio crossed the stage to hand a document to the Democrat candidate, Hillary Clinton, and was criticized for an invasion of her personal space. Lazio would go on to be crushed in the Senate election.

The final debate continued the pattern of the first two, with the relaxed Bush turning in his best performance while Gore's changing personalities heightened distrust of him and his ties to the scandal-plagued Clinton administration. However, even with the much discussed Gore stalking of Bush on the stage, 55 percent of viewers said Gore had beaten Bush in the third debate. The early perception among viewers of a Gore win, though, did not help the Democrat nationally as his numbers dropped. Prior to the first debate the vice president led the governor 45–41; however, after the third debate Bush led Gore 44–42.[43]

Bush's lead hurt his campaign as Republicans began a premature victory celebration, and Bush's campaigning pace slowed. The governor focused on Senate and House races in the final weeks of his campaign rather than spending time in presidential swing states. Bush only visited Florida again after polls showed his lead in the state declining.[44] Gore's campaign went into overdrive. Adhering to the Democrats' Get out the Vote (GOTV) efforts in the 1998 midterms, Gore focused on the party base of women and minorities, trying to maximize the turnout of these Democrat groups. Meanwhile, Bush's apparent stroll to victory was halted after his past was again revived.

Most campaigns worry about an October surprise, a news story breaking only days before Election Day. The 2000 election would have a November surprise. With Bush pulling ahead and the Gore campaign desperate for a break, news broke in Maine on Thursday night, November 2. The major networks reported that night that a Democrat operative had discovered Bush's 1976 arrest for driving under the influence (DUI). The news was not entirely unexpected in that Bush had revealed a hard drinking past that ended in 1986. The arrest did not include jail time, and Bush had his license suspended without further drinking and driving incidents; however, the record raised question whether Bush was hiding other arrests from his past.[45] The Gore campaign proceeded carefully, a full-scale attack on Bush's past likely producing a full-scale attack on the Clinton scandals, which went far beyond driving over the legal limit. Yet, this November surprise halted Bush's momentum and may have turned some undecided voters toward Gore.[46]

THE POLLS

The 2000 election was the most heavily polled of the presidential election upsets. George W. Bush opened an early lead in 2000: his separation from the Republican Congress and poisonous partisanship of the Clinton administration created the image of a Republican governor who could change Washington politics. After the conventions, Gore had a sizable lead in the Electoral College based on state-by-state polling. The vice president led in 27 states with 337 electoral votes whereas Bush had 197 electoral votes in 23 states. The sizable advantage though hid the fact that state polls were unreliable because they used smaller sample sizes than national polling and were not always conducted by professional pollsters.[47]

Through October, the Gallup–CNN–USA Today poll showed Bush with a point lead of two to four with the final poll at the end of October showing Bush leading 47 to 45. With both candidates below 50 percent, the election was deemed too close to call with the Bush campaign warning that the Texas governor could win the popular vote while losing the electoral vote.[48]

With Gore running partly on the Clinton administration record, the retiring president played a significant role in the election even as he was sidelined by the Gore campaign. As Clinton administration scandals dominated the news, the president's declining popularity was reflected in the polls. In March 1999 only 29 percent of Americans supported a third term for Clinton, and in August 55 percent of those polled said they had "tired of Clinton." Even the president's policies, perceived as his strongest asset in relation to his personal life, became less popular. In February, 54 percent of Americans wanted continuation of Democrat policies by the next president. By August that number had dropped to 44 percent.[49] Another poll from that month had 48 percent of voters wanting a new direction whereas 44 percent sought no change in policy—a clear opening for the Republican candidate.[50]

By October 2000 Clinton represented a drag on the Gore–Leiberman ticket. Only 17 percent of voters would vote for Gore based on his ties with Clinton whereas 40 percent would vote against Gore because of his Clinton ties. The numbers increased among independents with 45 percent opposing Gore because of Clinton whereas only 10 percent supported Gore for the same reason.[51] Those same independents who favored economic over moral issues proved decisive in the election. One-third of voters who approved of Clinton's economic policies, but were repulsed by his personal behavior, voted for Bush. This group was generally unconnected to the political process, and Gore lost them as he was unable to straddle economic and personal issues.[52]

While the 2000 election was hard fought, it was one of the cleaner campaigns in recent history. Gore forfeited any chance to make an issue of Bush's past indiscretions. Since 1992 Democrats had denounced attempts to tie Bill Clinton's sordid past to his qualifications for the presidency. During the Clinton administration Clinton's squalid personal behavior was papered over with the argument his personal life was irrelevant to his presidential performance. Having set the bar low for personal behavior, Democrats lacked legitimacy in questioning Bush's past of heavy drinking and drug use. The same could be said of his brief and mixed military record in the closing days of the Vietnam War.[53]

With negative attacks limited, both men built on strong personal appeals to voters. An October 20 *Newsweek* survey found 71 percent of voters found Bush personally likable, and 67 percent found Gore the same. Both men were tied on offering strong leadership while voters were split 50–50 on whether the candidates shared their views on issues.[54]

Gore led on some issues whereas Bush led on others though both men tended to rank well above 50 percent. Eighty-two percent of people agreed Gore was intelligent and well informed while 69 percent said the same of Bush. Sixty percent said Gore "cares about people like you" while 53 percent said the same of Bush. Sixty-three percent ranked Bush as honest and ethical, and 52 percent rated Gore as such. Only in the category of "Says what he believes not just people want to hear" did Gore fall below 50 percent with forty eight percent agreeing with the statement. Bush earned higher marks at 58 percent.[55]

Though preelection surveys showed a close vote was possible and that both men received high marks from the public, danger signs appeared as Gore struggled to hold onto southern states easily won by Clinton in 1992 and 1996. Gore's southern difficulties were starkest in his struggles in Tennessee: his home state which had elected him to

Congress, then the Senate. Throughout the campaign Bush held a lead in most Tennessee polls—the distance ranging from two to 11 points.[56] Gore's decision to return his campaign headquarters to Nashville was based on a desire to save money but also reestablish ties to his home state and region. In October members of Gore's family campaigned in west Tennessee and Memphis, struggling to rouse the black vote. Their efforts would go for naught as Bush won the state with 51 percent of the vote, taking Tennessee's 11 electoral votes which would have won Gore the presidency.[57]

Beside Tennessee Gore also struggled to connect in the most Democrat state in the south: Arkansas. With Bill Clinton in the White House and Gore originating from a neighboring state, it seemed Arkansas for the first time since the 1950s would vote Democrat for the third consecutive presidential election. However, with the president's popularity waning and scandals fresh in voters' minds, Gore used Arkansas to further separate himself from Clinton. The vice president rejected campaign events around the state house where Clinton had claimed his prize in 1992 and rejected Clinton radio advertisements targeting blacks.[58] The early polls showed a small Bush lead in the state, but the Republican easily won 51–45, taking six electoral votes from Gore.[59]

Another concern for Gore was the Nader effect. The Green Party candidate was below five percent nationally, but continued to appeal to left-wing voters in the swing states of Michigan, Minnesota, Wisconsin, Oregon, and Washington. Fearful that they were losing voters to Nader in those states, the Gore campaign stated that a vote for Nader was a vote for Bush. The media eagerly reported on the Nader problem, though the third-party candidate would turn none of those states to Bush.[60] However, the Nader effect and Clinton's influence would prove inconsequential compared to the decisions made in the offices of various Florida county clerks because local officials would become national celebrities during the postelection controversy.

As with many great historical events, the smallest change can have unforeseen and dramatic consequences, and in Florida that change was the requirement that a state constitution reform committee meet every decade to propose amendments to the state's constitution. The commission was formed in 1997, and the next year it proposed a seemingly minor change to ballot access for minor parties. As part of its Reconstruction past, Florida had raised high barriers to third parties appearing on the presidential ballot—seeking to prevent factionalism within the dominant Democrat Party that might split the party vote and elect Republicans.[61]

However, by the 1990s left-wing reformers sought greater ballot access for third-party presidential candidates; after the commission proposed, and Florida voters approved changes in the constitution, the number of parties on the ballot increased from four in 1996 to 10 in 2000. The six additional names crowded the ballot and forced county clerks to change the ballot arrangement.

In Palm Beach County the clerk of elections, Theresa Ann LePore, puzzled over how to handle the extended list of candidates. Smaller type for the names was rejected because of difficulties for older voters in seeing the names. Her solution was the butterfly ballot, with 10 names split over two facing pages, the voting circles alternating from one page to the other. At the top left was George W. Bush; at the top right was Al Gore; and directly beneath Bush was Pat Buchanan. After the election it was suggested that people pushed the slot for Buchanan with the belief they were voting for Gore. Democrats pointed to the fact that over 5,000 Palm Beach County voters pushed both the Gore and Buchanan slots, ruining their ballots, though voter intent, whether a vote for Buchanan or Gore, was not apparent.[62]

The arrangement did not excite controversy prior to the election. As required under state law, LePore distributed the sample ballot to the parties and published it for public comment. No objections were raised, and the butterfly arrangement became the Palm Beach ballot.

THE ELECTION THAT WOULD NOT END

The 2000 election was never to happen. After the disputed 1876 election between Rutherford Hayes and Samuel Tilden nearly descended into a constitutional crisis and a second civil war, Congress sought to prevent another dispute over how states chose electors. Acting with the usual alacrity, members passed the 1887 Federal Election law which set deadlines for the settlement of state electoral disputes. The law created a safe harbor where states were to certify presidential winners and assign electors. The December 12 deadline granted states a month for conducting recounts and hearing court challenges before choosing electors and allowing them to vote. The Supreme Court interpreted the law in the 1890 case of *McPhersen v. Blacker* which granted states near absolute power to set election rules. In addition, the Twelfth

Amendment set the third Wednesday after the second Monday in December for electors to vote. Under the 1887 act if a state completes its count by the safe harbor date; the electoral votes could not be challenged in Congress. The 1887 Safe Harbor provision would become critical to the Supreme Court's *Bush v. Gore* opinion and its ending of the interminable Florida recounts.

However, on the morning after the election neither the federal law nor the Court decision excited any interest; instead it was the confused and antiquated Florida election law which became the focus of both campaigns and the media. Florida mandated an automatic recount in the state, county, or citywide election if there was a 0.5 percent difference in the vote. The recount of the presidential election was triggered when the initial ballot count left Bush with less than a thousand vote lead out of six million votes cast. The recount was performed by machine using digital readers of punch card ballots and always within seven days of the election. When the machine recount was complete, a candidate could seek a hand recount with the challenger able to choose where the recounts occurred. Noting that the first machine recount had netted him nearly 600 votes, reducing George W. Bush's lead to just over 300 votes, Gore sought a recount in West Palm Beach and Dade Counties, the most heavily populated Democrat areas of the state. Certain he would gain the votes he needed, Gore pushed the two county canvassing boards to finish the recounts within the deadline of the Florida Canvassing Board. Much like in 1876, the board was composed of the state's highest elected officials: the Republican Secretary of State, Katherine Harris; the Democrat Attorney General Butterworth; and Governor Jeb Bush.

After reading Florida election law Harris determined the recounts had to be completed by November 14, giving the counties only a few days to go through hundreds of thousands of ballots. Gore appealed Harris's decision, and the all-Democrat Florida Supreme Court overturned her decision and set November 26 as the deadline. As hand counting bogged down in disputes, with election officials holding up ballots to lights, peering for dimpled or pregnant "chads," small swatches of paper punctured when a voter punched their candidate's name, the country was left wondering how the last days of the 20th century was dependent on 19th-century technology to choose the first 21st-century president. When the counties were unable to complete the recount by the state Supreme Court deadline, Harris rejected partial returns showing Gore gains and declared Bush the winner of

Florida's 25 electoral votes and the presidency. The announcement was made on live television and capped off by loud celebrations outside the building which could be heard through the walls.[63]

After Harris's announcement, the Gore campaign's only recourse was to contest the election and argue that the vice president had been denied his right victory. Much of their arguments focused on the undervotes: those ballots where no presidential vote had been recorded. The Gore campaign offered a two-front argument. The first was the confusion over the so-called butterfly ballot. Proof of the charge was based on Pat Buchanan receiving several thousand votes in the heavily Jewish county. Buchanan was the Reform Party candidate who excited controversy over his comments on the Iraq War, blaming it on "Israel and its Amen corner in the Pentagon."[64] The Gore campaign argued Jewish voters were unlikely to vote for Buchanan *en masse* because of those remarks. Some Palm Beach voters voted for Buchanan; later, they punched Gore's chad, creating an overvote where two candidates were chosen for the same office, thus spoiling their ballot. Gore argued that the overvotes should be counted in his favor as measuring voter intent.

A second argument was that undervotes were produced not by voters refusing to vote for any presidential candidate but rather difficulty at punching the "chad" free from the ballot. To remedy this, Gore argued ballots with indentations on the Gore swatch—pregnant chads— or those partially dislodged—swinging chads—were not counted by the automatic voting machine but should be tallied by hand counts as a Gore vote.

Not surprisingly the Bush camp rejected pregnant, dimpled, and swinging chads as overly loose definitions of votes cast. They argued a precise standard used in each county should be established before recounts could proceed. Without such a standard, voter intent was left to the subjective decision of county officials—many of them Democrats and Gore supporters. After the Florida Supreme Court decision extended the recount deadline, Bush appealed to the United States Supreme Court, seeking an end to the recount. A unanimous Court agreed, overturning the deadline extension and seeking clarification of the state court's ruling. It was a warning to the Florida justices to tread carefully in future disputes involving Bush and Gore. It was a warning the state Supreme Court chose to ignore only a few days later.[65]

While the Gore campaign focused on the recounts, other lawsuits proceeded in counties focused on ballot application. Two challenges were filed by Democrats in Seminole and Martin counties asking judges to throw out thousands of Republican ballot applications and ballots. The applications were partly filled out by a Republican Party official, and Democrats charged the official's involvement violated state law. Two Democrat judges, Terry Lewis in Martin and Nikki Clark in Seminole, refused to throw out the ballots by noting the parties could legally complete the ballot application numbers electronically and doing so by hand did not constitute fraud or vote-tampering.[66]

With the recounts halted, Al Gore sued Secretary of State Katherine Harris to continue the recounts. In contesting the election results and seeking its overturn, Gore was playing his last card. The case was heard by Circuit Judge N. Sanders Sauls, a Democrat with a penchant for garrulousness and running a loose courtroom. In a Saturday hearing he listened to witnesses and arguments, as Gore sought a finding of fraud or misconduct, necessary for a judge to overturn the canvassing board. Sauls refused, ruling there was no proof that restarting the recount would change the election.[67] Gore appealed Sauls's decision to the Florida Supreme Court, which was considered his last and best hope to continue the process. The state supreme court was unbowed by the first *Bush v. Gore* decision and in a four–three decision, the court overturned Sauls's ruling and ordered the recount to continue. The Court laid gifts at Gore's feet, ordering Harris to accept all previous ballots from the unfinished recounts in Dade and West Palm Beach Counties. The Court ordered a statewide recount and authorized local judges to develop standards for ballot counting. The Court set December 12, the safe harbor deadline under federal law, for the recounts to be completed. The justices also ordered only the counting of undervotes and accepted that the vote standard would be as broad as possible.[68]

It was a stunning reversal of fortune for Gore. By a single vote his hopes were revived, and as the recount progressed Gore appeared on the verge of overturning the Bush victory. Yet, there were dissenting voices, including three Democrat justices, who were quick to condemn the opinion and noting its broad reach. The Bush campaign and Republicans were quicker and harsher, noting that all four justices were Democrats and Gore supporters.

The Florida court decision was also a challenge to the U.S. Supreme Court. In the original *Bush v. Palm Beach County Canvassing Board,* which was derived from *Gore v. Harris,* a unanimous Supreme Court sought clarification of the Florida Supreme Court's extension of the recount deadline. However, instead of complying with the request for clarification, the Florida justices reinstituted the recount. Not since the battle over school integration had state judges treated the U.S. Supreme Court with such contempt. When Bush appealed it was a certainty the nine justices would hear the case—federal authority having been challenged and in need of being reasserted.

The Court's decision to hear the case was unexceptional as were dissents to the granting of cert. More unusual was Justice Scalia's concurring opinion as the outspoken conservative who reveled in inflaming liberal opinion declared "It suffices to say that the issuance of a stay suggests that a majority of the Court . . . believe that petitioners have a substantial probability of success." In answering the dissent from the liberal justices he warned that "Count first, and rule upon legality afterwards, is not a recipe for producing election results that have the public acceptance democratic equality requires."[69]

The *Bush v. Gore* case was argued on December 11, neither the justices nor the lawyers enjoying full preparation time, though the issues and arguments were well known. Washington attorney Theodore Olson headed the Bush team and focused on the equal protection clause and how pregnant, dimpled, and swinging chads were counted as votes in some counties while discarded in others. Olson's lips must have burned as a conservative lawyer arguing for equal protection rights which represented a reversal of 40 years of conservative efforts to limit the reach of the clause and the pursuit of equality.[70] Gore's lawyers, headed by David Boies, took the opposite view and denied that different standards used in different counties to count votes were an equal protection violation. Boies arguments upended half a century of Democrat arguments demanding federal judges override local officials.[71]

In addition to the equal protection argument, the Bush campaign invoked Article II's granting of power over choosing electors to state legislatures. Under the article, state legislators were granted plenary or complete power over the means of choosing electors. The Bush campaign argued that as soon as the legislature had set the rules for electors, the state Supreme Court lacked authority to change or overturn those rules. This argument foreclosed judicial intervention in the election and cast a pall over all federal judicial involvement in presidential elections. Only three justices accepted the argument which was based on an original reading of the constitution.

By the end of oral arguments, it appeared likely the Court would settle the issue, annulling the recount and ending the long national nightmare. The debate extended to the American public, which listened to audio tapes of the arguments only hours after their completion. As the clock ticked toward the December safe harbor deadline, Gore partisans bemoaned the stopping of the recount, realizing the Court was running out the clock on the election.

The gravity of the *Bush v. Gore* decision and the controversy certain to follow a ruling for Bush or Gore led the Court to issue an unsigned *per curiam* opinion, deflecting blame for the decision from a specific justice to all members of the majority. *Per curiams* were usually reserved for a brief opinion lacking a dissent or concurrence, but the Bush case was the most important *per curiam* since *Furman v. Georgia* when the Court struck down the death penalty.

Two decisions were handed down on December 12. In a seven–two decision, the Court struck down the recount ordered by the Florida Supreme Court. The opinion relied on the Equal Protection Clause, finding that the differing standards from county to county, precinct to precinct, election judge to election judge violated equal protection by counting the votes unequally. This violated the Warren Court's mandate of one man, one vote in state and federal elections. The justices' dismissed the debate over swinging, pregnant, and dimpled chads, the differing standards contributing to the equal protection violation.[72]

A coalition of liberal and conservative, Democrat and Republican justices joined the opinion with Justices Souter and Breyer from the Court's left wing joining five conservatives: Chief Justice Rehnquist, and Justices O'Connor, Scalia, Kennedy, and Thomas. Justices Stevens and Ginsberg dissented, dismissing the equal protection claim, a departure from their usual support for ensuring equal access and outcomes.

The seven-member coalition splintered over the remainder of the opinion which ended the controversy. The second portion of *Bush v. Gore* relied on the safe harbor date after which electoral votes would not be counted. The majority declared there was insufficient time to establish statewide standards and complete a recount to ensure the state's electoral votes were counted. If Florida missed the deadline, its electoral votes could be challenged in Congress, likely leading to another constitutional challenge to determine if Florida's votes could be counted and if not the electoral threshold for victory.[73]

Ending the Florida recount had the inevitable result of upholding Bush's Florida win, his acquiring of 25 electoral votes, and his electoral vote majority of 271. Ending the recount also left unanswered whether all Gore and Bush votes were counted though the confusion of the

Florida election system and the competing decisions of state and federal courts left that question unanswerable as no one could agree on what constituted a vote in the state's punch card ballot system.

Four justices dissented from the decision to end the recount. Justices Souter and Breyer from the seven-member majority joined Justices Stevens and Ginsberg in arguing for the recount to be continued and concluded within the safe harbor date. The angriest dissent came from the senior associate justice, John Paul Stevens, who lashed out at both the Court's use of the Equal Protection Clause and its involvement in settling the election dispute rather than allowing the state government machinery to count the votes. He noted that the decision ending the recount made it impossible to know the identity of the election winner but that "the identity of the loser is perfectly clear. It is the nation's confidence in the judge as an impartial guardian of the rule of law."[74]

The majority was almost as divided as the Court. Chief Justice Rehnquist composed a concurring opinion for Justices Scalia and Thomas focusing on Article II of the Constitution. Rehnquist argued the power to choose electors was plenary or total for the legislatures without interference of the other state branches. The Florida Supreme Court's order for a recount violated Article II by interfering with the legislature's power. Rehnquist echoed Justice Miller's warning during the 1877 Electoral Commission that allowing courts to rule on ballots and vote counting would turn elections into a judicial rather than political event. Known as a restrained judge, who deferred to legislatures on most issues, Rehnquist was offering a solution to the controversy that was unacceptable to activist judges.[75]

The chief justice offered not only a traditional separation of powers argument but also provided clues to the identity of the author of the *per curiam* opinion. Rehnquist's strong concurrence made it doubtful that he wrote the Court opinion and an opinion challenging the Court's opinion. The siding of Justice Scalia and Thomas with the chief also removed them as possible authors. This left the two swing or moderate justices, Sandra Day O'Connor and Anthony Kennedy, as the possible authors. As of 2013 neither justice had admitted to writing the opinion, the mystery unlikely to be solved until the justices' papers are made public.

If *Bush v. Gore* was not controversial enough, Democrats were angered by the majority limiting the reach of the opinion. Concerned their decision might open a new avenue for Equal Protection claims or challenges to election results, the majority declared the Bush decision had no precedential value and could not be used in future cases. The ruling heightened suspicion the five conservatives had composed a political rather than a legal document, overturning the Florida recount simply to make George W. Bush president. Controversial as the decision was, the justices correctly recognized the dispute was always political. Limiting the reach of *Bush v. Gore* shielded them from a wave of new disputes though it opened them to the inevitable charge of partisanship.[76]

The subsequent electoral vote count by Congress became both theater and anticlimax. Under federal law, if a House member and senator objected to a state's electoral votes, the two chambers would debate the issue then vote. If both rejected the state's votes, those votes would be excluded but a Republican House ensured no Bush votes would be so excluded. With the vice president serving his constitutional role of counting the ballots, the possibility of disruption threatened to extend the election controversy even as Gore made clear he rejected any challenge.

The count proceeded without incident, and Bush was declared the winner by a 271–267 electoral vote count, the closest such margin since Rutherford Hayes's single-vote victory in 1876. Gore could point to his 400,000 popular vote victory as proof he was favored over Bush, but that was thin gruel for Democrats who were convinced they had been cheated from a presidential victory. More agreeable were their congressional gains as the party picked up five Senate seats—the largest such gain for any party while suffering a presidential defeat.

Having entered the election with 55 senators, Republicans were guaranteed 50 and control of the chamber no matter what the result of the presidential contest. If Bush–Cheney won, then the vice president could cast the deciding vote for the Republicans to organize the Senate. If Gore–Leiberman won, then the Connecticut Democrat would have to surrender his Senate seat, and Republican Governor John Rowland would replace him with a Republican, ensuring a 51–49 split.

Republican Senate losses reflect the weaknesses of Bush's coattails but also the dominance of local issues and unusual circumstances that worked against the party. Republicans saw incumbent senators defeated in Delaware, Michigan, Minnesota, Missouri, and Washington—each election having its own story. In Delaware, Senator William Roth, creator of the Roth IRA, was running for a fifth term. The 80-year-old Roth, though, suffered from the twin indignities of poor health and a bad toupee. Twice falling during campaign stops, Roth was portrayed as too old and ill to win and was defeated in a close election. The remainder of the losses came from the Republican class of 1994, with several vulnerable freshmen being upset. In Michigan, one-term Senator Spencer Abraham was hurt by John McCain's charges that Republicans were anti-Catholic. In Minnesota, Senator Rod Grams was hurt by the arrest of his son in New Mexico and his own conservative record.[77] The state's voters had also shown a propensity for odd choices. In 1998, Minnesotans elected former professional wrestler Jesse "the body" Ventura as governor, and in 2008 they chose the hilariously unfunny *Saturday Night Live* writer Al Franken for the Senate, both choices casting doubt on whether the state's voters took their electoral choices seriously.

In Washington, incumbent Slade Gorton had an unusual electoral history. First elected in 1980 during the Reagan landslide, he then lost reelection in 1986. Two years later he won election to the state's other Senate seat and was narrowly reelected in 1994. Six years later he was defeated by 2,000 votes out of over two million cast by multimillionaire Maria Cantwell. The oddest election, though, occurred in Missouri, where incumbent John Ashcroft was challenged by Governor Mel Carnahan. Ashcroft enjoyed a narrow lead until Carnahan was killed in a plane crash days before the election. Missourians then elected a dead man senator—increasing the Democrat gain to five.

AFTERMATH

Unlike past disputed elections in 1800, 1824, and 1876, which produced legal and constitutional changes to the electoral system, the 2000 election produced little substantive changes in how presidents were chosen. George W. Bush entered office with a tattered mandate and a narrow congressional majority which disappeared in May, 2001 with the defection of Vermont Republican senator Jim Jeffords. This political earthquake was quickly forgotten after the September 11 attacks as Bush's response in Afghanistan and Iraq defined his presidency and set his legacy. His 2004 reelection campaign was based on foreign policy, the first such election since 1968 and the 2000 dispute seemed petty in time of national peril. Suffering from low approval ratings during his second term and the financial crisis at its end, Bush left office as one of the most unpopular presidents in modern history.

Al Gore's political career also came to an uneven end. Adopting the robes of an environmental Jeremiah, Gore produced a documentary and won a Nobel Prize hyping the effects of global warming. His predictions of imminent disaster mimicked his 1990 book and made him a darling of the left. An attempt at a political comeback in 2003 fell flat with many Democrats assigning him blame for his 2000 defeat. For a decade Gore traveled around the globe, trying to convince the public that the world was on the verge of extinction and seeking drastic measures to curb the effects of the industrial revolution.

Ralph Nader, once a darling of the Democrat left wing, became a pariah after 2000. Blamed for siphoning votes from Gore in Florida, his popularity plummeted; his speaking fees decreased, and his presidential prospects earned him less than one percent of the vote in the 2004 presidential election. On the opposite side of the political spectrum, Pat Buchanan quit the presidential campaign circuit, preferring to write alternate histories of American foreign policy in the 20th century while serving as a token conservative voice on the radical left-dominated MSNBC network.

The Supreme Court continued, unaffected by partisan attacks. Many Democrats were secretly relieved the justices ended the election rather than sending the issue to Congress where many members faced the type of difficult vote that destroyed careers. During a 2011 interview for his recently published book, Justice Scalia was asked about the *Bush v. Gore* decision. Scalia, blamed by many for driving his colleagues to make the final decision, responded with an annoyed "Get over it," to the Court's critics. One substantive change to the Court occurred because of *Bush v. Gore*. The arguments in the case were audiotaped much as thousands of cases before 2000. With public interest high, the tapes were released to the media on the day of the arguments, the justices and lawyers heard in action for the first time. The popularity of the recordings caused the Court to release future cases considered important and interesting—the arguments broadcast on CSPAN only a short time after they were made.

5

The Ugliest Campaign

ADAMS VERSUS JEFFERSON, 1800

George Washington's decision to voluntarily cede power in 1797 after two terms in office is considered as one of the most important precedents set by a chief executive. The two-term tradition remained sacrosanct until 1940 with Franklin Roosevelt's third term and then was institutionalized with the passage of the 22nd Amendment. Washington's successor, John Adams, set an even more critical precedent in 1801 after his election defeat as he acceded to the will of the people and involuntarily left office. Newly independent countries in the 20th century testify to the importance of Adams's decision as modern leaders have refused to abide by voters and instead used military violence to maintain power even after losing an election. The peaceful transfer of power in 1801 is a testament to Adams's belief in the wisdom of voters and importance of abiding by the constitution.

The Adams–Jefferson contest of 1800 was the last conducted election under Article II Section 1 and would be the only election that directly led to a constitutional amendment. The 12th Amendment was ratified in 1804 to prevent a repetition of the disputed election and correct the ramshackle system created by the founders. Operating under the old Electoral College system, the 1800 election produced two upsets: one in the Electoral College and the other in the Federalist-dominated House of Representatives.

The framers of the constitution spent months debating the proper method of electing the president. With only a single executive the framers were precluded from enacting another Great Compromise which ratified popular election in the House of Representatives and state legislative elections of senators. A plentiful number of electoral choices were offered starting with Pennsylvania delegate James Wilson arguing for popular election, but a democratically elected president generated little support as some framers worried that the process endangered the separation of powers. Another proposal granted authority to state legislators though concerns that the legislators would prefer that candidates from their region remained. After months of debate the framers created a vague, hybrid system of presidential electors with state legislative involvement and details to be announced at a later date. The resulting Electoral College system found in Article II Section 1 quickly broke down.

Under the original electoral rules each elector was given two presidential ballots in which they would vote for two presidential candidates. The candidate with the most electoral votes would become president; the candidate in second place would become vice president. The Electoral College created by the framers ensured that if a president was replaced because of illness or death, the vice president would be a capable candidate who enjoyed a broad following in the Electoral College. Unfortunately, the framers did not figure on the development of parties which produced a presidential administration where the top candidate represented one faction while the vice president represented an opposing faction. The first contested presidential election in 1796 saw John Adams elected president and his election opponent Thomas Jefferson elected vice president.[1]

Prior to 1796, the 1789 and 1792 elections offered little suspense as George Washington was unanimously elected with the ideologically compatible John Adams as his vice president. However, when Washington chose to retire in 1797 the electoral gloves were dropped, and the two competing philosophies, Federalists and Republicans, competed to replace him. The Adams–Jefferson rivalry began during the Washington administration which held the seeds for the 1800 election as three powerful figures—Adams, Hamilton, and Jefferson—battled for influence and the opportunity to succeed Washington.

WASHINGTON ADMINISTRATION

As the first president, Washington not only had to lead a new government but was responsible for establishing the traditions and boundaries of the presidential office. A man of caution, Washington saw his role as preserving the republic rather than embarking on innovative policies or a grand philosophy. His first duty was appointing the best men, and his first cabinet represented the best and the mediocre. His secretary of state, Thomas Jefferson, was a fellow Virginian, but beyond their home state the two men had little in common. Jefferson saw the American Revolution as the spark for a new republican era. His time in Paris stoked his imagination, and he lobbied Washington to tilt American foreign policy toward the new French government. Washington refused amidst concerns that the new American republic would be endangered if it became entangled in the petty quarrels and bloody wars plaguing Europe. When faced with a meddlesome French ambassador trying to recruit American systems to fight Britain, Washington sent him away with his tail between his legs—an implicit rejection of Jefferson's pro-France policies.[2]

Opposing Jefferson was Treasury Secretary Alexander Hamilton. The only New York constitutional convention delegate who approved of a new government, Hamilton was frustrated as he was outvoted by his New York colleagues. While his role in creating the new government was limited, his role in its ratification and interpretation was broader and historic. Joining James Madison and John Jay, Hamilton composed a series of newspaper editorials interpreting the words and philosophy behind the constitution, explaining how the checks and balance system worked and offering a benign view of creating a central government to replace the Articles of Confederation. The Federalist Papers would become the authoritative interpretation of the constitution and were used by politicians and judges alike.[3]

Hamilton was appointed to organize the republic's chaotic currency, taxation, and finance system—his time as Washington's adjutant during the revolution exhibiting his organizational skills. Hamilton realized the country could grow only with a constant stream of European loans which would be given only after war debts were repaid in full. His plan to turn worthless continental bonds into gilt-edged securities provoked conspiracy theories that the government was created to benefit bondholders, but Hamilton was a broader thinker than the economic determinists of the 20th century.[4] Hamilton proposed consolidating state debts into a national debt and creating a national bank to regulate the national currency. Hamilton's *Report on Manufactures* became part of the later Whig and Republican philosophy of using tariffs and subsidies to promote manufacturing. However, much like Jefferson's plans for spreading revolution, Hamilton faced the unyielding skepticism of Washington who refused to endorse his plan for economic centralism.

Washington's confidence in his own abilities was reflected by his inclusion of two strong and opposing minds side by side in his cabinet. Washington received all sides of an argument and then made decisions based on that information, usually disappointing both Hamilton and Jefferson who were convinced they were more brilliant and deserving of the presidency than the old general.

In addition to his appointments, Washington established other precedents, claiming executive privilege against a request from the House of Representatives for information on negotiations of the Jay Treaty. Washington tried to bully the Senate into quick ratification of the Jay Treaty only to be rebuffed by senators, who preferred a calmer and longer consideration. Washington further established openness to the office, allowing ordinary people to visit the president at regularly scheduled hours, an openness that would continue into the Franklin Roosevelt administration, after which the presidency would become more isolated from Americans.

Washington left office having served without the benefit of political party. His successor, John Adams, would not be as fortunate and spent his single term battling Alexander Hamilton for control of what became the Federalist Party. Hamilton considered himself de facto leader of the party, and the Hamilton–Adams rivalry proved more bitter and permanent than the Adams–Jefferson rivalry.

THE 1796 ELECTION

Without the benefit of a consensus candidate for president, Adams ran the first successful presidential campaign. In fall 1796 he was chosen by the Federalist congressional caucus to run for president. The choice of Adams excited little controversy, but the selection of his running mate revealed divisions within the Federalist Party. Hamilton was de facto leader of congressional Federalists and used his considerable influence to select South Carolina's Charles Pinckney as Adams's running mate. Pinckney was a Revolutionary War hero with a large following in his home state where Adams was at his weakest. Hamilton hoped Adams and Pinckney would share all of the New England Electoral votes—a Federalist stronghold—while Pinckney swept southern electoral votes and shut Adams out of the presidency. The combination would produce an electoral upset of the favorite Adams, who would receive the sop of a third vice-presidential term.[5]

In the 1796 election, the first electoral ballot served as the presidential vote with electors choosing between Jefferson and Adams. The second ballot, though, promoted favorite sons with 11 candidates receiving electoral votes for vice president though none would receive a majority. Electors and legislators struggled to make sense of the new electoral system, and anarchy in the voting produced unusual results with electoral votes split among 10 different candidates—the most in history.[6] One elector chose Adams for president and George Washington for vice president while another had Jefferson for president and Washington for vice president. Adams was paired with John Jay, Samuel Johnston, Charles Cotesworth Pinckney, and Oliver Ellsworth. Jefferson was paired with Thomas Pinckney, Adams, George Clinton, Justice James Iredell, and John Henry.[7]

The final result in 1796 had Adams defeating Jefferson by three electoral votes, 71–68, the margin of victory produced by Adams taking single electors in Jefferson-dominated Virginia and North Carolina. Amidst all of the confusion Adams had won the presidency, but the country's political leaders recognized more control had to be exerted over the electors with their decisions guided by party rather than personal preferences.

Hamilton's plans went awry as he expected Pinckney to receive Adams's votes, but South Carolina legislators divided their votes with Jefferson. With the Virginian elected vice president, a political odd couple sat at the top of the executive branch though Jefferson proved less problematical for Adams than did his Federalist rival, Hamilton.

ADAMS ADMINISTRATION

The Adams administration served during the bloodiest days of the French Revolution and the start of the worst European conflict since the Thirty Years War. During Adams's four years Europe was consumed by the French Revolution and later the Napoleonic Wars because the dictator imposed a secular monarchy on a bloodied people. Washington had maintained a deliberate distance from America's old friend France and old enemy Britain. In his farewell address he offered the same policy advice to his successors, advice that Adams took to heart. Neither Jefferson nor Hamilton appeared to listen to the old president's wisdom. Jefferson sought to use European chaos as a wedge to prove Adams was a secret anglophile and remove him from office.

Hamilton sought to enflame nationalism against the French, drawing power to the central government and acquiring influence by leading a large, standing military.

Their opportunity came after the humiliation of Adams's peace envoys by the French in the XYZ affair. Jefferson and the Republicans tried to exploit the controversy by demanding all diplomatic communications with the French be released to prove that Adams deliberately spiked negotiations. Adams was quick to comply with the Republican request knowing the communications would prove French perfidy rather than American incompetence. Anger swept the country as the newspapers told the story of French Foreign Minister Talleyrand demanding thousands in bribes for himself and millions in loans for his country before negotiations began. The Republicans, who had sided with the French, were attacked for placing love for France above love of country. While American nationalism appeared to sink Jefferson, it opened a new opportunity for Hamilton to implement his plans for military glory.[8]

The Federalist Congress reacted quickly to the XYZ affair, passing a land tax funding an enlarged army and navy to defend against a feared French invasion. Adams was an unwilling participant in the war hysteria, discounting Federalist warnings of an impending French invasion with a French fleet landing tens of thousands of troops on American soil. Adams declared he was more likely to see France invade heaven than the United States but eventually relented and appeared in public in uniform, a scene that made many Americans shudder at the thought of a military government.[9]

Having lost control of political events, Adams struggled to outmaneuver Hamilton by asking George Washington to head the new army. Adams was convinced Hamilton would not dare criticize the former president or attempt to shoulder him aside. However, Washington and his former treasury secretary had strengthened their friendship after the old general left office, and the former president endorsed his former aide as commander of the new army. Suddenly, Adams found himself isolated and without allies. The Republicans feared the new army was a means for crushing opposition and imposing a dictatorship. The High Federalists interpreted Republican opposition to the army as part of a Jacobin plot to leave the country defenseless against a French invasion.[10]

War fever continued into 1798 and into the midterm elections as France and national honor became the issues of the American equivalent of a Khaki election.[11] Federalists gained seats in the region most hostile to them, the south. In North Carolina they split 10 House seats with the Republicans and tallied a 7,000-vote majority out of 27,000 total votes. This put North Carolina into play for the presidential election. Federalists also picked up two House seats in Georgia and one in Maryland and nearly swept the South Carolina House delegation, taking five of six seats. Even in Jefferson's Virginia they gained four House seats with future chief justice John Marshall elected; he later served briefly before Adams plucked him from his district to serve as secretary of state. The Federalists would control the Sixth Congress with 60 House members, a gain of four from the previous Congress.[12]

Federalists swept into office all over the country, and the party appeared destined for a permanent majority while Republicans seemed on the verge of dissolution. Neither would be true. Heading toward 1800 both Adams and Jefferson miscalculated. Adams's mistakes were provoked by the purist High Federalists who tried to exploit the XYZ affair to eliminate the Republican Party. The High Federalist's strategy was enactment of the Alien and Sedition Act, a law against both French immigrants and Adams's domestic opponents. Knowing that the French ambassador and others campaigned for the Republicans, the Federalists mandated registration of foreign aliens and deportation of many. The sedition portion of the act targeted criticism of the Adams administration.[13]

As Republican critics were charged with criticizing the government, Jefferson overreacted. Using his political base in Virginia and influence in neighboring Kentucky, he convinced the state legislatures to pass the Virginia and Kentucky resolutions denouncing the Alien and Sedition Acts and offered a controversial means of overriding them. The resolutions suggested states could reject any state law they believed was unconstitutional. The argument became the starting point for John Calhoun's theory of interposition with states protecting their citizens from federal tyranny by annulling national laws. The resolutions drew immediate and negative reaction from all regions and factions which condemned the annulment as treason.[14]

As the Republicans self-destructed and Jefferson's presidential chances sagged, Adams purged his cabinet. After several months of vacation in 1800, Adams returned to the capital determined to root out Hamilton partisans from his administration. His first targets were Secretary of State Timothy Pickering and War Secretary

James McHenry. Pickering drew the president's ire by rejecting his diplomatic efforts toward France. With the election over and war fever cooling, Adams sought negotiations to prevent conflict. Pickering resisted and delayed sending the envoys because a peace agreement with France would eliminate the need for a large military and end Hamilton's efforts to snatch military glory.[15]

The purge set a showdown between Adams and Hamilton. The two men struggled for control over the Federalist Party and their battle at times seemed more important than defeating Jefferson and the Republicans. Hamilton faced a difficult choice in challenging Adams. While he could defeat the president it would lead to the election of his old rival Jefferson and potentially the rise of his New York rival, Aaron Burr.

HAMILTON VERSUS BURR

Political rivalries mark most of American history. Among them were Jefferson and Adams; Clay and Jackson; Lincoln and Douglas; Theodore Roosevelt and Wilson; Kennedy and Nixon; and Clinton and Gingrich. Each pitted powerful and influential leaders holding opposite views on the critical issues of the day. In each the disputes were settled in the political arena in either Congress or in elections with only the rivalry between Alexander Hamilton and Aaron Burr ending with a pistol shot.

Hamilton was born on the Caribbean island of Nevis either in 1755 or 1757—the actual date lost in the poor record keeping of the era. His father, James Hamilton, had the unusual talent of avoiding success though his father and son enjoyed financial and political success while James saw his endeavors repeatedly fail.[16] Alexander Hamilton's illegitimate status would become fodder for his political enemies, but his separation from the failed James Hamilton allowed him to develop his business acumen. A prodigy with finances, Hamilton operated a trading business on the island at age 14 and was responsible for buying and selling everything from flour to slaves.[17]

Hamilton sailed to America in 1772 and quickly became a participant in the budding revolutionary movement at King's College. It was as a student that he learned the effectiveness of the anonymous pamphlet, which would become his tool for lobbying for ratification of the constitution in 1787. When the war reached New York, Hamilton met Washington; the younger man was a part of the 1776 defense of the city, and later Hamilton was joined by another young soldier, Aaron Burr. Hamilton earned Washington's respect during the surprise attack on Trenton and subsequent retreat across the Delaware River. He became Washington's adjutant as the general used him for distasteful political missions ranging from requisitioning supplies from civilians to removing troops from the victorious General Gates after his victory at Saratoga.[18]

In his early 20s, Hamilton enjoyed a bird's eye view of Washington during his worst and best times, from Valley Forge to Yorktown. He was credited with leading an attack on a key British position at Yorktown, demonstrating his military and organizational skills.[19] His close association with the general drew whispers about the young adjutant's undue influence over the older man with similar suspicions following Hamilton into his tenure as treasury secretary.[20]

Hamilton's political career was crippled after his presentation to the constitutional convention on June 18, 1787. Rising before his fellow delegates, he hectored them on the need for an elective monarchy. The speech in an ostensibly secret meeting was leaked by Hamilton's enemies, ensuring it would be fodder for claims that Hamilton was a not-so-secret monarchist who could not be trusted with political power. No politician of the early republic could withstand offering such a proposal, and Hamilton was reduced to appointive positions and the designation as party elder at the age of 40.[21]

Aaron Burr enjoyed a less dramatic rise. Burr's life has elements of a Greek tragedy with a mix of potential, hubris, miscalculation, miscommunication, and greed all contributing to his downfall. Listed among early America's villains that include Benedict Arnold and George III, Burr's life has become more a caricature than reality. Born in New Jersey in 1756, Burr was orphaned at age two and lived with relatives before going to Princeton to study law. He joined the army at the outbreak of the revolution and saw considerable combat in New York City where he met Washington and Hamilton. After the war he returned to New York and became a successful lawyer and Hamilton's convivial rival. Occasionally working together for a client, the two men kept their disagreements professional, but in 1791 a political dispute would end their friendship.

Hamilton's father-in-law Philip Schuyler was one of the first New York senators. The framers use of staggered terms for the United

States Senate meant that one-third of the early senators would serve only two years; another one-third would serve four, and the last third would complete a full six-year term before having to stand for reelection. Schuyler was one of the two- year senators and faced the New York legislature in 1791. His reelection was expected with Hamilton influencing Federalist legislators, but the two men were stunned when Schuyler was replaced by Burr: the latter's election was a deliberate attack on Hamilton's power in Albany. Hamilton miscalculated in choosing Federalist Rufus King over a member of the powerful Livingston faction when selecting New York's other senator. Schuyler's defeat was a measure of revenge for Livingston. Burr's election ended the friendship between the two men as Hamilton came to distrust the man he had known for nearly a decade.[22]

With Burr in the legislative branch and Hamilton ensconced in the Washington administration, the two men built their own separate power centers. Hamilton worked with his main rival Jefferson in establishing the national capital and creating the first bank of the United States. As treasury secretary Hamilton returned to his military roots after leading the army to crush the Whiskey Rebellion. Hamilton accepted the duty after War Secretary Knox declined the job, fleeing to Maine to handle business affairs. When Hamilton left the Washington administration in 1794, he could point to his success at building the public credit while offering a vision of a manufacturing republic constructed through a protective tariff and government subsidies. Considered Washington's natural heir as leader of the Federalist Party, Hamilton dove into the task of keeping the presidency for his party.[23]

Freed of the constraints of public office Hamilton became a behind-the-scenes operator as he tried to manipulate the political scene. When Republicans took control of the New York legislature in spring 1800, Hamilton prodded Governor John Jay to annul the elections by changing the method of choosing presidential electors. Instead of allowing the new Republican legislature to choose, Hamilton proposed allowing voters in districts to select electors. The flip-flop was a temporary measure intended to preserve some electoral votes for the Federalists, but Jay recognized the danger of overturning the peoples' will and refused to change the rules.[24]

Adams's election did not cool Hamilton's partisanship. With political factions coalesced around political personalities, Hamilton became a secondary figure, lacking a formal portfolio and being reduced to influencing his congressional allies. As the Adams administration progressed, Hamilton created a separate power center challenging the president. Partly responsible for generating war fever during the XYZ affair, Hamilton seemed to lack a clear sense of direction in his quest to build a new American army. By 1799, he was in open opposition to Adams, developing brilliant but complicated plans to replace the president with an ally.

On reaching the Senate, Aaron Burr became a dedicated member of the Jeffersonian faction in Congress. The Jeffersonians were known as the Democrat-Republicans and then the Republicans. As one of only 32 senators, Burr rose quickly through the Republican hierarchy and in 1796 was chosen by Jefferson to run as vice president. Burr started the campaign with the expectation that he was the second choice of the Jefferson electors and would receive nearly the identical number of electoral votes as Jefferson. However, when the 1796 electoral votes were tabulated Burr was shaken to find himself in fourth place, receiving only 30 electoral votes—less than half of Jefferson's 68.[25]

When his Senate term ended in 1797 Burr returned to New York state politics, having recognized that real political power flowed from state legislatures which elected senators, created House districts, and controlled the Electoral College. Burr quickly established himself as the boss of New York Republicans and became the most powerful state leader in the republic. His ability to elect local and statewide candidates using a rudimentary political machine made him critical to Jefferson, who needed New York to defeat Adams.

THE STATE LEGISLATURES

After the confusion of 1796, states retreated from allowing voters to choose electors and shifted that power back to state legislatures which made the 1799 and early 1800 state elections critical in deciding the presidency. State candidates competed for office supporting the Republican or Federalist parties, and voters could choose their faction. Not all state legislative races were proxies for the presidential election because local, state, and personal issues decided many elections. Promises of patronage jobs could change state legislators' votes while threats of losing patronage could also change a vote though neither reason could be publicly revealed.

The first key state was New York. In 1796 Adams and the Federalists swept New York's 12 electoral votes, and Federalist Charles Pinckney took a dozen electoral votes from Aaron Burr. By 1798, the Federalist-dominated legislature was besieged by Republicans, and the Burr political machine began implementing plans for the electoral vote in 1800. To turn the legislature toward the Republicans, Burr focused on New York City districts by collecting the names of Republican voters, campaign volunteers, and potential donors to boost Republican turnout and finances.[26]

With lists of voters at his fingertips, Burr turned to choosing legislative candidates. Controlling the Republican selection committee he chose prominent military and political leaders for the 13 seats in Manhattan. Burr recruited former governor George Clinton, a prominent anti- federalist who bedeviled Hamilton during the constitutional convention. Burr used his persuasive powers to convince Clinton to accept a freshman legislative position, a move usually considered a demotion for a former governor. He did the same with the hero of Saratoga, General Horatio Gates, who agreed to muddy his military reputation with a jump into politics. Another military man, Colonel Henry Rutgers, joined the political fray. Burr picked off one of Washington's cabinet members, the first Postmaster General and hero of Bunker Hill, Samuel Osgood. Burr selected members representing his Republican faction; others who were included represented the Brockholst Livingston faction, and his choice of Clinton nailed down the support of the former governor's faction.[27]

Burr's slate would hold up well when compared with the middle-class candidates offered by Hamilton and the Federalists. Unfortunately for Hamilton, Federalist state legislators were also small businessmen who could not remain in Albany. Many of those elected in 1798 retired back to their businesses leaving Hamilton with a nondescript slate of candidates that included a shoemaker, a baker, and a grocer.

The central issues in the New York elections would be repeated in the general election as the candidates battled over the Revolutionary War, the constitution, and Anglophilia. The triumvirate of Jefferson, Burr, and former Governor Clinton were portrayed as fanatical anti-federalists who would use the presidential election to create a new constitutional order. Jacobinism, though crushed before the ascension of Napoleon, became a favorite Federalist charge against the Republicans. The heretical "Goddess of Reason" marching through the Paris streets by Robespierre was exploited by the Federalist as proof of Republican hostility to religion. Partisans from both sides warned that if the other party won, the country would be enveloped in chaos and anarchy.

The Republicans swept Manhattan and seized control of the state legislature for the first time. The state elections removed 12 electoral votes from Adams's total, forcing the Federalists to scramble to rebuild their 1796 electoral coalition. Suddenly, Jefferson and the Republicans were favored in the next election, and Aaron Burr became a national political star though his swift rise was followed by a sudden fall.[28]

Federalists turned to Pennsylvania in the search to replace New York's electoral votes. In 1796 Republicans had taken 14 of 15 Pennsylvania electoral votes; later, they elected a Republican governor in 1800. However, the Federalist senate blocked legislation that would have favored Republicans in choosing electors. As the election approached, Republicans were faced with having to compromise and allow the state's electoral votes to be divided with Adams or see the state's electoral votes not counted, taking 14 votes from Jefferson's expected total and undoing his New York gains.

In South Carolina, Federalists had taken all but one congressional seat in the midterm elections. Historically the state was known as a Jeffersonian, then Democrat state–turned–radical secessionist, but South Carolina also boasted a strong Federalist contingent. Most were located along the coast and in Charleston with coastal planters favoring a strong navy and closer ties with the British. In 1796 the state's electors had divided their vote between the Republican Jefferson and the Federalist favorite son Thomas Pinckney. In 1800 Hamilton's maneuvering placed Pinckney's cousin, Charles Cotesworth Pinckney, on the ballot with the hope of splitting the vote again.

With the South Carolina state legislature choosing electors, the state races could decide the election. However, the results were mixed as Federalists dominated the low country and Charleston while Republicans picked up seats in the growing western half of the state. A few legislators ran without a party label, and their votes would be decisive in choosing the president.[29]

THE CANDIDATES

The 1800 election would be the first of seven times in American history that two major party candidates faced each other for a second time in a presidential election. The Federalist congressional caucus was the first to choose the party nominee with Adams's nomination resisted by Hamilton and other High Federalists. Hamilton favored Charles Cotesworth Pinckney as Adams's vice president and potential replacement. Hamilton sold Adams–Pinckney ticket as a means of ensuring Jefferson's defeat rather than as part of a complex plan to replace Adams with Pinckney. Hamilton hoped that with Pinckney acting as the Federalist favorite son in South Carolina, he could unseat Adams. Hamilton received assurances from his South Carolina Federalist allies that the former ambassador was guaranteed all the state's votes on the second ballot.[30] Hamilton worked under the assumption that South Carolina legislators would choose Jefferson on their first electoral ballot and Pinckney on the second, leaving Adams without electors from the state. If the legislators performed as expected and Pinckney received the same votes as Adams in the New England Federalist strongholds but took all of South Carolina's votes, Pinckney would defeat both Adams and Jefferson.

Congressional Federalists nominated Adams and Pinckney without endorsing either candidate as the party's presidential favorite. The lack of an endorsement diverted pressure from the electors as it allowed them to support Cotesworth Pinckney without explicitly rejecting the caucus' announced candidate. However, Hamilton's maneuvering revealed his true intentions to Adams who realized his Federalist ally had become a dedicated enemy.[31]

The Republicans met on May 11, brimming with confidence over their New York victory and more united than the Federalists as they unanimously nominated Jefferson. He delegated the choice of running mate to his confidant and Republican congressional leader, Albert Gallatin, who proceeded to delegate the decision to his father-in-law, a well-known naval captain. The Republicans faced a choice of two New Yorkers: George Clinton and Aaron Burr. An opponent of amending the Articles of Confederation, Clinton had been New York governor during the constitutional convention. Using his appointment prerogatives he chose two opponents of national government—John Lansing and Robert Yates—along with a proponent of strong central government, Hamilton. Lansing and Yates used the New York vote to oppose the Virginia plan at the convention even as it granted the state considerable influence over the new government. Unable to reach agreement the New York trio left the convention during the break on July 4 and did not return, leaving New York without a vote during the critical late months of the convention. Clinton's deliberate sabotaging of the

New York convention delegation and his subsequent opposition to ratification opened the Republicans to a Federalist campaign painting the Republicans as opponents of the government and constitution.

His opponent, Burr, had his own problems as his New York City pedigree awakened suspicions of the large states of Virginia and New York dominating the new republic. Burr distrusted the Virginians after his poor showing in 1796 and actively pursued the vice presidency to Jefferson's detriment. Burr's eye for detail and grass roots politics would help the Republicans in New York but bred distrust of him as a grasping politician when compared to the more aristocratic Virginians. The need for the New York electoral vote overrode any concerns as Burr was nominated for a second try at the vice presidency. Burr provoked a constitutional crisis as he fought to ensure his election to the second office in the land; he later appeared poised to take the presidency from Jefferson, much to the chagrin of the Republicans.[32]

THE CAMPAIGN

The 1800 presidential election was one of the fiercest in history. In 1796 Washington foreswore another term in late summer, limiting the organization and campaign efforts of the two parties. In 1800 the two groups had four years to prepare exposes—both true and false against the opposition party. Some of the attacks were tempered by the Alien and Sedition Acts though its enforcement achieved the opposite of Federalist intentions as Republican papers increased in numbers and ferocity.[33]

The 18th-century libel and sedition laws were a form of campaign regulation focusing on promoting clean politics by limiting personal attacks and favoring discussion of issues. However, 18th-century America had its share of men willing to fight for their freedom while also seeking fame and fortune. Prime among these was James Callendar, who was paid by Jefferson to attack the Federalists and withstand the dangers of the sedition laws. Callendar was a political mercenary who spent his money as quickly as he made it and would return in 1804 to savage his benefactor Jefferson.[34]

The Republicans attacked Adams as a monarchist, a ridiculous claim against a man who risked all against the British monarchy. Adams's disgust with the bloody French Revolution and the dictator

Napoleon had seen him tilt toward the British, but his long history with England also made him suspicious of the British agenda. Republican charges struck a basic truth when charging that the Alien and Sedition Acts were undemocratic and limited public dissent. William Duane's *Aurora* was prosecuted under the Alien and Sedition Act and learned its lesson. Avoiding further charges of sedition, it directed its ire at Hamilton and revived charges of corruption against his Treasury Department. His attacks acquired legitimacy after a fire at the Treasury Department which destroyed much of the records from the Adams's administration.[35] The *Aurora*'s charges were published in other Republican newspapers around the country—the start of a tradition of a single party newspaper serving as a source of campaign material. Another charge focused on religion. With Federalists attacking Jefferson's supposed lack of religious fervor the Republicans responded with charges that Federalists approved of an established church as found in many New England states which charged taxes to fund the state church.

Jefferson's sympathy for the French Revolution was spun by the Federalists as proof he would impose a Jacobin regime on Americans when elected president. Republicans were equated with the murderous Jacobins wanting to introduce the guillotine onto American shores while adhering to a "creed of atheism and rebellion." Federalists questioned Jefferson's personal bravery by reviving a 1796 charge that he fled Monticello when the British approached during the revolution.[36] Federalist supporter Noah Webster published the soon-to-be-famous Mazzei letter in which Jefferson indiscreetly criticized Washington as a weak president who favored a monarchy, a ridiculous charge against a man who risked all to overthrow a monarchy.[37]

Jefferson suffered from the political malady of an ample paper trail. His greatest achievements were recorded in the written word, a habit he continued in his presidency when offering a written State of the Union address rather than orally presenting it to Congress. In his writings, Jefferson ignored his own warnings against mixing religion and politics and launched into indiscreet comments on both. In his *Notes on the State of Virginia* he launched into meanderings on Noah's Ark, Adam and Eve, and schools' use of the Bible as part of the curriculum. He declared "It does me no injury for my neighbor to say there are twenty gods or no God. It neither picks my pocket nor breaks my leg." Federalists repeated the phrase in campaign literature as part of general accusations against Jefferson as a nonbeliever who would attack religion when elected.[38] Jefferson's sneering at religious fundamentalists and other believers alienated a sector of the electorate unlikely to support him. The Federalist insults did not draw Jefferson from his shell as he followed a strategy of allowing his surrogates to defend him in newspapers.[39]

Jefferson and the Jacobins were linked because of his tenure as ambassador to France and open support for the French as secretary of state. However, guilt by association resonated mainly with partisans, and Federalists required a more tangible connection. It came with a planned slave revolt in the fall of 1800 in Virginia. Though the revolt never happened and the slave leaders were rounded up and executed, the Federalist's seized on what was known as "Gabriel's revolt." They fixed blame on the Republican's rhetoric of equality and liberty, two of the dictums of the French Revolution. The Federalists portrayed the slave-owning Jefferson as preaching an ideology that went against his self-interest. The charge targeted the south because slavery was being banned or had been banned in broad swathes of the north. While the message was received by large plantation owners who feared slave revolts, most southerners who lacked slaves favored greater equality for those at the lower end and found Jefferson's arguments more compelling than any fear of slave revolts.[40]

In addition to negative attacks the two campaigns offered arguments on their behalf. The Federalists ran on peace and prosperity—the Adams administration providing both for four years. They warned against changing leaders and trusting the Republicans with the presidency. Adams and the Federalists also used their offices to campaign throughout the country. Most public among these was Justice Samuel Chase. After having rejected a seat at the constitutional convention, Chase became a rabid Federalist. Appointed to the Court by Washington, he enforced the Alien and Sedition Acts while on circuit duty and used grand jury instructions as campaign platforms. During the summer of 1800 he traveled about his home state of Maryland praising Federalists and Adams and assuming a political role that would make a modern justice blanch.[41]

The Republican campaign focused on change and warned of the Federalists' creeping dictatorship. Jefferson composed letters to his supporters and spelled out his policies while criticizing the incumbent. He denounced Adams's large standing army and navy as a threat to the republic. In a Washingtonian statement, Jefferson declared his policy would be "free commerce with all nations, political connections with none."[42] By stating he would continue a neutral and isolationist foreign policy, Jefferson answered the charges he would ally the United States with Napoleon. Another letter laid out the states' rights under Jefferson which while promising a "frugal and simple" government, would leave states with a large role while warning that the Alien and Sedition Acts violated the Bill of Rights. Jefferson predicted that any government that limited freedoms would have a brief existence.[43]

While neither Burr nor Cotesworth Pinckney enjoyed the public acclaim of Jefferson or Adams, they suffered abuse from the opposition—Burr less so than the South Carolinian. Pinckney was tied to Hamilton and his alleged monarchist views. Their close relationship perpetuated the image of Pinckney as Hamilton's stalking horse, a candidate who would follow the treasury secretary's orders when elected. Republicans went further, declaring Pinckney incompetent and a military failure during the Revolutionary War as the British ravaged his state.[44]

The most dramatic campaign attack was also the first "October Surprise" suffered by a presidential candidate. The surprise came courtesy of Alexander Hamilton, and as a Federalist it was expected a Hamiltonian surprise would focus on Jefferson. Instead, Hamilton attacked the administration, attempting to apply the *coup de grace* to Adams's reelection effort. Hamilton was furious at Adams for firing his strongest allies in the cabinet as the departures of Pickering and McHenry denied Hamilton inside information on Adams's plans.

Using the stories provided by Pickering and McHenry and including his own issues with Adams, the former treasury secretary prepared his *Letter from Alexander Hamilton, Concerning the Public Conduct and Characters of John Adams, Esq. President of the United States.* According to lore, Hamilton had not intended for the letter to be distributed publicly but rather to Federalist electors to convince them to replace Adams with Pinckney. The publication rambled on for pages, describing Adams's disputes with his cabinet secretaries, his temper tantrums, and his alleged mistreatment of the most powerful men in government. The letter was the first tell-all book about a presidential administration and which when made public embarrassed Adams. Its publication came in late October and only exacerbated the divisions within the Federalist Party and may have convinced state legislators not to vote for Adams in states such as South Carolina.[45]

TIE

Election Day in 1800 was a hodgepodge of different days and was a true test of federalism as states set different rules for the presidential contest. Five states allowed citizens to choose electors: Kentucky, Maryland, North Carolina, Rhode Island, and Virginia. Three of the five states— Kentucky, Maryland, and North Carolina—chose electors according to congressional district. Three other states—Georgia, Massachusetts, and Pennsylvania—had changed their selection method after 1796, no longer allowing voters to choose electors and returning that power to the state legislature.[46]

Modern politicians are portrayed as master manipulators of the political process, changing electoral rules for short-term political gain. Their 18th-century brethren displayed the same tendencies. In Virginia, Republican ideology clashed with political expediency as Jefferson's calls for greater local control of government was cast aside. After Federalists won four House seats in the 1798 midterms and showed strength in other districts, Republicans feared the district system of choosing electors could divide the state against Jefferson. James Madison, at that time a state legislator after four terms as a congressman, proposed to change the voting system from district to statewide selection of electors and a winner take-all system. With Jefferson all but certain to win the state even as he lost specific congressional districts, he was guaranteed a sweep of Virginia's electoral votes. The change in the system undermined the calls of Jefferson and Madison for more local control. The district system had given local voters greater influence in the Electoral College. In a statewide electoral system, Federalist votes in certain districts were overwhelmed by a wave of votes from Jefferson strongholds.[47]

The Republicans were not the only manipulators of the electoral system. Massachusetts' Federalists also created a winner take-all system that ensured Adams would sweep the state's electors. In Pennsylvania, the state legislature reached an agreement, splitting the electoral vote, with the Federalists taking seven of 15 where Adams won only a single vote in 1796.[48]

Congress also proposed changing the electoral system. Pennsylvania Senator James Ross introduced a bill creating a federal committee composed of senators, congressman, and the chief justice to overseeing the counting of electoral votes. With Congress firmly in the hands of the Federalists, the commission would have had the authority to throw out Jefferson electors and likely hand the election to Adams. However, divisions within the Federalist Party prevented an identical bill from passing the House and the Senate, the High Federalists seeming to prefer a Jefferson victory to a Federalist-dominated body that would choose the hated Adams.[49]

As the election results tumbled in, uncertainty reigned. Poor communication and confusion among voters, electors, and candidates about the workings of the Electoral College prevented a clear picture of the result. There was also Hamilton's strategizing as he tried to manipulate electors into choosing Cotesworth Pinckney over Adams.

The 1796 election had seen nearly a dozen men receive electoral votes; however, four years later electors were more likely to identify themselves as Federalist or Republicans. Electors were expected to vote for their party candidate and were chosen for their demonstrated party loyalty rather than political independence.

Under the new partisan organization, Republican electors were expected to vote for Jefferson and Burr while Federalists were expected to vote for Adams and Cotesworth Pinckney—notwithstanding Hamilton's plotting. However, if party discipline reduced the chances of electoral chaos, the same discipline opened the possibility of a new political crisis—the electoral tie. If every elector who voted for Jefferson on their first ballot also voted for Burr on their second ballot, the two men would receive the same number of electoral votes. To prevent a tie, at least one Republican elector would have to vote for Jefferson, then cast a ballot for another candidate, thus giving Burr one less vote but the vice presidency. However, the number of electors not voting for Burr had to be limited because if he lost too many votes, his total could fall below Adams who, much like Jefferson in 1796, might be elected to the vice presidency even when he was running for the presidency. Most worried about this was Burr, who saw his 1796 electoral vote diminished when the Virginia electors refused to vote for him with their second ballot. Jefferson was also concerned because he needed Burr's support in New York to win the presidency and had to keep his vice president satisfied that he would win office this time. The difficulty was choosing the elector to vote Jefferson but not Burr.

Never to leave an election to chance, Burr dispatched his future son-in-law David Gelston to Virginia where he met Madison and Jefferson to ensure he received Virginia's electoral votes. Madison and Jefferson guaranteed Burr would receive all Virginia's electors, and Madison's influence went beyond the legislature as he was a Jefferson elector.

After the visit, Burr was satisfied that he had support of Jefferson electors and would be elected vice president if Jefferson won.[50]

Not unexpectedly Adams swept the New England states with 39 electoral votes for five states. He also took New Jersey and Delaware votes and was able to split the Pennsylvania votes after the state legislature reached a compromise. Adams also split Maryland's 10 electoral votes, and the president sloughed off a third of the electoral votes from North Carolina.[51]

Jefferson's strength was in the large states including New York because Burr's efforts in 1799 to elect Republican legislators tilted the state to the Republicans. His victory in Virginia and expected victory in the newer states of Tennessee and Kentucky gave him 65 electors tied with Adams and Burr. Hamilton's plan to unseat Adams and replace him with Charles Cotesworth Pinckney was foiled when a Rhode Island elector voted for John Jay, the disciplined Federalists ensuring Adams and Pinckney would not tie. However, the errant vote gave Pinckney only 64 electors while Jefferson, Burr, and Adams had 65 going into the South Carolina vote. If all eight electoral votes were given to Jefferson and Pinckney, then the former would be elected president, and the South Carolinian would serve as vice president.[52]

Uncertainty reigned in Columbia with both sides certain of victory. Federalists were confident they had a legislative majority while the Republicans were just as certain that Jefferson partisans controlled the chambers. The first legislative caucus saw the new members formally declare themselves as Federalists or Republicans, and the numbers showed a clear pro-Jefferson majority. Once the legislature was organized the legislators voted for individual electors who were pledged to Adams or Jefferson. The most votes received by any Adams elector was 69 while the fewest votes for a Jefferson elector was 82.[53] The result had eight Jefferson and Burr electors chosen even as poor communication confounded Jefferson's plans and nearly cost him the presidency. A letter from poet Philip Freneau, a Jefferson ally, recorded the electoral vote as eight for Jefferson and seven for Burr with a stray vote going for George Clinton to prevent an Electoral College tie. The information convinced Jefferson to send Burr a letter informing the New Yorker that they had been elected, but Burr had one vote less thus giving him the vice presidency. The final electoral vote count, though, would see the two Republicans tied with 73 apiece and the election would be decided in the House of Representatives.[54]

THE HOUSE

The Congress that met in February 1801 to decide the presidential election was an anomaly. Federalists enjoyed a 20-seat majority in the House, but Republicans controlled more state delegations—the key to winning the presidency. Able to block Jefferson's election but unable to elect Burr without Republican help, the Federalists considered several scenarios. One scenario had a permanent deadlock in the presidential vote. After John Adams left office on March 4, the scenario had the Federalist Congress continuing in office until December when the new Congress would be sworn in. Under the 1793 succession law, the Senate president pro tempore would replace Adams, and the 1800 election would be temporarily overridden until the new Republican Congress chose Jefferson in December. In future presidential elections, the delay of the inauguration to maintain a party's power would prove unacceptable, but in the heat of the election Federalists believed manipulation of the process was a constitutional method of delaying Jefferson's ascension.

The debate among congressional Federalists are found in Hamilton's extensive correspondence starting in the middle of December and continuing to February. Among the letters were those from congressmen and other leaders who expressed concerns about Burr and Jefferson, though to many, the latter represented a greater threat because of his political theories.

Delaware's single congressman, Republican James Bayard, agreed in a letter to Hamilton that Burr was untrustworthy, but Burr's lack of probity was less dangerous than Jefferson's adherence to radical designs that he could implement when elected president. Bayard also raised the widely held concern that Jefferson and the Virginians were planning to permanently seize the national government.[55]

Massachusetts Republican and House speaker Theodore Sedgwick agreed with Bayard's conclusions on the two men. He warned that Jefferson was "an enthusiastic democrat in principle," who would return the country to the old Confederacy. Jefferson was a "feeble and enthusiastic theorist," whereas Burr was a "profligate without character and without property." However, this negative characterization became a positive for Sedgwick when choosing a president. He was comforted that Burr was a "matter-of-fact" man and "held to no pernicious theories." With Jefferson tied to Jacobins and their foreign ideas,

Sedgwick believe the supposedly corrupt Burr offered less danger to the republic.[56]

South Carolina's John Rutledge also worried about Jefferson's theories of democracy and how he would change the constitution to allow greater popular involvement in government. Rutledge wrote to Hamilton about the threat of Virginia domination, which was sufficient reason for him to vote for Burr over Jefferson.[57]

Hamilton responded to these arguments with vigorous denunciations of Burr though his attempt to undermine his rival had little effect. Hamilton's bitter words revealed the depths of his grudge borne against his New York rival. The men who read his letters were rationalists—children of the Enlightenment who were more concerned with preserving the republic than engaging in personal vendettas. Hamilton denounced Burr to Sedgwick, bluntly stating the New Yorker would disgrace the country. Hamilton struggled to dissuade Sedgwick and his Federalist colleagues from striking a deal with Burr, trading votes in return for Burr agreeing to enact Federalist policies when elected. Hamilton warned that "no agreement with him could be relied upon. His ambition aims at nothing short of permanent power and wealth in his own person."[58]

Congressmen Bayard, holding the key Delaware vote in his hand, was bombarded by Hamilton with reasons not to support Burr. According to the New Yorker, his rival was guilty of "inordinate ambition," with "great management and cunning as his predominant features." According to Hamilton, Burr would sell out his country to the highest bidder and asked Bayard, "Will any prudent man offer such a president to the temptation of foreign gold?"[59]

However, Hamilton did not rely solely on personal attacks to convince his Federalist colleagues and offered pragmatic reasons why they should favor Jefferson over Burr. According to Hamilton, if Burr were elected by the Federalists he would become their political property, and all of his failings would be tied to the party. To Oliver Wolcott Jr., Hamilton warned that Burr was a Trojan horse intended to destroy the Federalists.[60]

One argument that Hamilton did not offer in his letters proved most important to Federalist congressmen. They began to fear public reaction if the House chose Burr, an unknown quantity in much of the country, over Jefferson. Voters clearly intended Jefferson as the president and Burr as the vice president. Fearful their party would be tarred with the brush of monarchy if they chose a usurper like Burr, the Federalists went in search of a compromise.

One of the compromises traded Federalist votes for Jefferson's agreement on future policies. Among the concessions sought was Jefferson's promise to maintain a large army and navy, retain Hamilton's Bank of the United States, practice neutrality in the European wars, and retain Federalist government employees.[61] Jefferson was not keen on tying his hands after an election in which he promised a second political revolution and refused to explicitly guarantee to a deal. Instead, after the election he focused on Burr and, in December 1800, penned a plea to Burr to agree he would not seek the presidency. As a sweetener, Jefferson alluded to additional duties for Burr including a cabinet position that would create a copresidency.[62]

Jefferson, though, was not diligent in his contacts with Burr, who saw an opportunity as Federalists began to line up behind his candidacy. He dispatched letters to his supporters though Burr enjoyed enough political savvy to know Jefferson was not the type to share power after two bruising elections.

Burr's House support was focused on the manufacturing centers of New York and Massachusetts. The merchant class saw Burr as a steadier hand than Jefferson, whose support of the Virginia and Kentucky Resolutions placed him at the fringe among the extreme states' rights supporters. Another selling point for Federalists was Burr's shrunken political base which was composed mostly of Federalists and northern Republicans. Burr's presidency would have been weak giving Federalists considerable influence while making him an easy target for defeat in 1804.[63] The same calculations were likely being made by Republicans, hardening their resolve for Jefferson. The machinations and plans soon met with the political reality of the delegations from the House of Representatives. Jefferson controlled eight states, needing only one more for victory. The Republicans targeted three states: Delaware, Maryland, and Vermont. The latter was split with one Republican and one Federalist House member. Without a switch in vote or the Federalist removing himself from the voting, the state would not vote. The Federalists enjoyed a majority of House members in Maryland until one obstreperous member rejected Burr and voted for Jefferson, thus placing the state in a deadlock.

February 11, 1801 was the legal date for the counting of the electoral votes with a tie between Jefferson and Burr.[64] For the remainder of the day and until three the next morning, the House took 15 votes. Jefferson won eight delegations, Burr six, and two states—Maryland and Vermont—split between the two. The next three days saw the pace of voting slow with only six votes occurring. With deadlock becoming more likely, some outside Washington offered a military rather than a political solution. In Virginia, Governor James Monroe made noises about military action, collecting arms in Richmond for a possible march on the national capital.[65]

Cooler heads were found among the candidates as Jefferson and Adams met on Saturday to seek an arrangement. The key meeting occurred in the Federalist caucus where Delaware Federalist Bayard revealed he was not voting on the next ballot. The decision would leave 15 states voting with Jefferson holding eight states—a majority. The Federalists begged Bayard off his plan as they waited for Burr to make an offer for their continued support. Bayard had contacted the Jefferson camp for assurances the Republicans would not punish the Federalists but received a stiff arm in response.[66]

Burr did make a pledge to cooperate with Federalists in return for their support, but the caucus was unimpressed and tired of the battle. The 34th ballot was cast on Tuesday, February 17. Federalists in Maryland, South Carolina, and Vermont abstained from voting, moving two states to Jefferson and ending the election.[67]

AFTERMATH

The delay in Jefferson's election heightened tensions between the parties, and Federalists began to fear the new Republican administration would take vengeance on them. On February 13, 1801, the Federalist Congress passed the 1801 Judiciary Act creating dozens of new federal judgeships which were immediately filled by Federalist supporters of Adams.[68] Known as the midnight judges, their appointment infuriated Jefferson. When Secretary of State James Madison refused to deliver the judicial commission to one of the judges, district justice of the peace William Marbury, a lawsuit followed. *Marbury v. Madison* would be the first real test of the constitution and judiciary as Chief Justice John Marshall declared the power of judicial review and used it to strike down a single section of the 1789 Judiciary Act.

The Marbury dispute was only one portion of the Republican attack on the courts, the one branch still controlled by Federalist. Another judiciary act was passed in 1802, repealing the 1801 act and cancelling the Supreme Court's 1802 term. Three years later the House of Representatives impeached Justice Samuel Chase, partly for his politicking for Adams in 1800 and partly for his strict enforcement of the Alien and Sedition Act. Chase ably defended himself and defeated the Republican war on the judiciary, likely saving Chief Justice Marshall from being impeached. Jefferson's nearly five-year vendetta against Federalist judges was a black mark on his record.

The Federalist Party suffered more from their 1800 defeat. Divided and leaderless as Adams returned home and Hamilton saw his influence wane, the party became regional—its New England base also shrinking. Adams's anger at his party influenced his son, John Quincy Adams, to forsake the Federalists in 1808 and join the Republicans. He would win the presidency under the party banner in 1824 in another disputed election. Hamilton would never again acquire the political prominence he enjoyed in the Washington and Adams administrations—dying in the famous duel with Burr.

The vice president spent four years in political purgatory as he was isolated from the administration and denied patronage in New York as his political empire was seized by his rivals. Denied renomination by the Republican caucus in 1804, he left Washington only to be dragged back the next year to answer charges of treason. Once again Burr would set constitutional precedent, this time in the use of the treason charge. The Jefferson administration's case against him was circumstantial at best and the presiding judge, Chief Justice John Marshall, serving in his circuit duties, adhered to a narrow definition of the crime. Marshall also ordered Jefferson to provide documents for Burr's defense, setting up an executive privilege claim which Marshall won. Burr's acquittal ended the Republican vendetta against him, and he died some 30 years later in New Jersey.

Jefferson would suffer through two terms of office: his singular achievement, the Louisiana Purchase, was overshadowed by his vengeful if feckless campaign against the federal judiciary. A disastrous embargo would bring the American economy to its knees and he would join the Adams's administration as a casualty of the European war. Jefferson and Adams would rekindle their friendship when the two men were out of office; the authors of the Declaration of Independence would both die on July 4, 1826—50 years to the day after publication of their grand document.

The final casualty of the election was the Electoral College. Created in a rush and as part of the compromise, the presidential electoral system was vulnerable to manipulation and deadlock. Unwilling to suffer through another extended election, Jefferson and the Republicans passed the 12th Amendment establishing a new Electoral College. Starting with the 1804 election, presidential electors voted for a single presidential and vice presidential candidate. The new system helped form the two-party system and eliminated the back room maneuvering so enjoyed by Hamilton and Burr. The new system produced only three disputed elections in two centuries of use. The 1824 election was the result of a single-party single party system with multiple candidates whereas the 1876 election was created by the unusual effect of southern Reconstruction. Only the election in 2000 could be blamed purely on an electoral system that counted popular and electoral votes separately.

6

Between Clevelands

After 24 years in the political wilderness, Democrats welcomed the long anticipated inauguration of Grover Cleveland on March 4, 1885, the first Democrat inauguration since 1857. Cleveland entered office as the leader of a political party chastened by its alliance with secessionists and white supremacists. By 1888 he struggled to convince voters to make him only the second Democrat president ever reelected. Cleveland's troubles began during the 1884 campaign which was one of the dirtiest in history. His narrow victory, based on a 1,000-vote margin in his home state of New York, left him without a political mandate.

Entering office Cleveland established himself as a fiscal conservative, vetoing private pension bills he characterized as a raid on the treasury, but stumbling on the key issue of the 1884 campaign—the protective tariff. Democrat opposition to high tariffs made a tax cut a key goal of the Cleveland administration, an unfulfilled goal by December 1887 after the president left the issue in the hands of feckless congressional Democrats who could not pass even a weak bill.

Cleveland's one unalloyed first-term achievement was his marriage to the 21-year-old Frances Folsom. While in Buffalo, Cleveland administered Folsom's father's estate—the two men were close friends up to Folsom's death. Cleveland's mentored the girl through her teen years, enjoying a close relationship with her mother. By the time he was president, she was a young lady, and on June 2, 1886 the 49-year-old bachelor and the 21-year-old were married in the White House. The marriage ended Cleveland's wild youth which had included an illegitimate child, which was an issue in the 1884 campaign.[1]

FROM SHERIFF TO PRESIDENT

Few presidents have experienced Grover Cleveland's rise from obscurity to the White House in a few years. At the start of 1881 Cleveland was the former sheriff of Buffalo and a successful local lawyer considering a run for mayor. Cleveland was elected as sheriff of Buffalo in 1870, serving a single four-year term; he was responsible for hanging a man—the only president to have performed that duty. In 1881 he ran for Buffalo mayor, chosen to run as no other prominent Democrat would run in a Republican-majority town. Winning a narrow victory, Cleveland did not shy from challenging the Republican establishment. When the city council authorized a grant from city funds to pay the Republican veterans' group, the Grand Army of the Republic (GAR), Cleveland vetoed the spending, angering Republicans but enthusing Democrats.[2] Desperate upstate Democrats considered Cleveland as gubernatorial material as he was untainted by the corruption of New York City's Tammany Hall political organization. Six months after becoming mayor he was the Democrat front-running gubernatorial nominee.

In his first statewide race Cleveland enjoyed the good fortune of running in 1882, a bad year for Republicans and against a New York Republican party decimated by the departure of its leaders, Roscoe Conkling and Tom Platt, in 1881. The Republicans bungled their own nomination as President Chester Arthur became embroiled in home state politics, plunging into the state convention in support of Charles Folger, his treasury secretary. The result was an overwhelming Cleveland victory.[3]

After a year in office Cleveland became a presidential front-runner—his battles with Tammany Hall and record of fiscal austerity popularizing his image as a steadfast and honest politician. From the moment of his presidential nomination Cleveland faced a torrent of accusations and smears about his professional and personal life, much of the latter focused on his illegitimate son. The 1884 presidential election was one of the dirtiest in history, and once again Cleveland benefitted from a Republican split as the party's reformers, known as the Mugwumps, abandoned the party for Cleveland. For the first time since 1856, the country elected a Democrat president, and a generation of Americans who knew only Republicans in the White House waited nervously to see if the party could run the government.

THE CLEVELAND ADMINISTRATION

Twenty-four years of Republican election campaigns created a caricature of Democrats as rebels and slave owners bent on reviving the Confederacy, offering pensions to Confederate soldiers, possibly repealing the 13th Amendment, and reinstituting slavery. Cleveland benefitted from this hyperbole because it lowered expectations for his presidency.

Cleveland treaded carefully, relying on appointments to reward his southern supporters. With a Republican-controlled Senate, he chose only men who would not excite sectional tensions. As interior secretary, he chose Alabama senator Lucius Lamar, who negotiated the end of the 1876 electoral crisis and elected Rutherford Hayes. Lamar's moderation and willingness to work with Republicans made him a respectable southerner and eventually earned him a seat on the Supreme Court. Cleveland's attorney general, Augustus Garland, had a more controversial record. The plaintiff in *Ex Parte Garland*,[4] he successfully challenged a federal loyalty oath required of state and federal officials; however, during his tenure at the Justice Department he avoided controversy. His secretary of state was Delaware Senator Thomas Bayard, a border state politician with southern sympathies. Bayard would play a key role in the 1888 election.

Cleveland's best appointment came at the end of his term after the death of Chief Justice Morrison Waite. Cleveland nominated Melville Fuller, an Illinois Democrat who fit in well with the increasingly conservative Supreme Court. Cleveland would be less pleased with Fuller when he voted to strike down Cleveland's 1893 income tax.

Cleveland's perceived moderation impressed American voters, and in the 1886 midterms Democrats crept within two votes of outright control of the Senate while losing only 15 House seats but retaining control of the chamber. The smaller-than-usual House losses and the unexpected Senate gains signaled hope for Cleveland's reelection and was the best result the Democrat party could expect in a majority Republican country.

However, Cleveland was not guaranteed reelection. His attempts to settle the major issues of taxing and spending fell flat. Cleveland faced an unimaginable situation for a modern president, a massive and growing budget surplus. In the first two years of Cleveland's term, the Treasury surplus tripled from $17 million to over $55 million—some six percent of the budget. That number would nearly triple again, by October 1888, to $140 million.[5] The source of the surplus was the

Republican protective tariff. For two decades Republicans were associated in the public mind with a protective tariff and high government spending. Proposals to cut tariff rates forced Cleveland to wade into a nearly century-old argument on federal taxation.

Originating with Hamilton's 1792 *Report on Manufactures*, the protective tariff became the means for creating an American industrial base and limiting imported goods and foreign competition. The protective tariff became a central policy of the Whigs and later of the Republicans when they enacted a policy during the Civil War in order to pay for the war, the costs of reconstructing the south, and the war debt. By 1880 the tariff became a tool for building American manufacturing by limiting low-cost imports and building an internal market. By 1888 the tariff was accepted by most Republicans as a central part of the party platform.

Democrats opposed the tariff as vehemently as Republicans supported it. Representing a rural constituency that needed to export goods and lacked an industrial base, Democrats denounced the tariff as punishment of the south. When Cleveland entered office his ears rang with Democrat denunciations of the tariff, but his first effort at tariff reform introduced in the 1886 Morrison tariff bill was defeated in the Democrat-controlled House by a coalition of Democrats and Republicans.[6]

Having served three years and failing to achieve meaningful tariff reform, Cleveland decided on a daring strategy, making the tariff the defining issue of the 1888 campaign. In his third State of the Union address in December 1887, Cleveland presented arguments why the protective tariff and budget surplus hurt the country; he then made a proposal how to reduce both.

Cleveland began by noting slow economic growth of the time and attributing it to heavy taxation which removed private capital from the market while building government surpluses. Reducing the tariff would return money to the private sector which could be used for productive means. Having recognized the surplus as an economic problem, Cleveland listed potential solutions to the problem. He dismissed a proposal for distributing the surplus through state banks for investment and preferred people to keep their own money rather than having it filtered through the government bureaucracy. He rejected using the surplus to repay the debt at a faster pace. Cleveland warned that bondholders would require a premium to surrender their bonds, thus costing the federal government more money than repaying the bonds on maturity. Finally, he refused to support a cut in federal alcohol and tobacco taxes by citing the immorality of these activities. Cleveland then proposed an across-the-board tax cut on raw materials and finished goods, the reductions benefitting manufacturing and rural states alike in the hope he could build a national coalition for cutting the surplus.[7]

The tariff battle consumed several months before the election and injured Cleveland's electoral prospects. His tax-cutting proposal, though, was only one-half of Cleveland's domestic agenda. During his term the president had struggled to impose an austerity plan on Congress which had been accustomed to large budget surpluses used to fund soldiers' pensions.

Interest group politics played a limited role in antebellum America because political divisions were sectional and based on ideology rather than economics. This changed with the Civil War and the formation of the GAR. For the first time since the revolution, a significant portion of the population was under the authority of the national government as Union soldiers were clothed, fed, and paid by Washington. After the war the GAR became a major political force and voted as a bloc for Republicans.

Through the 1870s Republicans rode the GAR to victory in national elections, but by 1888 the group's influence had begun to wane as its members aged and dwindled in numbers. Another group had risen against it: Confederate war veterans who received no benefits for military service because their government no longer existed. Bolstered by the rise of southern Democrats in Congress, former Confederates fought any attempt to institutionalize the pension system for all former Union soldiers.

By 1885 the pension system had taken on the tinge of the modern Social Security disability system as dodgy benefit claims used vague and unproven medical conditions to receive a government payment. A pension office was established to consider the claims, but rejection by the office did not end the quest for government largesse. Members of Congress used the private bill calendar which allowed them to offer individual pensions for their constituents without regard to need or medical claims. As soon as the private bill was passed by Congress and signed by the president, the pension was paid. While the number of pensions passed via private bill was a tiny proportion of all the pensions paid by government, the process was tinged with corruption and waste.[8]

Under Republican administrations the pensions were approved with hardly a murmur, but with the arrival of a Democrat administration, the process became a political issue. Cleveland was determined to halt the invisible patronage system greased by GAR influence. Reviewing private bills for pensions became an obsession for Cleveland, and instead of delegating the tedious task to a trusted advisor, the president became the final appeal for wounded GAR survivors and their widows.

Cleveland's veto of private pensions made him an instant outlier among 19th-century presidents. In his first term Cleveland vetoed more bills than all of his predecessors combined. In June 1886, he vetoed 56 bills, exceeding the number vetoed by the 21 presidents prior to him. Cleveland vetoed over 400 bills, many in his first term, and the number of vetoes was second only to Franklin Roosevelt's 600, which were issued over 12 years.[9]

The veto policy hurt Cleveland as he challenged the findings of local physicians who empathized with their patients and offered diagnoses intended to speed the process. Cleveland's direct involvement in deciding pension cases offered Republicans a tempting target for criticizing his decisions. In rejecting pensions Cleveland engaged in public debates over the supposed injuries offered by veterans and their families. Among these was a dismissed claim from a veteran that his measles were the direct result of military action two decades earlier.[10] In another case, Cleveland rejected a widow who sought a pension for her husband's death which she attributed to rheumatism, but dismissed by the president as drunkenness.[11] Others claims bordered on the ludicrous. One widow claimed a pension from her husband's 1881 death when he fell off a ladder, the accident caused by an 1865 injury to his calf while serving in the army. Another claimed a pension from an eye disease caused by diarrhea triggered by army rations during the war. There were also pension claims for deserters, though few would have criticized denying such claims.[12]

Charges of excessive harshness only reinforced Cleveland's image as a strong executive who denied pensions to protect the public purse from an out-of-control Congress granting benefits for political gain. Cleveland was consistent by opposing excessive spending in other departments, vetoing an agriculture bill providing free seeds to farmers. In his veto message the president thundered against government paternalism, arguing "government should not support the people but the people should support the government." He also vetoed funds for public buildings, a favorite pork barrel project for congressman seeking favor with constituents.[13]

Republicans made an issue of all Cleveland's vetoes, building a case that he harbored Confederate sympathies which prevented him from recognizing the needs of Union veterans. However, overturning his decisions proved nearly impossible. While a closely divided Senate offered some hope for override, the Democrat House, packed with former Confederates, ensured defeat. Of Cleveland's 343 vetoed pension bills, only two were overridden by Congress.[14] In July 1886 Republicans drew their line in the sand. After the president vetoed the pension bill for an army veteran, Joseph Romiser, who was wounded in the face during battle, Republicans mounted an override effort. Cleveland's point man on the debate was former Confederate Postmaster General, Texas Congressman John Reagan, whose leadership in trying to uphold the veto allowed Republicans to frame the issue as a former rebel versus a former Union soldier.[15]

In February 1887 Republicans challenged Cleveland's pension policies by avoiding the private bill process. They proposed the Dependent Pension Act which provided $12 a month to all Union soldiers who served a minimum 90 days. The pensions would be extended to family members bringing thousands more into the system in what would become the first form of old-age security offered by government. After the bill passed the Republican Senate and Democrat House, Cleveland vetoed it as a budget buster. Republicans seized the issue to accuse Cleveland of being uncaring toward veterans and their survivors.[16]

Beyond tariffs and spending Cleveland signed the law creating the Interstate Commerce Commission (ICC), one of the first federal regulatory agencies. The ICC began the process of regulating interstate railroad rates and fulfilled a Democrat promise to bring the industry under some federal control. While the ICC raised the ire of some railroad executives, Cleveland angered many in the north by ordering the return of confederate battle flags to various southern state governments. Though only symbolic, the decision favored one section. His decision to stoke Confederate patriotism awakened the worst fears of northern voters that the Democrats appealed mainly to former Confederates.

Cleveland's foreign policy was the least active and least controversial part of his administration. His secretary of state James Bayard was an old political hand who saw foreign relations through the prism of domestic policy and based many of his decisions on rejecting Republican policies. His abrogation of the 1871 Canadian fishing treaty appealed to the Democrats' Irish constituency but quickly developed into a crisis when the British Navy seized American fishing boats. When an angry Congress authorized Cleveland to respond with force, the president refused and sent his secretary of state to negotiate a new fishing treaty. When the Republican Senate rejected the treaty, Cleveland accused them of undermining foreign policy; he then sought to cease all trade with Canada, a bellicose overreaction to a dispute begun by Cleveland.[17]

Having bungled relations with the British, Cleveland then offended the Chinese government. With Chinese workers blamed for taking American jobs in building the transcontinental railway, Californians demanded immigration restrictions to dry up a source of cheap labor. By the 1880s state and local governments passed their own laws restricting Chinese laundries and forcing Chinese prisoners to cut their hair; however, both laws were struck down by federal courts.[18] Responding to California Democrats, Cleveland negotiated a Chinese exclusion treaty only to see it rejected by the Chinese government. Cleveland then proposed a bill prohibiting Chinese immigrants from reentering the United States. The reentry bill was severe though meaningless, but Cleveland signed it, promoting the law as an administration success.[19]

With his adequate record on domestic affairs and weak record on foreign affairs—an issue which rarely decides American presidential contests—Cleveland was poised for reelection. Cleveland's success would depend greatly on the Republican candidate with Democrats hoping the party would again nominate James Blaine, Cleveland's opponent in 1884, who sported a long personal and professional record vulnerable to attack. More worrisome for Democrats was a lesser known candidate free of Blaine's legislative record and scandalous past. Unfortunately for Cleveland, Republicans would choose such a candidate, further complicating the Democrat campaign.

REPUBLICAN CANDIDATES

The Cleveland administration provided a needed respite for Republicans, the party having been split for over a decade between conservatives and reformers. The narrow 1884 loss revealed an enemy that both sides could hate more than each other, Democrats. Yet, the Republican front-runner going into 1888, James Blaine, remained as controversial as when he first ran for president. Since 1876 Blaine played the role of Republican front-runner at presidential conventions, narrowly losing in that year and 1880. His nomination in 1884 was followed by a bitter campaign and a razor-close defeat. Blaine spent the next three years traveling the world and finishing an autobiography of his career in Congress.[20] As the 1888 election neared, Blaine's partisans and enemies waited for the former secretary of state and House speaker to make a decision on whether he would challenge Cleveland.

Blaine's entry into the 1888 nomination campaign began with his reaction to Cleveland's State of the Union address on the tariff. Travelling through Paris, Blaine critiqued the president's plan in a letter. In typical Blaine fashion he cast doubt on Cleveland's patriotic intent by noting the positive coverage the tariff speech received in the London press. He warned the end of the protective tariff would devastate business, laborers, and farmers and argued that the country should not focus on the small international trade but rather expand the already massive internal market. Blaine also offered his own plan for reducing the budget surplus including cutting the tobacco tax while using whiskey tax revenues to bolster coastal defenses. In addition, he proposed distributing more of the surplus to the states to provide property tax relief.[21]

Blaine's Paris letter became the official Republican response to Cleveland and indicated the "Plumed Knight" was preparing for his fourth nomination battle. However, just as the Blaine wave began to assemble, he put a stop to it. In January 1888, Blaine wrote from Florence, Italy requesting Republicans not to offer his name in nomination. He expressed concern that his nomination would split the party as it had in 1884; he then placed an impossible condition on any nomination attempt. Blaine would run only if the delegates unanimously nominated him, and with Mugwump Republicans suspicious of Blaine, no unanimity could ever be achieved.

However, the Florence letter had the opposite effect as Blaine's propensity for political manipulation fed speculation that his declining the nomination was part of a strategy to be drafted by the convention. Blaine ridiculed the notion he was engaging in a complicated political maneuver; however, up to the moment of Harrison's nomination, many Republicans expected a Blaine–Cleveland rematch.[22]

With Blaine apparently out of the running, the Republican field was wide open. The front-runner was former Treasury Secretary John Sherman. Marking 30 years in Washington, Sherman was the younger brother of William Tecumseh Sherman. The general had been aided in his rise up the military chain of command by his brother's influence within the Republican Party. The Sherman brothers, though, were very different men. William Tecumseh was a nervous, agitated fellow who had been considered insane by some of his early commanders. The general had no political ambitions and was naïve about Washington politics, as reflected in his disastrous attempt to get all Confederate armies to surrender in spring 1865. His distrust of politicians and desire to stay out of his brother's occupation led him to utter the most definitive refusal of any politician. Asked if he would accept the 1884 Republican nomination, Sherman declared "If nominated I will not run, if elected I will not serve."[23]

John Sherman was more definite in his desire to run if nominated and serve if elected. First elected to the House in 1854 he served six years before rising to the Senate. Serving as Rutherford Hayes's treasury secretary, Sherman guided the country through the transition from a greenback currency to a gold-backed currency. Defeated for the Republican nomination in 1880 and 1884, the 65-year-old Sherman recognized that 1888 was his last chance at the presidency.[24]

Sherman was handicapped by a divided Ohio Republican party. Republican Governor Joseph Foraker believed he was presidential material and tried to prevent the state convention from endorsing Sherman. Foraker was joined by his old rival Marc Hanna and Congressman William McKinley. Hanna feared a Sherman presidency would centralize the state's patronage in the White House and ruin McKinley's chances for the presidency. With Foraker and Hanna working against him, Sherman was a weak front-runner.[25]

With Sherman's candidacy weakened, other candidates maneuvered for delegates. Among these was Iowa Senator William Allison. In the midst of a 36-year Senate career, Allison chaired the Senate Appropriations Committee overseeing federal spending. Allison's major legislative achievement was the 1878 Bland Allison Act which moved the country toward a bimetallic monetary system with gold and silver serving as legal tender. Though respected in the Senate, Allison suffered from his connection to Iowa, which was in the midst of an anti-railroad fever as the state legislature created a railroad rate commission, not unlike Cleveland's Interstate Commerce Commission. During the spring the commission began setting rates far below what railroads considered profitable. Though Allison was not directly involved in these efforts, many of his Iowa supporters approved of rate regulation and awakened fear among railroad executives that President Allison might expand on federal rate regulations.[26]

Allison was not the only Midwest candidate as the convention included supporters of Walter Gresham, Russell Alger, and Benjamin Harrison. Gresham was a federal judge who had twice been defeated for Congress; he then served as Chester Arthur's Postmaster General and Treasury Secretary before his appointment to the federal bench.

Gresham had earned the reputation as a politically oriented judge after swatting down attempts by railroad speculator Jay Gould to reorganize the Wabash railway.[27] Gresham's tangle with unpopular Gould caught the attention of Chicago Tribune publisher Joseph Medill who mounted a newspaper campaign to nominate the judge.[28]

From Michigan came Governor Russell Alger, a wealthy industrialist who had a simpler strategy of winning the Republican nomination— buying delegates. Alger controlled the Michigan delegation, but his main target was southern Republican delegates who used their positions to acquire money and jobs. With an excess of the former, Alger prepared to become a first-tier candidate even as most Republicans sneered at his excessive spending.[29]

Competing with these candidates for the Midwest vote was Benjamin Harrison, the last member of a political dynasty that has been ignored through much of American history. Political dynasties are considered an aristocratic tradition overturned by the American Revolution, as being "born into greatness" was considered a violation of the American credo of social equality. However, dynasties have played a critical role in American history starting with the Adams and continuing with the Bayards, the Cabot Lodges, LaFollettes, Tafts, Roosevelts, Kennedys, and Bushes, much of their success based on family wealth and name. One of the lesser known dynasties that produced two presidents was the Harrison family.

Benjamin Harrison V was a founder of the republic and signer of the Declaration of Independence. His son, William Henry Harrison, was a hero of the War of 1812 and the first Whig president, though his one-month tenure in office was the shortest of any president. His great grandson, Benjamin Harrison, appeared destined for state or regional fame rather than national prominence.

After rising to the rank of general in the Civil War, Harrison returned to his Indianapolis law practice. His legal skills were respected when he served as a Supreme Court reporter who published official Court opinions.[30] In 1871 President Grant appointed him to defend the United States government in a lawsuit filed by Lambdin Milligan who claimed false imprisonment during the Civil War. Milligan was arrested in Indiana in 1864 and convicted by a military tribunal of plotting insurrection. After the war the Supreme Court overturned his conviction, ruling that Milligan should have been tried before a civilian tribunal. Milligan filed a $100,000 lawsuit against the government. In the civil case Harrison attacked Milligan's ties to pro- Confederate militias in Indiana and their insurrection plans. Milligan struggled to defend himself against these charges and while the jury ruled in his favor, their five-dollar award to Milligan made the decision a mere moral victory.[31]

After the trial Harrison became a popular figure in Indiana Republican circles, and his initial foray into statewide politics resembled that of Cleveland. Both men accepted a nomination for a candidacy that few in their party wanted. In Cleveland's case it was a nomination for the mayor's post of Buffalo; for Harrison, it was the governorship of Indiana. In 1876 Indiana Republicans nominated the extravagantly named Godlove Orth for governor. Orth was allied with Republican boss Oliver Morton and enjoyed close ties to the Grant administration, which appointed him ambassador to Austria. Orth proved unpopular with Republican reformers tired of patronage politics and seeking competent rather than politically connected candidates for office. After Republicans forced out Orth, they selected Harrison to fill his slot.

Running in the midst of the 1876 presidential election, Harrison performed poorly, basing his campaign on unpopular positions. Harrison focused on the currency issue, approving the administration's plan to remove paper money or greenbacks from circulation and replace them with gold. Unfortunately, Indiana had been swept by greenback fever with a greenback party challenging the return to the gold standard. In taking a stand firmly opposed by his constituents, Harrison was doomed to defeat. The Democrats' victory on October 10 was a warning to national Republicans the state would go for Tilden in the presidential contest.[32]

After his defeat Harrison continued in his law practice and later won a seat in the United States Senate in 1881. At the time state legislatures chose senators in the months between the presidential election and the inauguration, and Harrison's election was crucial for the Republicans to maintain control of the chamber.

Harrison's influence in the Senate was limited by his freshman status, but he was a loyal Republican who worked hard to maintain the party majority. As chairman of the Senate Territories Committee, Harrison pushed for statehood for sparsely populated South Dakota with the expectation that the new state's voters would choose two Republican senators and keep the chamber in the GOP's hands. Opposing him were southern Democrats who could taste majority power, and the Democrat-controlled House killed the bill. It was not until Harrison was in the White House that South Dakota and five other Republican-leaning states joined the union, though Republicans lost the Senate in 1892.[33]

Harrison's single Senate term was unexceptional, and his reelection defeat exemplified the narrow partisan balance in Indiana as he lost by a mere handful of votes in the state legislature. By the time Harrison left Washington in early 1887, it appeared his family's political dynasty had come to an ignominious end, but many of his supporters saw the presidency in the former senator's future.

Representing the swing state of Indiana enhanced Harrison's candidacy as did his isolation from the internal Republican squabbles of the 1870s and early 1880s. None of the major candidates had clashed with Harrison, making him an acceptable compromise. His lack of national experience was not troubling as the Republican candidate in 1888 would focus on the tariff and use the issue against the Democrats.[34]

The tariff battle of 1888 widened the ideological divide over the role and size of government. Republicans favored spending the additional revenue provided by the tariff, and the Harrison administration would preside over the first billion-dollar budget in history—the money used to construct a two-ocean navy and supply veterans' pensions. Democrat complaints about higher tariffs were ignored by voters who recognized that without the war debt created by Confederate secession, the tariff would not have to remain at high levels. The Republican candidate's success would depend on his ability to sell the protective tariff as a positive economic force and convince voters that Cleveland's proposal to cut the tariff would lead to economic disaster.

CLEVELAND AND THE DEMOCRATS

The Democrat convention was one of the calmest in the party's history. Cleveland was the first Democrat president to be nominated for a second term since Martin Van Buren in 1840 and the first since Andrew Jackson in 1832 to have a realistic chance at reelection. Yet, the path to a second term was rocky as protectionist Democrats such as former

Speaker Samuel Randall opposed reducing the tariff and warned that Democrats would lose his home state of Pennsylvania if they cut the tariff. In New York, Governor David Hill, part of the Tammany faction which despised Cleveland, was even less interested in a second Cleveland term.

The president's strained relations with his home state party hurt him in the general election but did not threaten his nomination. Hill mounted a campaign to convince the state Democrat convention to endorse the governor for president or at the very least deny Cleveland his home state endorsement. Hill ridiculed Cleveland, noting the 200,000-vote victory the governor earned in 1886 and comparing it to Cleveland's 1,100-vote victory in New York in 1884. Hill also quoted a mail survey of Colorado Democrats which put the governor ahead of the president for the Democrat nomination. However, Hill had little chance of unseating Cleveland in New York. A final appeal to rally pro-tariff Democrats against Cleveland received only passing interest. Hill would play a key role in suppressing the Democrat vote in the general election and electing Harrison.[35]

Cleveland was nominated by the Democrats on the first ballot. The party platform and choice of vice president proved more controversial. The Democrats carefully avoided the tariff issue, the plank supporting tariff reduction while denouncing any claim that they favored free trade. The platform tied the tariff to higher prices but also recognized the tariff protected American jobs. The fence-sitting was intended to attract both pro and anti-tariff forces but undermined Cleveland's strong tariff reform speech of December 1887.[36]

The death of Vice President Thomas Hendricks in 1885 opened the second spot on the ticket. The vice presidency was considered unimportant in governing, but the candidate was responsible for much of the public campaigning. Democrats suffered from a death of candidates, their weakness in national politics producing few men of note. Their southern base offered strong politicians, but selecting a former Confederate or sympathizer to the national ticket would only reawaken northern concerns. Desperate, the Democrats chose 74-year-old Allen Thurman, former Ohio senator and member of the 1877 Electoral Commission. Out of office since 1880, Thurman had lost touch with national issues and lacked a national following. His advanced age was tested by the rigor of the campaign with William Barnum, chairman of the Democrat National Committee, indelicately noting the Democrats were "nominat(ing) a corpse."[37]

With Cleveland remaining at the White House during much of the campaign, Thurman took to the hustings, speaking in the swing states of Ohio, Michigan, New Jersey, New York, and Indiana. His rambling speeches degenerated into complaints about his declining health, and reporters covered his speeches as a form of a deathwatch. On three occasions Thurman collapsed or nearly collapsed on a platform, his tottering health becoming the message of the campaign. He noted during one speech "I am not quite as well as I ought to be and I am in no condition to speak to an immense audience like this tonight. I want to speak but I am unwell." With that he was helped from the platform— all but ending his viability as a national candidate.[38]

Cleveland remained in Washington during much of the campaign, his Rose Garden strategy presenting the image of a chief executive engaged in the peoples' business while Republicans campaigned for office. The focus of his summer was the Mills Bill, the congressional attempt to turn his tariff speech into legislation. Cleveland's gambit to make the tariff an issue resembled Henry Clay's 1832 strategy of granting the Bank of the United States a new charter in the face of presidential opposition. When President Andrew Jackson vetoed the new bank, Clay had a campaign issue.

However, the national bank proved a millstone for Clay, who went down in defeat. The same proved true for Cleveland. Though he may have intended 1888 to be a "solemn referendum" on the tariff, Cleveland awakened strong business opposition that had been quiescent during much of his pro-business administration. The Mills Bill, fashioned by Roger Mills, Texas Congressman and Chairman of the House Ways and Means Committee, proved an ineffective method of lowering the tariff.

Mills presented an uncompromising southern bias in cutting taxes. Mills drove the bill through the committee, ignoring Republican objections and making it a purely partisan piece of legislation. To combat opposition to the bill he cancelled the committee's hearings. Mills excluded Republicans during markup of the bill when the bill's details are amended and approved. The resulting bill favored southern interests and maintained high tariffs on the raw materials used by northern manufacturers. Among the tariff changes was a significant reduction for hemp, used almost exclusively for tying cotton bales which was the basis of much of the southern economy. Other products such as sugar, coal, tobacco, and rice, which were produced mostly in the south and faced significant foreign competition, remained protected by a high tariff wall. The Mills Bill was approved by the House, but its sectional tone made Senate passage doubtful.[39]

The subsequent rejection of the Mills bill created a campaign issue for Cleveland, and he accused Senate Republicans of failing to pass significant tariff reform. However, the partisan and sectional nature of the bill hurt his argument by creating an image of Democrats using tariff reform not to lower taxes on ordinary Americans but only to help narrow southern interests. As the campaign proceeded, Cleveland and the Democrats were dismayed as voters rejected their carefully plotted campaign theme.

REPUBLICAN CONVENTION

The Republicans gathered in Chicago on June 21 without a true frontrunner. Sherman entered the convention with the most pledged delegates, but his total was less than half of the majority needed for the nomination. Half of his votes came from southern black Republicans who showed a propensity for trading their loyalty to the highest bidder. Hovering over the convention was Blaine's on-again, off-again candidacy. On May 1, he sent another letter while passing through Paris, calling for Republicans not to offer his name to the convention. However, a few days later, after Blaine had crossed the English Channel, his denials were contradicted by Andrew Carnegie, the steel magnate and Blaine's host. When asked by a reporter about his guest and the presidency, Carnegie responded Blaine would run if nominated—something much less than a Shermanesque rejection.[40]

With or without Blaine in the mix the other Republican candidates continued to maneuver for delegates. John Sherman's well-financed and organized campaign paid to transport scores of black delegates pledged to him. Upon their arrival several delegates received a better offer from Governor Alger, whose campaign then isolated them in a room to ensure they were not tempted by a more lucrative offer. Alger combined Michigan and Missouri delegates and a double-digit number of delegates from Arkansas, Alabama, and South Carolina to rise through the ranks. Sherman struggled to maintain his hold on Florida and Mississippi and was forced to divide Virginia with Alger.[41]

As his southern vote totals declined, he faced a revolt from within the Ohio delegation. Governor Foraker worked behind the scenes to promote Blaine—his followers wearing buttons with Sherman's name on one side and Blaine's on the other, the delegates willing to shift loyalties with the turn of a button. Marc Hanna was maintaining lists of southern delegates whose votes he purchased for Sherman. If the senator's campaign stumbled, those same delegates could be used to support William McKinley's dark-horse candidacy.[42]

Among the large northern delegations, Pennsylvania and New York remained wild cards. The chair of the Pennsylvania delegation, Senator Matthew Quay, was not a beloved figure in his state or among national Republicans, but he respected power more than popularity and used the former well to get what he wanted. Quay had worked his way up the state Republican machine run by Simon Cameron and later by his son Don Cameron.[43] Quay's rise was helped by his dedication in keeping political records of all Democrat legislators including their votes and speeches, then using that information against them. Republican legislators received the same treatment with Quay using personal and political information to restrain their opposition to legislation. His data collections became known as Quay's coffins.[44]

Quay used his "coffins" to rise from state treasurer to United States Senator and chair of the state's convention delegation. He was determined to make Pennsylvania a key player in choosing the party nominee. Under the Camerons, Pennsylvania delegates became tools to advance the boss's political ambition—Simon Cameron's 1860 presidential run—to settle political scores; Don Cameron refused to let his delegates vote for rival James Blaine in 1876 or as the junior partner in a coalition with New York boss, Roscoe Conkling—part of the 300 delegates who supported Grant in 1880. Quay recognized that Republican division between the Mugwumps and Stalwarts defeated Blaine in the 1884 election and decided to make the Pennsylvania delegates available to the most attractive candidate—even Blaine.[45]

The New York favorite son candidate, Chauncey Depew, controlled the single largest slate of delegates. The Chairman of the New York Central Railroad, Depew, served as a placeholder for Blaine if he chose to run, but his candidacy was also a serious attempt to win the nomination for New York. Depew lacked a second choice for the nomination but was clear in his opposition to Senator Allison. With Iowa clamping down hard on railroad rates, the railroad industry and Depew was determined to defeat Allison.

One candidate seemingly missing from the early convention maneuvering was Benjamin Harrison. Still considered a dark horse, Harrison had the advantage of a weak Republican field and a representation of the key swing state of Indiana. Harrison's main struggle during the convention's early days was fighting off Judge Gresham's attempt to poach Indiana delegates from him. However, even with a solid Indiana delegation, Harrison's hope for a nomination was dependent on help from men like Quay and Depew and most critically James Blaine.

Indiana attorney general Louis Michener acted as Harrison's campaign manager and wisely struck up a friendship with Stephen Elkins, Blaine's 1884 campaign manager, who was telegraphing back news to the noncandidate in Scotland. A fabulously wealthy speculator in New Mexico land grants, Elkins enjoyed considerable influence among Republicans, particularly Blaine supporters. His ability to swing Blaine delegates at the behest of the candidate made him the most important man at the convention, even more powerful than many of the state bosses. Elkins latched onto Harrison as his second choice after rejecting John Sherman as too old and concluding that the other Republican candidates lacked the gravitas to defeat a sitting president.[46]

Michener and Elkins convinced state delegations to pledge second and third ballot support for Harrison. Both men realized no candidate would have an overwhelming first ballot vote total, and only by building momentum in subsequent ballots could any candidate break free from the pack.

However, as his campaign began to build momentum, Harrison's stubbornness threatened to derail all of Michener's efforts. When Matt Quay sent a letter to Harrison seeking cabinet positions for his state in return for his delegates, Harrison responded angrily to the demand for control over his cabinet and scribbled a hurried *"No"* on the letter margin and returned it to Quay. The Harrison rejection of the deal kept Pennsylvania delegates uncommitted to a candidate and enhanced the possibility of a deadlocked convention.[47]

The convention's first ballot revealed the weakness of the Republican field. The front-runner, John Sherman, scraped together only 229 of the 416 votes needed for the nomination. Judge Gresham was second, Chauncey Depew third, and Harrison fourth. Neither Sherman nor Gresham appeared on the verge of victory, and the convention adjourned to allow the bosses to coalesce around a favorite candidate.[48]

The first challenger to Sherman and Gresham was William Allison, whose cause was advanced by the chair of the Massachusetts delegation George Hoar. Hoar met with Midwest delegates and the New York delegation and proposed shifting votes to Allison.

The Iowan had received 72 votes on the first ballot; however, if combined with Depew's 99 and a smattering of Midwest delegates, the number might be enough to overtake Sherman and nominate Allison. The New York delegation gave conditional approval, but Depew vetoed the deal, refusing to accept any Iowan who approved of radical rate legislation.[49]

The convention reopened after a long weekend of negotiations and was greeted by another Blaine message that broke the logjam. Blaine definitively declared he was not a candidate because his first ballot total of 35 fell far short of his earlier demand for a unanimous convention. In sending his message to Elkins, Blaine made clear his support for Harrison, directing his campaign manager to tell his supporters to vote for the Indianan. At the same time, Depew endorsed Harrison, and soon the convention was a two-man fight between Sherman and Harrison. Michener's strategy of building momentum in the second and third balloting helped Harrison. Depew's endorsement of Harrison on the fourth ballot moved him closer, and by the fifth ballot Harrison was in second place with 213 votes, 11 behind Sherman who had barely moved from his first ballot vote total. Sherman was approached with a proposal to drop out and support Harrison to which he responded with another Shermanesque statement that would have impressed his brother "I prefer defeat to retreat."[50]

With victory close, Michener lobbied for the support of southern black Republicans who had originally declared their allegiance to Sherman for a price, then to Alger for more money, and finally to Harrison for an additional stipend—approximately $5,000 for 100 votes. The final push for Harrison was Allison's release of his votes to the Indianan, and the Harrison stampede drove him to victory on the seventh ballot. The final act of the convention was the choice of New York's Levi Morton for vice president, and then one of the closest elections in history began.[51]

THE CAMPAIGN SPIN

Pulitzer Prize–winning biographer Allan Nevins has set the narrative of the 1888 campaign. His 1931 biography of Cleveland established the president's reputation as a forthright and honest politician who was defeated by a corrupt Republican machine and Democrat politicians who put self-interest above public interest.

Nevins painted the 1888 election as a Manichean struggle between Cleveland and pro- tariff Democrats who infiltrated his campaign. One of his managers, William Barnum, owned iron ore mines in Michigan and built a fortune on the profits earned under the protective tariff. Barnum was a member of the Iron and Steel Association, one of the groups mobilized against the Mills bill. Cleveland's campaign finance manager, Calvin Brice, was the worst of progressive bogeymen, the railroad lawyer. Nevins intimated Brice sabotaged Cleveland's campaign and in return received a Senate seat two years later.[52]

According to Nevins Cleveland worked on the assumption that the public was uninformed about the costs of the protective tariff and the benefits of tariff reduction and would use his campaign to educate them.[53] As Nevins and other writers portrayed Cleveland as the honest candidate, Harrison was presented as having assembled one of the most corrupt campaign staffs in history. To Nevins, the Republican campaign chairman Matthew Quay was a perfect representative of the corrupt big city boss, willing to steal elections to maintain his hold on patronage. Nevins portrayed the Republican campaign treasurer W.W. Dudley as a political hack who used his position as federal pension commissioner to buy the votes of Civil War veterans. Nevins denounced Dudley as a "second rate lawyer" and party hack while glossing over his war record which included the loss of his leg during combat.[54]

However, the failure of the campaign rested with Cleveland who was responsible for his election strategy. His speech in 1887 made the tariff the central issue, and the subsequent Mills bill, which was based more on sectional than national interests, hurt Cleveland's chances. The president's decision to run a rose garden campaign flopped as his time in Washington isolated him from the campaign and the slow but steady erosion of public support for the Democrats. Having set the agenda for the campaign, Cleveland ceded the argument to the Republicans and was unprepared to battle the interests aroused by his tariff reform plans.

THE MILLS BILL

When the Mills bill passed the House of Representatives on July 21, the battle was joined between opponents and supporters of the protective tariff. Lined up for protection was the American Iron and Steel Association, the group that included not only William Barnum but also

Andrew Carnegie, James Blaine's host during the Republican convention. The association distributed pamphlets backing Harrison's tariff policies. Another group, the Protective Tariff League, was chaired by Harrison's vice-presidential running mate, Levi Morton. A third group, the Home Market Clubs, focused on New England states and workers arguing that the protective tariff benefitted both domestic industry and labor.[55]

The anti-tariff side included academics and industrialists. Among these were Charles Deering, founder of John Deere; Marshall Field of department store fame; Philip Armour, the meatpacking tycoon; and Cyrus McCormick. Among academics, the field was weaker though the father of American Social Darwinism, Columbia's William Graham Sumner, offered his support to the Democrats. All of this talent and influence proved remarkably inept at raising money and fell behind the pro-tariff side on funds available for the movement.[56]

As the Mills bill reached the Senate, the Republican leadership faced a difficult decision. Their nominee, Benjamin Harrison, and former nominee, James Blaine, were campaigning on the benefits of the protective tariff. The Cleveland administration effectively framed the issue as cutting taxes for ordinary consumers and promoting economic growth. If Republicans rejected any tariff reduction, they would face Democrat attacks for maintaining high tax rates. Proposing to cut the tariff would undermine Harrison and dilute a potent issue. Facing this quandary and the strong desire to deny Cleveland an election-year legislative victory, Republican leaders Senator Allison and Rhode Island's Nelson Aldrich offered a competing plan cutting internal taxation and reducing some tariffs while leaving most of the protective taxes in place. They focused on reducing farm tariffs to appeal to a Democrat constituency—Midwestern farmers. The proposed tariff reduction forestalled Democrat accusations of Republican obstructionism while slowing the momentum of the Mills bill, which eventually died a quiet death.[57]

With the promise of the Republican platform to eliminate the whiskey tax while Allison and Aldrich offered eliminating the federal tobacco tax, the Cleveland campaign saw an opening in the competing tax proposals. The Democrats quickly labeled Republicans the party of free whiskey and free tobacco. In his nomination acceptance letter of September 10, Cleveland declared "unnecessary taxation is unjust taxation" and reminded voters that when Americans called out for tax relief, Republicans offered them "free tobacco and free whiskey."[58]

Harrison roused from his front porch campaign and offered his acceptance letter two days later. The Indianan came out squarely in favor of the high tariff, an unusual position as most presidential candidates offer lower taxes, and offered his own epigram, accusing Democrats of being "students of maxims, not of the markets."[59]

Proposals to eliminate the whiskey tax provoked another interest group—the prohibitionists. The Women's Christian Temperance Union (WCTU) expressed dismay at the proposal to lower the price of whiskey. Its president, Frances Willard, condemned their usual allies, the Republicans. Responding for the party was former Blaine supporter Robert Ingersoll who offered an unusual defense for the reduction in the whiskey tax by noting, "temperance walks hand in hand with liquor." He warned that without a cut in the federal whiskey tax, Americans would pay more for domestic than foreign whiskey but preferred that, "those who wear foreign velvets and drink *Chateau y quem* pay the taxes." His comment reinforced the nationalistic defense of the tariff and a preference for American alcohol over European spirits.[60]

Ingersoll's comments were not an isolated attack. The Republican defense of the tariff combined economic nationalism with protecting American jobs. A Republican pamphlet "An English Invasion" conjured the specter of England reasserting economic dominance over the states if the Mills bill passed. The pamphlet told the story of the Denver Rail Company purchasing 5,000 tons of castings from a British firm, which managed the lowest bid even with a hefty tariff attached to the import of the castings. Republicans used the Denver example to demonstrate that without a tariff more contracts would be given to foreign firms, ruining American industry and throwing thousands of Americans out of work. The pamphlet drew scorn from the anti-tariff *Nation*, whose editors complained Republican policies forced Denver to pay more for their equipment. The magazine noted that higher costs were passed onto riders of their train system which hurt Americans with higher taxes and costs.[61]

Republicans defended the tariff with the one constituency, farmers, who almost universally opposed limits on trade. In an open letter published on October 27, the party warned that the defeated Mills bill would have opened American wheat markets to India and Russia, both of which would flood the country with cheap wheat. Without the wheat tariff to protect American farmers, they would lose their internal market and be driven into bankruptcy.[62]

A pro-tariff Boston newspaper, the *Commercial Bulletin,* offered a regional view of Cleveland's Mills bill. Noting congressional Democrats hailed overwhelmingly from the south, the *Bulletin* revealed that much of the tariff cuts in the bill rewarded southerners, including eliminating the tariff on hemp used for cotton baling while making northern manufacturers pay more for imported natural resources.[63]

The Republican campaign's unwavering front for a higher tariff did not always transfer to their business supporters. John Wannamaker, a Harrison advisor and hefty political contributor advertised for lower foreign goods at his stores. His advertisements asked "The money is yours. It is wholesome to bolster Troy at the cost of a third of your money? We are not such ninnies as to seriously ask you." The question conflicted with Wannamaker's assertion that the tariff protected American workers from low wage competition and guaranteed employment and prosperity.[64]

Even Harrison stumbled on the tariff issue during a speech he made prior to his nomination. In a March 1888 speech he ridiculed those who equated cheaper goods with American prosperity. According to Harrison, "I cannot find myself in full sympathy with this demand for cheaper coats which seems to me necessarily to involve a cheaper man or woman under the coat." Harrison's inelegant phrase about cheaper men and women was interpreted as an attack on those lacking means for expensive, tariff-laden clothing. Later, he clarified his comments, noting if any "man or woman who produces any article cannot get a decent living out of it, then it is too cheap." Unaccustomed to the sound-bite politics that existed even in 1888, Harrison's garbled message intended to highlight that tariff reduction directly led to a flood of cheap imports. American companies could only compete by lowering wages, and while overall prices declined, family income would also decline, leaving Americans with less purchasing power and possibly unemployment.[65]

Republican tariff arguments went from the convincing to the outlandish. The Harrison campaign chair, William Kelley, argued that western farmers benefitted from lower railroad shipping rates because of the American-made steel protected by tariffs. Kelley could not explain the connection between American-produced steel rails and farmers' costs.[66]

Modern readers might puzzle over the Republican arguments for higher taxes during an election year, but the economic and currency system of the time supported some of their arguments. A protective tariff was one means of building a manufacturing economy by creating a domestic market for goods. The gold standard of the period also sup-ported the high tariff. Imported goods were paid for with gold and as the supply of the metal declined, a country's money supply also declined, sometimes causing a recession. A protective tariff prevented large gold outflows while attracting foreign currency to build up the money supply even as it raised prices of staple goods that helped cre-ate industrial monopolies. Unfortunately for Cleveland, his appeal for a lower tariff did not pierce the Republican arguments for protection.

DEMOCRAT CAMPAIGN

During the debate over the Mills bill, Cleveland remained in Wash-ington, unable and unwilling to reach out to voters and the various Democrat organizations in the states. His decision to spend the sum-mer fighting for the Mills bill also trapped his cabinet members in Washington, limiting their campaign opportunities. With members of his administration unable to campaign, Cleveland was forced to rely on members of Congress, but the president lacked credibility with many Democrats when he sought their campaign support. During his 1884 campaign Cleveland focused on reform and eliminating patron-age influence in government, a typical campaign promise for a chal-lenger seeking the presidency. While the public responded positively to criticism of Washington politics, Washington Democrats jeered at the rhetoric. With his campaign stand against patronage and excessive spending, Cleveland offered members of Congress little in return for their votes. In addition during his first term Cleveland earned a reputa-tion for stubbornness and vindictiveness, two unsuitable traits in a sys-tem that required compromise and working across the political aisle.[67]

Cleveland's attack on corruption and unwillingness to cater to "cor-rupt" politics hurt him in New York. Governor Hill's weak challenge to Cleveland's nomination was not an accurate indicator of his politi-cal strength. The governor's influence over the Tammany political ma-chine ensured an overwhelming voter turnout and gave him control of the campaign message. Cleveland did not help his cause when New York Democrats sought his endorsement of the governor, and he re-fused with the comment "Each tub must stand on its own bottom."[68] A Committee of Democrats and Independents, filled with Cleveland supporters and Hill opponents, promoted split ticket voting for Cleve-land and against Hill's Tammany Hall candidates. Hill responded during his campaign stops around the country, focusing his speeches on a potential Hill presidential campaign for 1892 rather than electing Cleveland in 1888.[69]

Republicans also hurt Cleveland in his home state. The GOP-controlled New York legislature offered two bills: an election reform bill and legislation setting licensing for saloons—certain to split the governor and the president. The state election reform act gave state and local governments control over ballot printing and distribution. The act replaced the tradition of parties distributing single party ballots to be used by voters on Election Day. Reformers, who had little chance of having their name on party ballots, sought a general ballot printed by the government with the names of all candidates. Where the reform ballot promoted split ticket voting by giving voters choices from both parties, the old ballot system discouraged it. New York Republicans encouraged split ticket voting with New Yorkers selecting local Democrat candidates but national Republican candidates. When the bill reached Hill's desk, he vetoed it to protect his Tammany supporters who vigorously disapproved of a ballot system they could not control.[70]

The second bill established license fees for New York saloons. The bill was intended to appeal to prohibitionists who were in the midst of a nationwide campaign to regulate and eliminate saloons. The movement used licensing fees to prevent new saloons from opening and for making the cost of maintaining saloons so high many would close on their own. The prohibition movement had originally supported Republicans, but their voters slowly drifted away from the party. The licensing bill was expected to bring back that vote. Once again Hill vetoed the bill, claiming the minimum and maximum licensing fees were too high and were simply a different means of prohibiting alcohol. With Tammany Hall Democrats dependent on saloons for support, the veto was not surprising. However, Hill created an instant issue for Republicans who pounded New York Democrats for being pro-alcohol and antireform. Both issues hurt the president because many reformers refused to support Cleveland and Tammany Hall.[71]

Republicans also benefitted from a divided Democrat party in New York City—usually a center of Democrat strength. The incumbent Democrat mayor faced off against a Tammany Hall Democrat and a Republican. The interparty squabbling suppressed the Democrat vote as the two Democrat machines worked at cross-purposes. The Republican reform candidate, Warner Miller, was nominated to attract the Mugwumps or reform Republicans and independents who voted for

Cleveland in 1884. New York Republicans hoped Miller's popularity would transfer to Harrison with voters choosing a straight party ticket.[72]

The efforts of New York Republicans to win back the state after their narrow loss in 1884 were not matched by the Cleveland campaign to hold the state. Having expected to face Blaine again, Democrats struggled to run an effective campaign against the relative unknown Harrison. Instead, national Democrat campaign lacked focus and stumbled from one crisis to another. During the summer Cleveland was struck with Anglophobia when challenging Canadian fishing rights. His calls for military authority to use against the British were seen as an election year conversion because he had refused to use such authority when given to him by Republicans in 1887. The Cleveland administration provoked a crisis in Anglo-American relations with the Sackville-West imbroglio. Republican activist George Osgoodly set a trap for Lord Sackville-West, the British ambassador in Washington. Sackville-West was the type of Briton sporting an aristocratic title and a hyphenated name that produced sneers from most Americans. In September, Sackville-West received a letter from a Charles Murchison—George Osgoodly in disguise—asking for guidance on whether to vote for Cleveland.[73]

A bungler with little knowledge of the American electoral process, Sackville-West composed a letter praising Cleveland as the best candidate and suggested his anti-British policies were intended only for domestic political consumption. When the ambassador's letter was published in October, Cleveland and the Democrats were stunned. They argued the original letter to the ambassador was a Republican provocation, but Sackville-West's words stung Irish immigrants and nationalist Americans who believed the British were limiting American international influence. An influential Irish newspaper, the Boston *Pilot*, made clear its dislike of the ambassador and the need for sending him back to Britain. Even the struggling Senator Thurman, offered a memorable quote, saying he was unable to "make up my mind whether the British minister was more rascal or more fool."[74]

Cleveland then overreacted, demanding Sackville-West's recall, and when the British refused he had the ambassador declared *persona non grata*, a condition usually reserved to dangerous or inflammatory foreigners. The British were displeased by their ambassador's humiliation, and Cleveland's actions did not satisfy Republicans who emphasized British interference in the American election. The Murchison letter may have suppressed the Irish vote in New York, but more importantly it diverted Democrats from their anti-tariff message and gave Republicans an additional issue on which to pummel the president.

HARRISON CAMPAIGN

On the opposite side, the early glow of Harrison's nomination, especially among reformers, began to dim as the Republican establishment seized control of the campaign. The party chose Matthew Quay to run the campaign, striking fear in the hearts of reformers that Harrison was little more than a tool in the hands of party bosses, and in Democrats, who realized Quay's coffins would now be used against the national party.

As Cleveland and the Democrats suffered from an absence of talent on the campaign trail, Republicans faced the opposite with too many powerful personalities competing for media attention. Benjamin Harrison remained in Indianapolis, his front porch campaign serving as a template for future Republican presidents William McKinley and Warren Harding. Crowds of interested voters journeyed to Indiana to hear the future president make one of his 94 speeches in the summer and fall of 1888. Each speech reached a national audience through favorable coverage in Republican-oriented newspapers. Harrison's sedate campaign made few ripples: his speeches were composed mostly of defending the protective tariff and appealing to the Republican base.[75]

On August 11, Harrison declared James Blaine Day in Indianapolis, welcoming the former presidential candidate from his year-long European tour. The holiday included a parade in Blaine's honor and a platform for him to denounce Cleveland and the Democrats. In sharing the stage with Blaine, Harrison closely allied himself with the controversial figure even as he could deny he was Blaine's ally. In return for the recognition of his years of service, Blaine became a frenetic campaigner for Harrison, seemingly hell bent on defeating the man who had denied him the White House.[76]

Sneeringly called the "Greatest Living Statesman" by Democrats, Blaine traveled around the country, recycling many of his 1884 campaign issues, hitting hard on the tariff and at times overshadowing Harrison, who was referred to as the "nominal candidate" and White House caretaker.[77] The debates over the tariff, prohibition, voter reform, the British ambassador, and Canadian fishing rights may have distracted and even entertained voters, but it was only part of the 1888 campaign. While Cleveland struggled to raise money and develop a coherent political message, the Harrison campaign focused on winning two key states: Indiana and New York.

As Republican campaign chairman, Matthew Quay reached back to his days in Pennsylvania state politics and his use of systematic data collection and applied it to a national campaign. His focus was on New York which Blaine had lost by a little over 1,000 votes. Quay used the 1884 results to denounce voter fraud in New York City and turn the issue against Democrats by promising to end it. In offering the image of a Republican Party wronged in 1884, Quay was deploying a defense against Democrat claims he was manipulating the New York vote through means fair and foul.

One of those means was a large contingency fund that paid informers $1,000 if they identified voter fraud in New York City. The existence of the fund in the name of campaign reform put a positive spin on a political slush fund that could be used to prevent fraud or practice it by buying votes.[78] Quay went beyond offering money for information and began collecting it in the most massive private census ever taken of New York City. He created a boiler room arrangement with a fake storefront and a cover story to explain hundreds of census takers spread across the city, Quay collected detailed records of every New York City voter, a complex effort in an era of paper and pencil data collection. The names were assembled in a directory, an enlarged example of Quay's coffins, and could be used as evidence of voter fraud if a ballot was cast by anyone other than the registered voter. Quay put Democrats on the defensive and forced them into a weak response claiming that Republicans had stolen the election through their census and slush fund. Few contemporary observers believed Tammany Hall, who controlled the election machinery in the city, would allow widespread fraud by the opposition party.[79]

Quay was less involved in Indiana, his New York effort taking much of his time and energy. Instead, he delegated the state to the party treasurer, William Dudley, who knew the state as an Indiana politician. Indiana had been a swing state with Democrats winning the state in 1876 and 1884, when their presidential candidates had won a national popular vote plurality, whereas in 1880 Republicans took Indiana and the presidency. Party leaders openly commented on vote buying and ballot box stuffing in the state. At a dinner in 1884 the then president

Chester Arthur declared Indiana was a Democrat state–turned Republican by liberal use of bribery or "soap" as Arthur put it.[80] As a former Indiana governor and longtime politician, Harrison was familiar with voting felonies in the state. His former law partner, W. P. Fishback, told stories of national Republicans buying votes, paying repeat voters, and bribing election judges to stuff ballot boxes and falsify vote counts. According to Fishback, Republicans spent $400,000 in 1880 to turn the state to Garfield.[81]

During the summer of 1888, Democrats conducted a 60-day poll, a 19th-century form of political survey that saw hundreds of thousands of Indianans questioned over two months about their presidential preferences. The poll showed Cleveland winning the state with a small plurality, but Harrison's Indiana origins helped him more in Indiana than Cleveland's New York citizenship helped him in his home state. The Republican campaign treasurer William Dudley was a fellow Indianan and could manipulate the system. Dudley ran the Indiana campaign from Washington, his many letters to the state attracting the attention of a Democrat campaign worker who noticed the many pieces of correspondence while working on the mail car. His curiosity provoked him to steal one of the letters and turn it over to the Democrat Party. Inside the envelope was a frank discussion of the Republican strategy to win Indiana through the systematic use of floaters.[82]

When a party lacked a majority of registered voters, they became creative and felonious, paying individuals from the state or from out of state border areas to "float" from precinct to precinct casting ballots for the candidate paying their bills. Dudley suggested a systematic approach to this form of voting fraud with Indiana Republicans forming blocks of five floaters who would be organized and watched by local Republican leaders who would then pay them for their repeated votes.[83]

The "blocks of five" letter became the one genuine scandal Democrats could use against the Harrison campaign. However, as the party of Tammany Hall cringed in horror at the Republican plan for voter fraud, many voters tuned out their selective outrage. By 1888 most Americans were familiar with the stories of urban political corruption—much of it in New York City—and dismissed the charges as politics as usual.

Whether or not Republicans implemented Dudley's block-of-five plan, Indiana went for its favorite son, an unsurprising result even in a swing state. As the election approached, Cleveland and the Democrats faced a close election, but as the solid south closed ranks behind them and Democrats competitive in the Midwest and the key states of Pennsylvania and New York, reelection seemed a strong possibility.

THE MINORITY PRESIDENT

The 1888 election was not only an upset but also one of the most unusual. Benjamin Harrison won the presidency after losing the popular vote by second largest margin of any president. It would be another 112 years before a presidential candidate lost the popular vote but won the electoral vote. Benjamin Harrison's election was the fourth straight in which no candidate won a popular vote majority—setting a record yet to be matched. The postmortems on the 1888 election offered competing answers to the unusual results. Cleveland's popular vote victory in the face of an Electoral College defeat can be attributed to overwhelming Democrat support in the south. By 1888 southern Democrats were practiced hands at suppressing the black vote—which was overwhelmingly Republican—through a combination of violence, threats, and discriminatory laws. In six southern states Cleveland won by a margin of two to one, winning in Texas by nearly three to one. Cleveland's 100,000-vote popular victory came entirely from his 150,000-vote win in Texas. The Democrat built up nearly a 400,000-vote lead from the old Confederacy which Harrison would have to overcome if he was to win the popular vote. In states where there was an absence of free voting through systematic harassment and intimidation, Harrison won by some 300,000 votes.[84]

Analysis of the election focused on two states—Indiana and New York—and one man, Matthew Quay. Cleveland's home state of New York provided the electoral vote margin of victory with Harrison squeaking by with a 13,000-vote plurality.[85] Many Cleveland supporters took aim at David Hill while others pointed to Quay and his large slush fund and personal involvement in the New York City results. There were accusations of vote buying, the only method of voter fraud available to Republicans as Tammany Hall Democrats controlled the electoral machinery and could stuff ballot boxes at will.[86]

The *Nation* magazine probed the New York vote, examining four Brooklyn precincts. In each precinct, Cleveland outdistanced Hill while the Republican mayoral candidate Miller outdistanced Harrison, who won each precinct. The Cleveland vote was well below the Miller vote suggesting that Mugwumps had voted straight Republican, boosting Harrison over the top. Hill proved a drag on the Democrat ticket as disgust with Tammany corruption turned many reform voters back to the Republicans.[87]

Cleveland's weakness in New York and Indiana was matched by Harrison's weakness in Connecticut and New Jersey—both Democrat states in past presidential elections. Cleveland won Connecticut by a mere 350 votes out of the total casted votes of 150,000.

AFTERMATH

Benjamin Harrison and Grover Cleveland would compete in a rare presidential rematch in 1892—the only time a sitting president faced a former president in a two-party race. Harrison was dogged by questions of corruption: his campaign manager's comments about felonies committed to get Harrison into the White House stoking Democrat ire. His term as president would earn him obscurity in presidential annals though his achievements were not insubstantial. The Sherman Antitrust Act continues as a major regulation of American industry, but the Sherman Silver Purchase Act doomed the economy for Harrison and later Cleveland. Deemed the "human icicle" by his old manager, Quay, Harrison stumbled into the 1892 election all but certain of defeat.

Grover Cleveland would be the first defeated president to receive a second shot at the White House. The Democrats' weakness made him the party's front-runner in 1892, and a poor economy earned him four more years. They proved a disaster, the worst since the Buchanan administration as depression doomed his legacy and cancer threatened his life. The Democrats turned left in 1896, rejecting Cleveland who did not vote for the regular Democrat candidate.

Matthew Quay continued as the boss of Pennsylvania Republicans and exerted influence over one more presidential candidate. In 1900 the death of William McKinley's vice president, Garrett Hobart, left a vacancy. New York Republican boss Tom Platt had clashed with Republican governor Theodore Roosevelt and wanted him out of the state. Platt teamed up with Quay in elevating Roosevelt to the vice presidency and all of the obscurity associated with that office. The end result would be different than Quay and Platt hoped with Roosevelt becoming president and leading to the end of the careers of both men.

The Hand of God

JACKSON VERSUS QUINCY ADAMS VERSUS CLAY VERSUS CRAWFORD, 1824

Americans are duly proud of their two-party heritage. The battle between Republicans and Democrats was preceded by Whigs versus Democrats that originated from the Federalist and Republican competition animating the republic's early years. By 1820 the Federalist Party was in the midst of its long decline into irrelevance with President James Monroe winning an uncontested reelection. The consensus of Monroe's "Era of Good Feeling" hid factions within the dominant Republican Party which led directly to the four-way split in the 1824 election.

MONROE ADMINISTRATION

Monroe's two terms had been preceded by the two-term Madison presidency which followed the two-term Jefferson presidency, the only time in American history with three consecutive two-term presidents. The stability masked growing public unease as slavery and the economy became potent political issues. In his first term Monroe faced the depression of 1819 and agitation over slavery when Missouri applied for statehood. The depression was the result of the second tightening of credit by the Bank of the United States (BUS), leading to mass bankruptcies, bank failures, and the worst depression in the country's brief history while awakening suspicions of public monopolies and the inherent corruption of concentrated economic power. Though Monroe's reelection was not derailed by the troubles, the populist revolt generated by economic problems was a foreshadowing of political turmoil to follow.[1]

When Missouri applied to enter the Union, it revealed sectional splits over slavery. Congressional debate on the issue focused on the extension of slavery beyond the Mississippi. The result was a compromise allowing both Missouri and Maine into the union to balance slave with Free State and contain slavery below Missouri's southern border.

Monroe began his second term with a tour of traditional Federalist strongholds as part of a policy of absorbing factions into the Republican Party. However, his efforts to create a one-party system foundered on public disenchantment with the political system and the growing belief that national politicians were focused more on expanding their power than the good of the country. One target of this popular discontent was the congressional caucus, the party nominating system begun during the Jefferson administration.[2]

The congressional caucus system delegated to members of Congress authority to nominate their party's presidential candidate. Even at the height of its influence the caucus had its detractors who worried the system undermined the separation of powers. With Congress choosing the presidential candidates, concerns arose that the branch would favor presidents who deferred to congressional power rather than checked it. The caucus proved useful in giving each section of the country input into presidential candidates as members from north and south discussed and voted. With two national candidates, one Federalist and one Republican, offering an Election Day choice, the caucus' choices were still accountable to voters or the state legislators who chose electors. The disappearance of the Federalists limited the election to a single party with the caucus decision serving as the de facto election.[3]

Opponents denounced "King Caucus" and demanded greater democracy in the presidential system. The term "king" was used to stir a public that still equated a monarch with tyranny and war. The shift in popular sentiment against the government complicated the campaigns of the men maneuvering to succeed Monroe. Instead of focusing on the support of state and national elites who could manipulate legislators and win electors, candidates would shift their focus to issues and personal leadership with General Andrew Jackson's campaign reflecting the new political reality.

The ultimate outsider, Jackson was seen by supporters and opponents as a leader prepared to dramatically change governance. His talk of greater democracy and his reputation for decisive if not always wise leadership, transformed Jackson into a folk hero. The other candidates, John Quincy Adams, Henry Clay, and William Crawford discovered too late that their carefully cultivated political experience and administrative skill garnered little interest as voters sought a leader who challenged rather than represented the Washington elite.

Those who feared democracy or mob rule worried about Jackson's propensity for violence, and when the election moved from the voters to state legislatures and later to the House, Jackson's chances were diminished. The thought of President Jackson stirred old enemies to set aside political animosities for the goal of stopping Jackson.

THE CAMPAIGN BEGINS

From the start of Monroe's second term, potential candidates within and outside the administration jockeyed for political advantage and stifled his domestic agenda. As cabinet secretaries used their offices to campaign, Monroe struggled to maintain peace within his administration. His efforts were hampered early by the battles between War Secretary John Calhoun and Treasury Secretary William Crawford.

Calhoun's career is generally associated with states' rights and the doctrines of interposition and nullification that justified states overriding federal laws they found unconstitutional. However, Calhoun began his political career dabbling in Federalist ideology—his time in Washington strengthening his faith in an active federal government. Appointed as the youngest war secretary, Calhoun became a political star seemingly destined for the presidency. His sudden rise became a threat to more senior politicians, who plotted to derail his presidential hopes. Chief among these was Treasury Secretary William Crawford, a representative of the old Jeffersonian Republican values of limited government, states' rights, and intense hatred of everything Federalist.

Crawford worried Calhoun could develop a national following by courting Federalists in New England and the Mid-Atlantic states of Pennsylvania and Maryland and gather votes from his South Carolina base where the treasury secretary was the strongest. In response to this threat Crawford and his congressional allies went on the offensive.[4]

Congressional Republicans used their committee oversight to make near-daily demands on Calhoun for information on War Department spending. The department's contracts were scrutinized and questions posed on mundane topics such as the numbers and locations of cadets at the national military academy with all the questions intended to create the appearance of impropriety.[5]

The Crawford campaign against Calhoun took a dangerous turn when Congress proposed to slash national defense. Any reduction in federal spending would cut disproportionately from the War

Department budget which represented 35 percent of government spending, some nine million dollars out of less than the $26 million federal budget. Crawford used the budget cuts as an exhibition of Calhoun's political weakness and an appeal to the tradition Republican disdain for a standing army and government spending. Congress slashed army manpower and payroll, reduced appropriations for forts, and even cut the ammunition budget—affecting troop training.[6]

However, Crawford learned quickly that congressional investigations can be turned against any department of government, and during the lame-duck congressional session in December 1822 the Treasury Department was attacked by Calhoun partisans in search of scandal amidst all of the monies collected and spent by the Treasury. Audits of government accounts uncovered discrepancies in the department—the problems trumpeted in newspapers friendly to Calhoun as evidence of Crawford's corruption. Another line of attack came from the "A. B." letters written by Crawford opponent, Ninian Edwards of Illinois. The letters continued the assault against the Treasury Department and its dispersing of federal funds through state banks. The public attacks heightened pressure on the secretary and may have contributed to a break in his health in late 1823.[7]

Outside of Congress, Calhoun and Crawford partisans used friendly newspapers to attack the other. After a Georgia newspaper accused Calhoun of corruption, one of his allies, George McDuffie, was challenged to a duel that left him alive but with a bullet floating next to his spine. Newspapers wars in Washington were less violent but just as nasty. The Washington *Republic*, a paper allied with Calhoun, accused Crawford and his allies of factionalism in attacking Calhoun. In response, a Crawford-affiliated paper, the Washington *Gazette*, responded with personal attacks on Calhoun that included charges of malfeasance in office.[8]

The attacks on Calhoun within the Senate eventually drew Monroe into the dispute. After Monroe made several military appointments with the advice of Calhoun, Crawford's Senate allies Martin Van Buren and Thomas Hart Benton accused Monroe of usurping senatorial power. Monroe was surprised to find that Crawford was working to undermine the administration even as the president unsuccessfully lobbied for the appointments.[9]

While Calhoun's and Crawford's surrogates tried weakening their rival's presidential hopes, another political front opened as House Speaker Henry Clay critiqued Monroe's foreign policy and Secretary of State John Quincy Adams. During his two terms Monroe struggled to develop a coherent plan for recognizing new Latin American republics formed from the disintegrating Spanish empire. Secretary of State Adams pursued a cautious policy, refusing to grant immediate diplomatic recognition to the new republics. Clay was disturbed by the administration's timidity and was unafraid to criticize the president of his party and turned his formidable abilities toward foreign policy after having built the House Speaker position into one of the most powerful in government.

Clay enjoyed a long professional but not always friendly history with John Quincy Adams. The two men were lead negotiators during talks leading to the Treaty of Ghent, ending the War of 1812. The two men clashed during the negotiations, and their relationship worsened when Adams joined the Monroe administration as secretary of state. With the State Department considered the final step to the presidency as Jefferson, Madison, and Monroe had served in the position, Clay considered Adams the front-runner to succeed Monroe and the main obstacle to his White House plans.[10]

The Speaker jabbed at Monroe for his weak response to Latin American events and the Adams–Onis Treaty which ceded Florida to the United States. Reading the treaty the sharp-eyed Clay discovered that the Spanish had inserted a clause allowing the king to keep large land grants in Florida after Spain abandoned the territory. The oversight was sloppiness on Adams's part but also the result of State Department's poorly trained and small staff. The oversight forced Adams to resubmit the treaty to the Spanish government sans the land grant— the extended wait affording Clay more time to undermine it.[11]

While he enjoyed no formal influence over ratification—a Senate duty—Clay mounted a one-man campaign against the treaty, criticizing Monroe and American relations with the Spanish empire. Unconstrained by having to make real decisions with consequences for the country, Clay attacked allies and enemies alike, lashing out at Europeans for their interference in Latin America and attacking America's favorite whipping boy, Great Britain. The crux of the Speaker's argument had Monroe and Adams ignoring American's dedication to freedom and refusing to recognize Latin American republics so as not to offend the Spanish monarchy before it acceded to American annexation of Florida. Clay had problems with the western boundary set under the treaty, leaving the Texas territory outside the American sphere of influence and practically demanded annexation of the territory—a position he would yield during the frenzied 1844 campaign.[12]

Clay displayed Churchillian determination to get the United States to recognize Latin American republics, ignoring much of his party, his president, the jeers, and ridicule from partisans of Calhoun, Adams, and Crawford. Yet, the cautious diplomacy of the president and secretary of state secured the Gulf Coast and eliminated a military threat. Recognition of the republics came later without inflaming the Spanish during negotiations and without undermining the country's reputation for promoting liberty.

The Calhoun–Crawford and Clay–Adams battles consumed official Washington and caused the Republican establishment to miss the rise of a political outsider, General Andrew Jackson. By 1820, the old general was an iconic figure among the public and a controversial figure within Washington. The hero of New Orleans had handed the British their worse defeat during the War of 1812, imprinting his name in American history and the public's mind. His later actions in Spanish-controlled Florida solidified his popular appeal while generating fear of Bonapartism and an American military dictator in the minds of the Washington establishment. Jackson's southern roots placed him in direct competition with Clay, Crawford, and Calhoun—all working from a southern political base. With Jackson's addition to the list of presidential hopefuls, five major candidates, Adams, Calhoun, Clay, Crawford, and Jackson, were staking a claim to the White House.

WILLIAM CRAWFORD

A native Georgian, William Crawford rose from what was considered a political backwater in the south. Elected senator in 1807 he did not start as the purist Republican candidate he was in 1824. As a senator he chaired the Senate committee assigned the task of chartering the first Bank of the United States (BUS) and defended the institution on the Senate floor as a necessary and proper function of government. Crawford voted for the bank even as it went down to defeat.[13] In 1813 he was appointed minister to France and served during the dying days of the Napoleonic regime. When he returned to the United States he replaced James Monroe as war secretary. During this time Crawford developed a yearning for the presidency.

By 1824 William Crawford was Monroe's self-anointed successor. His claim to the presidency rested on his refusal to challenge Monroe at the 1816 congressional caucus. The caucus of that year was held to choose James Madison's successor. Secretary of State James Monroe was the front-runner, but many Republicans feared he was too weak and a continuation of the unpopular Virginia dynasty. Monroe's opponents offered William Crawford with Martin van Buren, the New York political boss, supporting his candidacy.[14]

The brief but nasty campaign before the caucus vote saw Crawford's allies portray him as a Republican outsider who could challenge the capital's corruption. In response, Monroe partisans, writing under the anonymous *Americanus,* accused Crawford of favoring miscegenation among Indians and whites while serving as war secretary and harboring secret Federalist tendencies by supporting John Adams's Alien and Sedition Acts.[15] Crawford hesitated at directly challenging Monroe because he realized that if he lost, his political career would be over. Instead he mounted a half-hearted campaign that left his supporters uncertain whether he was serious about the party nomination. When the congressional caucus met on March 16, 1816, Monroe won by six votes, 65–54: his margin of victory was provided by eight Crawford supporters who voted for Monroe believing the war secretary was a not a candidate.[16] Crawford would be rewarded for his loyalty and refusal to split the Republican Party as Monroe appointed him treasury secretary.

Crawford was better prepared for the 1824 caucus, allying with Van Buren who controlled the New York congressional delegation in the caucus and the state legislature which determined the state's electoral votes. As part of the campaign Van Buren visited Thomas Jefferson and sought out his endorsement of Crawford, but the wily old ex-president preferred reminiscing about past political battles.[17]

In a daring maneuver, Crawford convinced his congressional allies to pass the Tenure in Office Act of 1820, which set a four-year term of service for government officials. After four years the officials would have to be reappointed by the president. As treasury secretary, Crawford enjoyed influence over hundreds of officials including the powerful head of the New York customs house. Using these patronage positions for his benefit, Crawford hoped to pack as much of the federal government with his supporters, though Monroe recognized his secretary's plans and simply reappointed all of the former officials when their tenure ended.[18]

The hopeful signs for Crawford were overshadowed by events on the ground. In 1823 the House elected Henry Clay as Speaker rather than Crawford ally Philip Barbour because Speaker Clay would have the advantage if the presidential election deadlocked and was sent to the House. Shortly after, another blow struck Crawford as Tennessee elected General Andrew Jackson as governor. The Speaker and treasury secretary discussed a fusion ticket as Crawford was strongest in the deep south where Clay was weak while Clay was strongest in the old northwest where Crawford was weak, but the two men could not agree on any arrangement.[19]

In September 1823 Crawford was felled by illness, the long hours as treasury secretary and the pressures of the campaign breaking his health. As part of the medical consensus of the time, Crawford was subjected to a bodily purge which was intended to remove the illness from his system. Instead the treasury secretary suffered a stroke—his right side paralyzed and affecting movement, speech, and eyesight. Crawford spent the next six months suffering through a cycle of recovery and relapse which kept him from his office for much of early 1824. A hasty return to Washington caused a relapse ending his direct involvement in the campaign.[20]

Even without his illness, Crawford faced an uphill struggle to the presidency. A master of inside politics of the congressional caucus, Crawford had lost touch with the changing public mood. Outsiders like Andrew Jackson preferred a populist campaign that appealed to the growing influence of voters while casting Washington insiders as the enemy of the people. In focusing his efforts on winning the congressional caucus, Crawford cast himself as the insider candidate.

The caucus met on February 14, 1824, with only one-third of the Republican members of Congress participating and representing the party's radical wing. The members preferred a partly disabled Crawford to a fully functioning candidate who did not hold purist Republican views. The members represented the South and Mid-Atlantic states with few from New England or the west. Crawford received the caucus endorsement, earning 64 of 67 votes, but the nomination proved to be the highlight of Crawford's campaign.[21]

JOHN QUINCY ADAMS

As the son of a former president, Adams endured the burden of high expectations among Federalists that he could revive the party; however, instead of rebuilding the Federalists, the president's son abandoned the party his father built. Elected as a Federalist senator from Massachusetts, he defied his party in supporting Jefferson's Louisiana Purchase, voted for the 12th Amendment, and in a bold move, supported Jefferson's embargo. The embargo vote followed by his involvement in the Republican congressional caucus nominating James Madison caused the final split between Adams and the Federalists.[22]

Appointed as minister to Russia by Madison and later turning down a Supreme Court appointment, Adams became Monroe's secretary of state in 1817. Yet, for all his accomplishments Adams was distrusted by his adopted party, which treated him as an apostate always under suspicion of backsliding. Having connections with the two parties, Adams represented the best candidate to continue Monroe's amalgamation policy of creating a single Federalist-Republican party.

Being under suspicion from both sides, Adams had to tread carefully in appealing to either faction. A full-throated appeal to Federalists would be interpreted by purist Republicans as proof that the former Federalist remained loyal to his old party. Rejecting the Federalist would cost him New England support. The balancing act forced Adams to privately accept Federalist support while publicly refusing it. In 1822 he accepted the nomination for president by the Massachusetts' legislature but with the condition that all Federalist members be excluded and only Republican members vote for him. This convinced some Federalist leaders that Adams was a full-fledged Republican who would not appoint Federalists to high office if elected.[23]

Adams' political and diplomatic skills were on full display during his tenure as secretary of state. Adams skillfully used Andrew Jackson's rampage through Florida to negotiate the Adams–Onis treaty which annexed the territory. The treaty would become controversial during its ratification as Clay attacked the agreement to keep Texas outside of the American sphere of influence. Adams responded to Clay ally Jonathon Russell who accused him of surrendering to the British on fishing rights and Mississippi navigation. Having maneuvered the country through a difficult international scene, Adams could campaign on genuine achievements while appealing to Federalists and Republicans in New England and the old Northwest.[24]

JOHN CALHOUN

John Calhoun was one of the original war hawks who seized control of Congress after the 1810 midterm elections. Calhoun barely survived the 1816 congressional election which was marked by voter fury at a congressional pay raise and led to the defeat of two-thirds of House members. Calhoun's political stock rose after he accepted Monroe's offer of the War Department after Clay refused the appointment. Early in his term he confronted the Florida crisis and joined Crawford in condemning Jackson's rampage through Spanish territory. Crawford leaked Calhoun's criticism of Jackson to the press, hoping that the general's supporters would campaign against the war secretary. However, Calhoun's battles with the treasury secretary made him more popular with many Federalists and some Republicans who thought Crawford too radical.[25]

By 1823 Calhoun had attained a favored status among Pennsylvania Federalists. The state's Federalists were divided between two factions: the Family Party and the Amalgamators. The Family Party was led by George Dallas and took its name from the familial relations between the faction's leaders. The party was built around disgust with the dominance of the New York and Virginia Republican parties which dominated the presidency and vice presidency for two decades. Dallas and others believed the war secretary was a candidate capable of generating a support across factions and sought an alliance with Ohio and South Carolina to create a national movement.[26]

Dallas struggled to pack Pennsylvania government with Calhoun supporters, using patronage positions to build support for his campaign. However, his favoring of an obscure Calhoun partisan for governor over a more prominent candidate led to a revolt among Pennsylvania legislators, hurting Calhoun's cause and strengthening his political rivals in the state.[27]

Opposing the Family Party were the Amalgamators. Led by Federalist congressman James Buchanan and future Supreme Court Justice Henry Baldwin, the faction sought a fusion of Federalist and Republican voters. Unlike the Family Party which was based in urban areas such as Philadelphia, the Amalgamators depended on rural voters. As early Jackson supporters they promoted the old general both to stop Calhoun but also seize control of the state party from Dallas's Family faction.[28]

Calhoun ignored Jackson while focusing on Crawford as his main rival. Relying on his Pennsylvania allies, Calhoun hoped the state party endorsement would be followed by endorsements in Maryland and North Carolina. However, the Jackson political whirlwind swept aside Calhoun's carefully laid plans. Few Washington leaders took Jackson seriously even as his iconic status and heroic story appealed to ordinary voters. Jackson partisans also organized local meetings as a form of voter caucus to discuss Jackson and then pass resolutions for the old general by overwhelming margins to create the image of a wildly popular candidate. For the first time, a presidential candidate appealed to the grassroots rather than the elites to advance his cause, and neither Calhoun nor his Pennsylvania allies could halt the momentum.[29]

Calhoun's hopes ended in the fall of 1823 at the Pennsylvania state Republican Convention. Buchanan and his amalgamator faction swept the convention, and 125 delegates endorsed Jackson for president with Calhoun receiving a single vote. To soothe the feelings of the Family faction, Calhoun was nominated for vice president, which would serve as his highest office in government, first under Adams, later under Jackson. The vote caused a seismic shift in George Dallas's position on a Jackson presidency. Dallas denounced his own pro-Calhoun movement as a fad or "effervescence that can accomplish nothing" and the pro-Calhoun faction as a "miserable, infatuated minority." The Orwellian turn in loyalties did not hurt Dallas in Pennsylvania among Jacksonians, a voluntary surrender seemingly better than a coerced one.[30]

Losing Pennsylvania struck at the core of Calhoun's campaign. After his bitter battles with the treasury secretary and his allies, Calhoun could not grasp the possibility of a Crawford presidency but knew that if he split Federalist votes in North Carolina, Alabama, and Louisiana with Jackson, Crawford might slip in and win those states. Certain he could not beat Jackson and fearful his campaign would elect Crawford, Calhoun ended his campaign, giving the old general a clear field against Crawford in the Deep South.[31]

HENRY CLAY

The 1824 campaign for Clay was the culmination of a decade of work making him a national political figure. From his arrival after the midterms in 1810, Clay was the leader of the War Hawks, the cohort of Republican legislators who sought war with Britain. The War of 1812 proved a disaster for the country though Britain was firmly and finally expelled from American territory. Clay was emboldened, taking the once ceremonial Speakership and turning it into the most powerful position on Capitol Hill. From his perch Clay controlled committee slots and bill scheduling and could reward loyalists with plum positions and punish opponents with meaningless positions.

Clay acquired a national reputation that he hoped to transfer into a presidential campaign. The Speaker's penchant for working compromises began in 1820 after New York Congressman James Tallmadge offered an amendment to the Missouri statehood bill requiring gradual slave manumission in the state as a requirement for statehood. The bill passed the House, but southerners bottled it up in the Senate. Clay offered a compromise drawing the Missouri compromise line that allowed slavery to expand in the south but not in the Northwest Territories. Clay would work two other compromises in 1832 and 1850, but his congressional efforts hurt his claim to the presidency.[32]

The Speaker's propensity for compromise handicapped his presidential run as voters sought a leader who did not retreat from his position. Clay's image became that of a politician willing to toss aside principles and allies with equal ease in the name of legislative victory. His logrolling and vote trading would haunt him after 1824 with the taint of a corrupt bargain as he traded principles for a cabinet position. As the campaign settled into a four-candidate race, Clay recognized the president would not be chosen by the voters or state legislatures but by the House of Representatives where the Speaker could nearly guarantee himself victory.

ANDREW JACKSON

Andrew Jackson was the unlikeliest candidate and for the Washington establishment the most dangerous. The last president to have served in the Revolutionary War, the then 14-year-old Jackson earned a scar when a British officer struck his face with a cutlass. This generated a deep and abiding hatred of the English which bubbled up during Jackson's assignment in New Orleans in the War of 1812 and in Florida during Monroe's first term.

The War of 1812 is generally considered a failure for American arms, but Jackson's successful defense of New Orleans made him an icon among ordinary Americans. Faced with an overwhelming British force, Jackson constructed defenses that drew the English soldiers into a devastating line of fire. While all celebrated his military victory, his military–civil relations left some fearing a military dictator. Faced with a recalcitrant populace and press, Jackson moved to curb dissent while the British were threatening the city. His decisions were challenged in court and overturned by a judge who was then jailed after citing the general for contempt. After the battle was won, Jackson revived normal civil institutions, released the judge, and paid the assessed fine. That fine would become part of Jackson lore as Congress voted in 1843 to repay it.[33]

As one of the few generals to escape the war with his reputation intact, Jackson was assigned the task of halting Indian raids from the Spanish territory of Florida. This supposedly limited goal became a full-fledged invasion as Jackson's troops burned settlements, killed Indians, and executed two British agents believed to be inciting the Indians. The resulting furor was a diplomatic crisis which had Adams defending the actions of the man who would become his bitterest enemy.[34]

Upon returning home, Jackson was elected governor of Tennessee and later as senator. The old general arrived in Washington and immediately conducted a charm offensive to convince the Republican establishment he was an able leader not bent on military tyranny. The new senator greeted old enemies such as Missouri Senator Thomas Hart Benton as new friends. Jackson and Benton served together during the war then became rivals and enemies, ending in a duel that wounded Jackson, but the old general required Benton's influence in the old northwest.[35]

Few leaders in Washington took Jackson seriously as a presidential threat, but public disapproval of King Caucus was exploited by the general, whose message of egalitarianism and economic growth was well received by a population tired of economic depression and Washington politics. Moreover, Jackson also attracted Federalist support with his Senate votes for the 1824 tariff raising tax rates to help domestic industries and his vote for a survey bill that prepared for internal improvements. Jackson, though, also approved of Monroe's veto of the Cumberland Road bill as a federal intrusion on state powers, a position appealing to Republicans.[36] Jackson's victory in Pennsylvania over Calhoun launched him as a national candidate, the Tennessee slaveholder earning the endorsement of a powerful state Republican Party. His association with Federalists like James Buchanan also attracted that party's declining but still significant number of voters

Jackson's lobbying of the Federalists proved most fruitful with his position on an issue dear to them: proscription. In retaliation for Federalist attacks during the 1800 presidential election, Thomas Jefferson purged the government ranks of loyal Federalists, and his successor James Madison continued the policy. Lacking access to patronage,

Federalists could not reward their followers, forcing many, including John Quincy Adams, to join the Republicans.[37]

Madison's successor, James Monroe, offered some hope that proscription would end. Seizing upon this General Jackson composed three letters on behalf of Federalist William Drayton recommending him for war secretary. The first was written before Monroe was elected, another in November and a third in January. In each letter, he was lavish in praise of Drayton who during the War of 1812 had "abandoned private ease and lucrative practice for the tented field," and "will always act like a true American."[38] In another letter he noted "Drayton is the best selection that can be made."[39] In his third letter, Jackson took aim at the proscription policy and the Hartford convention that had provoked it. In typical Jackson hyperbole he wrote "had I commanded the military department where the Harford Convention met—if it had been the last act of my life I should have punished the three principle leaders of the party."[40] Jackson made clear his preferred punishment was execution of the leaders.[41]

When the letters were published in early 1824 Jackson became a political star. His appeal for inclusions of Federalists heartened the remnants of the party, offering them hope that President Jackson would appoint them to high office. Jackson made clear his disdain for the Federalists in the Hartford Convention, writing "these kind of men altho (sic) called Federalists are really monarchists and traitors to the constituted government," but then in a quintessential Jacksonian moment, welcomed the Federalists by noting "There are men called Federalists that are honest, virtuous and really attached to our government." From that moment Jackson was a national rather than a regional candidate.[42]

With its Pennsylvania victory and the proscription issue improving its popularity among Federalists, the Jackson campaign moved to another Calhoun stronghold: North Carolina. Calhoun's main rival in the state had been Crawford though Jackson's sudden rise transformed it into a contest between the general and the treasury secretary.

Targeting North Carolina in 1823, Crawford used his treasury post to mobilize federal employees for the state legislative elections. Crawford's faction was able to gain a plurality of seats which were then used to choose a Crawford slate of presidential electors. Calhoun supporters won the second largest number of seats and for the next year battled over the election system.

The North Carolina election system reflected the chaos of the 1824 Electoral College. Crawford and Calhoun partisans joined together to vote down an election reform that would have chosen electors based on congressional districts allowing a candidate who won the most votes in a district to claim a single electoral vote from that district. The legislature then voted in a Crawford electoral ballot with all 15 electors going to the Georgian. Calhoun scrambled to assemble electors for a People's Party ticket though the men on the list were not committed to any candidate. Jackson later ran under the People's Party label after Calhoun's campaign collapsed.[43]

The People's Party had a Jackson–Calhoun ticket competing with Crawford's regular Republican ticket. Jackson could thank Crawford, whose partisans had aided his rise with the belief that he would weaken Calhoun while not affecting Crawford's chances. The opposite would prove true. With North Carolina voting as a state for electors, Jackson swept most of them. However, when the House of Representatives voted, the North Carolina delegation voted for Crawford after they were initially elected as the treasury secretary's supporters.[44]

The statewide battles over state legislators, electors, and voting lists would be repeated all over the country. One key state, New York, would produce a titanic battle that would build the reputation of two prominent political manipulators of the *ante bellum* era.

WEED VERSUS VAN BUREN

The electoral votes of New York State determined the outcome of several 19th-century presidential upsets. By 1824 the state boasted the largest population and enjoyed the status as a growing financial center but was the scene of bare-knuckled political battles dating back to the fierce and deadly conflict between Aaron Burr and Alexander Hamilton. The four-way contest of 1824 built on that tradition as the two preeminent political minds of the *ante bellum* era, Martin Van Buren and Thurlow Weed, clashed over the state's electoral votes and House delegation.

Thurlow Weed started his career in Albany as a lobbyist then moved into the newspaper industry working part-time at an Albany newspaper while also serving as a state legislator. Weed became publisher of the Albany *Evening Journal* and transformed it into the country's leading Whig and later Republican newspaper.

Weed's reputation as a master political operator was built on the 1824 election when he engineered Adams's upset victory in the state legislature's electoral vote. An additional benefit for Weed in Adams's success was the exclusion of his rival, Henry Clay, from the final House vote.

The New York battle triggered a two decade Weed–Clay rivalry for control of what would become the Whig party. In 1840 and 1848 Weed denied Clay the presidential nomination and later successfully elected a Whig president. Besides Clay, Weed would also match wits with Martin van Buren, who would never forget Weed's maneuvering and defeat of Van Buren's favorite: William Crawford.

A native of Kinderhook, New York, Martin van Buren started as a state legislator and moved through the state machinery to become a U.S. senator. In that rise he clashed with Dewitt Clinton who was the boss of the state's Jeffersonian faction and four-time governor of New York. In 1824 Clinton was in partial retirement, serving on the Erie Canal Commission, a project he promoted as governor. The position lacked political influence, but Van Buren's allies feared the ex-governor's power and had him removed from the commission. The dismissal drew scorn from New Yorkers and generated a grassroots movement to nominate Clinton for governor under the Peoples' Party Banner. Clinton was elected with popular acclaim, and many Republican legislators lost their seat with his victory radically changing the presidential election. Crawford depended upon New York electors to reach the final three in the House, and Van Buren promised that his state legislative allies would provide the critical votes. The election undermined that influence because Van Buren's Republican allies came to believe that the little magician had led them astray.

However, Van Buren was distracted by efforts to build a national Republican organization in the Mid-Atlantic and southern states. His plans at national party building lagged when faced with opposition from state party leaders who refused to surrender their authority and independence in the name of efficiency. By focusing on events outside of the state, Van Buren lost control of his New York organization and nearly destroyed Crawford's campaign almost allowing Clay to move from fourth to third place in the electoral count.[45]

THE CAMPAIGN

Multicandidate elections are a rarity. The 1824 and 1948 elections were the only upsets featuring more than two major candidates though

Henry Wallace and Strom Thurmond in 1948 could not measure up to Jackson, Adams, or Clay in 1824. The Electoral College combined with a winner- take-all approach to electoral votes favors two-candidate elections. The 1824 winner-take-all system was a growing but not the only method of choosing electors. Some states divided up electors according to the congressional district which usually meant more than one candidate won electors in a state because few candidates managed to win the most votes in each congressional district. Some states allowed legislatures to choose electors and added to the problem as a candidate's state legislative allies compromised and divided electoral votes according to their numbers in the legislature. The 1824 deadlock convinced states to adopt a winner-take-all system that had the candidate who won the most popular votes in a state take all of the state's electors which tended to settle elections immediately and cleanly.[46]

None of the candidates in 1824 were under the illusion the election would end in November and realized a four-candidate field would divide along sectional lines forcing the House of Representatives to make the final decision. The single Republican Party with its political and regional factions created this division, but there have been other times in American electoral history where parties deliberately tried to clog the electoral machinery. In 1836 the Whigs offered three presidential candidates hoping to produce an electoral deadlock and election by the House. In 1860 southern Democrats expected to prevent a Republican victory and northern Democrat victory and again send the election into the House. In neither of these instances did the parties succeed—their plans foiled by the winner-take-all system of choosing electors.

Other multicandidate elections were based on real rather than contrived divisions. The 1912, 1924, 1948, 1968, and 1992 elections reflected factional disputes within parties. In every year except 1992 the faction was led by a prominent elected official including Theodore Roosevelt, Robert LaFollette, Henry Wallace, and George Wallace. Only in 1992 was the faction leader a true independent with Ross Perot running against George H. W. Bush for reasons of personal pique and ego. In 1948 the candidates had no effect on the outcome; however, in three of the other four, candidates captured electoral votes and in 1912 and 1968 changed the outcome though in 1992 Perot took 19 percent of the vote—most of his supporters being Republican. Unlike 1824 each of these elections was settled on Election Day.

The lack of an opposition party might be expected to calm partisan rancor and in 1824, most of the Republican candidates agreed on the basic functions of government. Three of the candidates—Adams, Clay, and Jackson—shared a nationalistic vision of the country: their specific views were shaped by experience and section, which also allowed them to attract voters who shared their views and regional loyalties. Jackson favored a Hamiltonian president, an energetic executive willing to use the enumerated and inherent tools of the presidency to effect change. Jackson distrusted public monopolies such as the Bank of the United States which were created under special privileges granted by Congress

Clay was the opposite. As a creature of Congress he opposed Jackson's theory of a muscular presidency. Clay's distrust of executive power conflicted with his American system which was a plan for activist government using taxes to raise revenue, aid domestic industry, and provide for internal improvements constructing roads and harbors while creating federal institutions such as a national military academy. The contradictory element of Clay's ideas had Congress rather than the president offering leadership.

John Quincy Adams favored a presidential model more active than Clay's vision of the executive but more restrained than that of Jackson. Adams sought a presidency that implemented internal improvements but worked within the political process and Congress to create it. Adams's model represented the old Hamiltonian and Federalist belief of "energy in the executive": a view that coincided with the beliefs of voters in his New England base. With Clay, Jackson, and Crawford originating from slave states where the Federalists were weak or nonexistent, Adams was the only candidate who reflected Federalist values. While Clay used policy to appeal to Federalists, the Adams family and regional ties to the party made him a favorite to sweep New England and advance to the House of Representatives.

Alone among the four was Crawford whose dedication to the ideal of a Jeffersonian democracy made him suspicious of a strong president and activist national government. His campaign focused on old Republican ideals as an alternative to the Monroe approach to fusing Federalists and Republicans into a single party. Crawford found fault with Monroe's foreign policy focusing on the Florida incursion, the Latin American revolutions, and the Monroe Doctrine promising military action against European states. Crawford partisans favored states' rights and strict construction of the constitution, the use of the phrase a smack at the Marshall Court which had stretched congressional powers in cases like *McCulloch v. Maryland* and *Gibbons v. Ogden.* Crawford was also on record opposing internal improvements, a core policy for both Clay and Adams.[47]

Crawford's campaign also tried to link him to Jefferson when his congressional caucus allies nominated Albert Gallatin, Treasury Secretary of both Jefferson and Madison, for vice president. Gallatin's ties to the traditional Republican administrations could not overcome his troubled political past. Gallatin was the first senator expelled from the chamber after a dispute over his Virginia citizenship. The Swiss-born Gallatin struggled to shake the perception he represented foreign values, and his opponents raised questions about his loyalty with voters who were suspicious of foreigners and Switzerland.[48]

Republicans held Gallatin in high regard for his Senate expulsion, seeing it as a Federalist Party effort to destroy a bright political career. After being isolated from politics for over a decade, Gallatin had changed, becoming an abolitionist, the first national candidate to represent those views. As controversy raged around him, Gallatin stepped aside as vice presidential candidate, much to Crawford's relief, but the issue hurt Crawford's image as the controversial Gallatin was considered a poor choice for a national position.[49]

STALEMATE

The United States of 1824 sported four overlapping regions controlled by factions of the Republican and Federalist parties. Adams ties to the northeast saw him sweep the electoral votes of the region's six states.[50] The South Atlantic states boasted the strongest Republican faction as Jackson and Crawford competed for votes in the Carolinas and Virginia. The men split the region as Jackson won the Carolinas, whereas Crawford took Virginia and Georgia. The closest vote was in North Carolina where Crawford's close second-place finish allowed him to claim the state House delegation when the full House of Representatives voted for president. The Crawford–Jackson battle pitted the old guard Republicans of limited government and weak presidency against the new Republican Party that favored egalitarianism and an activist presidency. The remainder of the south would go for Jackson though his Louisiana victory was razor-thin and based on serendipity rather than political popularity.[51]

In the old northwest there was a three-candidate battle with Jackson, Clay, and Adams fighting for states ranging from Ohio to Missouri. Jackson's policy of expansion and cheap land appealed to western settlers who sought freedom from the strictures of the old economic system.

However, the settlers' aversion to slavery, which they saw as cheap competition, hurt Jackson because of his slaveholder status. Clay's support for federally funded internal improvements such as rivers and harbors offered farmers cheaper transport for their goods. Adams's popularity was based on suspicion of Clay and Jackson as southern slave owners and fealty to the region.

The old northwest produced the closest popular margins. In Illinois Jackson won with a small plurality, 40 percent, because Clay with 33 and Adams with 22 percent divided the opposition vote, and Jackson's election victory but subsequent loss in the House vote was deemed part of the corrupt bargain. Yet, Jackson's opponents polled 55 percent of the Illinois vote, much less than a popular endorsement of the old general. Indiana had similar results with Jackson winning 46 percent of the vote while Clay earned 34 percent and Adams 20 percent. It was a weak victory for the general though he held onto the state's delegation in the House vote. Ohio was Clay country, but the Speaker managed a narrow 38 to 37 percent victory over Jackson with Adams a distant third at 24 percent. Ohio was another example of Jackson's opponents earning a large combined victory with 62 percent of the vote.[52]

The old general won his own landslide with victories in Pennsylvania—his one large northern victory—and in his home state of Tennessee and the Deep South states of Mississippi and Alabama where he tallied oversized majorities giving him a clear claim to those states in the House. Clay could lay claim to the old northwest and parts of the south while Adams also enjoyed support in the same region along with New England. Crawford was the weakest of the four with the votes of southern states and New York, if Van Buren could swing the state legislature in the treasury secretary's favor.[53]

By mid-November, voting trends began to appear. The popular and electoral vote totals showed a sizable Jackson plurality among voters but a small plurality among states. His large majorities in the south and unexpectedly large margin of victory in Pennsylvania put him in the lead with 153,000 votes. Adams was behind with 114,000 while Clay and Crawford battled for third. Clay enjoyed a 300-vote plurality over the Georgian from a total 90,000 votes shared by the two men, but popular votes served only as helpful guides to the congressmen who would decide the election while the electoral vote count produced a different result. The final vote tally had Jackson with 99 while Adams was a close second with 84. Crawford and Clay battled for the third and final spot for consideration in the House of Representatives. Entering the House election, Jackson's lead in the popular and electoral vote made him the front-runner, but he had won only 11 of 24 states, two short of the state delegations he needed for victory.[54]

Jackson's best hope for victory was to have both Adams and Clay included in the House vote. Each man appealed to the supporters of the other two men, and their combined votes in the northwest had swamped Jackson. If Adams reached the House without Clay, the secretary of state could lay claim to the House Speaker's states while retaining his New England votes. If Clay defeated Crawford and entered the House as a candidate, he would split his votes with Adams, offering the general the chance to squeeze out a victory. If Crawford was one of the three, it was inevitable that the states of Adams and Clay would combine to support Adams over the treasury secretary and the old general. Though popular lore has the election decided in the House of Representatives because of a corrupt bargain, the decision was made earlier by state legislators in New York which included Adams while excluding Clay from the House vote and ensuring the New Englander would become president.

By the time the New York legislature voted, it was clear no electoral winner would be declared as Jackson could not take the state and win an electoral majority. The state would decide which candidate would join Jackson and Adams with Clay and Crawford competing and the treasury secretary enjoying the advantage of his alliance with Martin Van Buren.

Once the national election results filtered into New York, Van Buren called a meeting of his caucus and ensured the selection of a solid Crawford slate of electors. The little magician's failure in the gubernatorial race forced him to compromise with the Clay faction, and the Kentuckian was guaranteed seven electors if his supporters also voted for Crawford.

New York had a complicated process with the senate and general assembly drawing up competing lists of electors that would be approved by the full legislature. The state senate vote on November 10 put Crawford in the running to win 29 votes and catapulted him into third place above Clay. However, Van Buren scotched the agreement between Crawford and Clay partisans as the general assembly prepared to vote. With the assembly divided among three factions representing each of the candidates, Van Buren proposed an end run around Clay supporters, forming a new alliance with Adams's faction while offering 15 electoral votes for Clay. Van Buren worked out an agreement to combine the Crawford and Adams factions in the general assembly and guarantee Adams some electors when the entire state legislature voted.[55]

The weekend intervened, and Van Buren saw his grand plans for Crawford unravel as Adams's managers, led by Thurlow Weed, struck. Meeting with disgruntled Clay supporters, Weed convinced them to cut out Crawford and vote for Adams with the secretary of state receiving seven votes in return. Clay's supporters were furious with Van Buren's maneuverings and agreed but in doing so doomed their candidate. The Clay faction discarded Van Buren's promise of electors for Clay and instead took the fewer guaranteed electors from Thurlow Weed to demonstrate their anger with Van Buren and Crawford.[56]

The vote on November 15 stunned Van Buren when he realized Weed and the Clay faction had outmaneuvered him. With 157 legislators, Weed enjoyed a tiny margin for error with Clay receiving seven electoral votes because 95 legislators supported him. Adams received 25 electors with the support of 78 legislators while only 76 supported Crawford's electoral claims. Three blank ballots created a loophole for Adams, who was one short of a complete majority but enjoyed a plurality with only 154 of 157 ballots counted. Crawford received exactly 50 percent, dooming his claim for New York.[57]

Van Buren's allies demanded a revote, and when their request was rejected, stomped from the legislature. Adams was ensured a second place showing in the Electoral College while Clay remained in the running to continue to the House. The next day the general assembly met again, and it was Weed's turn to be double-crossed as the remaining four electors were assigned to Crawford, vaulting him ahead of Clay and moving the focus of the election down to Louisiana. However, Clay's bad luck continued as his allies in the Louisiana legislature lost a 30–28 vote against a combination of Jackson and Adams supporters denying him any Louisiana electors and preventing the Speaker from being considered in the House. Clay watched as two legislators were unable to attend after being seriously injured in a carriage accident and several others did not attend having heard rumors the Speaker dropped out of the race. Thus, Weed's acquiring of extra electors from New York for Adams and Clay only helped the former.[58]

Van Buren blamed his loss on the perfidy of Clay supporters, but his maneuvering on behalf of the disabled Crawford and his handling of Republican legislators were pivotal to that defeat. Some legislators were angry at Van Buren's alliance with Adams's supporters in the general assembly and attempts to cut out Clay. Rumors about

Crawford's illness preventing him from serving further tilted Clay supporters away from the favored Republican candidate. Crawford could never get elected in the House while Clay enjoyed an overwhelming advantage.

CORRUPT BARGAIN?

Once it became clear Jackson, Adams, and Crawford would be competing in the House, the campaigns began maneuvering for the vote of state delegations. By 1824, 24 states were represented in Congress and with each state delegation granted a vote, 13 states could elect a president. Many state delegations were set in their support before they reached Washington. Adams enjoyed his New England base of six states. Jackson enjoyed Deep South support along with some old northwest states and Pennsylvania if the state delegation followed their constituents' lead. Crawford enjoyed less support with Georgia and Virginia along with North Carolina and Delaware serving as his base with New York and some Mid-Atlantic states possibly voting for him. Crawford's main influence was in his control of four delegations because he limited the number of available states for Adams and Jackson and left the election even more firmly in Clay's hands.

The old northwest offered the best opportunity for shifting loyalties. Clay had won his home state of Kentucky along with neighboring Ohio—two critical votes for Jackson and Adams. Clay had taken Missouri and his second-place finish in Louisiana earned him influence over the delegations of both states. However, not all House members would follow their constituent votes. In Delaware, Congressman Louis McLane represented a state with a strong Federalist presence and one of the few outside of New England and New York where Adams had taken an electoral vote. Crawford had taken two votes, but few in Washington expected the treasury secretary to be president. McLane though enjoyed a close friendship with Van Buren and during his tenure as chair of the Ways and Means Committee had a long working relationship with Crawford at Treasury. McLane's Federalist sympathies would later garner him an appointment as Jackson's treasury secretary, but as the sole congressman in the state he could vote for Adams with little damage to his reputation. Instead, he stayed with Crawford, refusing to trade his vote for a cabinet post. This decision may have earned him Jackson's respect even as he did not place Delaware into the old general's column.

In neighboring Maryland the state was split among Republican Crawford supporters, uncommitted Republicans, Federalist Jackson supporters, Adams supporters, and at least two undecided members. Adams had won the state's popular vote while Jackson had taken seven of 11 electors, making the state a swing vote in the House. Adams was petitioned by the large Federalist congressional contingent to end proscription, and he agreed not to automatically exclude members of his father's party from government. The key vote came from outgoing congressman Henry Warfield, who was serving his last days in the lame-duck session and likely held out hope for an appointment in the Adams administration. Adams used the most prominent Federalist politician, Daniel Webster, to soothe Warfield's worries and tilt the state away from Jackson.

Even as he lost some states, Jackson maintained control over Tennessee along with Indiana, Pennsylvania, and New Jersey while his southern supporters giving him a solid seven states. This compared to Adams's 12 states and Crawford's four.

The first ballot was scheduled for February 10 and was Adams's best opportunity for the presidency. His shaky agreements with the Maryland delegation and deals with single member delegations in Missouri and Illinois might not extend to a second ballot. Any weakening of his support would spell disaster, and members could slide to Jackson. The key state was once again New York with congressmen generally divided between Adams and Crawford with a few stray Jackson votes. The near tie drew attention and pressure on an old Van Buren friend and member of a politically connected New York family. Stephen van Rensselaer III had inherited his congressional seat from his cousin, Solomon. At 64 years, van Rensselaer lacked the stamina to cast a critical vote, wilting under the pressure of his old friend Van Buren on one side and the dominating personalities of Thurlow Weed and Clay on the other. Initially, Van Rensselaer was considered a Jackson supporter, but with the old general unlikely to take New York he was forced to choose between Adams and Crawford. Daniel Webster and Clay warned him of political turmoil if the House did not make an immediate decision on president. Van Buren played on the congressman's dislike of all things related to Adams—his disdain for the old president an open secret. This face convinced Van Buren that his old friend was a solid Crawford vote, even as everyone knew the Georgian could not serve as president.

However, when the old congressman reached the House floor on February 10 he suffered a crisis of confidence, stumbling to his seat with the other members of the New York delegation and bowing his head in search of divine guidance. It came in the form of a printed Adams's ballot at his feet. Spotting this sign from above, Van Rensselaer snatched it up and plunged it into the New York state ballot box, making it the 13th and decisive state that gave Adams the presidency. The final tally was as follows: Adams: thirteen; Jackson: seven; and Crawford: four—the various bargains between the secretary of state and the swing delegations holding up.[59]

John Quincy Adams, the candidate with the smallest following and operating from a weak New England base had outmaneuvered two of the most effective politicians of his era: Martin Van Buren and Andrew Jackson. His victory was a combination of ruthless exploitation of opportunities, a mix of bad luck and bad decisions by his opponents, and an electoral system that did not reflect the wishes of voters or their representatives. Upon receiving news of his election, Adams's reaction was one of a condemned man, telling his messengers he preferred to refuse the office and noted he was "oppressed by the magnitude of the task."[60]

The defeat was not forgotten by the little magician. In his memoirs, Van Buren told the Van Rensselaer story—casting doubt on tales of a corrupt bargain that would become the Jacksonian argument against the legitimacy of the 1824 election. However, the story of divine intervention may have been a face-saver for Van Buren, covering up another blunder by the manager who cost his candidate the election. In 1822 Solomon Van Rensselaer, the congressman's cousin, sought appointment as the Albany postmaster, a lucrative position for a Federalist supporter. President Monroe and the New York congressional delegation supported the request until Van Buren and his Regency allies objected. A petition was distributed in the state legislature to register opposition, and disagreement over the appointment became so heated that Monroe was forced to call a cabinet meeting to announce the choice.[61]

Suddenly, New York was consumed with the debate over whether a prominent and loyal politician who was wounded in the War of 1812 and was a true patriot deserved a government appointment. Though the elderly man was appointed by Monroe, his cousin Van Rensselaer likely recalled Van Buren's attacks during that moment of divine guidance in the House of Representatives in 1825 and turned him away from Crawford toward Adams, a decision based on personal rather than divine belief.

AFTERMATH

Adams's victory was one of the most controversial in presidential history, but the hard feelings and partisan attacks were not immediate in coming. The day after Adams's election, Monroe held a reception for the president-elect and invited his rivals, Clay and Jackson. Adams and Jackson shook hands while Clay received friendly greetings from all. A few days later Adams announced his appointment of Clay as secretary of state and suddenly the details of the supposed bargain became part of public lore. Jackson and his supporters cried corruption, an unusual charge from a man who would start the spoils system which relied on party loyalty for government employment.[62]

Neither Adams's job offer nor Clay's acceptance was unexpected. Adams had asked Crawford to return to the Treasury Department, but the ill secretary refused the offer. Adams likely would have offered a cabinet position to Jackson if hard feelings had not already enveloped their relationship. By 1825 Clay had reached the height of his power in the House, and higher office was his next goal. As the candidate who was closest ideologically to Adams, Clay's alliance made the most political sense as neither Jackson nor Crawford shared his views on an activist national government. Another reason for Clay's support of Adams was his conversation with two living ex-presidents. Between the election and the House vote, Clay visited Charlottesville, speaking with Thomas Jefferson and James Madison, neither man sharing any Federalist ideals. Jefferson was adamant in his opposition to Jackson, expressing concern about the militaristic general seizing power. He threw his support behind Crawford and Adams, the son of his old enemy though the two had since reconciled. The advice of the two old presidents and founders of the republic strengthened Clay's resolve in favor of Adams, who represented the establishment and had a close if at times contentious relationship with the Speaker. The public reaction to charges of a corrupt bargain should not have surprised Clay.[63]

The Speaker would have realized that the presidency was different than any other legislative bargain he had struck. However, the presidency was not a private bill or obscure piece of legislation where a bargain could remain hidden in the recesses of the House cloakroom. Instead, any deal struck between Clay and one of the three presidential candidates would explode into public view the moment the House voted and the political payoff to Clay followed closely on its heels. While such logrolling was an acceptable part of congressional compromise, the political culture had changed as insider politics was rapidly being replaced by an obsession for greater democracy and voter participation in government. Suddenly people thought themselves better judges than the elite, and the lifting of property limitations on voting marked the turn toward greater democracy and away from the backroom politics that doomed Adams's presidency.

Andrew Jackson was not a man to forget a political slight, and for the next four years Jackson's partisans relentlessly attacked the administration and its agenda. The 1828 rematch was no contest though one of the dirtiest campaigns in history. Jackson was vindicated in his claim of a stolen election while Adams left the White House for the House of Representatives, serving nearly two decades. Jackson won reelection against Henry Clay, another 1824 rival, and had an era named after him. Clay served a full term as secretary of state, returned to the Senate, built the Whig Party as a challenge to Jackson's Democrats, and lost two more presidential elections. Possible the greatest American politician never elected president, his legacy is secure, his achievements greater and better known than many presidents. William Crawford would recover physically from his stroke, dying in 1834, but his political career ended in 1824. The House of Representatives would never again choose a president. Two disputed elections, in 1876 and 2000, were decided by a compromise electoral commission or a Supreme Court decision.

8

The Election That Would Not End

TILDEN VERSUS HAYES, 1876

As the country marked its centennial, it braced for a close presidential election that would become a rare constitutional crisis over the Electoral College. The Hayes–Tilden dispute of 1876 capped two decades of political turmoil including war, assassination, and presidential impeachment. The year began as the best chance since 1856 for Democrats to regain the White House but soon became a nightmare for the party and its nominee, Samuel Tilden.

By 1876, Republican control of the national government sagged under the plagues of corruption, economic depression, and political stalemate. Ulysses Grant's second term was an unexpected disaster after his easy reelection in 1872 when he posted the largest popular majority since Andrew Jackson. Grant's victory reflected Democrat weakness rather than his strength, the opposition unable to nominate a candidate and instead endorsing the quixotic campaign of newspaper publisher Horace Greeley under the Liberal Republican label. The Democrat endorsement of Greeley highlighted how far the party had fallen.

Greeley's crushing defeat and subsequent death created Electoral College–chaos as six candidates received electoral votes while one state, Louisiana, had its votes rejected by Congress after charges of corruption. From that point the Grant administration began a slow, steady decline starting with the 1873 panic and depression and growing public disenchantment with Reconstruction policy. The 1874 midterms marked resurgence by the Democrats, the party regaining the House of Representatives for the first time in 16 years. The threat of the Democrat House broke the congressional logjam, and during the lame-duck session in December 1874, Republicans passed two bills that would become issues in the presidential election. The Specie Resumption Act tried to untangle the confused currency system, setting a target year of 1878 to return the country to the gold standard.[1]

The 1875 Civil Rights Act, passed in the session's waning days, enforced social equality by banning discrimination in public accommodations. The act infuriated southerners who grew more determined to regain control of their state governments. The act would never be fully enforced and was struck down by the Supreme Court in 1883.

Upon taking power in 1875, House Democrats launched investigations of the Grant administration, their public hearings part oversight, part political theater. The House Judiciary Committee uncovered corruption in the Indian Bureau and forced Interior Secretary Columbus Delano to resign. More corruption was found in the War Department, causing Secretary William Belknap to resign then be impeached—the first and only impeachment of a cabinet officer by the House of Representatives. Even as scandal enveloped the Grant administration and the Republicans, Democrats broadened their political attacks to include the declining economy.

Democrats blamed the depression on a massive railroad investment bubble, spurred by a Republican Congress that benefitted as railroad companies liberally sprinkled stocks and bonds among members in return for land grants and subsidies. Grant's first vice president, Schuyler Colfax, was forced from office after accepting Credit Mobilier stock in exchange for helping the railroad company. The mixing of corruption and economic depression worked well for Democrats while Republicans struggled with its legacy of "Grantism."

The Republican establishment split on civil service reform with Grant ally, New York Senator Roscoe Conkling, manipulating the spoils system to build a political machine funded by "voluntary" contributions from government workers. Opposing Conkling was a collection of liberal Republicans who split from the party in 1872. The faction's leaders were the German American Carl Schurz and the youngest member of the Adams political dynasty, Henry Adams.

Liberal Republicans faced a difficult choice of working within the party to reform it or mount another independent campaign. The internal reform plans focused hopes on Treasury Secretary Benjamin Bristow, who had been appointed by Grant to clean up the department after the scandal-tarred tenure of William Richardson. Bristow burnished his reform credentials by testifying before House committees as Democrats investigated the Grant administration. His willingness to reveal the inner workings of the administration made him popular with Democrats and Liberal Republicans but earned him powerful enemies in the party establishment.[2]

Bristow was targeted by Republican newspapers who charged him with paying off fraudulent claims and aiding smugglers with favorable rulings as treasury secretary. The same newspapers tied him to William Belknap, the impeached former war secretary. Reporters dug into Bristow's Kentucky record and found more charges of bribery while serving in state government. The charges only reinforced public views of a corrupt administration even as Bristow fought to clean up the Treasury Department.[3]

With Bristow under attack, reformers considered the alternative of splitting from the Republican Party. At a meeting on May 15 on New York's Fifth Avenue, reformers split on the issue. The politically savvy Schurz convinced the other liberals to remain within the party and attempt to mold its platform to include a reform plank. The meeting issued a strong statement for civil service reforms and decided to make the Republican Party the party of change.[4]

Even with the party united, Republicans faced a difficult election cycle: their strategy of tying Democrats to the Confederacy was undermined by the three-year economic depression that had worn down voters. In search of a new wedge issue that could put Democrats on the defensive and neutralize economic issues, Republicans reached back to their Know-Nothing roots and mixed the volatile issues of immigration and religion to attack Democrats. By the 1870s, the subject of public schools was a salient issue as Catholics sought public funding for parochial schools. Democrats split on the issue with some approving of parochial schools while Republicans demanded that children be taught exclusively in public schools. Under the direction of Maine Congressman James Blaine, congressional Republicans launched a crusade for a strict separation of church and state.

Much of the energy and organization went into passage of "Blaine" amendments to state constitutions banning public funds for parochial schools. At the national level, Blaine offered a constitutional amendment that was "an extension and clarification of the Establishment and Free Exercise clauses."[5] Ulysses Grant joined the effort, warning against parochial schools, and offered full presidential backing to the amendment and ban on using tax dollars to fund religious "sects." While the amendment mentioned no specific religion, Blaine played upon protestant concerns that Catholics would use land grant money to establish parochial schools and colleges.[6]

Blaine offered the public pose of defender of constitutional liberty from the secret designs of the authoritarian Vatican even as he used the issue to bash Democrats. The Blaine Amendment was applauded by liberal Republicans, who were suspicious of the church and its opposition to secularism. Blaine even reached out to the remnants of the Whig Party in the south who shared opposition to immigration. Though the Blaine amendment earned overwhelming support in the House after some modifications, it was defeated in the Senate and never sent to the states; however, Blaine had made his point.[7] His efforts raised him to status of Republican front-runner going into the 1876 convention.

THE CANDIDATES

With Republicans working overtime to distract voters from economic and corruption issues, Democrats struggled to find a candidate appealing to northern voters and strong enough on the patriotism issue to defuse the bloody shirt issue. Listed among the front-runners in a weak field was Delaware Senator Thomas Bayard, a political survivor par excellence. Serving in a border state during the Civil War and Reconstruction era, Bayard had straddled the major issues of the time, though a flirtation with the Confederate cause in the early years of the war tinged him with the copperhead label. A favorite of southerners who saw him as a staunch ally during their worst days, Bayard did not instill confidence in northern Democrats who feared he could not withstand Republican attacks.[8]

The sole Midwest candidate was former Indiana governor and senator, Thomas Hendricks. Hendricks's opposition to the postwar amendments including the banning of slavery placed him within the Democrat Party mainstream but in the far extreme of American politics. During his two years as governor in 1873, Hendricks appealed to populist voters by favoring greenbacks over gold as a single currency. The party's eastern wing, which financed the presidential campaigns, was unsettled by Hendricks's currency positions. Lacking eastern support, Hendricks's campaign floundered as Democrat financiers turned to one of their own: New York governor Samuel Tilden.[9]

A strongly Democrat state, New York had nominated the first postwar Democrat candidate—Governor Horatio Seymour. The election was a disaster, the popular Grant crushing Seymour, but the 1868 convention established the dominance of the Democrats' eastern financial wing. Eight years later New York promoted another governor, Samuel Tilden, who enjoyed an anticorruption record. A favorite of grassroots Democrats for attacking the establishment, Tilden earned the support of that same establishment who welcomed his personal wealth as a means to finance a national campaign.

During his career Tilden was a Democrat rebel, having joined the Van Buren Democrats or Barnburners, who opposed the Hunkers or party regulars who used patronage as a means to power.[10] Tilden supported Van Buren in his failed 1848 third-party candidacy and, along with the Little Magician, was relegated to the political wilderness. He reemerged in 1868 to lead the state party and backed Seymour for president. As party chair he battled Tammany Hall, the political "club" that for most Americans represented corrupt urban politics. He challenged Tammany control of New York City by offering a reform slate for mayor and other citywide offices and defeated the Tammany candidate. After Seymour's defeat, Tilden continued his reform efforts first as a state legislator then as governor after winning in the 1874 Democrat sweep. As governor, Tilden's assault on the "canal ring" added to his popularity while earning him powerful enemies in the New York Democrat establishment.[11]

Having attacked Democrat corruption, Tilden seemed the perfect candidate for cleaning up the mess in Washington, but he faced state and national challenges to his candidacy. Tilden's silence during the Civil War protected him from the copperhead label but cast doubt on the depth of his unionist sympathies. In defeating Tammany, Tilden raised his national stature and the ire of men such as Tammany leader "Honest" John Kelly, who warned against Tilden's nomination as president.[12] Kelly openly opposed Tilden's nomination at the state and national convention though he pledged support when Tilden became the nominee. Another opponent was Fernando Wood, the former copperhead New York City Mayor who touched off the city's 1863 draft riots. The staunch Democrat financier August Belmont preferred anyone to Tilden though when he was nominated, Belmont donated to the Tilden campaign.[13] The first major test for Tilden came in the New York State Democrat convention where Tammany held considerable influence, but the governor's supporters jammed through the unit rule to ensure a united New York delegation for Tilden.[14]

With his New York base secure, Tilden prepared for the Democrat national convention which opened on June 27 in St. Louis. Newly arrived delegates were greeted by a Tammany sign predicting Democrat defeat if Tilden was nominated. However, Tammany power weakened when it left the state, and Tilden supporters exploited the organization's opposition as a sign that their candidate supported reform. As Democrats rode or floated into the city, delegates experienced a rush they had not experienced since 1856. The convention went quietly, the party platform accepting the inevitable—pledging enforcement of the 13th, 14th, and 15th Amendments even as the Democrats were silent on enforcing social equality. The platform was filled with criticism of Republican mismanagement and corruption, high taxes, and also economic depression.[15] The platform condemned anti-Catholic bigotry while making vague promises about solving the currency problem and returning to the gold standard.

In his nominating speech for Tilden, Robert Kernan noted how the New York governor had cut taxes while Republicans raised them and credited Tilden with cleaning up the corruption in New York. With little competition, Tilden was nominated on the second ballot, sweeping in most of the favorite-son delegates in one of the quietest conventions since Andrew Jackson's nomination in 1832.[16]

After Tilden's nomination, two more battles remained: the currency plank of the Democrat platform and the vice-presidential nomination. Tilden's reputation as a Wall Street hard moneyman hurt him in the far west and agricultural Midwest. While many grassroots Democrats wanted the 1875 Specie Resumption Act repealed, the party regulars refused. Wall Street Democrats favored the gold standard, whereas farmers and western Democrats recognized the deflationary effects of a return to the gold standard as it drained money from the economy.

With the party divided, Democrats nominated Thomas Hendricks for his soft money views. Hendricks balanced the ticket on the currency issue while aiding Democrat efforts to win his home state of Indiana. The choice of Hendricks as candidate produced a public split within the ticket with the vice-presidential candidate making speeches opposing the Specie Act and forcing Tilden to repudiate those views and support the Specie Act.[17] Hendricks's nomination also provoked criticism in the press: his inclusion on the ticket was labeled as "a ridiculous nomination" with his election to the vice presidency promising to become "worse than ridiculous."[18]

Overall, the Democrats' choice was praised by critics of the Grant administration. According to the *Nation*'s editors, when compared with past Democrat nominations including the disastrous fusion with the Greeley campaign, Tilden's nomination was a sign that Democrats acted with "sagacity and common sense." Democrats offered change, whereas Republicans proved unable to move—the *Nation* approving of the Democrat's "outspoken anti Mongolian plank" attacking Asian immigration.[19] The *Nation* editors advised Hayes to focus on distancing his campaign from the Grant administration and criticize its patronage abuses.[20]

Yet, the St. Louis convention did not heal all wounds or guarantee a Tilden victory. Many voters dreaded the thought of a Democrat president "armed with authority and discretion," after the disastrous Buchanan administration descended into civil war. Hendricks's inclusion on the ticket and his appeal for an inflationary monetary policy had "alienated (voters) beyond recall." Democrats were aided by Republican inaction on the economy and voters' expression of a "readiness and widespread desire for change."[21]

The nomination battle exhibited Tilden's strength; his campaign revealed his weaknesses. Responsible for funding much of the Democrat effort, Tilden maintained tight control over the campaign. Having suffered a minor stroke a few years before the election, Tilden labored under periods of high and low energy. All but certain he was going to be elected, Tilden expended his limited energy in the general election and was unable to summon any more for the postelection battle, leaving the Democrats leaderless after November 7.

The glow from the St. Louis convention was dimmed by news from the frontier and Washington DC. While the convention was nominating Tilden, George Custer made his last stand on the Little Bighorn. The massacre and resulting outcry raised the public stature of Grant as Americans demanded a military solution—a policy area where Grant and Republicans excelled. The second piece of news reinforced the public distrust of Washington politics as the Senate began the impeachment trial of former war secretary Belknap, who resigned after discovery of his involvement with the Whiskey Ring. Senators spent much of their time debating the impeachment power rather than sifting through the evidence against Belknap with senators eventually bowing to the constitutional reality that impeachment could not be used against a private citizen. Many senators also realized that the Belknap impeachment was an election-year ploy by Democrats to embarrass the Grant administration.

THE REPUBLICANS

The Democrat convention occurred three weeks after the Republicans, who were more divided in their choice, a sign of trouble for the general election. James Blaine entered the campaign season as the front-runner at the 1876 convention, the first of four in which Blaine entered as the favorite. A master politician who manipulated issues and voters with equal ease, Blaine was the Nixonian figure of his time. Brazen and bluff, he rarely sat on principle, instead adopting once rejected positions all in the name of victory. In 1880, Blaine convinced Republicans to hang up the bloody shirt in national campaigns and replace it with the protective tariff. However, it was his response to a political scandal that earned him the enmity of Democrats and Republicans.

The House Democrats' zeal to uncover Republican scandals hooked Blaine as they focused on his ties to the Union Pacific railroad. Blaine had purchased and sold railroad bonds at a profit, but when the bonds collapsed, he used a railroad loan to reimburse angry investors, a loan never repaid. Similar dealings with railroads had forced Schuyler Colfax off the Republican ballot in 1872, and the same seemed possible for Blaine in 1876 without any dramatic action on his part.

When a Union Pacific official revealed the existence of letters detailing Blaine's relationship with the railroad, Blaine retrieved the letters before the Democrats could seize them and later refused to hand them over. Angry Democrats hammered Blaine as another example of the Republican culture of corruption and taunted him to release the letters. Blaine responded by calling their bluff. On June 5, he stood in the well of the House of Representatives and defended his work with the railroad. Holding up the letters as a prop, Blaine selectively read from each—the excerpts exonerating him. The speech was met with raucous applause from the House gallery, shutting down the chamber after Blaine denounced Democrats with the very evidence they had hoped to use against him. The so-called Mulligan letters became another footnote in American history, and Blaine's speech, emotional and manipulative, would be repeated in form and tone by Nixon's emotional Checkers speech during the 1952 campaign.[22]

The Mulligan letter speech was one of many political maneuvers used by Blaine to become the Republican front-runner. Blaine recognized in 1875 that Ulysses Grant was his most formidable opponent and maneuvered behind the scenes in support of a House Democrat resolution denouncing a third Grant term even as he did not vote for it. The resolution served its purpose, halting the third-term movement with Grant rejecting a third nomination. In January 1876, Pennsylvania Democrat Samuel Randall offered a bill restoring political rights for all former Confederates including Jefferson Davis. Seizing the opportunity, Blaine offered an amendment specifically denying Davis his political rights. The proposal quickly descended into a debate over the former Confederate president with Democrats trapped into defending Confederate rights, an unpopular position with northern voters. In a speech, Blaine raised the specter of the Andersonville prison and provoked former confederates including Georgia Democrat Congressman and Confederate General Benjamin Hill into a full-throated defense of the lost cause.[23] Blaine's goading of his enemies into defending unpopular positions immediately transformed him into a national figure while making him the man every Democrat wanted to defeat.[24]

Democrats were not the only ones to suffer under Blaine's lashing tongue because he infuriated some Republicans with character attacks. In a scathing speech on the House floor, Blaine targeted Roscoe Conkling, ridiculing his outlandish dress and personality. Stung by the attack Conkling made it is his goal to hold New York delegates back from Blaine, making Blaine's climb to the nomination that much harder. However, the Maine congressman remained the most popular Republican in a weak field.

Among Blaine's less illustrious challengers was Indiana governor Oliver Morton, who boasted a pro-Reconstruction record but also a troubling support for soft money policies. The Cincinnati convention offered Morton a home-field advantage, its proximity to Indiana allowing his campaign to bring in his supporters to dominate the gallery. Unfortunately for Morton, two other announced candidates, Rutherford Hayes of Ohio and Benjamin Bristow of Kentucky, shared a similar advantage. Morton locked in the Indiana delegation, the state Republican convention unanimously endorsing him while his support of Louisiana Senator P.B.S. Pinchback drew the support of southern black Republicans who endorsed him at their southern Republican convention in Nashville.[25]

Yet, Morton was caught between the demands of Indiana Republican and the national party over the currency issue. Many in Indiana opposed the 1875 Specie Resumption Act, and the state Republican Party called for its repeal. Morton straddled the issue, agreeing that the act should be repealed if found to be unenforceable but refusing to endorse outright repeal.[26]

Corruption charges during his service as a wartime governor also bedeviled Morton. During the war Morton received a quarter of a million federal dollars to arm a militia. Democrats accused him of fraud while the governor reminded voters of Confederate private militias including the Sons of Liberty and the Knights of the Golden Circle. Morton produced a federal audit showing he had accounted for half and returned the other half of the money unspent. Although winning the battle over the militia, Morton lost the war with the Democrats, suffering a stroke that cast a shadow over his candidacy. The Republican delegates were reminded of Morton's declining health during the convention as his nominating speaker defended Morton on the health issue.[27]

Joining Morton was Benjamin Bristow, the candidate of the party's reform wing. After separating himself from the Grant administration and burnishing the image of a reformer, Bristow looked to be Blaine's main opponent. However, Bristow would have his reform credentials challenged by the Ohio governor, who enjoyed support of the state most critical to Republican hopes.[28]

Rutherford Hayes ran on his reform record as a three-term Ohio governor. Ohio was the easternmost part of the northwest and the keystone to any Republican victory because no Republican president has been elected without winning Ohio. Hayes separated himself from the Blaine movement and tried to appeal to reform Republicans who held the key to nomination.

Hayes enjoyed the undying loyalty of Ohio Republicans during his 15 years as a leading politician in the state. Elected to a safe House seat, Hayes left to run for governor in 1867 where he learned the effectiveness of a bloody shirt campaign. He tied the inoffensive Allen Thurman to the treasonous Democrat congressman Clement Vallandigham and defeated Thurman by 3,000 votes.[29]

Originally a Grant supporter, Hayes became disillusioned with Washington corruption while remaining true to the administration's Reconstruction policies. His signal achievement in his first term was pushing the 15th Amendment through the state legislature, capping off Republican attempts to protect the freedman. Running for reelection in 1871 Hayes campaigned on government reform while running another bloody shirt campaign against his Democrat opponent, George Pendleton. As George McClellan's running mate in 1864, Pendleton proved the perfect foil as he reminded voters of Democrat defeatism. After an easy reelection, Hayes struggled to wean the state from the patronage system and pushed for an elected judiciary. He also extended voting rights while expanding state services that included building an asylum and an orphanage.[30]

Hayes's second term ended in 1871, and he was boosted by some liberal Republicans as a challenger to Republican Senator John Sherman in 1872. However, Hayes refused to join in a state Republican civil war, instead accepting nomination to Congress. His loss in 1872 seemed to end his career, but in 1875 Republicans nominated him for governor, hoping Hayes could help Republicans regain momentum after the disastrous elections of 1873–1874. Hayes won a difficult campaign, and Republicans hoped his victory was a harbinger for success in 1876.[31]

REPUBLICAN CONVENTION

With a front-runner in Blaine, the three challengers had to hope he stumbled in order to overtake him. Blaine's first setback occurred in the rules committee as it approved the unit rule, preventing Blaine from peeling off delegate votes from New York and Pennsylvania. Instead, the state delegations remained under the control of Blaine's enemies, Roscoe Conkling and Don Cameron. Blaine won a victory as the party platform endorsed civil service reform and a protective tariff. Blaine won another victory when Republicans endorsed ratification of the Blaine Amendment and reiterated support for the separation of church and state.[32]

The convention's second day was consumed by nominating speeches with Blaine, Bristow, Morton, Conkling, and Hayes nominated by their handpicked speakers. Blaine's speaker, the famed atheist Robert Ingersoll, offered a compelling and emotional speech. According to Ingersoll Blaine was the "grandest combination of heart, conscience and brain beneath the flag." Ingersoll unrolled the bloody shirt noting, "he preserved in Congress what our soldiers won on the field." Ingersoll then gave Blaine the name that would follow him through his career. "Like a plumed knight James S. Blaine marched down the halls of the American Congress and threw his shining lance full and fair against the brazen foreheads of the defamers of his country." Ingersoll's all-out offensive against the Democrats appealed to the Republican base with the delegates on the verge of nominating Blaine; however, darkness intervened; the hall was not lit, and the convention adjourned.[33]

As the delegates returned to their hotels, Conkling and Cameron went to work to defeat Blaine. To keep Pennsylvania delegates in line, Cameron offered former governor John Hartranft as a favorite son and placeholder to prevent his delegates from breaking for Blaine. Conkling promoted his own candidacy in New York, maintaining a tight hold on the largest delegation at the convention. With the dawn of the next day, the plan of Cameron and Conkling promised to deadlock the convention.[34]

The convention's first ballot showed Blaine with 285 delegates—93 short of the majority of 378. Morton was in second place with 124 votes though much of his support was focused in Indiana and the rotten boroughs of the south. Blaine led through five more ballots, whereas Morton sank to 85. Both New York and Pennsylvania remained outside the fight, preferring Conkling and Hartranft respectively. By the sixth ballot, Blaine had risen to 308 votes, Morton's delegates from Arkansas and Florida switching to him.[35]

As Blaine seemed destined to go over the top on the next ballot, one opponent broke ranks. Don Cameron of Pennsylvania offered Blaine all of the state delegates in return for a cabinet seat in a Blaine administration. Blaine's campaign manager, Eugene Hale, rejected the offer, possibly believing he did not need the votes and did not want to make promises to Cameron.[36] However, the rejection convinced Cameron that Blaine would oppose him in Pennsylvania, and he went in search of another candidate. Blaine's enemies eventually agreed on an alternative, Rutherford Hayes, who was swept into third place with 113 votes. His sudden popularity was driven by a switch of Michigan delegates, the last time that state would do anything for an Ohioan named Hayes.[37]

By the seventh ballot, Bristow's manager, John Marshall Harlan, switched the Kentucky delegates to Hayes, ending Bristow's campaign. An appreciative Hayes would appoint Harlan to the Supreme Court in 1877. As Hayes's delegate count mounted, Blaine's opponents latched onto the Ohioan's candidacy, less out of respect for Hayes than antipathy toward Blaine. The final push coming as the Pennsylvania delegation went for Hayes, and Conkling released the New York delegation, giving Hayes the nomination even as Blaine reached his zenith with 351 votes—27 short of victory.[38]

For the first time since 1852 a political party had nominated a dark horse. Hayes was unprepared for a national campaign, his close elections in Ohio being neither a sign of widespread popularity nor public adulation. Suddenly, the congressman and former governor was the leader of the country's dominant party in a difficult election cycle, following an unpopular incumbent during a time of deep economic depression.

Not all Republicans were pleased with Hayes's nomination as reformers split on his candidacy. Schurz backed Hayes, while Henry Adams rejected Hayes's promises on civil service reform and joined the Tilden campaign. His move to the Democrat party was a far cry from Adam's plan to create a movement filled with "men of intelligence, breeding and ability."[39]

As the Republican candidate, Hayes had to deal with the Camerons and Conklings in the party who opposed civil service reform as patronage oiled the workings of their political machines. While Hayes was closer to the reformers, the Grant wing of the party controlled the organization, reflected in their choice for party chairman and Hayes's campaign manager, Interior Secretary Zachariah Chandler. A three-term Michigan senator, Chandler represented the worst of the patronage system. Having been denied reelection by a combination of liberal Republicans and Democrats, he held men like Schurz in low regard, believing them politically naïve for wanting to eliminate patronage.[40]

After his defeat, Chandler was appointed interior secretary and during the campaign drew two salaries: one as interior secretary and another as leader of the Republican campaign. The choice of Chandler cast doubt on Hayes's reform promises—the secretary described as "one of the most disreputable, coarse and unscrupulous politicians in the Republican Party" and representing "the base and corrupt elements in our politics."[41] However, Chandler proved an effective party chair, raising money in hard times and dragging Hayes to victory under conditions where few expected the Republican to win.

Chandler rescued Hayes from some of his worst reform impulses. As the depression progressed, political donations dipped precipitously. Democrats relied on Tilden's personal fortune to fund their campaign, but Hayes enjoyed no such advantage. Chandler struggled as state parties offered less money than in 1872. Massachusetts Republicans offered only a third of the total from the previous election while Chandler dipped into national funds and provided $5,000 to struggling Ohio Republicans. Without state donations, Chandler returned to the practice of federal employees "voluntarily" contributing to the Republican campaign, a kickback to the party for providing secure government jobs. Schurz and other reformers denounced the practice, but Hayes exercised little control over the chairman.[42]

With his campaign team established, Hayes introduced himself to the American voter using an acceptance letter spread across the country's leading Republican newspapers. In his letter Hayes endorsed the Blaine amendment, approved civil service reforms, and promised the establishment of a professional bureaucracy while offering compromise to the south. Hayes signaled that if elected he would allow "responsible" southerners to take control of their state governments, ending federal occupation.[43] Hayes also distanced his campaign from Grantism and the Belknap scandal unfolding in the Senate.

Hayes's rejection of the spoils system did not prevent Grant from using the executive branch to enforce party loyalty. Grant fired Bristow along with the Postmaster General Marshall Jewell who refused to appoint Republican postmasters in Indiana to shore up Republican support. The new postmaster general, James Tyner, proved more flexible to Grant's wishes and tried to turn the state toward Hayes. The department was cleansed of reform Republicans including the commissioner of internal revenue—a powerful position of collecting taxes and hiring thousands of employees—a district attorney in Indiana, the treasury solicitor, the federal treasurer, and several auditors, the newly opened positions filled by Grant supporters.[44]

THE CAMPAIGN

The Democrat campaign began with the publication of Tilden's acceptance letter on August 4. Hayes had eased Tilden's task by foreswearing Grant's Reconstruction policy, allowing Democrats to ignore the issue. Tilden instead focused on the depression, blaming high taxes and excessive spending, much of which was used to pay off war debt, for the economic problems. He offered soothing words on the southern issue, promising to protect all citizens' rights, a wink at southern voters intended not to scare away northern voters. Tilden also condemned the Specie Act, warning that Republicans were unprepared to change the currency system though he refused to call for repeal.[45] On one issue Tilden and Hayes agreed, both men promising to serve a single term.

As Congress marched into the fall, the two parties jockeyed for advantage, using their majorities to pass legislation in their chambers and force the opposition to take embarrassing votes. Blaine pushed his amendment through the Democrat House, a difficult process, though Democrats were able to remove the clause granting Congress authority to enforce a strict separation of church and state. The Republican Senate then considered a different amendment which failed.[46]

House Democrats repealed the Specie Act, appealing to farmers and swing state voters in Indiana and the Midwest who supported retaining greenbacks. The Republican Senate did not even consider the repeal, but the House action made the Specie Act an issue.[47] The positions staked out by each party in Congress melded with negative attacks that were part of every campaign.

Mudslinging commenced almost from the moment Tilden and Hayes were nominated. With the candidates agreeing on the end of reconstruction, the currency question, corruption, and a civil service system, partisans lacked wedge issues to attract voters. Hayes was accused of being a Know-Nothing with a hatred of Germans. Democrats obtained a letter from Hayes to the American Alliance, an anti-immigrant group that endorsed him. Democrats seized upon the connection and hammered home Hayes's ties to nativist groups to German voters. Republicans weakly responded that the letter was one of many hundreds sent to those who endorsed him. The *Nation* greeted the explanation with disbelief as Hayes defended himself by trumpeting Carl Schurz's endorsement as spokesman for German Americans.[48]

Republicans returned with the bloody shirt though with less success. In Bangor, Maine Robert Ingersoll argued the choice was clear with Republicans "hopeful in defeat, confident in disaster, merciful in victory," while Democrats and southerners were "friends and allies of persons who regarded yellow fever and smallpox as weapons of civilized warfare." Republicans raised the old issue of compensation for Confederate soldiers, a charge made against every Democrat though such a bill would never survive Congress. Tilden deflected these charges, his Wall Street pedigree making him the opposite of a southern redneck Confederate sympathizer.[49]

Another line of attack was Tilden's signature on a law allowing Catholic nuns to teach in public schools. The bill generated controversy and another Tilden signature, this time on the law's repeal. Republicans leaped on the opportunity, saying Tilden's signature on the first bill was a sign he favored parochial over public schools and opposed the Blaine amendment.[50]

Republicans lashed out at Tilden's Wall Street connections, tying him to Jay Gould, the controversial financier partly blamed for the

1873 crash. Much like Robert Vesco of the 1970s and Enron of the early 21st century, Gould was a symbol of an out-of-control, insider system. Republicans reminded voters that Tilden and Gould were being sued over failed railroad bonds while Tilden was using his personal wealth to fund the Democrat campaign.[51]

In a speech at Xenia (Ohio) James Blaine raised the specter of Tilden as a tax cheat. Displaying a piece of paper he declared, "I hold in my hand a semi official letter from an officer in the Treasury Department." The gist of the letter, according to Blaine, was Tilden owed over $200,000 in federal taxes. After making the allegations, Blaine denied he was attacking Tilden's honesty then declared, "I have, of course, no personal knowledge of the subject but I make this statement on the best authority in the United States." It was a typical ploy as it placed the onus of proof on Tilden while protecting Blaine from charges of deception if the allegations proved false.[52]

Republican attacks on Tilden turned personal as Zachariah Chandler declared Tilden a "hermaphrodite because he was a bachelor."[53] The New York governor had been a "legal spider" who represented "cunning and heartlessness." Ingersoll echoed Chandler in noting Tilden never married, offering the explanation "the Democratic (sic) Party has satisfied the longings of his heart" and then made a sly attack in suggesting Tilden "courted men because women couldn't vote."[54]

The viciousness of the campaign was limited only by its spread through the country. A lack of campaign funds prevents wide dissemination as Republicans' "voluntary donations" from government workers and Tilden's personal fortune proved insufficient for a full-fledged campaign on the lines of 1872. Democrats enjoyed one advantage in the financial portion of the campaign because the party focused on the northern tier of states, the "redeemed" southern states solidly Democrat. Republicans divided their resources between swing states including Indiana and Ohio while also forced to finance campaigns in southern states controlled by Republican governors.

REDEEMING THE SOUTH

Grant had swept the southern states in 1868 and 1872, Republican governments working hard to ensure the freedman vote while suppressing the Democrat vote. The depression weakened public interest in civil rights, and dwindling northern support led to the "redeeming" of reconstructed states to southern Democrat governments. By 1876, only three of the original 11 Confederate states—Florida, Louisiana, and South Carolina—remained under Republican control. The obsessive quest to redeem those states among Democrat officials overrode any interest in electing Tilden.

For southern Democrats black voters were the sole impediment to political power, and they utilized all means at their disposal to eliminate the black vote. With Republicans controlling each state's election machinery, Democrats used a combination of harassment, intimidation, and murder to suppress the black vote. Rifle clubs such as the South Carolina red shirts—a takeoff of the bloody shirt waved by Republicans—roamed the states' backcountries, threatening blacks and Republicans with death or worse if they voted.[55] On June 8 in Hamburg, South Carolina, groups of armed white Confederates attacked black militia, killing five after they had surrendered. In support of the brutality, the Charleston *Journal of Commerce* declared the freedman would not "be treated as prisoners of honorable warfare, according to the laws of nations."[56] The massacre signaled to blacks and Republicans that Democrats would stop at nothing to "redeem" South Carolina.

The massacre became Republican campaign fodder after Ulysses Grant sent troops to protect black voters and bolster Governor Chamberlain. However, South Carolina was not the only state where Democrats' violence suppressed the black vote. Massacres and black voter intimidation in Louisiana made a free and fair election impossible. The 1873 Grant Parish Massacre saw some 200 freedmen murdered as part of a campaign against black voters. Suppression of the black vote was matched by Democrat efforts to pack ballot boxes with Tilden votes.[57]

Southern Democrats were emboldened by Hayes's refusal to make Reconstruction an issue. Convinced by his advisors, including Carl Schurz, that civil service reform was the decisive issue of the election, Hayes left it to surrogates to wave the bloody shirt. This single-minded focus on a procedural issue of government rather than substantive change also suppressed the vote of discouraged Republicans throughout the country.

EARLY VOTING

Among the states conducting early voting in 1876 were bellwether states in the northeast and swing states in the Midwest—all critical to the Tilden and Hayes campaigns. Two early states, Maine and Vermont, recorded Republican victories as the party exceeded its vote total of the year 1875. The newest state of the union, Colorado, also went Republican confirming the party's rush to approve statehood. In the swing state of Indiana, the Republican candidate for governor was defeated, but the party gained four congressional seats.[58] The mixed results were a worrisome sign for Republicans who needed Indiana to elect Hayes.

A more critical state for Republicans was Ohio. Hayes and the Republicans knew that not since 1844 had a candidate lost his home state and won the presidency. Ohio buoyed Republican spirits when they won the governorship and picked up five House seats, a clean sweep of contested seats.[59]

With Midwest results mixed, attention turned to New York. The largest state in the union boasted 36 electoral votes and was considered a swing state until the Democrats nominated Tilden. Turnout and split-ticket voting were key factors in the state: the Tammany organization in New York City was key to turning out voters and ensuring they voted a straight Democrat ticket. The top of the state ticket, governor, was a key slot as many New Yorkers were more concerned with statewide rather than national politics. Not unexpectedly, Democrats were divided on their gubernatorial selection. A compromise candidate, former governor and 1869 presidential candidate, Horatio Seymour, refused the nomination. Finally, Democrats chose the most obscure candidate, the state comptroller, a sign they believed Tammany and the Tilden candidacy would tilt the election in their favor. Republicans nominated a former governor Edwin Morgan but even with a well-known candidate, the party was doomed in the state.[60]

Unlike most presidential elections, the 1876 contest had most of its action and controversy after voting ended. With the depression and disgust with Washington corruption in the north and a desire to redeem Reconstruction states in the south invigorating voters, over 80 percent of registered voters went to the polls. In the west the Specie Act and its possible repeal drove western voters while the Republican bloody shirt campaign and fear of a Democrat takeover of the national government bolstered weak Republican enthusiasm.

VICTORY?

November 7 offered the best hope in 20 years to Democrats that they would elect a president. However, instead of victory, the campaign was the longest presidential election in history, extending another four months beyond the voting and not concluding until hours before inauguration day, March 4. The initial returns showed Democrats sweeping the south after 16 years and taking critical states such as New York and Indiana. Tilden went to bed election night certain he was president-elect.

Republicans were able to keep major states of Illinois, Pennsylvania, Massachusetts, and Ohio in their column, but on election night Zachariah Chandler returned to his room and reportedly drank away his worries. However, not all were convinced of the Democrat victory. The pro-Hayes *New York Times* began investigating the election returns, focusing on three southern states, South Carolina, Florida, and Louisiana, and the far west Oregon. The closeness of the election in each offered Hayes hope for if he won the electoral votes from all four states, Tilden would be stuck at 184 votes, one short of victory.

It was on the morning after the election that history becomes hazy with two different versions of who convinced Chandler to fight for the three southern states. One version had the New York Times sending out the call to southern Republican to hold their states. Another version has two visitors to the Republican national headquarters spurring Chandler. Chester Arthur, master spoilsman who ran the New York Customs House that oversaw the collection of tariffs, and Daniel Sickles, former congressman, Civil War general, and also a criminal defendant, were convinced Hayes had won. Arthur, a close ally of Roscoe Conkling, feared for his job, knowing that if Tilden was elected, he would be replaced by a Democrat. Even with the animosity between the Conkling machine and Hayes, Arthur was more concerned with his own authority than settling a score with Hayes.

Sickles had earned the reputation as a loose cannon. Prior to the Civil War he had been charged with the murder of Philip Barton Key II, the son of Francis Scott Key. Sickles had shot Key after the discovery that he was having an affair with Sickles's wife. A jury acquitted him, and Sickles continued his political career that became a military career as a general in the Army of the Potomac. During the battle of Gettysburg, Sickles ignored orders from General Meade and moved his troops into a salient, exposing them to attack from three sides by the Confederates. The resulting battle saw Sickles's forces nearly destroyed while retreating under fire with heavy losses. Sickles was among them, his leg shot off during the retreat, thus ending his military career.[61] Hobbling around Washington on the morning of November 7, he decided to make another thrust against orders, this time trying to convince the

Hayes campaign to declare victory and fight for the presidency in various state boards and courts. The biographies of both Sickles and Arthur do not note their involvement—either an extraordinary oversight or confirmation they were not involved.[62]

Arthur and Sickles roused Chandler, convincing him the election was not over, and Tilden was yet to be assured victory. Chandler sent off the famous order to state Republican parties "Hold your states," the first shot in Sickles's foray into presidential politics, which would prove more successful than his military plans. On November 8, Chandler declared Hayes the winner even with preliminary vote totals in Florida and Louisiana showing Tilden had won. Republicans and Democrats dispatched a phalanx of lawyers to the south, hoping to influence the canvassing and county boards to rule for their candidate. Ulysses Grant got into the act, dispatching additional troops into the three southern states to ensure a fair counting of the votes. Each of the three Republican states had their story of Reconstruction and their contribution to the Hayes–Tilden battle.[63]

THREE STATES

The internal politics of Florida, Louisiana, and South Carolina had the Democrats and Republicans placing local concerns over the national party. Southern Republicans recognized they were losing their strongest advocate as Ulysses Grant's presidency wound down. They faced a difficult choice as they could fight for their state office and Hayes, uncertain whether they could depend upon continued federal support, or they could compromise with Democrats, elect Tilden, lose federal support, but build a coalition with conservative Democrats and former Whigs. Hayes and reform-oriented Republicans saw the southern governments as an unwelcome extension of the corrupt northern patronage system. To keep their promises on government reform, Republicans would have to abandon their southern brethren and allow Reconstruction governments to fall to Democrats.

In South Carolina, much of the state's electorate and political class were focused on the governorship rather than the presidency, many southern Democrats having given up on Tilden and northern Democrats to help them. South Carolinians were new to the electoral process, the first gubernatorial election occurring in 1868 as the state legislature had chosen the governor prior to then.

The governor's race between Republican Daniel Chamberlain and Wade Hampton III, Democrat and famed Confederate cavalry general, became an obsession with South Carolinians, to the detriment and eventual defeat of the Tilden campaign. Republicans coalesced around Chamberlain who was seeking a second term based on his own reform platform after cleaning up the corruption of former governor Frank Moses.

Democrats were split between moderates or fusionists and hard-core elements or Straight-Outers. Moderate Democrats sought coalition with Republicans, offering to work with Reconstruction in return for greater influence in government. The Straight-Outers wanted Republicans and carpetbaggers ejected from South Carolina's government, by force if necessary. The Tilden campaign feared the Straight-Outers and their leader Hampton, whom Tilden blamed for the Democrats poor showing in the 1868 election. The national Democrat party sent a representative, John Coyle, to speak against Hampton at the state convention. Despite that opposition from the Democrat establishment or because of it, Hampton breezed to the nomination, Tilden's opposition never to be forgotten.[64]

With their candidate in place, South Carolina's Democrats focused on the black vote, which was crucial to any Chamberlain victory. Democrat's initiated the "preference plan" applying economic pressure to black voters. Those who favored Chamberlain saw their jobs and credits disappear, but those voters favoring Hampton were unaffected. The plan weakened Chamberlain's support but proved unsatisfactory to Democrats who resorted to violence to suppress the black vote. Future senator Martin Gary and his red shirts murdered some two dozen black men during a three-week period in late September and early October. The Democrat vigilantes terrorized local law enforcement and made them "as powerless as the wind to prevent these atrocities."[65]

On Election Day, Gary led the effort in Edgefield and Lauren counties to stuff ballot boxes with Hampton votes, his efficiency leading to vote totals exceeding the number of registered voters. Phony ballots were printed with Hayes's picture beside Hampton's name, a tool to trick illiterate black voters dependent on the visual rather than printed word. Swarms of Georgians and North Carolinians crossed the border to vote for Hampton while red shirts surrounded black polling places, eyeing the black voters who dared cross their lines.[66]

In Edgefield County a standoff between red shirts at a white polling place and black voters backed by federal troops saw the outnumbered and outgunned federal troops retreat. With black turnout diminished and Hampton's vote totals inflated by fraud, Democrats seemed destined for victory. The day after the election, Republican and Democrat newspapers in the state claimed victory for their candidate, much as national papers had claimed victory for Hayes or Tilden.[67]

When the national battle was joined, the state's inherent parochialism took center stage as the battle over the state house overshadowed the Hayes–Tilden dispute. The South Carolina canvassing board was responsible for announcing the winners of all state contests. Composed of the state treasurer, comptroller, secretary of state, and attorney general, the board had four Republicans certain to favor Chamberlain and the Republican state legislature.[68]

Democrats began to fear their campaign of intimidation and murder of black voters was for naught and sought remedy before the state Supreme Court overruled the canvassing board's decision. Chief Justice Franklin Moses Sr., father of former governor Moses, was a doddering and ill man who would die less than six months later. He summoned a last burst of strength to convince two Republican justices to join the single Democrat on the Court to order the canvassing board to turn over all voting records to the Court.[69]

The injunction was too late, though, with the canvassing board certifying a victory by Hayes and Chamberlain and certifying a Republican majority in the legislature. Reaching these results required some sleight of hand with the board throwing out the results from Edgefield and Laurens counties: the overwhelming Democrat victories in those states were seen as the result of fraud. The board members then dispersed to avoid the injunction.[70]

Foiled in their attempt to manipulate election results, the Court jailed each board member on contempt charges. A federal judge released them and by the end of November South Carolina appeared headed for civil war. Governor Chamberlain received federal troops from the Grant administration, but lacked broad public support. At that point events turned dangerous as the Republican legislature opened on November 28 with Democrat legislators barred from entry. Two days later the Democrats charged the state house and forced their way into the chamber.[71]

For a 24-hour period South Carolinians were treated to the sight of two legislatures operating simultaneously in the same chamber house. Legislators recognized different House speakers, made simultaneous speeches, and occasionally engaged in fistfights. Outside the state house, armed red shirts gathered, guns ready in a scene reminiscent of the Sans Culottes of the French Revolution. Facing the red shirts was a smaller number of black rifle groups, the Hunkidories, a single mistake threatening to trigger a bloodbath. Cooler heads prevailed, and the Democrat legislators left under the prodding of Hampton.[72]

For the next four months, South Carolina had two state governments. Governor Chamberlain, protected by the guns of the Union army, passed a bill banning the creation of an opposition government. The law provided for a $100,000 fine and prison sentences ranging from 10 to 40 years. The target of the law was Hampton though his arrest and imprisonment was beyond Chamberlain's means. Another law criminalized serving in the opposition government and sported a $3,000 fine along with a prison sentence of one to 10 years.[73]

While Chamberlain was trying to hold onto power in Columbia, Hampton was seeking a compromise to seat him as governor and Hayes as president. Hampton had returned from the war to find his mansion burned to the ground, convincing him that compromise was better than conflict. One compromise leader, Mississippi Congressman Lucius Q. C. Lamar, told reporters that southern Democrats would support any candidate who allowed "honest" men to run the state government.[74] Hampton rejected calls for punishing black Republicans and promised to end the white boycott of blacks. He further promised enforcement of equal protection for blacks in education and voting. Hampton even enforced Presidents Grant's ban on rifle clubs marching in Washington Birthday parades.[75]

The new "moderate" Hampton was at odds with the reality of the red shirts and voter intimidation, but as the crisis in Washington lengthened into February and threatened Hayes's inauguration, Republicans realized that losing the south and gaining the White House was a reasonable compromise when considering the alternative of losing both. Hampton expressed little concern for Tilden's claim to South Carolina's votes, never forgetting how the Democrat establishment opposed his nomination.[76] As South Carolina simmered, the vote count in Florida threatened to break into violence.

FLORIDA

Memories of the disputed presidential election of 2000 in Florida make modern readers flinch at the seemingly endless legal and political disputes 125 years after the first disputed election in the state. In 1876 Florida was a shadow of its future: much of the population was located in Jacksonville and Tallahassee, with a smaller rural population fueling the controversy over Florida's electoral votes. Throughout 1876, white Democrats conducted an intimidation campaign against black Republicans. Klansman seized black voters and placed nooses around their necks to demonstrate the consequences of voting Republican. The Republican governor was threatened with assassination if the state enforced election laws. Sharecroppers were threatened with loss of credit by stores and loss of land by landlords. Stores threatened to raise prices for anyone found to vote Republican while railroads provided numbered ballots to their employees to keep track of who voted Republicans. Black railroad workers were sent into Alabama and kept there until after Election Day to suppress the Republican vote. The result was a 93-vote victory for Tilden in Florida.[77]

Florida Democrats showed little concern with legalities in their question to redeem the state. Two Republican poll watchers in Polk County were greeted at the border by armed Democrats who offered to accompany them, ostensibly to prevent Republican theft of votes. The Democrats made clear a refusal of the escort would result in a gunshot blast to the back. General Lew Wallace was forced to use troops to get black voters to sign affidavits of their vote for Hayes because intimidation and violence suppressed the Republican vote.

When the votes were tallied in each county, the state's canvassing board had the task of counting and recording the votes. The board was composed of Secretary of State Samuel McLin, State Attorney General William Cocke, and the State Comptroller Clayton Cowgill. McLin and Cowgill were Republicans, whereas Cocke was the sole Democrat.[78] The board members immediately noted the dramatic decline in the Republican vote as Democrats swept counties by margins of four or eight to one. In Jackson County, the Democrats enjoyed a 436–111 majority while Monroe County / Key West Republicans managed only 59 votes to 401 Democrat tallies. Jasper County offered a closer division with Democrats leading 323–185. All three counties had fielded a Republican majority in 1872. In response to affidavits alleging both fraud and violence against black voters, the canvassing board tossed out the offending precincts and eliminated Tilden's majority.[79]

Democrat totals were not the only ones challenged. The board considered Alachia County where Republicans enjoyed a 399–136 majority. Poll watchers tallied the Republican vote at 180, but the party offered affidavits of 300 voters who had cast votes for Hayes. Baker County offered its own challenges as the canvassing board considered three sets of returns. McLin supported the highest Republican vote total and convinced Cowgill to throw out a 238–143 Democrat majority and approve a 130–90 Republican majority—further reducing Tilden's total.[80]

The board's two Republicans were divided on how far they would change the county results. The weakest of the group, Clayton Cowgill, was a Delaware surgeon who moved to Florida to reform its government. Easily influenced, Cowgill enjoyed a working relationship with a Republican operative, Francis Barlow, who tilted him toward the Democrat side. The New York Attorney General Barlow came to Florida determined to elect Hayes but after spending time in the state became convinced that Tilden had won the state. His doubts saw him exiled from the Republican camp, but he attempted to convince Cowgill to uphold the Tilden vote.[81]

The Republican-dominated board heard claims of intimidation and fraud from rural counties and then began tossing out entire precincts with suspiciously large Tilden majorities, turning his narrow victory into a 45-vote Hayes victory. The board then declared the Republican Marcellus Stearns as governor and assigned Florida's four electoral votes to Hayes.[82]

The canvassing board's decision did not last long. The state Supreme Court ruled against the board's decision, and the new Democrat governor appointed three Tilden electors, whose votes were sent to Washington to be counted. The controversy would be the first to be considered by the Electoral Commission and set the tone for the Hayes–Tilden controversy

LOUISIANA

Louisiana election officials struggled with local Democrat corruption, massacres of black voters, and a political system that accepted vote fraud as a commonplace event. The first of the Confederate states to be reorganized, Louisiana served as an experiment in nation building with carpetbagging northern politicians such as Benjamin Butler and Nathaniel Banks flocking to New Orleans for ideological as well as economic reasons.

Working with the northerners were the southern "scalawags," the most prominent being former Whig and plantation owner J. Madison Wells.

Described by General Phil Sheridan as sallow-faced and a snake, Wells first joined the Lincoln Reconstruction efforts and was elected lieutenant governor. However, as Reconstruction policy in Washington changed, so did Wells. During Andrew Johnson's failed presidential Reconstruction, he sought an alliance with Johnson to build a new southern Whig party. Wells's offer was rejected, and he was defeated for reelection. The Grant administration rewarded Wells with a post in the New Orleans customs bureau, a lucrative position that gave him influence as he dispensed patronage to Louisiana Republicans.[83]

After the Republicans passed Reconstruction acts and seized control of southern policy, chaos reigned as the state stumbled through three governors in five years including the luxuriously named Henry Clay Warmoth. The 26-year-old Warmoth proved a disaster as governor. Widespread corruption in his administration precluded a second term, but Warmoth's manipulation of the election process led to his impeachment to curb his powers.[84]

By 1872 Louisiana was in a state of political chaos and gridlock. The state recording board announced William Pitt Kellogg as the winner of the governor's race though only the presence of federal troops allowed him to rule. The board also reported the state for Grant though Congress rejected Louisiana's electoral votes after claims that the board miscounted ballots. The political chaos translated into a breakdown of law and order in the up country.

By 1876 Louisiana Democrats had perfected their suppression efforts, focusing on registration and the voting process. Many parishes enforced a rule that required one white voter to register followed by one black voter until all of the white voters had registered. Registration would occur at odd or unannounced times, and when black voters appeared, registration would cease. One parish placed the poll place on an island reachable only by boat with the effect of eliminating most voting. There was even a fusion between Democrats and a Republican faction loyal to former Governor Warmoth. When these efforts did not succeed, Louisiana Democrats resorted to violence to end all black voting.[85]

On April 13, 1873 the Grant Parish Massacre marked the comeback of Louisiana Democrats as dozens of black men were trapped in the parish courthouse, which was set on fire, the parish sheriff and his posse gunning down any who tried to escape. The murders produced a Supreme Court case, *United States v. Cruikshank*, which weakened civil rights laws and protections for the freedmen. In Red River Parish, the northern-born sheriff was shot and had both arms amputated while his family was gunned down by members of the White League, a virulently racist militia bent on restoring Democrat rule over the state.[86]

With federal judicial and executive protection denied them, Louisiana Republicans were left to fend for their own survival. Their tactics, sometimes illegal and always skirting ethical standards, were mostly ineffective in the face of Democrats' campaign of threats and murder. As the Republican vote plummeted, Tilden appeared headed for a state and national victory, but once against their plans would be stymied by the state returning board.

Unlike the Florida and South Carolina canvassing boards whose members were elected state officials, the Louisiana board was composed of political appointees. Fresh from his job at the New Orleans port authority, J. Madison Wells served as chair of the board and influenced the other three members. Among these was Louis Kennar, a freedman who operated a saloon that may have doubled as a brothel, Gedana Cassonave, a free black, and T. C. Anderson.[87]

Once the Louisiana results rolled in and the final tabulation showed a sizable Tilden victory, Republican observers rolled into New Orleans. Among them was John Sherman, James Garfield, Edward Evarts, two state bosses—John Logan of Illinois and Matt Quay of Pennsylvania—and General Lew Wallace. Democrats managed a less distinguished field—only two recognizable names, Lyman Trumbull and William Graham Sumner, challenging Republicans. Democrats were just as active, none more so than Tilden's nephew. William Pelton discussed terms with Wells while the head of the canvassing board travelled to Washington and offered his vote to the Tilden campaign for a million dollars. When Tilden's manager rejected the offer, Wells dropped his price to $200,000 and then returned to Louisiana empty-handed.[88]

As the returning board considered parish vote totals, Tilden enjoyed a 6,000-vote win, considerably larger than the plurality overturned in Florida. However, like in that state, stories of intimidation and ballot box stuffing offered Republicans an opening. Sherman and Republicans collected over 300 witnesses to tell personal stories of harassment and intimidation of black voters.[89] The board focused on bulldozed parishes that saw dramatic declines in the black vote. Among these was East Feliciana Parish which recorded 1,700 Republican votes in 1872 but not a single Republican ballot in 1876. Grant Parish showed a similar decline, the 1873 massacre having scared most black voters out of the parish or away from the voting booth. As Wells and the board heard witnesses and read affidavits, they threw out the results in Grant and East Feliciana parishes along with others for a total of 15,000 votes. Tilden suffered the most, losing over 13,000 while Hayes lost 2,500. The final result was a Hayes victory and Republican electors chosen to vote in December.[90]

The process in all three states enraged congressional Democrats who were forced to witness Republican state officials discount Democrat votes and erase Tilden's presidential victory. Republicans countered that a truly free and fair election would have produced a Hayes victory, and only Democrat violence against black voters turned the states toward Tilden. The fraud and intimidation had forced canvassing boards to reject returns from the rotten precincts. As the election controversy moved to Washington, a constitutional crisis nearly consumed the government as Congress lacked the proper system for counting disputed electoral votes.

Scholars and experts on the election point to a decision by the Republican Senate as the precipitating factor in the crisis. In 1865 the Republican Congress passed the 22nd joint rule that allowed a majority of either house of Congress to reject the electoral votes of any state. The rule may have been in response to Reconstruction plans and concerns about Democrats seizing powers in southern states and manipulating presidential elections. The rule granted the Republican Congress plenary power in denying Democrats the opportunity to elect a president based on illegal southern presidential votes.

The rule was first implemented in 1872 against Grant electors from Louisiana. Grant's overwhelming victory prevented the decision from changing the electoral outcome, but the congressional rejection of the electoral votes raised concerns about the viability of southern Reconstruction governments to run a proper federal election. With the election of a Democrat House in 1874, Senate Republicans repealed its part of the joint rule, leaving Congress without a system in place for accepting disputed electoral votes. Lacking a coherent set of rules, Congress was forced in 1876 to create an ad hoc compromise for settling the Hayes–Tilden dispute.[91]

That compromise would be created in Congress with little input by the presidential candidates. Tilden's passivity during the December congressional session was in stark contrast to his nephew's efforts. According to the uncovered cipher telegrams, Pelton had offered thousands to Republican members of the returning boards only to see Hayes win the electoral votes. In Oregon, Pelton sent $8,000 to swing a disputed electoral into his uncle's column. Money exchanged hands, but Hayes swept all three electoral votes.[92]

Pelton's bare-knuckled strategy clashed with Tilden's more passive approach to the dispute as he remained out of the public eye during the debate in the states and the electoral commission and ceded control of the campaign to his nephew and other Democrats. Having defeated Tammany Hall with power politics, Tilden appeared to lose his nerve, ignoring that the debate over electoral votes would be won at the state rather than federal level. Tilden offered a legal argument that the Florida Democrat electors should be accepted by Congress even though they were chosen a day after the date required under federal law. It was the proverbial bringing a knife to a gunfight.[93]

While Republicans and Democrats battled in statehouses and the capitol, Tilden obsessed over constitutional and electoral tradition, trying to draw comparisons between the 1876 election and past disputed elections. His strategy of watchful waiting as the state canvassing boards assigned electoral votes to Hayes placed Democrats at a severe disadvantage when the debate moved to Washington. Republicans reached the capital with electoral votes in hand, needing them only to be officially counted. To win, Tilden would have to stop the electoral count, convince the commission to overturn at least one Hayes vote in a state, and replace it with a Tilden vote.[94]

CONGRESS AND THE ELECTORAL COMMISSION

With a crisis on the horizon, members of Congress scrambled to work out a compromise. With the 1865 joint resolution no longer accepted by the Senate, there were no rules for challenging a state's electoral votes. When the electoral votes reached Congress, Republicans interpreted the 12th Amendment as allowing the Senate president pro tempore to count the ballots and choose which electoral votes to accept. The death of Vice President Henry Wilson thrust the duty of counting electoral votes onto Republican Senator Thomas Ferry of Michigan, the senator who became president pro tempore.[95]

Democrats rejected the Republican's interpretation, preferring to limit Ferry's role to that of a clerk, opening and announcing the votes. According to Democrats, disputed votes would not be counted and no winner declared as Tilden would fall short of the necessary 185 electoral votes. The Democrat-dominated House of Representatives, according to the 12th Amendment, would then choose the president. Not unexpectedly Republicans rejected this outcome, and with neither chamber budging from their position a deadlock ensued that could not be broken until Congress settled the election.[96]

On December 7, 1876, Iowa Congressman George McReary offered a bill creating Washington's favorite solution to a crisis—the bipartisan commission. The House and the Senate established separate committees to work out the details with Republicans controlling the Senate side and Democrats controlling the House. For two months the commission proposals were debated and amended, Congress setting the rules for choosing the president with little input from the men at the center of the dispute. Before the commission was approved, Tilden held a meeting in the mansion of Democrat financier, August Belmont; Tilden spoke vaguely of arbitration to settle the dispute, but did not openly oppose its formation. Uncertain of the candidate's views on the compromise, his lieutenants allowed it to pass Congress, setting the stage for Hayes's victory.

Congress created a 15-member commission composed of members from both chambers and five Supreme Court justices. Though drawing fire from both sides, the commission seemed the only process for avoiding a full-blown constitutional crisis and potential civil war.[97] The commission act passed Congress with an unusual partisan divide. House Republicans suspected a trap, and less than a third voted for the commission, which was overwhelmingly supported by Democrats. The vote was different in the Senate with Republicans voting three to two for the commission while less than a majority of Senate Democrats voted for the bill.[98]

Under the law the commission was divided evenly between five senators—three Republicans and two Democrats—with five congressmen—three Democrats and two Republicans—creating an even partisan division. This gave the deciding votes to five Supreme Court justices. Unfortunately for Democrats, the Court leaned heavily Republican with only two Democrats—the aging Nathan Clifford and raging Stephen Field—expected to vote for Tilden's electors. Democrats' only hope was to find the most moderate justice—their choice being David Davis, former Lincoln campaign manager and nominal Republican who had declared himself a political independent. Democrats believed Davis was the most likely justice to agree to a reexamination of ballots rejected by the states' canvassing boards.

In his nearly 15 years on the Court, Davis had exhibited a streak of independence. His opinion in *Ex Parte Milligan* overturned Lincoln's policies of military trials for civilians during the war. In 1872, he was a leading candidate for the liberal Republicans challenging Grant. Davis's alienation from the Republican heartened Democrats, but Hayes's criticism of Reconstruction and promise of civil service reform also appealed to Davis. The justice never received an opportunity to vote. The Illinois legislature, under the prodding of William Pelton, Tilden's omnipresent nephew and Democrat financier, Cyrus McCormick, elected Davis to the U.S. Senate, replacing another Lincoln ally, Lyman Trumbull. Democrats may have believed Davis's election would earn Tilden the justice's vote, but Davis responded by resigning from the Court and leaving Democrats scrambling for a replacement.[99]

The attempt at political manipulation doomed Tilden because Grant appointee Joseph Bradley was appointed to the commission. Bradley had been part of the tandem of new justices who overturned the one-year-old Legal Tender cases, upholding the 1863 Legal Tender Act which financed the Civil War. Overturning the one-year-old precedent had put Bradley and Justice Strong in the Democrat crosshairs, and their criticism likely rang in his ears when he sat down in the commission six years later.

Bradley had exhibited openness to southern arguments on reconstruction. Sitting as a circuit judge in the Louisiana district, he had struck down the Louisiana law creating a slaughterhouse monopoly, utilizing the 14th Amendment for the first time, only to be overruled by the Supreme Court. In 1874 he limited the reach of civil rights acts in the Cruikshank case and had this decision upheld by the Court.[100] Bradley was suspicious of the Louisiana Reconstruction government, which could translate into a vote to overturn that state's electoral count. However, Tilden's troubles extended beyond the justices on the commission. Neither Ohio Senator Allen Thurman nor Delaware Senator James Bayard was friendly with Tilden, and neither man was assertive on his behalf. Hayes enjoyed stronger support among the Republican members with future president James Garfield, Senator George Edmunds, and future secretary of state Frederick Frelinghuysen fully engaged in helping elect a Republican president.

With the commission in place Congress began counting electoral votes in February 1877. Under the federal act when a state's electors were challenged, the dispute was placed before the commission, which would determine the electors to be counted. The commission's decisions would stand unless both chambers rejected it. With a Democrat House and Republican Senate unlikely to agree to overturn a commission decision, Congress had granted the 15 men authority to determine the winner while also taking the political heat for that decision.[101]

The electoral count moved alphabetically, placing Florida first among the disputed states. Florida was the state that offered equal arguments as South Carolina's election results favored Hayes, and Louisiana favored Tilden. When Florida's Hayes electors were objected to by Democrats, the Florida canvassing board's decision to announce Hayes as the winner went before the commission.

Both sides employed the best legal talent for their arguments. The Democrats used Jeremiah Black, Buchanan's attorney general and briefly secretary of state who had also been involved in negotiations to end the Civil War. Joining Black was New York attorney, David Dudley Field, the older brother of Justice Stephen Field. His presence raised ethical concern though Justice Field was expected to rule for the Democrats, his brother's presence on behalf of Tilden not changing the outcome. In response, the Republicans offered Stanley Matthews and William Evarts, both at the top of the party's hierarchy, good posts; Matthews would be appointed to the Supreme Court while Evarts would become Hayes's secretary of state.

The Florida argument focused on the process to be followed. Democrats asked the commission to delve into the charges of corruption in Florida and the decision by the canvassing board to throw out Tilden votes. Republicans took a more limited view of the commission's authority. With Hayes declared the victor by the canvassing board, Republicans wanted the commission simply to ratify the board's decision.[102] Matthews and Evarts warned that a drawn-out investigation of voting fraud in Florida could delay the inauguration and provoke a constitutional crisis.[103] The arguments were the flip side of each party's political philosophy on states' rights. Democrats had argued for the sanctity of state governments making decisions while Republicans had used the military to enforce federal control over state governments, weakening their sovereignty.

The commission hearings was dominated by the justices as they enjoyed a home-field advantage—the hearings were conducted in the Court's chambers—and the format resembled the arguments presented by lawyers during the Court's terms. Most aggressive was Justice Stephen Field who tangled with Hayes's counsel, William Evarts.

Field challenged Evarts's argument for deferring to Florida's canvassing board and Governor Stearns who certified Hayes's victory. Field offered a hypothetical case of canvassing board members being taken hostage and forcibly made to sign false documents. Evarts refused to surrender his argument that the canvassing board enjoyed the legal power to declare election winners. Field offered several more hypotheticals, each echoing Democrat charges against the Florida decision including bribed election officials, miscounted ballots, and corrupt canvassing boards. The seasoned advocate Evarts stayed on point, maintaining a staunch states' rights defense for states running elections. The other members of the commission ignored Field's questioning and blatant attempt to maneuver Evarts into making absolutist arguments.[104]

After three days of argument the commission settled in for its members to discuss the competing issues. On February 9, less than a month before the planned inauguration, Justice Field offered the Democrat view for the commission. He argued that the Florida canvassing board could not reject ballots but rather was bound to accept the vote totals given them by each county government. He stood by a Florida Supreme Court ruling that the board had violated state law in tossing Tilden ballots.[105]

Justice Strong offered the Republican view, finding the Florida canvassing board acted properly in allowing Hayes electors to cast their ballots. When the electors had voted, this ended the Florida debate as the commission had no authority to overrule the state canvassing board. Strong noted the Florida Supreme Court decision was moot, having been issued after the electors cast their ballots. In declaring the issue settled by the electors' votes, Strong was setting the argument for the Louisiana and South Carolina appeals. Justice Miller, another Republican and a Lincoln appointee, agreed with Strong, but took the additional step of warning that if state courts were allowed to overturn canvassing boards, it would open the floodgates for any state Supreme Court to become the final arbiter of federal elections which would then be transformed into judicial rather than political contests. Miller's plea for judicial restraint reflected his Slaughterhouse Cases opinion rejecting a broad interpretation of the 14th Amendment.[106]

The justices' opinions meant little without Justice Bradley's approval. Strong's and Miller's support of Hayes was no more unexpected than Field's defense of Tilden's position. While modern readers know the outcome, those sitting in the Supreme Court chamber could only guess and hope. Bradley did not immediately reveal his hand. Like any experienced judge he ranged across the various points, picking at the arguments of both sides. He began by handing the Democrats a victory, rejecting the Republican argument that the Senate president pro tempore could rule on which electors to accept. His dismissal of the extreme Republican decision may have given Democrats hope, but few outside the Senate had taken the argument seriously. However, after raising Democrat hopes he dashed them, agreeing with Miller and Strong that state courts lacked authority to overturn decisions of a state canvassing board. He agreed state control of elections ended the moment the electoral votes were cast. Once the votes were cast, control of the process reverted to the national government. He rejected the Democrats' calls to probe the canvassing board's decisions, ruling the commission could only act if there was a claim of fraud in the certifying of electors. Without that, Hayes had won Florida, and his electors must be counted by Congress.[107]

When the commission's eight–seven decision reached Congress, the House voted to reject it while the Senate upheld it. Florida was the first test, and Tilden and the Democrats had lost. Some held out hope for the votes of three other states—Louisiana, Oregon, and South Carolina—all with different issues that could still tilt the election toward Tilden. When Louisiana electors were objected to by Democrats, they wagered Bradley would change his mind on the sanctity of the state canvassing boards' decisions having witnessed firsthand the corruption of Louisiana politics.

Arguing for Tilden was Lyman Trumbull—a close friend of Abraham Lincoln and the main author of the 13th Amendment. His partner was former Supreme Court Justice John Campbell, who resigned from the Court in 1861 to join the Confederacy. It was an unusual partnership—the architect of slavery's abolishment working with a man who had destroyed his political career to defend the institution. Trumbull's presence proved a public relations boon for Democrats while Campbell's awakened old fears of southern dominance of the Democrat Party.[108]

Louisiana offered Tilden his best chance for victory as the canvassing board had thrown out thousands of votes rather than the few hundred discarded in Florida. Unfortunately, Tilden had the Florida precedent working against him, the legal and political momentum working for Hayes. A neutral observer of the Louisiana election would note how violence and intimidation had suppressed the Republican vote, and the canvassing board's decision to throw out the results of the bulldozed parishes was more than simple partisanship. While the canvassing board's actions might be seen as corrupt and overreaching, it was a reaction to a decade of Democrat efforts to destroy the Reconstruction government using murder and mobs. The eight Republican members of the Commission again voted together to accept the decision of the state canvassing board and accept the Hayes electoral votes. This decision cast a pall over Tilden and the Democrats as the House rejected the commission's report while the Senate accepted it.

When a single Oregon elector was challenged by Democrats, the commission turned from the contentious issue of reconstructed states to the obscure 12th Amendment ban on federal officials serving as presidential electors. The framers placed the ban to protect the independence of the electors to ensure their vote for president was based on merit rather than a desire for a government job. The framers understood the promise of government employment might be sufficient inducement for electors to base decisions on personal rather than national interest.

An Oregon postmaster, John Watts, was a Hayes elector. As a federal employee, he could not serve in both positions prompting Watts to resign prior to Election Day. His resignation was not accepted until after the election, and Democrats seized on the fact he remained a federal employee on the day he was chosen as a member of the Electoral College. The Oregon governor, a Democrat, appointed a Democrat elector to take Watt's position, giving Tilden the deciding electoral vote for election. On the third Wednesday in December, Hayes's electors met and rejected the Tilden elector and cast Oregon's three electoral votes for Hayes. The Democrat governor sent a fourth electoral vote for Tilden to Washington, creating another disputed state for the commission.

The single Oregon vote would decide whether Tilden or Hayes reached the magical 185 total, and Democrats had renewed optimism that Bradley would rule for them, freed from the politically sticky issue of Reconstruction. However, the Democrats' arguments proved no more convincing than for Florida and Louisiana. The general rule was that replacement electors were chosen for those who became ill or ruled ineligible. The popular vote in a state does not choose electors, but rather chooses the party that has selected electors to cast the electoral vote. Democrats did not dispute that Hayes had won Oregon, the will of the people being that Hayes chose the electors to cast their votes. Allowing a Tilden elector to replace a Hayes elector would override the will of the voters and change the election. With Bradley providing the key vote, the commission again voted eight–seven for Hayes, and Democrats knew they were doomed. Once again the House rejected, and the Senate upheld the commission report, an increasingly dreary political dance that allowed Democrats to vent their feelings even as those outside Congress sought redress beyond meaningless votes.[109]

As the electoral commission ruled against Hayes, northern Democrats became more belligerent. The Democratic Veterans Association of Union Troops formed groups of armed minutemen, ready to battle Republicans at a minutes notice. The publisher Joseph Pulitzer warned of bloodshed if Hayes were elected while some Democrats offered union generals, William Franklin and Winfield Scott Hancock, as leaders of an armed force to prevent Hayes's election.[110] Neither of the generals took such talk seriously; neither did southern Democrats nor Republicans as most of those predicting bloodshed had been "invisible in war and invincible in peace."

Lacking options, congressional Democrats prolonged the pain and uncertainty, offering dozens of procedural motions to slow the process while continuing to object to electoral votes, including the votes from South Carolina, the weakest of the cases for Tilden. The state that provoked the Civil War would be responsible for ending the era. Democrats ignored public relations, declaring South Carolina was not a republic but a federally controlled government maintained only with army bayonets. Democrats argued all South Carolina results should be thrown out, an argument that would have forced Republicans to declare Reconstruction a failure. Not unexpectedly the commission rejected the argument eight–seven, the House voting down the report and the Senate accepting it.[111]

Defeated in the commission and seeing their hopes of a Tilden victory slip through their fingers, northern Democrats delayed the final counting of electoral votes possibly with the hope of preventing a president from being declared and provoking a constitutional crisis. Southern Democrats were initially supportive and then saw an opportunity for redeeming the final three southern states.

THE GREAT COMPROMISE

Having spent the last decade denouncing Republican carpetbaggers, southern Democrats were forced to swallow their pride and seek a compromise with their former enemies. Chief among these was Wade

Hampton III, battling for the South Carolina governorship and alienated from Tilden who had opposed his nomination. When Hampton approached the Hayes's campaign, it signaled southern Democrats wanted to end the election crisis while also ending reconstruction.

Southern Democrats' dalliances with Hayes drew a sharp response from Tilden supporters. The *Washington Union*, published by Tilden ally Montgomery Blair, accused southerners of a conspiracy to elect Hayes. House Speaker Samuel Randall accused the region's politicians of treachery and called for the appointment of Secretary of State Hamilton Fish as president and for a new election.[112] Southerners fired back, accusing their northern brethren of ignoring the section of the country that had provided Tilden with two-thirds of his electoral votes. The *Louisville Courier Journal* was one of the first to call for Hayes's election, completing a transformation from "bellicose and uncompromising" against Hayes to expressing strong support. The *Memphis Avalan*che editorialized against Tilden continuing his fight: its editor Andrew Keller was one of the leaders of the southern movement to work with Hayes. Without southern support, the die was cast against Tilden.[113]

However, the Hayes–Democrat alliance disturbed many Republicans who feared Hayes was on the verge of abandoning freedman to the Democrats.[114] Hayes's supporters tried to soothe Republican concerns, suggesting the compromise would include a Republican coalition with former southern Whigs to elect Republican James Garfield as House Speaker. Democrats had their own plans including a southerner appointed to a low-level cabinet position in the Hayes administration. Neither party would see their plans to fruition as cooperation ended almost the moment Hayes crossed the White House threshold.[115]

When Hayes and southern Democrats had made their agreement, northern Democrats made a last-ditch attempt at stopping the electoral count. House members began a filibuster, using delaying tactics to drag out the vote past the inauguration date of March 4. The pivotal vote came on February 20 when enough southern Democrats joined Republicans to defeat an adjournment motion intended to further slow the counting process. When Democrats saw opportunities to wring more compromises from Hayes or worried about his willingness to enforce their deal, they would threaten a filibuster until their demands were met.[116]

The 1876 election would not be settled until March 2, 1877—only two days before inauguration day though Hayes took the oath a day early for fear of Democrat disruption of the official ceremonies. While

Hayes was in the White House for an uneventful single term, the disputed 1876 election would not be forgotten. Infuriated Democrats in and out of Washington heaped abuse on Bradley, who was perceived as the deciding vote as he was the final commission member chosen. The justice was burned in effigy, a rare burst of unpopularity for a Supreme Court justice. Bradley also heard criticism from within the court. Justice Field was never one to mince words, and he charged Bradley was improperly influenced by businessmen and Republicans, two groups Field protected in his judicial opinions. The charge originated from the period between the end of the arguments over the Florida electoral votes and the commission's decision on Florida. During that time the commission members worked together to reach a conclusion but were also available to be influenced by other side. According to witness accounts after the decision, Republican businessmen had visited Bradley, who had apparently decided for Tilden in the Florida dispute.[117]

According to the story, Bradley had an epiphany while meeting with the Republicans and changed his vote in favor of Hayes. A different story had Bradley's wife, a Hayes partisan, influencing him toward the Republican. Both stories ignored the fact that Bradley's only documented visitor at the time was Justice Field, who tried to influence his colleague to vote for Tilden—a visit that Field conveniently ignored when criticizing Bradley.

Public anger at Bradley subsided, and during his 20 years on the Court he developed a reputation as a conservative jurist. Hayes would not escape so easily. Forever known as "Rutherfraud" Hayes, he completed a relatively successful term under a cloud of suspicion. He struggled to enact civil service reform and angered spoilsmen such as Senator Conkling with his reform of the New York Customs house. Hayes did not reward the loyalty of Chester Arthur, who was critical in convincing the Republican to challenge the results in three southern states. Hayes removed Arthur as head of the customs house in 1878 as part of his promise to reform and professionalize government though Arthur would bounce back as he was elected vice president in 1880 and later became president after James Garfield's assassination.

Tilden would never recover from his loss. Physically weakened by the long dispute, he was criticized by Democrats for bungling and then saw his reputation for honesty undermined during a House investigation of the election when the telegrams between Tilden's nephew and operatives in four disputed states revealed attempts to bribe those officials. A desultory draft campaign was launched for Tilden's "reelection" in 1880, but a physically and mentally weakened former governor pulled out of the race and settled into obscurity.

In the south, the losers of the national campaign won the war over controlling state government, overturning Reconstruction, and reinstituting a feudal economic and political system. Leaders such as Wade Hampton III kept their promises to allow black voting and enforce laws equally for blacks and whites, but were replaced in the 1890s by Ben "Pitchfork" Tillman and other populist Democrats who returned the Democrat party to its violent, racist roots. A system of economic and political segregation ensued, Democrats dominating the region until the 21st century.

The end of Reconstruction also saw a whitewashing of history as the new Democrat narrative of the postwar era turned reality on its head. For southerners, Hayes "saved" southern society and the political system from Grant, who was snidely referred to as "the man on horseback" seeking to enforce a military dictatorship on the south. It was Hayes and his fellow liberal Republicans who halted the third-term movement for Grant and were among the "thinking men" who rejected outlandish ideas of Reconstruction including black and white equality.[118]

Even the South Carolina carpetbagger Daniel Chamberlain earned some praise: his administration was supposedly reformist until brought into line by the Grant administration. According to this view, black militias were the true source of violence, particularly in South Carolina, the militias attacking black and white Democrats alike and the violence being exploited by Grant who sent federal troops to the state during the election. In response, the Democrats started the Red Shirts, a militia that took its name from the "bloody shirt" campaigns of Republicans. The Red Shirts engaged in violence as defense from the black militias and used harassment and intimidation in response to the same against white Democrats.[119]

The southern narrative would become part of the region's lore and proved a powerful argument for many who had tired of Reconstruction and saw the economy rather than the civil war as the issue of 1876. By the 1980s, states such as Florida and South Carolina were transformed into a GOP bastion, the former state the focal point of the 2000 election with the Hayes–Tilden controversy rekindled and partisan lines drawn even after a quarter century had passed.

9

Give 'em Hell Harry versus the Bridegroom

TRUMAN VERSUS DEWEY, 1948

The 1948 presidential election is considered the gold standard of presidential upsets. In that year, a weakened incumbent president struggled to hold together a divided Democrat party while battling a revitalized opposition and public opinion polls predicting that President Harry Truman would lose to Thomas Dewey. The election would be the first four-way race since 1860 and only one of two upsets with four candidates, dating back to 1824. However, the resemblance between 1948 and 1824 ended there. The earlier election sported four factions within a single party, whereas 1948 saw a two-party system with the Democrats split among three factions, ensuring almost certain doom for the incumbent. However, Truman was aided by party loyalty which was irrelevant in the single party 1824 election and the fact that in 1948 many Democrat voters "came home" and voted for the regular party candidate. Truman's startling comeback is ranked as the fourth greatest presidential upset in history.

In 1948 Harry Truman faced long odds in his bid for a second term. Following in the footsteps of Franklin Roosevelt, whose four consecutive presidential victories earned him the title of "the champ," Truman tried to extend the streak to five straight Democrat presidential victories, an accomplishment that had not occurred since 1876. Congressional Democrats understood the magic of the Roosevelt name at the top of the ballot. In the 1938 midterms Democrats lost 75 House and seven Senate seats, whereas in 1942, Democrats lost 46 House and seven Senate seats with Republicans coming within seven seats of taking the House. The only factor that saved Democrats in the period was the seats gained when Roosevelt ran for reelection, those gains allowing them to maintain their congressional majorities. In 1946 Democrats suffered even greater losses with 11 Senate and 55 House seats won by the Republicans who also took control of Congress. Without Roosevelt heading the ticket in 1948, Democrats appeared headed for another defeat.

The 1948 presidential election marked the height of the party's control of the executive branch. Over the next 60 years only Lyndon Johnson and Bill Clinton won a second term with Johnson's victory coming less than a year after the Kennedy assassination. During that same period four Republican presidents—Eisenhower, Nixon, Reagan, and George W. Bush—won reelection. The final Truman campaign also represented the last gasp of the original New Deal coalition.

Truman benefitted from the Roosevelt mystique, but also suffered from comparisons with the man who created the modern Democrat Party. Truman's struggles after the end of World War II cast doubt on his ability to continue Democrat dominance of the White House and forced him to run a purely negative campaign.

TRUMAN ADMINISTRATION

Six American presidents had died in office before Franklin Roosevelt's death in Warm Springs, Georgia on April 12, 1945. His vice president, Harry Truman, may have been the least prepared vice president of the previous six who took office as he was excluded from presidential decision making during his brief tenure.

A veteran of the Kansas City Pendergast political machine, Truman had failed in the business world, but thrived in government. He was elected Missouri senator in 1934, casting himself as a thorough New Dealer within the constraints imposed by his patron, Pendergast. His 1940 reelection campaign would be difficult and an education for Truman. His loyalty to the Kansas City machine earned him few friends in the White House, and Roosevelt made little effort on Truman's behalf, considering the one-term senator as a lost cause. Truman barely escaped the Democrat primary, but with his narrow reelection he adopted an independent agenda, chairing a committee investigating excessive defense spending during the war and embarrassing the Roosevelt administration.[1]

After Roosevelt was nominated for a fourth term in 1944, the Democrat convention split over the vice presidency. The incumbent, Henry Wallace, was perceived as a leftist radical. Many in the party noted

Roosevelt's poor health and were unwilling to allow the unstable Wallace to become president. Wallace's opponents preferred the safer choice of Harry Truman who could appeal to both wings of the party.[2]

After the election Truman was excluded from discussion of war strategy including the development of the atomic bomb, which he learned about after Roosevelt's death. Truman's first months in office proved the most triumphant of any president. Within five months he presided over the surrender of Nazi Germany, the use of nuclear weapons, and the Japanese surrender. However, the war's end brought new problems of rising inflation, labor unrest, consumer shortages, and a slow-motion military demobilization at home while starvation, European rebuilding, and the rise of Soviet Communism challenged his foreign policy team.

Truman cobbled together a strategy to handle both while battling Roosevelt holdovers who denounced his policies. Truman's popularity dipped precipitously in 1946 with Republicans seizing control of Congress. However, the status of opposition leader revitalized Truman whose battles with congressional Republicans proved an effective distraction from Truman's many domestic ills.

The Republican victory convinced party leaders that the public had rejected the New Deal; the 80th Congress began passing legislation dismantling the welfare state. Truman used his veto of the Taft Hartley Act to reassert his political relevance. The act banned the closed shop, a tactic from the 1930s that required workers to join a union prior to being employed. The act granted states authority to pass right-to-work laws prohibiting closed shops and gave businesses rights when faced with union boycotts. Truman's veto appealed to his labor base even as many congressional Democrats joined Republicans to override the veto.

By 1948 the Republican Congress had failed to repeal the New Deal but had curbed the excesses of the union movement, reinstated the two-term tradition for presidents with the 22nd Amendment, reorganized the armed forces and defense establishment with the National Security Act of 1947, and approved the Marshall Plan to rebuild Europe. With a record of achievement behind it, Congress provided the Republican nominee with a legislative platform to use against Truman. Squaring off against a revitalized Republicans, Truman faced long odds as many Americans perceived the president as incapable of solving the country's problems with some quipping "To err is Truman."[3]

Complicating Truman's election campaign was division within the Democrat Party. Disaffected New Dealers including Harold Ickes and Henry Wallace publicly attacked Truman while southern segregationists opposed Truman's civil rights policies. In two short years Truman saw his 80 percent approval ratings dip into the low 40s, and anxious Democrats wondered if a new Republican era was about to begin. As 1948 dawned, the Republicans searched for a candidate who could end their presidential losing streak.

REPUBLICAN CANDIDATES

As Democrats worried, Republicans entered the 1948 campaign season revitalized by the productive Congress and confident they had a candidate to defeat the Democrats. The 1944 Republican nominee New York Governor Thomas Dewey was the front-runner, his unsuccessful run against Roosevelt preparing him to challenge Truman.

Dewey made his name as New York City district attorney, taking down some of J. Edgar Hoover's most wanted gangsters and setting a new tone for law enforcement in the city. His prosecution of Lucky Luciano made him a household name and a front-runner for the 1940 Republican nomination.[4] After losing by the greatest landslide in presidential history in 1936, Republicans lacked effective leaders to challenge Roosevelt, who was running for a third term in 1940 though his second term had been disastrous, upending the two-term tradition begun by Washington. At age 39, Dewey lacked the gravitas necessary for the presidency: his youth and inexperience were considered too much of a risk as Hitler rampaged through Europe. Dewey lost the nomination to the even less qualified Wendell Willkie, a former Democrat who ran as a Republican in his only political campaign.

In 1942 Dewey was elected New York governor in a very good year for Republicans. Two years later he won the Republican presidential nomination in what was a more difficult race than 1940 because American voters were unlikely to change presidents in the midst of a war. Dewey's campaign was controversial in its attacks on the "tired old men" of the Roosevelt administration which appeared to exploit Roosevelt's poor health. The campaign produced a campaign story for the ages. Republicans attacked Roosevelt for use of a destroyer, noting it had sailed to retrieve his dog. In one of his radio addresses, Roosevelt ridiculed his opponents, noting he and his family did not mind the attacks, but that his dog Fala was distressed when criticized by the Republicans. The Fala speech would be the highlight of a dismal election because ill health prevented Roosevelt from conducting a full-fledged campaign.[5]

Dewey focused his fire on Roosevelt's allies including Sidney Hillman, head of the CIO, and the ties between the administration and domestic communists, which would become an issue only after Roosevelt's death. Dewey refused to raise the issue of what the American military knew prior to the Japanese attack on Pearl Harbor. The Republican acquired information on American code breaking that suggested the military knew about a plan to attack Pearl Harbor. After a request from General George Marshall, Dewey buried the evidence of the code breaking, which might have tilted the election in his favor.[6]

Dewey's defeat in 1944 was attributed to his negative campaigning and weakened his resolve to run a full-bore attack against Truman. Instead, Dewey focused on his governing philosophy as if guaranteed victory in 1948. It was a strategy leading to a stunning defeat at the hands of Truman's demagogic negative campaign.

Unlike the Democrat Party, which divided along regional lines, the Republican Party of the 1940s was split along ideological lines. The division between the conservative and progressive wings of the party began during the 1912 campaign and reopened during the 1940 Republican convention as the party's progressive wing nominated former Democrat, Wendell Willkie. Dewey's nomination in 1944 continued that trend as the governor was the quintessential Wall Street Republican and leader of the northeastern liberal wing. His nomination in 1944 seemed to place the Progressives in control of the party, and his nomination in 1948 would solidify that control. However, the right wing of the Republican Party fielded a competitive candidate in the person of Ohio Senator Robert Taft.

The Senate majority leader had taken the place of his father who had also battled a New York governor, Theodore Roosevelt, for control of the party in 1912. Taft was responsible for many of the bills that passed through the 80th Congress including the Taft Hartley Act which slowed the pace of unionization in the country and earned him the undying enmity of organized labor. Taft and other congressional isolationists were suspicious of the attempts by Roosevelt and Truman administrations to broaden American international responsibilities. Labeled as isolationist, Taft opposed the formation of NATO in 1949 by arguing the Soviet Union represented no threat to Western Europe much less the United States.[7] Taft warned that the International Monetary Fund (IMF) created under the 1945 Bretton Woods Agreement would make countries dependent on American largesse.[8] Taft voted for the Marshall Plan but only after failing to reduce its funding by a third.[9]

Taking his cue from Wendell Willkie, whose "one world" philosophy was not unacceptable to the Roosevelt administration, Dewey countered Taft by supporting American financial and military involvement in the world. He publicly separated himself from the Isolationist wing of the party by endorsing the Democrat opponent of New York Republican Congressman Hamilton Fish, who represented Roosevelt's Hyde Park district. Fish was a leading Isolationist with ties to German American groups and openly expressed anti-Semitic views that had become unacceptable in the United States with the war against the Nazis. Fish lost his seat in 1944, and Dewey was able to achieve in one election what Roosevelt had been unable to do in six elections.[10]

The conservative-progressive Republican division was complicated by an influx into Washington of young Republicans elected in the 1946 landslide. Among these was California Congressman Richard Nixon, who favored an aggressive campaigning style focusing on communism at home and abroad. Nixon had made his name with his anticommunism campaign against Congressman Jerry Voorhis. Joining the House Un-American Activities Committee (HUAC), Nixon began collecting evidence of communist infiltration of the Roosevelt administration. In the midst of the 1948 campaign, the committee interviewed former *Time* editor Whittaker Chambers who alleged that former State Department official Alger Hiss was a communist. The Hiss case would break after the election, but the hearings made domestic communism a campaign issue and put the Truman administration on the defensive. The attacks on the Roosevelt legacy infuriated New Dealers who targeted Nixon for destruction throughout his career.[11]

The three-way split among Republicans had little effect on the 1948 campaign, the battles between conservatives and Progressives ending when Dewey won the nomination. Dewey's defeat convinced the party's right wing that moderation and a refusal to attack Truman had doomed the party and reopened the battle between left and right.

Bolstered by an overwhelming reelection victory in 1946, Dewey announced his presidential candidacy in January 1948 and immediately became the man to beat. For the third consecutive election, he faced off against Taft, who favored a low-key campaign focused on rounding up convention delegates and ignoring the primaries.

A third candidate was already in the field. Harold Stassen was known as the boy governor of Minnesota, elected to that office in 1938 at the mere age of 31. A liberal from the Willkie wing of the party, Stassen began his campaign in 1946 and two years later came closest to winning the nomination. The three Republican front-runners would battle for becoming the Republican nominee who for the first time since 1928 seemed destined to become the president.

THE MEMO

Faced with a recalcitrant Congress at home and a hostile Soviet Union abroad, Truman struggled to maintain support among Democrats and New Dealers who saw him as a usurper of their beloved Franklin Roosevelt. Liberals criticized Truman for not battling congressional Republicans and extending New Deal programs. Those same critics accused Truman of following overly confrontational policies toward the Soviet Union and destroying the wartime alliance built by Roosevelt.

The party's conservative wing, located mainly in the solid Democrat South, approved of Truman's hard-line anticommunist policies but opposed his decision to expand on Roosevelt's racial policies. Among these was the Fair Employment Practices Commission (FEPC), a forerunner of the Equal Employment Opportunity Commission. The FEPC was used by the Roosevelt administration to enforce antidiscrimination clauses in federal defense contracts in the South. Forcing southern employers to hire black workers infuriated southern Democrats, and when the war ended they sought a return to the old segregation policy, but Truman proposed making permanent the FEPC and granting it new powers.

After his FEPC proposal was blocked by a southern filibuster, Truman turned to administrative efforts to advance civil rights. Attorney General Tom Clark drafted a report, "To secure these Rights," and proposed the following: a federal antilynching law; a ban on racially discriminatory poll taxes; and a creation of a federal civil rights division in the Justice Department to investigate and prosecute civil rights violations. Though none of the proposals passed Congress, Truman's efforts convinced southern Democrats that his reelection threatened segregation.[12]

Attacked by the right and left, Truman depended upon a few allies and campaign experts. Foremost among these were Clark Clifford and James Rowe, two political consultants responsible for composing a memo offering a blueprint for victory. Their first advice to Truman was to ignore southern angst over his racial policies. They noted that southern Democrats were unlikely to vote for Dewey because the Republicans were still seen as the party of civil rights. Clifford and Rowe proved wrong in dismissing the possibility of a southern splinter party, but were correct in discounting the effect of southern opposition to Truman. The memo counseled that instead of pandering to segregationists Truman should focus on the northern and western states where Roosevelt had transformed reliably Republican regions into Democrat-dominated states.[13]

Clifford and Rowe next advised Truman to use labor unions to replaced urban machines, a conclusion that must have pained the president who had clawed his way up the Kansas City Pendergast machinery to the White House. Prior to the New Deal, political machines had provided economic support for city voters in return for their votes. New Deal welfare programs federalized that system, and voters switched loyalties from local leaders to the national Democrat Party. Replacing urban machines were labor unions which organized their members along the same lines as urban machines. Unions generated membership dues that could be used to fund a candidate, making labor the most important interest group of 1948. In addition to acquiring union support, Clifford pushed Truman toward aggressive civil rights enforcement to turn the black vote permanently from the Republicans.[14]

The progressive challenge to Truman drew scorn from Clifford and Rowe who were contemptuous of the party leader Henry Wallace. The memo advised Truman to attack Wallace from the left, drawing in Progressives and preventing a party split. This left turn included a populist, fearmongering attack on Republicans and big business, a type of campaign that appealed to Truman who was described by columnist Westbrook Pegler as a "thin lipped hater."[15]

Clifford and Rowe went beyond merely advising Truman and created an opposition research division, offering the Democrats negative information on Dewey and the Republicans. The division, which included a group of advisors on Truman's campaign train, provided positive facts about the next whistle-stop ranging from major employers to elected officials and sports teams. Truman wound the information into his speeches: his listeners were convinced that the president's knowledge of their town was the result of his folksy personality rather than a highly organized political operation. Truman also leaned heavily on his campaign manager, J. Howard McGrath, future attorney general and federal felon. Despite all their good advice, Clifford and Rowe made one glaring error by operating under the false assumption that voters made their voting decisions by July. Fortunately for Truman, their assumption was incorrect as the president trailed Dewey by over 10 points during the summer. Instead, undecided voters broke decisively for the president.

Truman's reelection campaign began in April 1948 during a western trip where he was to receive an honorary degree from Stanford. This nonpolitical train tour included stops in Cleveland, Chicago, and Omaha before wending through the far western states of Idaho and Oregon. The trip did not go well, the president stumbling through his speeches and creating the image of an administration in disarray. During the trip Truman attacked what would become his favorite election year target—the 80th Congress. He compared the Taft Republicans to the Radical Republicans of the Reconstruction era, an odd contrast from a president whose platform included reviving the civil rights laws passed by those same Republicans in the 1870s. His appeal to the lost cause was a reminder to the South that Truman originated from a former slave state that included a strong pro-Confederate strain. Truman's trip provoked Senator Taft to denounce the tour as a whistle-stop campaign. The president jumped on the phrase, labeling it an insult to rural America and the small towns that merited only a quick stop and a whistle from passing trains.[16]

Truman tested his populist message during the trip, speaking as a folksy everyman, whipping up voter antagonism in the tradition of William Jennings Bryan and Robert La Follette. It was a return to the old stem-winding speeches, something that had been missing during the 1940s as Roosevelt's health declined and his campaign appearances became rare.

The populist message also implemented the advice from Clifford and Rowe of attacking Henry Wallace. The former vice president represented the New Deal cohort of Harold L. Ickes, Frances Perkins, Francis Biddle, Henry Morgenthau, and Wallace who left the Truman administration during 1945–1946. Some former New Dealers coalesced around the Progressive Party which Ickes had helped lead during the Taft and Wilson administrations. The Progressives began as a faction within the Republican Party that challenged the party's orthodoxy on economic regulation and tariffs. Progressives' distrust of big business was matched by their belief in the ability of professional elite in Washington to guide the economy through difficult periods. The movement became a party after Theodore Roosevelt lost his challenge to William Howard Taft at the Republican convention of 1912 and sought a vehicle for an independent presidential campaign. However, the party crumbled after 1912 with Roosevelt returning to the Republicans. In 1924 Wisconsin Senator Robert LaFollette revived the party to run another third- party campaign but won only his home state, and the Progressives returned to political hibernation.

Franklin Roosevelt's 1932 election was a victory for progressive principles if not the party as the New Deal implemented many of the party's policies from 1912 to 1924. Building a coalition of progressive liberals from urban areas and rural conservative Democrats, Roosevelt won four presidential elections. His death slowed progressive momentum, and Truman proved a disappointment for those who demanded even greater government control of the economy.

Truman's anticommunist policies alienated some Progressives who recalled the closer relationship between the Soviets and the Roosevelt administration during the war. Challenging Truman's foreign and domestic policy became the driving force behind a new progressive party which, like its predecessor in 1912, went in search of a prominent political figure to lead the ticket. That figure was former vice president Henry Wallace.

HENRY WALLACE AND THE PROGRESSIVES

One of the New Deal's true believers, Henry Wallace, put the truth to the proverb that there is nothing more fanatical than a new convert. Born in Iowa, Wallace followed his father's footsteps as Henry C. Wallace spent four years as agriculture secretary in the Harding and Coolidge administrations. His son earned a reputation as a plant geneticist, creating a form of hybrid corn to improve yields. Appointed Roosevelt's agriculture secretary, Wallace enacted radical farm policies that included removing farmers from unproductive land and creating price supports for commodities. It was a reversal of the decadeslong Republican policy of granting land to homesteaders and leaving the details of farming to the individual. Wallace's unapologetic liberalism and dedication to centralized planning earned him Roosevelt's attention and the vice presidency in 1940.[17]

Wallace's single-term vice presidency formed around his ideal of the "century of the common man." Given responsibility to run the Board of Economic Warfare, Wallace lost his battle to impose his egalitarian vision on the war effort.[18] By early 1944, Wallace had lost favor in the White House and was sent on a fact-finding mission to Siberia, the furthest place from Washington while Democrats plotted to replace him.[19]

The vice president returned just in time to see Harry Truman nominated to replace him; he then was appointed as commerce secretary to salve his bruised feelings. Dismayed at the slow unraveling of the New Deal and the disintegration of the Soviet–American alliance during the Truman administration, Wallace tried to reorient American foreign policy during a Madison Square Garden speech on September 12, 1946. Wallace criticized Truman's foreign policy and was fired by the president for disloyalty.[20]

Progressives who opposed Truman's foreign policy were attracted to Wallace because of his opposition to the Cold War. They faced off with mainstream liberal groups like Americans for Democrat Action (ADA) which favored his anticommunist policies while promoting civil rights, nationalized healthcare, and strong unions. Among its members were Arthur Schlesinger Jr. and Eleanor Roosevelt, who supported Truman by tearing at Wallace for underestimating the Soviet threat. The mainstream media joined in the campaign, even producing one article entitled "Old Testament Stories, crossed Pansies and four weeks in bed," in which Wallace was described as disheveled and brooding. His old New Deal rival, Harold Ickes, described Wallace as "present in the flesh but usually absent in the spirit" during cabinet meetings. The attacks followed the Clifford and Rowe memo that identified Wallace and the Progressives as the greatest threat to Truman's reelection.[21]

Wallace's comments and associations offered plentiful targets for Truman supporters. His argument for nuclear disarmament and accommodation of Soviet power in Europe included blaming American policy for provoking the communist coup in Czechoslovakia in the summer of 1948. During the campaign Wallace accepted the endorsement of the American Communist Party and packed his campaign with known communists including Paul Robeson and Woody Guthrie or labor leftists such as Lee Pressman and Harry Bridges, Congressman Vito Marcantonio, and John Abt. Wallace was also aided by his former agriculture department assistant and dedicated leftist, Rex Tugwell.[22]

The height of the Progressive campaign came with the upset win in an open 24th Congressional seat in the Bronx as Leo Isacson of the American Labor party defeated the regular Democrat candidate. Isacson favored the progressive foreign policy line of opposing the Marshall Plan and a separate air force.[23] The victory drew out the long knives from Truman's allies in the labor movement which attacked Wallace for his ties to communists and opposition to the Marshall Plan and peacetime draft.[24]

The Progressive Convention in Philadelphia was anticlimactic as Wallace was nominated for president and joined on the ticket by first-term Idaho Senator Glen Taylor. Before his senatorial career, Taylor was a sideshow entertainer who traveled the country singing and dancing. Taylor was a fervent New Dealer who saw Wallace as the right heir to Roosevelt's legacy and was denied his rightful place in the White House by a conspiracy of southern Democrats, union bosses, and machine politicians.

Taylor's politics may have impressed Idaho voters, but in a national campaign he suffered ridicule as his sideshow antics antagonized southern Democrats. Taylor visited Birmingham, Alabama, attending a black church and entering through the black entrance, and was subsequently arrested and banished from the city. While gaining headlines, Taylor was mostly ridiculed for his clownish efforts which lost more votes than they gained.[25]

Wallace's moment of triumph was overshadowed by his confrontation with former sportswriter-turned–political columnist, Westbrook Pegler. While being vice president, Wallace had been involved with a Russian guru, Nicholas Roerich, a half-demented spiritualist who held séances in the White House. Pegler acquired the letters of Roerich and Wallace and published them much to Wallace's embarrassment. During a convention press conference Wallace lashed out at Pegler and his "stooges" including H. L. Mencken, who peppered him with questions. Pegler did not back down, sneering at Wallace who refused to take questions from anyone he considered as Pegler's ally. The entire scene was reported in the newspapers and reinforced public doubts about Wallace.[26]

The Progressive campaign ran on a shoestring as the party struggled to attract large donors. The progressive resorted to an old-time tent revivalism, charging entrance fees for Wallace's speeches. Then in a scene reminding observers of a Sinclair Lewis novel, party leaders sought donations from the audience, praising those who pledged, shaming those who did not. A typical rally managed to raise enough money to pay for that night's festivities with little left for the campaign. Lacking advertising and organization, the Progressives faced long odds as their campaign was reduced to a spoiler role trying to prevent Truman's election or Wallace serving as a martyr for the cause.[27]

Enjoying their strongest support in large cities, the Progressives' best hope was appealing to urban liberals and radicals angry at Truman for his foreign policy and bungling of domestic policy. Wallace could take enough liberal votes from Truman to throw the contest into the House of Representatives and play kingmaker. The former vice president, though, lacked the skill of a political manipulator; instead, he played the role of true believer, his message more important than his vote total. In August 1948 he turned South, taking his crusade to the one region where he had little chance of converting his listeners. Surrounding himself with southern blacks—a deliberate affront to racist southern Democrats—Wallace preached on the evils of segregation and in favor of civil rights. In North Carolina he survived a barrage of eggs, Wallace reveling in the controversy that only alienated rather than attracted voters. Wallace chose to interpret southerners' violent reaction as a sign he had touched a nerve in denouncing the evils of a segregated society.[28]

His speeches went further, drawing out some of the southern populism of Cotton Ed Smith and Theodore Bilbo, denouncing capitalism and the wealthy as coconspirators in maintaining segregation to divide workers on racial rather than class lines, an analysis that would have made any Marxist nod in agreement. Populist economics attracted some southern votes, but Wallace's rhetoric recalled the paranoid fantasies of the 1930s. Wallace blamed arms makers for the Cold War, associating anticommunism with an economic plot to maintain corporate power. At times Wallace sounded like Charles Lindbergh, the prewar isolationist who ignored the threat of totalitarianism for the siren song of isolation from the rest of the world. Throughout the campaign, Wallace undermined his appeal with public relations stunts, one of which was a public letter to Joseph Stalin seeking negotiations and "peaceful coexistence" without interference in internal affairs. Wallace's letter reiterated the communist party line and reinforced the public perception of him as a communist dupe.[29]

The lack of an organization and Wallace's focus on message rather than electoral votes ensured the Progressive Party remained the fourth of four parties when it came to ballot access. His name was not on the ballot in many southern states, where the Democrats also removed Harry Truman from their ballots. In Minnesota, where Wallace's message was preached by the Farmer–Labor Party, party leaders rejected a fusion ticket that would have provided Progressives use of a state party apparatus.

By September the polls showed Wallace dropping from a respectable 10 percent of the vote in the spring to just over three percent, a number unlikely to hurt Truman in any state. Some local and state Progressive parties shattered, fearful a vote for Wallace would become a vote for Dewey. By Election Day, Wallace's toothy grin and loose hair dropping over his eye became a source of amusement as the former vice president became a forgotten man, relegated to trivia questions. The election would end Wallace's political career and the Progressives as an effective third party.[30]

DIXIECRATS

The Truman administration's civil rights policies worried southern Democrats who feared federal interference with segregation. Truman's efforts matched the decline in the virulent racism of southern politicians such as South Carolina's Cotton Ed Smith, who was defeated in 1944 by Governor Olin Johnston, a New Dealer supported by Roosevelt. However, when the Supreme Court struck down the white primary in *Smith v. Allwright*, Johnston led South Carolina's drive to pass more restrictive laws against black voters. The most "moderate" southern Democrats established their white supremacist bonafides by fighting hard against ending segregation even as a new cadre of senators including Al Gore Sr. of Tennessee, William Fulbright of Arkansas, and Georgia's Richard Russell rejected the South's political isolation while fighting to integrate the region into national politics.[31] Within the administration, Secretary of State Jimmy Byrnes had been one of Roosevelt's closest advisors, acting as the president's liaison with southerners and then serving as a Supreme Court justice, war czar, and Truman's first secretary of state. Byrnes and the others would face a difficult decision as their southern compatriots tried to split the Democrat party.

As 1948 approached, Southerners promised to fight any change in the party's civil rights plank of 1944. To exhibit their seriousness, southern political leaders made plans for an independent presidential run. The first to act was Alabama Governor "Big Jim" Folsom, who announced his presidential candidacy on January 20, 1948. Folsom was not the stereotypical Alabama governor as he criticized Truman's foreign policy as overly harsh toward the Soviet Union. Following the Wallace line he accused Truman of propping up the British Empire. Folsom did not represent a threat to Truman and was considered too far to the left to carry the southern Democrat banner.

During the spring, state conventions throughout the South chose uncommitted delegates to the national convention instead of delegates pledged to Truman. The leader of the movement, Mississippi Governor Fielding Wright, sought a separate southern party focusing on the constitutional issue of states' rights that was considered less controversial than segregation. In May, 1948 Wright welcomed over 1,000 delegates to Jackson, Mississippi, with the participants agreeing to establish a third party if civil rights became an issue in the Democrat convention.[32]

The president's campaign seemed unconcerned with southern threats, focusing on destroying the Wallace campaign and protecting his left flank. Following advice from the Clifford and Rowe memo, Truman gambled that southerners would use the period before the convention to vent for their voters then rally around the Democrat Party, preferring Truman to Dewey and the hated Republicans. The gamble failed, and Truman saw his party base erode.

Democrats gathered in Philadelphia during July 13–14 and tried to soothe southerners with a vague call for civil rights balanced with states' rights. After Truman's nomination the delegates assuaged southern feelings by nominating Kentucky Senator Alben Barkley as vice president. However, Barkley was seen as a Roosevelt puppet, having defeated in 1940 the segregationist candidate for Senate Majority leader with the president's help. Barkley's nomination could not calm southerners after northern liberals proposed an extensive civil rights plank to the platform.

The original civil rights plank was borrowed from the 1944 platform with platitudes about equal voting and economic rights, but with no specific mention of racial or religious discrimination and any proposed civil rights legislation. Limited debate over the platform was intended to paper over the party's internal divisions.[33] One opponent of the watered-down plank, Minneapolis Mayor and Minnesota Senate candidate, Hubert Humphrey, mounted the podium and blasted the weak civil rights plank. Using the same moralistic tones that would mark liberalism for 75 years, he implored Democrats to escape "the shadow of states' rights" and "walk forthrightly into the bright sunshine of human rights." That bright sunshine was a strong civil rights plank demanding federal legislation promoting equal and voting rights, anathema to the South. Humphrey dismissed calls for more delay in civil rights or a slow, measured approach, declaring "we are 172 years late."[34] Humphrey's speech swung delegates toward his view, and the plank passed by 31 votes. Upon passage, the Alabama and Mississippi delegations left the convention while the remaining southern delegates made a halfhearted push for Senator Richard Russell who was easily defeated by Truman 948–266.[35]

The southern walkout was well planned with delegates utilizing two reserved trains for a rushed trip to Birmingham and a convention to choose a southern Democrat candidate to replace Truman in the old Confederacy. The Birmingham gathering was a mixture of racists and segregationists mixed with old-line populists. Gerald L. K. Smith and Bull Connor were present as defenders of segregation while the 87-year-old former Oklahoma governor, "Alfalfa" Bill Murray, lauded the benefits of segregation.[36] The convention hid its defiant defense of racial separation under the states' rights mantra, besmirching the constitutional argument with the stain of white supremacy. It accused the federal government of dictatorial powers and promised to revive the 10th Amendment. Though united on the overreach of the federal government and Harry Truman, the convention was split on the proper political strategy for challenging the president. In a reversal of his previous rhetoric, Fielding Wright wanted to remain within the Democrat Party but one that included prominent southern politicians and acceptance of southern segregation.

The Birmingham convention failed to unite southern Democrats. The American preference for a two-party system saw third parties as destructive while many southern Democrats who benefitted from patronage and Democrat programs were repelled by the possibility that a southern party would defeat Truman. Powerful southern politicians including Richard Russell, William Fulbright, and Sam Rayburn ignored the convention and publicly endorsed Truman.

The star of the convention was not even there. South Carolina governor Strom Thurmond swore off an invitation by noting a prior meeting with the state militia. As South Carolina governor, Thurmond established a moderate record of having improved state education for black and white students, ended poll taxes, and pushed for prosecutions for lynching. Thurmond favored Wright's version of a southern Democrat Party that would not rejoin the regular party until the civil rights issue was removed from the party platform. Knowing the South could not elect a purely regional candidate, he hoped to deny Truman his base and throw the presidential election into the House of Representatives where southerners would hold the decisive vote for president. Upon his nomination, Thurmond selected Fielding Wright as his vice-presidential candidate and then embarked on a campaign focused more on his political future than a realistic chance of winning.[37]

At 46, Thurmond entered the presidential race at a time most men were approaching the peak of their influence and were settled in their world views. However, the governor would experience several setbacks, battling the state and regional establishments, his influence burgeoning in his 60s and well into his 80s.

Born in 1902, Thurmond was too young to volunteer for World War I and considered too old for World War II combat. His father was a judge who advised South Carolina's leading politicians ranging from Pitchfork Ben Tillman to James Byrnes. Watching Governor Coleman Blease demolish an opponent on the stump, Thurmond decided to go into politics and was never to be outdone in the quantity or fierceness of his rhetoric. Serving as a state judge in the 1930s, Judge Thurmond proved a vigorous proponent of the death penalty as an answer to racial tensions. After Pearl Harbor, Thurmond volunteered for the paratroopers at age 39 and was part of the vanguard dropped behind enemy lines at Normandy, earning a bronze star and a reputation for foolhardy bravery. Returning from the war, he was elected governor in 1946 but more importantly for his political career, he found a wife.[38]

Nineteen-year-old Jean Griffin was the newly crowned Miss South Carolina, and when the 44-year-old governor married the beauty queen, many South Carolinians snickered at the scandal, but Thurmond reveled in the attention and his new wife. In a famous *Life Magazine* article, Thurmond was pictured standing on his head, outfitted with tennis shorts while his wife watched beaming.[39]

Once the southern Democrat movement was dubbed the Dixiecrats, Thurmond was trapped in a mainly southern campaign. Much like Henry Wallace, Thurmond lacked the funds for a strong media campaign. Major newspapers in the north and south treated the Dixiecrats with contempt and ignored Thurmond's speeches. Without the backing of the national Democrat Party, Thurmond relied on state parties, limited to the Deep South, to manipulate the voting process.

The campaign focused on Strom Thurmond. While his running mate Fielding Wright lacked the populist touch and avoided crowds, Thurmond thrived in his stump speeches—part of the South Carolina populist tradition. Though Dixiecrats claimed their movement went beyond racial politics, Thurmond's speeches tended to focus on the issue. A late-August speech in Mariana, Arkansas was typical as the candidate warned of a movement to integrate public accommodations including busses, restaurants, and schools—all of which would destroy southern traditions. The FEPC was another target as Thurmond denounced it as a communist plot to control the workplace using federal power.[40]

Thurmond's stump speeches focused on segregation and the dangers of mixing races if integration was forced on the South. He tossed out the usual racial fears of miscegenation at dances, office parties, and restaurants.[41] In Savannah he warned that the federal government's racial policies were leading the country toward dictatorship. According to Thurmond "The Jeffersonian Democrats have spewed out their mouths that mongrel outfit which captured our party in Philadelphia." Thurmond did receive an unexpected endorsement from the aging commentator H. L. Mencken who declared Truman was a "shabby mountebank" while Dewey was a "limber trimmer," and that Wallace had lost "what little sense he had formerly if instead he ever had any at all." According to Mencken the South Carolina governor was the "best of all the candidates," but worried that "the worst morons in the South are for him."[42]

Thurmond made a single trip to the north, a speech in Boston near the end of the campaign, but his attempts to soft-pedal the racial issue was not well received in the north and earned him pungent comments from newspapers and tough stories from *Time* and *Newsweek*. With northern support nonexistent Thurmond's focus was on maximizing the southern vote and taking the election away from Truman. The Dixiecrats won only the four states that had thrown Truman from the ballot; in the remainder of the South the president easily defeated the Thurmond–Wright ticket. Thurmond's split from the regular Democrat Party opened a schism between the upper-class conservative Democrats and the rank-and-file populist Democrats who were willing to use segregation as a tool to pry power from the regular Democrats. Thurmond would ride that wave to a write-in victory in the South

Carolina Senate race of 1956—the first Senate write-in victory ever.[43] Later, he led the Southern Democrats into the Republican column.

THE GROOM ON THE WEDDING CAKE

If Truman's reelection campaign was complicated by the Wallace Progressives and the Thurmond Dixiecrats, it was made easier by the Republican who ran against him: Thomas Dewey. The New York governor began his campaign focusing on building organization in key states, polling, and enjoying his fundraising advantage over his Republican opponents. Dewey's drive to the Republican nomination revealed his strengths and weaknesses as he fought off challengers. Having sewn up a large segment of delegates chosen by state conventions, and busy with his gubernatorial duties, Dewey virtually ignored the limited primary schedule.

In Wisconsin, Dewey faced Minnesota governor Harold Stassen, and the war hero, five- star General Douglas MacArthur. Dewey's campaign staff saw the state as a lost cause with Stassen's proximity to the state making him a favorite while MacArthur's childhood ties to Milwaukee gave him a home state advantage. Certain he could not win Dewey campaigned only two days so as not to raise expectations.

The primary on April 6 began a troublesome period for Dewey and drove his campaign to the edge of collapse. Stassen easily won Wisconsin, all but eliminating MacArthur and making the Minnesota governor the alternative to Dewey. Stassen's momentum picked up with a win in Nebraska the next week. To the Dewey campaign it appeared the Republican grass roots had spoken and was unhappy with Dewey's front-runner pose. Longtime Republicans could not forget the 1912 nomination battle when the insurgent Theodore Roosevelt swept the Republican primaries against President Taft but was beaten in the party convention by a deluge of Taft votes. Yet, 1912 had not turned out well for the Republicans, and Dewey needed to win primaries to show he was the choice of Republican voters rather than party bosses.

While the Dewey campaign struggled with a strategy, Stassen made a mistake. Heady with his two victories he turned to Ohio, challenging its favorite son Senator Robert Taft. In 1948 it was considered a breach of political ethics to challenge a candidate in his home state, but Stassen smelled weakness after Taft polled a distant third in the Nebraska primary. With Dewey conceding Ohio, Stassen believed he could deliver a knockout blow to both of his opponents. Knowing he could not sweep Taft's southern Ohio supporters, Stassen focused on industrial cities in northern Ohio with its abundance of blue-collar union workers who disliked Taft–Hartley. Stassen also appealed to Democrats who could vote in the Republican primary.[44]

The election results were mixed, Taft taking a majority of delegates with Stassen winning just over one-third. Unfortunately for the governor, the Ohio campaign broke his momentum and allowed Dewey to campaign alone in the next primary state—Oregon. The New York governor arrived on the coast, tossing off the yoke of inevitability, and running a personal campaign of palm-pressing and picture-taking—the most famous had the suited Dewey grinning with several men dressed in cavemen skins.[45]

The Dewey campaign controlled the radio airwaves, reintroducing the governor by emphasizing his farming experience in New York in order to connect with rural Oregonians. By the time Stassen reached the west coast from Ohio, Dewey had gained the upper hand. Hoping to deliver another knockout blow, Stassen agreed to a radio debate on whether to ban the Communist Party. Stassen was an unapologetic cold warrior, demanding that the federal government prevent communist subversion. Dewey, challenging public opinion and the right wing of his party, took the opposite view, offering another reason for conservatives to distrust him.

During the debate, Stassen offered the emotional if not effective argument that the American Communist Party was an agent of a foreign government and could be banned. True to his education and profession, Dewey was lawyerly in his response, warning against restricting political speech because it was unpopular. His reasoned argument sounded more presidential while the debate reenergized Dewey, who used his large organization to campaign across the state. Stassen lacked the organization and money and relied on his Paul Revere Raiders composed of enthusiastic grassroots activists. Four days after the debate, Dewey defeated Stassen by 9,000 votes, ending the Minnesota governor's chance at the nomination. Stassen would continue to run for the Republican nomination, with his last campaign occurring in 2000, though he last won Republican delegates in 1968.[46]

With the primary season moving him back to front-runner status, Dewey strolled confidently into Philadelphia on June 21, 1948. The city was picked as part of an experiment to televise the convention. Television cameras were set up in the hall, but viewing was limited to the east coast, requiring a northeastern city to allow transmissions. Unfortunately, the city was caught in the worst heat wave in the past century, making the delegates miserable.[47]

Dewey's convention managers were the same men who led his national campaign. The New York lawyer, Herbert Brownell, had state legislative experience but little experience on the national scene. Russell Sprague headed the Republican machine in Nassau County, whereas Ed Jaeckle was a politician from Buffalo. The trio easily manipulated delegates but was less effective at connecting with ordinary voters, their insulated New York experiences offering little experience with the type of Democrat campaign awaiting them.[48]

As front-runner, Dewey was the target of all the second tier candidates: Stassen, Taft, and *Chicago Tribune* publisher Robert McCormick. None was capable of defeating Dewey alone, but together they might stop him and open the convention for a dark horse. The strategy had worked for Wendell Willkie eight years earlier with the former Democrat slipping by Taft and Dewey for the nomination. Dewey's managers had learned their lesson, preparing delegates to jump on the Dewey bandwagon as the voting moved from the first to the second and the third ballots. After the partisans of favorite son candidate such as Earl Warren of California screamed their voices raw in support, the delegates were available for the leading candidates. The Pennsylvania delegation agreed to swing behind Dewey on the second ballot, and the California delegation backed him after a deal with Warren. The voting went for two days, June 22–23, and three ballots. The Pennsylvania break for Dewey settled the issue, and after his nomination Dewey chose Warren as his running mate, the last time a major party fielded candidates from states with the two largest electoral vote counts. However, even this political strategy could not save the doomed campaign; the 1948 nomination would be the peak of Dewey's political career.

DEMOCRAT CAMPAIGN

The Republican divisions were minor when compared to the Democrats. Even prior to the convention, Truman was buffeted by calls for him not to seek a second term. Dissident Democrats in search of a different candidate offered the nomination to Dwight Eisenhower while Truman offered the vice-presidential slot to Justice William Douglas;

however, both men rejected the offer—a sign many high officials expected the Democrats to lose. This left Truman as the sole candidate, a president distrusted by a large fraction of his party that had not wanted him as senator, vice president, or president.[49]

Truman did not give his acceptance speech until two in the morning, the convention chaos resembling that of 1972 when George McGovern the Democrat presidential nominee gave his speech at three in the morning. However, even with poor timing, the speech signaled Truman's intent to conduct a raucous campaign. In his speech he called Congress into a special session, the first in nearly a century, and challenged Republicans to pass bills on issues such as housing, inflation, and unemployment.[50]

The recalling of the 80th Congress was a master public relations success as Truman tied Dewey to the Republican Congress and blamed them for the issues, such as inflation, unemployment, and high taxes, which had all but ruined his administration. Not having to run for president in 1944, Truman did not face Republican reminders of broken promises from that campaign. Instead Truman almost ran as a challenger, attacking Dewey and the Republicans as if they had controlled the government in the previous four years. Dewey was forced to defend the 80th Congress filled with members who did not share his ideology.[51]

With Truman launching his first attack of the campaign, Dewey assumed his usual pose as front-runner returning to his farm and granting Truman a monopoly on the news cycle. As Congress stumbled through the three-week session, Truman attacked the do-nothing Republicans even though as a former two-term senator he knew three weeks was insufficient time to pass even small legislation much less anything dealing with inflation, unemployment, or other economic ills. By demagoguing the issue Truman distracted voters from his own poor economic record though his attacks would not soon be forgotten by Republicans.[52]

As August days dwindled, Dewey grew more confident that Truman's frenetic campaign was not succeeding. Throughout the summer the Republican enjoyed a point lead of eight to 14 over the incumbent, but in each poll Dewey never rose above 45 percent, raising concerns he had reached his highest support. Most of the swing voters in August were southern Democrats or northern Progressives—neither of whom likely to vote for Dewey—offering Truman a chance for a comeback if they returned to the Democrat Party.[53]

Dewey remained confident in his lead and voter disgust with Truman and ran a positive campaign, refusing to attack Truman while offering vague promises of what his administration would do when in office. Truman also ignored the party's conservative wing by distancing himself from the Republican Congress. The governor realized while campaigning in a Democrat- majority country that he could only win by blurring partisan lines and soft-pedaling Republican policies.

Truman suffered no such limitation, and his campaign enjoyed new electoral techniques; all of which would become the norm in modern presidential elections. One of those techniques was the focus group. A Democrat official, Leslie Biffle, drove around Kentucky and Ohio conducting interviews with ordinary people, seeking their input into critical issues. Though the participants were not randomly chosen and Biffle employed rudimentary surveying techniques, the results offered grassroots views used by Democrats to pound popular issues. Truman was also the first to utilize advance men. During the whistle-stop in the fall, Democrat staffers arrived at towns ahead of Truman, identified local issues and officials, and wrote short blurbs that were passed to Truman upon his arrival. This allowed the president to appeal to voters on those issues and convinced many that he enjoyed an intimate knowledge of their town and state.[54]

Throughout much of 1948, Dewey assumed the posture of an incumbent while Truman seized the role as underdog challenger. Their different approaches were reflected in their speeches. In a foreign policy address, Dewey promised that his administration's foreign relations would be more "effective" and run by people who "understood peace," while being "vigorous, knowledgeable and experienced." Amidst the vague promises Dewey warned there were "no trick answers or easy solutions."[55]

Truman was more direct. During the Democrat convention he said promised "I will win this election and make the Republicans like it." Later when speaking of the improved conditions for farmers he declared, "Never in the world were the farmers . . . as prosperous (as now) . . . and if they don't do their duty by the Democratic Party they are the most ungrateful people in the world." Later when calling for the Republican Congress to act on the country's economic ills, he also demanded a new law on displaced persons to replace "the anti semitic, anti Catholic law which this 80th Congress passed."[56]

At a speech in Dexter, Iowa in October Truman continued with the divisive rhetoric as he declared the election "issue is the people against the special interests." It did not take much imagination to discover the identity of those interests as Truman denounced Republicans as "gluttons of privilege," and called them "cold and cunning men," who "stuck a pitchfork in the farmer's back." He warned that a "Republican blight would wipe out your prosperity" using the "economic tapeworm of big business."[57]

In another speech in October, the president said the Republicans represented "the most reactionary elements" and if they took power would "skim the cream from our natural resources to satisfy their own greed," while allied with "bloodsuckers with offices in Wall Street." In Philadelphia Truman spoke to raucous crowds, calling out that "we don't believe in the unity of slaves . . . or sheep." In Buffalo he complained Republicans used "a butcher knife and meat ax . . . on every forward-looking proposal," the president had offered them.[58]

The demagogic rhetoric appealed to many in Truman's audience who still held a hatred of the very Republicans Franklin Roosevelt had denounced in four presidential elections. Dewey's main tactic was to ignore the attacks and remain on a higher plain. During a Los Angeles campaign stop the governor focused on the communism issue promising not to "ignore the communists nor outlaw them." Dewey reinforced the arguments he made during his Oregon debate with Stassen on outlawing the communist party and promised "In this country we'll have no thought police. We will not jail anybody for what he thinks or believes." Dewey's speeches were described by columnist Stewart Alsop as "a trifle too ostentatiously noble" and that his words had the "faint flavor of Batten, Burton, Durstine and Osborn."[59]

Dewey demonstrated some emotion during an accident in Illinois when the train engineer backed the cars into a gathering crowd of people. The Republican stormed "That's the first lunatic I've had as an engineer, he probably ought to be shot at sunrise." To this the engineer was reported to have responded "I think as much of Dewey as I did before and that's not much."[60]

It would be Earl Warren who would launch a counterattack in a Tulsa speech where he characterized the Democrat Party as "a sorry spectacle of warring factions, city machines, rebellious elements, pressure minorities, fellow travelers and left wingers."[61]

It will never be known whether Truman's demagogic attacks or the natural return of the Democrat majority to Truman's side led to his upset victory, but the speeches were characterized by friendly reporters and historians as the president "giving them hell," when in reality it was Truman accusing his opponents of antisemitism only a few years after the fall of the Nazis and comparing them to leeches and tapeworms, terms usually not used in a presidential campaign.

THE POLLS

Public opinion polling was a new technology in 1948. Though used in the 1940 and 1944 elections, the lack of any history or study of electoral politics led to misinterpretation of results and a mistaken belief that voters made their decisions during the summer of election year and maintained their support through Election Day.

Truman's summer began with bad news as a Roper poll had him trailing Dewey by 23 points, a larger deficit than anything seen in the 1940 or 1944 polls.[62] However, the polling results did not tell the whole story. Truman's deficit was the result of a divided party, and his comeback was enabled by the return of dissident Democrats. Independent party movements start fast, the novelty of their candidates and ideas attracting disaffected voters seeking change. As the campaign proceeds, though, their support dwindles, their positions attacked by the major parties, a lack of organization and fundraising placing them at a disadvantage and the powerful influence of party identification pulling voters back to the major parties. Only in instances of weak candidates in the two major parties, such as in 1968 and 1992, or the presence of a well-known third-party candidate such as an ex-president, as in 1856 and 1912, can a third-party maintain a high level of support and threaten the major parties. Neither Wallace nor Thurmond boasted these characteristics while Truman and Dewey remained relatively popular among their voters.[63]

Wallace was the first to see his support decline. The Soviet coup in Czechoslovakia and Wallace's apparent support of Soviet military action to promote stability reinforced voters' doubts about Wallace. Those doubts were reinforced by the ADA and Truman-allied labor unions that cast the progressive candidate as a communist dupe. Denied mainstream liberal support, Wallace saw his support fall below five percent nationally.

Thurmond's decline was less dramatic and focused entirely on the issue of ballot access. Thurmond's plan to deny Truman the southern votes required replacing the regular Truman–Barkley ticket with the Thurmond–Wright ticket. If southern Democrat voters faced a choice between Thurmond and the hated Republican Dewey, they would choose the Dixiecrat.

The Thurmond–Wright ticket replaced the regular Democrats in Alabama, Mississippi, and South Carolina but struggled for ballot access through the remainder of the South. In Florida state election law placed the name of the electors rather than the candidates on the ballot; however, with two list of Democrat electors, fears arose that voters would be confused, splitting their votes between the two sets of electors and potentially allowing Dewey to win the state. To prevent this, the legislature changed the law and allowed Thurmond to place his name next to Truman. Dewey's name would also be on the ballot, whereas Henry Wallace supporters would have to find another state to vote as their candidate was excluded from the ballot.[64]

Louisiana offered a different challenge to Thurmond. The Truman–Thurmond contest was overshadowed by local politics and a bitter battle between a rooster and a donkey. Earl Long was the successor to his governor brother Huey Long. The younger Long was nearly as unpopular as Truman with rural Democrats, and his support of Truman did not help the president. Facing the question of ballot access, the Louisiana state legislature chose a compromise, allowing both Truman and Thurmond on the ballot. The Truman victory was tempered by the states' rights ticket acquiring the rooster symbol, which was the official symbol of the state Democrat party. With the high illiteracy rate of Louisiana Democrat voters, the symbols next to the candidate's name would cue their vote; the rooster was more popular than the donkey, the symbol of the national Democrat party and the one assigned to Truman on the ballot.[65]

Several southern states rejected the Thurmond ticket in part or whole. In Georgia Herman Tallmadge, son of former governor "Whipping Gene" Eugene Tallmadge, won the Democrat gubernatorial primary. His white supremacist roots appeared to place him among the Dixiecrat sympathizers, but Tallmadge refused to support a move to replace Truman with Thurmond on the Georgia ballot. The president's low polling numbers may have helped him in the state as Georgia Democrats were certain that Truman would lose and did not want to face recriminations from the national party if they contributed to the defeat of a Democrat president. Senators Walter George and Richard Russell also fought to keep Truman as the regular Democrat on the ballot and in doing so locked down the state's electoral votes for the president.[66]

Truman was even more successful in Texas, where the state legislature under the thumb of House Speaker Sam Rayburn, forced Thurmond–Wright to run on an independent ticket, ensuring Truman would win the state's critical 23 electoral votes. Fear of Republican victory in Virginia and Tennessee stymied Thurmond's efforts in those states. Both states sported a strong Republican vote of over 40 percent with Republican Warren Harding winning Tennessee in 1920 and Herbert Hoover winning Virginia and Tennessee in 1928 for the first break in the solid South. Concerned that a States' Rights Democrat would split the Democrat vote, the two state parties rejected the Thurmond ticket outright.[67]

The surprising Truman win would be anything but a shock to modern pollsters who would have recognized the trend toward the president: the inability of Dewey to rise above 50 percent as a sign of weakness and the tendency of voters to make up their minds during the waning days of the campaign. Truman managed 303 electoral votes to Dewey's 189 and won two million more popular votes.

Dewey swept much of the northeast losing only Massachusetts and Rhode Island with the early Republican tide convincing the *Chicago Tribune* to publish its embarrassing headline "Dewey defeats Truman." However, the Dewey steamroller lost a wheel as it moved toward the Mississippi. Democrats swept nearly all of the states west of the river, Dewey winning only the four plains states and Oregon which offered little in electoral votes when compared to the 15 states won by Truman. The president won most of the narrow victories taking Illinois by just over 30,000 votes out of nearly four million polled votes. He won California by 18,000 votes out of 3.9 million and won Ohio by 7,000 votes out of 2.9 million polled votes. Dewey's narrowest victories came in Michigan and surprisingly in his home state of New York.[68]

The two spoiler candidates accomplished little. Thurmond polled just 18,000 more votes than Henry Wallace, his 1.175 million votes limited to the old Confederacy. Thurmond won three states that replaced the Truman–Barkley ticket with the Thurmond–Wright ticket— Mississippi, Alabama, and South Carolina—while the rooster topped the donkey among the Louisiana Democrats. Lacking support of the state parties in the rest of the south, Thurmond performed poorly. In Arkansas, Florida, North Carolina, Texas, and Virginia Dewey outpolled Thurmond, a shocking result in the supposedly solid South that revealed Thurmond's weakness when challenging state parties.[69]

Henry Wallace won no states and just over 1.1 million votes. His presence on the New York ballot where he received his highest percentage was greater than the one percent Dewey victory in his home state.

AFTERMATH

Harry Truman's comeback win set the conditions for a failed second term and the lowest approval ratings for a modern president, lower than Nixon's in August 1974. In demagoguing the 80th Congress and the Dewey campaign, Truman confirmed Westbrook Pegler's description of him as a thin-lipped hater. The fifth consecutive election loss also heightened Republican desperation. Having suffered a vituperative campaign in 1948, the Republicans unleashed their dogs of political war, ripping Truman's foreign policy failures in Korea and his domestic failures including widespread government corruption. The Republican attacks ended Truman's drive for a third term in 1952 while poisoning political discourse. After leaving office, Truman assumed the role of political gadfly for his own party, intervening in the party's presidential politics for the next two decades.[70]

Thomas Dewey returned to New York, completing his gubernatorial term and then settling into the role of senior statesman and backroom operator. His influence within the Republican establishment was undiminished by his loss, and he promoted Eisenhower's nomination much to the chagrin of Robert Taft and the party's conservative wing. Dewey supported Nixon in 1960 and 1968 and was offered the position of chief justice by Nixon in 1969, which he refused. Dewey died in 1971, a year before Truman expired.

Dewey's failure is generally mentioned as the worst defeat for any presidential candidate, but he held up under the strain. Republicans and Democrats agreed he mismanaged his campaign and claimed defeat from the jaws of victory. Earl Warren, his running mate, would enjoy the most successful career, appointed chief justice by Eisenhower in 1953, though his tenure would prove controversial and provide fodder for Nixon's 1968 campaign.

Beside Dewey, the biggest loser in 1948 was the public pollsters as Gallup and Roper saw their credibility sink. Their misplaced predictions of a Dewey landslide were blamed on several factors. The pollsters had ended their surveys weeks before the election, not measuring the opinion shift in Truman's favor. The third-party candidacies also wreaked havoc with the polls as southern Democrats and urban liberals returned to the Democrat fold once it became apparent Strom Thurmond and Henry Wallace had no chance to win the election or even change the result. The expected Dixiecrat revolt was contained in four states and with Republicans noncompetitive in the state, southern voters lacked any choice beyond Truman. After 1948, pollsters tightened their methods and ensured a continual stream of surveys up to the weekend before the election to measure every change in public opinion. For the next 60 years the pollsters faced no surprises, hedging their bets by emphasizing the margin of error and refusing to declare an outright winner. The greatest failures occurred in the 2000 and 2004 presidential elections with the exit polls predicting Al Gore as the winner of Florida and then John Kerry defeating George W. Bush nationally in 2004. Both predictions proved wrong and forced the pollsters to again reevaluate their techniques.

The Smartest Election

HUGHES VERSUS WILSON, 1916

The victory of a sitting president is not generally considered a presidential upset, but the contest between incumbent Woodrow Wilson and Justice Charles Evans Hughes in 1916 saw the challenger enjoy considerable advantage in terms of running in a Republican-dominated country and during a time of foreign turmoil that cast doubts on Wilson's competence. Only two Democrat presidents were elected between 1860 and 1932: Grover Cleveland and Woodrow Wilson. Cleveland's two terms seemed more a continuation than an interruption of the dominant Republican era. Wilson's two terms would be revolutionary in comparison.

Serving between the conservative William Howard Taft and Warren Harding, Wilson was the most liberal president up to that time. His election in 1912 resulted from a divided Republican party as Taft and Theodore Roosevelt split their party's vote and allowed Wilson to win with a popular vote plurality of 43 percent.

Wilson's narrow victory did not prevent his pursuing an aggressive domestic and foreign policy agenda known as the New Freedom. Facing reelection in 1916 Wilson confronted a united Republican Party in a majority Republican country with his best hope for victory making the campaign a referendum on his New Freedom program.

WILSON ADMINISTRATION

Not since the First Congress and the Republican Congress of the period 1861–1863 did more important legislation pass from the capitol to the White House than in the 63rd Congress that met from 1913 to 1915.[1] During the period Congress passed the Federal Reserve Act, creating the first central bank since 1835 and granting it the task of smoothing out economic excesses while stabilizing the currency. The Clayton Act modified the 1890 Sherman Antitrust Act by creating the Federal Trade Commission to investigate and prosecute restraints of trade. The act immunized labor unions from prosecution for antitrust violations, overturning the 1895 *In Re Debs* case upholding a federal judge's injunction against unions. The Debs case pitted unions against the Cleveland administration and was supported by Cleveland's chief justice, a sign how much the Democrat party changed in 20 years.

The Federal Reserve and Clayton acts targeted the financial industry and manufacturers, but Wilson's other reform, the Smith–Lever Act, targeted farmers, who suffered from excessive debt and an unstable currency. The act created federal extension services that offered information on planting and expanding yield to local farmers. The educational services focused on the small homesteader who lacked basic agricultural knowledge and tended to struggle to survive.

The president moved beyond changing policy to also strengthening the presidency by centralizing power in the White House. Wilson came to depend on Colonel House, a Texan who reflected the president's belief in expert control of government policy. House was a controversial figure as reflected in Henry Cabot Lodge's complaint about him for having excessive influence in the White House. The colonel's views on the government can be found in his dystopian novel, *Philip Dru: Administrator*, a paean to a Platonic dictatorship, run by an intellectual elite.[2]

Wilson's domestic reforms appealed to Democrats on the left and Republican Progressives, but Wilson's foreign policy appealed to few. The assassination of Archduke Ferdinand in Sarajevo in July, 1914 quickly spun out of control into a worldwide conflagration. Finely tuned European diplomacy failed for the first time in a century to settle issues among the major powers before they mobilized.

Watching the war from across the Atlantic, the United States stood as a world economic power whose leaders and people shrank from international involvement. From August 1914 through the presidential election, European governments and their supporters in the United States battled to sway public opinion to their side. Opposing them was a mass of Americans who strictly interpreted Washington's admonition against entangling alliances. Referred to by their opponents as isolationists the antiwar faction believed the United States could only be hurt by international involvement. Its members included the powerful Secretary of State William Jennings Bryan and scores of members of Congress from the Midwest and Mountain West and also millions of ordinary citizens who preferred to stay out of European quarrels.[3]

As Wilson maneuvered between combatants, Bryan pushed for absolute neutrality. In 1915 he took exception to Wilson's sharply stated complaint to the Germans over the sinking of the Lusitania, and fearful that Wilson was leading the country to war, he abruptly resigned. Bryan's departure clarified Wilson's foreign policy as his replacement, Robert Lansing, agreed with the president's view of America's role in the world.

However, if Bryan thought Wilson was too warlike, many thought he was too weak. Primary among these was Theodore Roosevelt, who barnstormed across the country condemning the German military menace and arguing for American intervention. His attacks nettled Wilson who responded with a preparedness program that his War Secretary Lindley Garrison denounced as insufficient and showed his displeasure by resigning.[4]

As continental war raged across the ocean, Wilson was plagued by an older foreign policy problem: political instability in Mexico. The crisis began in the closing days of the Taft administration when General Madero overthrew the Diaz government. Weeks before Wilson's inauguration, General Huerta replaced Madero and began reinstating the Diaz regime. Taft refused to recognize Diaz, leaving the decision to the Wilson administration.[5]

Wilson and Secretary of State Bryan were infused with the fervor of democratic reform and rejected the Huerta regime. The decision angered the Catholic Church which was allied with the regime. When General Venustiano Carranza challenged Huerta, the rebel general was granted American aid including weapons and diplomatic support. A civil war followed, and Wilson ordered a naval blockade to prevent Huerta from receiving German arms. Eventually, Huerta was overthrown, and Carranza installed; however, almost immediately the Wilson administration threw support behind a former Carranza ally, General Pancho Villa.[6]

Carranza created a revolutionary state, forming so-called red battalions to battle Villa and writing a new constitution targeting the Catholic Church by banning its schools, eliminating special rights for priests, and nationalizing church lands. When Villa was defeated, Wilson recognized Carranza's government even as it transformed Mexico into a haven for European socialists exiled from their home countries—the most famous being Leon Trotsky. In 1917 Carranza flirted with the Kaiser's government, the famous Zimmerman telegram promising Mexico the return of its northwestern territories—Arizona, California, and New Mexico—in return for attacking the United States. Wilson's Mexico policy was the one glaring failure in his first term and made an opponent of the Catholic Church, but Wilson's election depended mostly on a divided Republican Party.[7]

REPUBLICAN CANDIDATES

Even with a relatively successful president seeking reelection, opposing Republicans lined up for what would be a hard-fought campaign. The three leading Republican candidates were all from New York, a reflection of the dominance of the party's eastern faction. Senator Elihu Root was the favorite of the conservative wing, whereas Theodore Roosevelt retained the loyalty of Progressive Republicans and Democrats. The third candidate, Charles Evans Hughes, was best positioned to combine both wings of the party, but each man came with electoral baggage.

Elihu Root's support for the protective tariff and opposition to federal economic regulation made him popular with the Republican right wing. His tenures as war secretary and secretary of state offered the necessary foreign policy experience when facing a global war. As senator, though, he took an antiwar stance, voting against Wilson's ship purchase bill that would have spent millions on armoring the American merchant marine. However, Root supported Bryan's policy of selling weapons to all belligerents as a sign of neutrality. Both positions reflected the center of the Republican Party on the war issue.[8]

By 1916, candidates were expected to travel the country, using the rail system to meet and speak to large segments of the population raising concerns that Root at his advanced age—he was 70 in 1915—could not withstand a vigorous campaign. Root also lacked the charisma necessary to inspire swing independent voters who would have to be convinced to vote Republican.

However, Root's liabilities were overshadowed by the advantages of representing New York where he enjoyed broad media coverage and a home advantage at carrying the state's 36 electoral votes, some 15 percent of the total needed for victory. The New York media offered national coverage for Root when following his role as chair of the New York state constitutional convention. In typical New York media fashion, the public referendum on the finished document was treated as a test of his presidential viability. When voters rejected the constitution, the papers pronounced postmortems on Root's candidacy.[9]

When Root delivered the keynote speech at the New York state Republican convention, the New York media hyped it as an opportunity for the senator to revive his candidacy. In his speech Root challenged Wilson's foreign policy credentials, warning American "diplomacy has lost its authority and influence because we have been brave in words but irresolute in action." Root characterized Wilson's Mexico policies as interference in a neighbor's politics.[10]

Reaction to the speech was as divided as the Republican Party. Conservatives worried Root had moved to the left, embracing Roosevelt's bellicose calls for American involvement in the Great War. William Howard Taft declared the speech ended Root's candidacy. Progressives were unconvinced by his attacks on Wilson, remembering Root's opposition to Roosevelt in the 1912 convention and demanded more than a speech to correct that apostasy. Roosevelt's reaction was tepid, and he privately declared he would vote for his old friend rather than Wilson though it was less than a full endorsement considering his views of the president.[11]

Through it all Root remained the preferred establishment candidate, a safe alternative to the unpredictable Roosevelt and the unwilling Hughes. Among Root's partisans were two future secretaries of state, Republicans Frank Kellogg and Henry Stimson from New York, who were economically conservative but internationalist in their foreign policy. Columbia University President Nicholas Murray Butler lobbied Republicans to endorse Root over Charles Evans Hughes.[12]

In addition to the establishment Root garnered some grassroots support. In the winter of 1916 two rudimentary polls offered insight into how the country perceived Root. A poll of Republican newspaper editors, who were influential in molding opinion in the country, had Root leading Hughes. Another smaller survey of Republican state party chairs, responsible for choosing and leading delegates in the party convention, had Hughes leading with Root in third place behind the relatively unknown: Iowa senator Albert Cummins.[13]

At the end of March 1916 Root met with Roosevelt, General Leonard Wood, and Henry Cabot Lodge. The newspapers breathlessly reported it as either Roosevelt endorsing Root or Root welcoming Roosevelt back into the Republican fold. Progressives fretted that their man had rejected them for his old party by meeting with two powerful conservatives. Conservatives worried Root might be endorsing Roosevelt for another presidential run. Neither was true, and the meeting aided neither man.[14] A late April *Literary Digest* poll showed a decline in Root's popularity as Progressive state legislators favored the unannounced candidate Justice Charles Evans Hughes with 758 votes, placing Roosevelt a distant second at 275 and Root in third with 138.[15]

Root's candidacy faltered during the New York Republican convention. Supporters of former New York governor and current Justice Charles Evans Hughes prevented a Root endorsement by the convention. Unable to corral his home state, Root bowed to the inevitable, declining a formal campaign based on his age while holding his delegates to prevent a sudden convention stampede for Roosevelt.

Theodore Roosevelt's hovering presence over the Republican field proved to be both a liability and a benefit to the party. The most popular and best-known Republican politician in the country, Roosevelt had been in a two-decade battle with the party establishment. His election as New York governor ignited a movement by Republican bosses in New York and Pennsylvania to sideline him with a vice-presidential nomination, believing the insignificant job would lead him to political oblivion. William McKinley's assassination put "that damn cowboy" in the White House, and even then President Roosevelt was forced to battle the Republican establishment to earn his nomination in 1904.[16]

Roosevelt appeared to hand back the party to conservatives with his endorsement of William Howard Taft in 1908, but the honeymoon ended abruptly in 1912 when Roosevelt challenged Taft for the Republican nomination and then ran as an independent. Four years had not healed the wounds, and Republicans of all beliefs waited for the former president, still young and brimming with ideas, to announce his intentions. Chastened by Wilson's victory, he deemed a second Wilson term as the greater of two evils even if it meant another Republican was elected. Roosevelt had learned that without a Republican president or Congress his influence was diminished; his speeches on the war and preparedness were ignored in Washington. Reclaiming that influence became more important than personally regaining the White House.

However, a third term appealed to Roosevelt, and he had the choice of two parties to achieve his ambitions. One party, the Progressives, was welcoming while the other, the Republicans, was more disdainful and suspicious of his motives. After 1912, Progressives learned they needed Roosevelt more than he needed them. In the presidential election with Roosevelt heading the Progressive ballot, the party became the most successful third party in terms of electoral votes. However, in the 1914 midterms, without Roosevelt at the top of the ticket, Progressives suffered considerable losses, their 1912 gains nearly wiped out. Maintaining Progressive viability required a second Roosevelt run, and the party's leaders became obsessed with the task of convincing him to accept the party's nomination.[17]

The Progressives labored under weak and contentious leadership, its members occupying the fringes of political power. Among them was a Wall Street lawyer, Bainbridge Colby, New Mexico senator Albert Fall with a prison term in his future, acid-tongued Harold Ickes whose predilection for infighting made him a political liability, and William Allen White, publisher of the *Emporia Gazette* and every liberal's favorite conservative. These men enjoyed little influence within Washington and except for White were unknown among most Americans. Fall and Roosevelt agreed on Mexican policy, forging their relationship. Pancho Villa's raid into New Mexico was blamed on Wilson's bungling of the crisis because Fall and Roosevelt supported more aggressive action against the Mexican bandits. Fall favored the former president as either the Republican or Progressive nominee and delivered the nominating speech for him at the Republican convention.[18]

During much of Wilson's first term, Roosevelt sounded like a presidential candidate. His strong stand on the Great War and criticism of Wilson's weakness hurt him among Progressive allies in the isolationist Mountain and Midwestern states. Many Progressives were natural pacifists who perceived war as a distraction from domestic problems.

Knowing that his presence in the Republican primaries would draw out the long knives of his conservative opponents, Roosevelt made a quiet announcement of interest in the presidency. He began his unofficial presidential campaign while vacationing in the West Indies. In December 1915 he issued his Trinidad statement, both an announcement and a renunciation of the Republican presidential nomination. Roosevelt rejected any interest in the 1916 campaign "unless the country has in its mood something heroic."[19]

The statement alluded to both domestic activism and military preparedness as Roosevelt tossed the gauntlet at Republican conservatives who sought less action and more normalcy. He sought their unconditional surrender to his will and policies in return for riding his coattails to victory. Conservatives, though, seized on Roosevelt's claim of no interest in running another campaign, believing they were finally finished with the "cowboy." Progressives were of two minds. They wished for a Progressive–Republican fusion ticket with Roosevelt at the head. An alternative was a Republican candidate other than Roosevelt running on a Progressive platform to satisfy most in the party and prevent another third-party campaign.[20]

The manager of the Roosevelt boomlet in early 1916 was James Garfield Jr. An Ohio Progressive and the eldest son of the assassinated president, he worked to pull together Progressives from the Midwest, rebuilding the coalition that nearly unseated William Howard Taft in 1912. If Roosevelt was unwilling to run, Progressives sought out potential candidates ranging from Roosevelt's 1912 running mate, Hiram Johnson, to General Black Jack Pershing to run instead of the former president.[21]

The third Republican man was the first major party candidate to be nominated by a political draft. In the early decades of the republic it was considered bad form for a politician to actively seek the presidency. Instead, a man was to be chosen by leaders and the people, a bow to the illusion of a popular "draft". By the 20th century, eagerness for office was considered not only proper but a necessity when seeking the presidency. Justice Charles Evans Hughes's posture of disinterest in the presidency in 1916 seemed like a return to a simpler time.

Hughes's place on the Supreme Court did not preclude a presidential run as several of his judicial predecessors had run for the White House while serving as a justice. Most frequent among these was Justice John McLean (1829–1861). Starting in 1832 and continuing until 1860, McLean sought nominations from various parties: Anti-Masonic, Whig, Free Soil, Know Nothing, and Republican. His best chances came in 1848 when he was the Whig front-runner and in 1856 when he finished second in the Republican convention. In 1848, McLean was joined by Democrat Justice Levi Woodbury, who failed to win his party's nomination. In 1872 Justice David Davis was favored for both the Liberal Republican and Greenback nominations though he never officially announced his candidature. In 1880 and 1884 Justice Stephen Field ran an expensive campaign backed by railroad money for the Democrat nomination but finished far back in the pack.

However, Hughes lived in a different time and under a code of ethics that he believed prohibited a presidential run while serving on the

Supreme Court. Although he rose through the New York Republican ranks until elected governor, he put aside his political ambitions on reaching the Court as associate justice.

By 1910, Hughes was on the cusp of a great political career. Reelected in a Democrat state, the Republican governor had the reputation as a reformer who shared Republican views on the tariff and economic regulation while challenging corruption and rejecting the reactionaries in both parties. One barrier to Hughes's continued rise was President William Howard Taft, who would be seeking reelection in 1912. Taft may have recognized Hughes as a Progressive threat to his nomination. Eliminating the threat was a delicate assignment as Taft sought a position high enough to attract Hughes while removing him from the political scene. Fortunately for Taft during his four years as president, six Supreme Court vacancies opened. Justice Rufus Peckham's death provided Taft the opportunity to appoint Hughes associate justice, and he dangled the chief justice's office before Hughes when it became vacant. The governor accepted the nomination and would later become the first justice to serve two separate terms on the Court.

Hughes became the junior member of the Supreme Court whose membership seemed to change by the month. Within two years he was the fifth most senior member, and when he left in 1916 was the de facto leader of the progressive bloc. His six years witnessed the Court retreat from a strict reading of the interstate commerce clause, a weakening of the liberty to contract doctrine and offering new protections for criminal defendants. Hughes redefined old doctrines and was on the verge of a career as a great justice before he was nominated. His greatness as a justice would come 14 years later when he was appointed chief justice by Herbert Hoover.

Hughes wrote two critical opinions during his six-year tenure. In *Houston, East and West Texas Railway CO v. United States* he ruled intrastate commerce that had a close and substantial effect on interstate commerce could be regulated by Congress.[22] This opened new paths for federal regulation and fit neatly with the Wilson administration's desire to regulate all areas of commerce. In *Bailey v. Alabama,* Hughes continued the Republican tradition of fighting for civil rights in the south. In Bailey he used the 13th Amendment to strike an Alabama peonage law as a violation of the involuntary servitude clause. Under Alabama law, petty criminals could have their fines paid by others and then be forced to work at private employment until the fine was paid off. Hughes noted the peonage statute was used most frequently against black defendants and continued the southern tradition of involuntary servitude.[23]

Hughes public successes shielded his private troubles as he struggled with the workload, writing decisions with little help, and wading through hundreds of cases, many of them minor and irrelevant. His struggles dropped him into a state of depression, and Hughes sought out the help of psychologists who used electric shock treatments to cure his problem. Hughes's colleague Chief Justice Edward White witnessed one of these treatments and noted it in his diary.[24]

However, Hughes refused to run, publicly rejecting attempts to draft him. In 1915 as a draft-Hughes campaign gained steam, the justice issued repeated denials of interest in the presidency. In a letter dated May 20, 1915 Hughes announced "I have no right to be a candidate openly or passively. I must, therefore, ask that no steps be taken to bring my name before the convention."[25] Nine months later when his name was mentioned along with Root and Roosevelt as Republican front-runners, Hughes released a statement that "I am entirely out of politics, I am totally opposed to the use of my name in connection with the nomination."[26]

The justice's efforts to withdraw from the nomination process were for naught. In April 1916, William Howard Taft prodded him, confiding that Hughes was the only man who could build a Progressive–Republican coalition. Taft dismissed Root as a weak candidate and Roosevelt as unelectable while former vice president Charles Fairbanks was stale. According to Taft's reasoning this left the field open for the justice, and he correctly predicted Roosevelt would support Hughes when he was nominated.[27]

As Hughes became a front-runner against his wishes, the justice received advice about his future from unexpected sources. Wilson's vice president Thomas Marshall praised him for refusing to campaign, his words revealing the party's nervousness at a Hughes nomination and the belief they could dissuade him by dropping hints that the justice would be promoted to chief justice after the aging Edward White left the bench. Even White, a Grover Cleveland Democrat, advised Hughes that he was next in line for the Court's center chair. Some doubt likely entered Hughes's mind having being passed over for the position of chief justice by the Republican Taft and wondering if the Democrat Wilson would appoint a Republican to the seat.

However, the draft campaign continued, and when a petition drive gathered enough signatures and put his name on the Nebraska ballot,

Hughes threatened a lawsuit. On May 3, the Michigan state Republican convention endorsed him, and two weeks later the noncandidate won the Vermont and Oregon primaries, knocking his closest competitor Senator Cummins out of the race and making the justice the front-runner. At the convention he would be the most unusual front-runner in history because he lacked a campaign structure that otherwise would have distributed signs and buttons while paying supporters in the gallery to cheer his name. However, Hughes enjoyed one large advantage, a scared and quiescent party that feared a repeat of 1912. With neither Root nor Roosevelt able to attract sufficient support from either wing of the Republican Party, the decision was made to drag an unwilling Hughes to an unwanted nomination.

With neither Roosevelt nor Root announcing their candidacy and Hughes rejecting even a draft campaign, lesser known Republicans sought to fill the vacuum. Boomlets lit up the Republican field in 1915 and 1916 including one for Idaho Senator William Borah, a Progressive Republican whose record suggested he could appeal to both the Progressive and Republican vote. Borah was safe for conservatives on the tariff, battling against the tariff rates cut of the Underwood Tariff Act. Borah had Roosevelt's tacit approval, but being from a small state his support was limited to the Mountain West, and he was not considered a serious threat for the nomination. Albert Cummins, Iowa senator and Progressive, seized the opportunity to sweep several primaries with Hughes and Roosevelt not on the ballot. Campaigning as a fusion candidate who could combine Progressive and conservative ideals, he opposed the Underwood tariff while warning Eastern Republicans against appointing a regional candidate who could not appeal to the Midwest and Mountain West voters. Cummins's advice would be ignored.[28]

California Governor Hiram Johnson offered his name as the Progressive candidate. As Roosevelt's vice-presidential running mate in 1912 Johnson enjoyed the undying loyalty of the Progressives and the unrelenting enmity of conservative Republicans. Johnson's California base was less critical in 1916 than in future years as the state boasted only 13 electoral votes. Johnson had also crusaded against strict partisanship, introducing referendums and primaries that allowed candidates to win the Republican and Democrat nomination at the same time. His ideas were unappealing to most of the country and after announcing an interest in the nomination quickly withdrew after support dried up. Instead, Johnson played a negative role in the presidential election, hurting Hughes in California and handing the election to Wilson. Other favorite sons including Roosevelt's old vice president Charles Fairbanks and Wisconsin Senator Robert La Follette entered the early primaries.

DEMOCRAT CONVENTION

The 1916 Democrat convention was the calmest Democrat gathering since Grover Cleveland's nomination in 1892. Wilson lacked appreciable opposition though his managers feared the presence of William Jennings Bryan, who was attending the convention as a journalist rather than politician. Denied delegate credentials for the 1916 convention by his home state of Nebraska, which also defeated his brother Charles for the Democrat gubernatorial nomination, Bryan acquired press credentials for his newspaper, the *Commoner*, and watched the convention as observer rather than participant for the first time in 20 years.[29]

The dull nominating speech of New York governor Martin Glynn for Wilson awakened Democrat yearning for the stem-winding Bryan, fresh from his Chautauqua tours. As the delegates demanded that the three-time nominee speak, Bryan mounted the rostrum while Wilson's men watched the convention's one unscripted moment with trepidation. They feared Bryan would sink their candidate or even seize control of the convention, much as he had in 1896. However, Bryan was unconcerned about the man in the White House, instead using the speech to place his final imprint on the Democrat party. He began by praising the New Freedom domestic agenda, much of it reflected in his three presidential platforms.[30] However, it was the war in Europe about which Bryan cared the most: his declaration that Wilson "kept us out of war" was foisted upon the party as a campaign slogan. Bryan was greeted by each of the 1,200 Democrat delegates—a sign of his continuing popularity though as an icon rather than a leader.[31]

The president's advisors struggled to use the old commoner during the fall campaign. Memories of three presidential defeats and the taint of radicalism attached to Bryan made Wilson and Colonel House wary of using him. However, Bryan refused to be sidelined. His nationwide Chautauqua tour earned him a generous income and offered a public platform that could be used against Wilson's foreign policy. An angry Bryan could damage Wilson by suppressing the populist and Progressive vote in the plains and Mountain West.

The Democrats initially planned a Bryan tour in the decidedly un- friendly east and Mid- Atlantic with stops in Pennsylvania, New York, and Massachusetts, states considered solidly in the Republican col- umn. Colonel House and Wilson feared that Bryan would offend these voters, his brand of populism unlikely to sway residents of industrial states. After a discussion with Wilson's son-in-law William McAdoo, Bryan agreed to change his tour to the more friendly territories of the plains, including his home state of Nebraska and the Mountain West with their silver mining interests.[32]

Starting on Constitution Day, September 17, Bryan made his first speech for Wilson in Reno, Nevada, focusing on the issue closest to his heart, an isolationist foreign policy. Bryan told the assembled crowd that Wilson shared his desire to prevent every "single Ameri- can mother's son from bleed(ing) and dying in the settlement of some kings' dispute."[33] His tours through isolationist areas allowed Bryan to openly express his disgust with war while promoting the Wilson ad- ministration. In using Bryan, the Wilson campaign implicitly tied itself to the antiwar cause while retaining the ability to hedge on the war issue in parts of the country where Bryan's pacifism was unpopular. The former secretary of state performed two large favors for the presi- dent, leaving his administration to allow Wilson to conduct a more effective foreign policy and campaigning for Wilson on the war issue and helping the Democrats win the west and plains states.

NEW FREEDOM COMPLETED

Modern elections consume an entire year with presidents unable to pass significant legislation while the campaign rages. Wilson proved the rare exception as the summer of 1916 proved an unexpectedly ac- tive legislative period. While Hughes campaigned around the country, Wilson was busy enacting the remainder of his agenda including the first federal minimum wage for rail workers, a ban on child labor, and in the spring his preparedness bill that included the Hayden amend- ment for a peacetime military draft.

Wilson's Democrat predecessor, Grover Cleveland, had attempted the same strategy in his reelection campaign. Cleveland had remained in Washington during the summer of 1888 trying to pass the Mills tariff bill but was stymied in his efforts by a Republican Senate, dashing his reelection hopes. Wilson's decision to focus on legislation rather than campaign was a calculated gamble, much as it had been for Cleveland. However, Wilson enjoyed one critical advantage over Cleveland, a Democrat-controlled Congress. In 1888 Cleveland depended on Republicans who had little incentive to help a Democrat president, but in 1916 Democrat members of Congress were willing to pass legislation.

Through the first half of 1916 the nation faced a strike as railroad workers threatened to walk off the job if their wages were not raised or their working day cut from 10 hours to eight. Wilson faced an economic disaster as most passenger and freight traffic was carried by railroads. Fortunately for him railroad workers were considered as part of interstate commerce which allowed the federal government to act.

Instead of a long arbitration process, Wilson supported a bill proposed by Georgia Democrat Congressman William Adamson, chairman of the House Interstate Commerce Committee, setting an eight-hour workday for railway workers. It passed in August 1916 and became the template for New Deal and state laws mandating an eight-hour workday. The act proved popular among rail workers, who saw their pay for every hour of work increase but displeased many railroads and those not associated with the industry. The Adamson Act benefitted Wilson in Ohio, known as the home of Republican presidents, because many railroad workers in the state saw their wages increase.[34]

Passing child labor legislation proved more difficult. The employment of children in textile and furniture mills in the south offered a competitive advantage to the region over the same mills in northern states—many of which had banned child labor under the prodding of Progressives and labor unions. With industries moving south to take advantage of cheap labor, a federal ban on child labor was proposed to save northern union jobs. Wilson was cast between two large constituencies, loyal southerners representing the Democrat base and Progressives and unions that provided the key votes in northern states. Balancing these, the president guided the Keating–Owen Act through Congress. The law banned the interstate shipment of products made by child labor and was a broad and controversial expansion of federal authority over labor issues, usually considered the province of the state. Keating–Owen would not survive Wilson's second term, the Supreme Court in *Hammer v. Dagenhart* striking the law as exceeding the commerce powers of Congress.[35]

The burst of legislating by Wilson coincided with the end of the Progressive courting of Roosevelt. Wilson interpreted the 1914 midterms as Progressives returning to the Republican fold with most the GOP congressional gains coming from Progressives rather than Democrats. Wilson likely surmised without Roosevelt in the field that the lackluster Hughes would struggle to attract Progressives while Wilson's child labor and minimum wage laws appealed to disaffected Roosevelt voters in the Midwest and Mountain West.[36] Wilson's success at fusing the Progressive and Democrat parties changed the latter as he co-opted the third party's agenda with Progressives such as Bainbridge Colby, Harold Ickes, and Henry Wallace serving in high office in the Wilson or Franklin Roosevelt administrations.

Wilson's legislating handed the Democrats control over the message of the campaign. Republicans were forced to react to the new laws and generally criticized Wilson's activism. Hughes in particular took issue with the minimum wage law but in doing so alienated key groups including blue-collar workers and farmers.

PICKING HUGHES

As the Republican convention approached, the draft-Hughes movement was on the cusp of victory. The movement was operated by former Postmaster General Frank Hitchcock and investment banker Frank Meyer, who agreed to finance a Hughes candidacy after a happenstance meeting in late 1915. Hitchcock had strong political instincts, whereas Meyer was the financial genius whose acumen on Wall Street impressed even J. P. Morgan who said the trader could "end up having all of the money on Wall Street." Hitchcock sought out Meyer's advice on commodities' trading and also to measure his support for a Hughes's candidacy. Meyer was bullish on the former New York governor, and he agreed to fund the draft effort while Hitchcock collected Republican delegates for the summer's convention.[37]

Hitchcock's and Meyer's participation in the draft-Hughes movement raised red flags for Progressives. They remembered Hitchcock as Taft's 1912 campaign manager and the man who bullied Republican delegates to deny Roosevelt the party's nomination. Meyer was also the financier of more than one Republican old guard campaign, and his Wall Street connections were another tie to the very faction from which the Progressives wanted to wrest the party.

Hitchcock faced a slowly forming primary system that included a healthy number of state conventions which chose a majority of the national delegates. It was the same primary system used by Theodore Roosevelt in his 1912 challenge to William Howard Taft. Roosevelt scored victory after victory in states such as Wisconsin, Iowa, Nebraska, and Oregon, showing his popularity with American voters. Yet, most of the national party convention delegates were chosen at state party conventions controlled by state party leaders loyal to Taft, who was easily nominated. Four years later regional candidates would seek to use the primaries to enhance their national stature and their case before the convention, but once again the primaries would serve only to stop candidacies rather than propelling them to victory.

The early primaries of spring 1916 saw Senator Cummins roll up primary wins in Iowa, Minnesota, South Dakota, Nebraska, Colorado, and Montana, states where Republicans had lost or narrowly won in 1912. Unfortunately for Cummins his election victories and his experience would not overcome his weakness as a stump speaker. Progressives were spoiled by their candidates William Jennings Bryan and Theodore Roosevelt who held audiences' attention with their style and ideas. Cummins was better suited for the set-piece speeches of the Senate, the type of delivery that chased away Progressive voters.

Even as Cummins won smaller primaries against favorite son candidates, he struggled against Hughes. In Vermont, Hughes and Cummins faced off with the justice winning without campaigning. The end for Cummins came in Oregon, where Hughes easily defeated him. The senator was reduced to favorite son status after failing to beat nothing with something. The biggest loser was the Republican primary system. The lackluster 1916 primary season showed a lack of interest among voters and candidates and sparked a shift in state support for primaries as two Progressive states, Iowa and Minnesota, eliminated the elections in 1917.[38]

Even though he was not a formal candidate, Hughes enjoyed media coverage of his public appearances. In early 1916 Hughes addressed the New York State Bar Association, his words parsed for any sign he was considering a presidential run. Instead of a political speech, Hughes offered a boiler plate judicial speech, complaining about the difficulties faced by judges forced to interpret poorly drawn legislation, a perennial complaint of judges usually ignored by legislatures. Hughes went further with a *sub silentio* endorsement of the Wilson–Progressive agenda of delegating government decision making to expert commissions rather than through democratic legislation. Favoring elite rule Hughes was at odds with the Bryan Progressivism that sought community action through democratic means and the Republican belief in free markets solving problems. The *Nation*, journal of Progressive elitism, offered fulsome praise for Hughes, writing that his speech should be "read and pondered and that the justice's view represented a combination of fruitful experience and a singularly rich mind."[39]

After his victory in the Oregon primary and with Root and Roosevelt unable to spark a movement, Hughes was the front-runner entering the Chicago convention on June 17. The only obstacle for Hughes was the unexpected, such as the Progressive convention meeting a short distance away.

Even with the Progressives hovering offstage and preparing a Roosevelt nomination to rekindle the 1912 party split, the Republican convention was a dull affair. New Mexico Senator Albert Fall received tepid applause after nominating Roosevelt. On the first ballot Hughes collected 253 delegates with Root as his closest competitor with 103 and Roosevelt far back in third place with 65. Hughes widened his lead with 328 votes in the second ballot. At this point the convention adjourned, seeming to stop Hughes's momentum to the nomination and reaching the point where past Republican front-runners such as James Blaine, William Seward, and Ulysses Grant saw their hopes dashed.[40]

However, Hughes faced a divided opposition. Returning to their Chicago hotels, conservative leaders were unable to agree on a candidate as Root was unable to ignite the convention. Progressives held out hope for a third-party Roosevelt run but enjoyed no influence with the Republican delegates. The next day the convention nominated Hughes on the third ballot and chose Charles Fairbanks, Roosevelt's vice president, for vice president. Hearing of his nomination via telegram Hughes sent a return telegram to the convention accepting the nomination and then composed a terse resignation letter to the man he would spend the next five months trying to unseat.[41]

The Republican campaign started slowly as Hughes struggled to adjust from the cloistered halls of the Supreme Court to the active days of a national campaign. Wilson who enjoyed speechmaking and debate had the inherent advantage of having running a national campaign in 1912. The president even revived the tradition of the George Washington era of making the State of the Union address in person rather than delegating the duty to a House clerk.

Hughes's first campaign speech in Carnegie Hall was a clarion call for a dull campaign. Entitled "America First and America Efficient," Hughes sounded like a justice reading an opinion in a tax case, focusing on policy minutiae rather than offering broad and bold proposals. With war raging in Europe, Hughes proposed international law enforced by an international court but offered no thoughts on whether he would maintain neutrality when confronting a widening world conflict. Hughes struggled with his stump speeches over the campaign's first five-week period between the middle of August and the end of September. His route took him through the Midwest, plains states, Mountain West, and Pacific West. Making daily speeches, Hughes resembled a nervous novice, offering only platitudes with promises of greater "efficiency" "effectiveness" and "consistency" in domestic and foreign policy. His speeches offered little reason for undecided voters to reject Wilson; instead, his words were tailored to ensure that neither Republican conservatives nor Progressives were offended.[42]

With Wilson's victory in 1912 fresh in his mind, Hughes adopted the conventional wisdom that he could defeat the president simply with a unified Republican Party. He focused his campaign on maintaining party unity, offering no policy to offend either faction. Yet, his deliberate blandness did not appeal to a generally contented public and offered no basis for removing Wilson in favor of a new president. This was particularly true for many westerners who were suspicious of eastern candidates with Wall Street ties. Hughes's five-week campaign swing through much of the country proved a disaster. According to the editors of the *Nation*, Hughes was campaigning as if following a "predetermined plan" that was a "woeful disappointment." Hughes fell back on a "routine and humdrum Republicanism" that "offended nobody and won nobody," while he "left the country cold."[43]

WILSON CAMPAIGN

As he focused on his legislative agenda for the summer, Wilson turned campaign planning over to Colonel House who chose a grassroots campaign, announcing he would "run the president as Justice of the Peace." Working on the assumption that each of the two parties enjoyed a base support of 40 percent no matter who the candidate was, House focused on the 20 percent of independents or swing voters. Among these swing voters were those in the plains and Mountain West, a region that swung Democrat during William Jennings Bryan's three runs and voted with Wilson in 1912. Using local and state Democrat organizations, House identified Progressive voters, and the Wilson campaign flooded them with information. The Democrat campaign also taunted Hughes during his cross-country tour, taking out full-page advertisements in newspapers of the cities he was visiting. The advertisements posed questions for Hughes to answer during his visit, hoping to either embarrass the Republican or distract him from his campaign speeches. While the advertisements did not seem to affect Hughes, they did offer a counterargument to the Republican campaign.[44]

Wilson collected endorsements from prominent politicians and business leaders, most of who were expected to support Hughes. Among these was Bainbridge Colby, Progressive leader and wholehearted Roosevelt supporter. Colby's endorsement represented slippage for Hughes among Republican Progressives. Wilson would not forget his endorsement and appointed Colby secretary of state in 1920. Enjoying greater public acclaim was industrialist Henry Ford and inventor Thomas Edison, both of whom joined the Wilson reelection effort. The Republican Ford endorsed the president but with conditions. The consummate capitalist Ford agreed to fund billboards for Wilson but only if Ford's name also appeared. Edison was less concerned with self-promotion, endorsing Wilson and answering Republican charges the president was a bungler by noting Wilson "usually blunders ahead," a smack at the supposedly reactionary opposition.[45]

Individual endorsements attracted brief, positive newspaper attention, but group endorsements were more valuable. Wilson and Hughes struggled to gain the support of two key ethnic groups, the Germans and the Irish, with their endorsement tied closely to the American government's response to events in Europe.

HYPHENATED AMERICANS

Mass immigration of the mid and late 19th century had changed the country's ethnic makeup from an overwhelming Anglo-Saxon majority to a mixture of Irish, German, and southern Europeans. The start of the Great War reignited old world prejudices with German immigrants cheering the advances of Kaiser and his armies in the early days of the war while cursing the English blockade of their country. Support for the German war cause was strongest in cities with large immigrant populations including Cincinnati, St. Louis, and Omaha. The German language press offered a different interpretation of the war than English-oriented newspapers which described the bloodlust of the "Huns'" and the brutality of their occupation of Belgium.[46]

The American press focused on atrocities and condemned German militarism and predicted an eventual allied victory, whereas German language papers attacked any American politician seeking U.S. entry into the war. Their first target was Theodore Roosevelt, who lobbied for immediate American entry on the allied side, pressing and criticizing Wilson for a feckless foreign policy. The German American leadership targeted Roosevelt for defeat during the 1916 primary and convention season though their opposition had little effect on the former president's chances as he had collected enough Republican enemies to already deny him the nomination. The same was true for Elihu Root as Germans took offense at his hard-line speech at the New York Republican convention.[47]

One influential German American leader was George Viereck, publisher of the German American daily The *Fatherland*. Viereck became an American propaganda arm of the German government though he was unable to convince the Kaiser's government to finance his efforts. Viereck was dedicated to the mission of presenting the German side of the story, denouncing pro-British stories that portrayed German atrocities in Belgium and France. Instead, Viereck presented an idealized version of the German occupation of those territories, passing on official German military reports to his American readers. With Wilson's disdain for the German American press and suspicions about the loyalty of German Americans, it was inevitable Republicans would become the default party for German voters. However, Hughes was hurt by Theodore Roosevelt, who made speeches echoing Wilson's attacks on hyphenated Americans and chased away some German voters. As the election approached, a frustrated Viereck declared that if Hughes lost it was because he "permitted his Machiavellian advisor, Theodore Roosevelt, to drive the German-Americans into the Wilson camp."[48]

Instead of courting the German vote, Wilson clashed with the German press accusing the newspapers of serving as an extension of the Kaiser's government. Germans suspected Wilson favored Great Britain even as he preached neutrality: his friendly relationship with the British government was a sign he favored the Allies over the central powers. German criticism of the President drew a stern rebuke as Wilson launched an attack on hyphenism or the practice of immigrants identifying themselves as German-Americans or Irish-Americans. This revived an old American suspicion that immigrants remained loyal to their home country. He warned these groups were undermining U.S. security to aid their homelands and proposed federal laws banning anti-American conspiracies, a broad and vague term that would become the Espionage Acts of 1917.[49]

Wilson's war policy was perceived by many Irish Americans as tilting toward Britain. Irish immigrants had formed a powerful interest group in large urban areas on the east coast including Boston. These immigrants—some who were two generations separated from their homeland—aided their compatriots with money and weapons to fight the English. With the British Army occupied in Flanders and the Somme, the Irish made their bid for independence, and the Easter Rebellion of 1916 spelled the eventual end to British occupation. As the war ground down the British, the Irish realized a continuation of the conflict weakened their enemy, and a German victory was likely to lead to immediate independence. Any American help to prop up the British might make the fight for Irish independence longer and bloodier. The usual Irish affinity for Democrats was tempered by Wilson's perceived anti-German and pro-British tilt, but Theodore Roosevelt's pro-war speeches and attacks on Germany also made Republicans suspect. As the Wilson campaign's tenor turned nasty toward immigrant groups, the Irish faced a difficult choice in their adopted homeland.

The president used the same approach to Irish opposition as he did to German Americans by dividing the ethnic group. His main weapon was the O'Leary letter, an Irish Catholic activist's attack on the president which included a prediction that Wilson would be defeated if he refused to change his Irish policy. Wilson responded pugnaciously, declaring O'Leary had greater "access to many disloyal Americans," and the president did not want their vote.[50] The president went further, attacking immigrants for practicing hyphenism and denouncing "small alien elements" such as O'Leary who were more loyal to their homeland than their adopted land. It was a rare to witness a president seeking reelection publicly attacking a major voting bloc, but Wilson and his advisors decided to run on a patriotism platform, using immigrants as a "wedge" issue and tying Hughes to foreign elements and hostile governments. The Democrat campaign was quick to assert that a Hughes presidency would lead to conflict, offering their campaign slogan of "Hughes with Roosevelt and War." The accusation could not be taken seriously as Hughes's lack of foreign policy experience was a more believable attack line than an accusation he was the dupe of some foreign cabal.[51]

THE CAMPAIGN

With Wilson stoking ethnic tensions while appealing to the native American vote, Republicans struggled to find an issue to excite voters against the president. Since the 1880s, Republican candidates had hammered at the tariff issue, tying it to employment and nationalism. While Democrats decried high taxes and high prices created by tariffs, Republicans focused on the threat of foreign goods flooding the country. They warned that without a tariff, domestic manufacturing could not compete with low cost Europeans goods. Competition would not only hurt big business but also the workers they employed with mass unemployment and economic disaster following any cut in the tariff much less the free trade policies that Republicans accused Democrats of supporting.

By 1910 the tariff issue had sagged in importance. The battle over the Payne Aldrich tariff in that year led to Republicans losing their congressional majorities because voters came to believe high tariffs benefited special interests while raising the prices for consumers. The Underwood tariff, passed by a Democrat Congress in 1913, lowered tariff rates and cut the price of goods while the lost revenue was made up by imposition of the newly ratified income taxes that affected mainly the wealthy. The *Nation* was quick to assert that the tariff issue was a "prehistoric and unthinking doctrine."[52]

The European war complicated the tariff question for Republicans. With the Europeans desperate for supplies, the American economy boomed, providing food and manufactured goods for the allies. The economy was lifted out of a brief recession while the amount of imports into the United States declined because much of the European continent was cut off by naval blockade. The Republican warning that the Underwood tariff cut would cause mass privation and a flood of imports was not supported by events as the economy expanded. Prosperity with a lower tariff required Republicans to shift their arguments. Agreeing that foreign competition was not a danger during the war, they argued that when the war ended Europeans would again become economic competition for the United States; without a tariff, dire Republican predictions would come true. Republicans noted Wilson would not raise tariffs, but a President Hughes would enact a protective tariff and save jobs.[53]

The Democrat legislative success during the summer offered several tempting targets for the Republicans, but Hughes was unable to use them to spark public interest in his campaign. During a Nashville speech, Hughes criticized the Adamson Act, arguing the law eliminated the freedom for business and workers as the government set wages and hours. Workers could no longer decide their workday, whereas wages would be set by government rather than through what the business thought a worker was worth. On a less abstract level Hughes lashed out at Wilson for surrendering to unpopular unions and providing special benefits to a special class of workers. When Hughes's denunciation of Adamson provoked questions about his support for repeal, Hughes offered a memorable epigram while dodging the question by noting "a surrender cannot be repealed." In attacking the eight-hour law, Hughes alienated the rail workers in swing states such as Ohio that benefitted from it; however, in tying the law to unpopular labor unions, it showed up as another form of special interest legislation that benefitted the politically powerful at the cost to ordinary workers.[54] The *Nation* complimented Hughes's renewed vigor, complimenting him for not pandering to the German population while in St. Louis and taking on unions in Nashville. The Tennessee speech was seen as the "turning point in the campaign."[55]

Hughes's struggles on the stump were matched by his difficulties in uniting the Republican Party. Hughes understood he would have to convince Progressives and conservatives to coalesce around his candidacy, but divisions among Republicans in Ohio and California doomed the justice. In Ohio a regional split among the conservative northern half and the more Progressive southern half of the state threatened the Hughes's campaign. In 1914 Warren Harding had won the first popular Senate election held in the state. Harding's manager, Harry Daugherty, was already planning the senator's presidential run having managed to get Harding named as chair of the 1916 Republican convention. In the spring of 1916 Daugherty sought the Republican nomination for the other Ohio Senate seat. His opponent was former governor Myron Herrick, who represented the Progressive wing that included another Progressive governor, Walter Brown. When Hughes spoke glowingly of Herrick and the governor won the primary, Daugherty blamed the justice for his defeat.[56]

The bitterness between Republican factions placed Hughes in the impossible position of trying to build a winning coalition of the two Republican regions. Winning Ohio was critical for the justice because as modern commentators repeat endlessly, no Republican has won the presidency without the state.

The problems in Ohio were less a split between conservatives and Progressives and more a dispute over patronage and political power. Beyond Ohio, Hughes struggled with Republican Progressives who saw him as the conqueror of their hero Roosevelt and as too close to Republican conservatives such as Root, who controlled the party apparatus. Hughes was dismayed to be classified as too conservative, his New York record of fighting utilities and signing Progressive laws, combined with his Progressive voting record on the Supreme Court, placing him in the left wing of his party. Moreover, Wilson had moved the political debate decidedly to the left—passage of the Federal Reserve Act, creation of the Federal Trade Commission, and the Clayton Acts' strengthening of the antitrust law going beyond Hughes's state centric progressivism. Wilson's use of the presidency as the focus of domestic policy—as an activist executive beyond even Roosevelt's frenetic presidency—exceeded Hughes's philosophy of federal–state relations. Wilson represented the progressivism of the future, his new freedoms inspiring the New Deal. Hughes represented the progressivism of the past, focusing on state over federal power with a suspicion of national authority.

The justice also suffered the slings and arrows of his Republican rivals who considered themselves more deserving of the party nomination than Hughes. Among these was the egotistical Roosevelt—his campaign speeches sounding more presidential than those of Hughes, his calls of intervention in Europe hurting Hughes who tried to straddle the issue of the Great War and pull in the ethnic vote that Wilson had alienated. In California, Governor Hiram Johnson was running for the Senate, using his progressive party machine to run against the establishment Republican machine.

After Roosevelt refused to run as a Progressive, Johnson lived under the delusion he was the one true national Progressive politician, and his anger at Roosevelt was turned against Hughes. The governor declared he saw no reason to "break our necks on this campaign," and complained "I never did submit to discipline and I am not going to now." In his official endorsement of Hughes, Johnson made it a personal endorsement, saying he would vote for Hughes but would not direct his Progressive followers to do the same. Johnson's unwillingness to support the Republican national ticket was not the actions of a mature political mind but instead resembled an adolescent temper tantrum.[57]

However, Johnson was not the only California politician to place control of the state party above Hughes's presidential chances. California conservatives had been scorched by Johnson's attacks and antics as governor. Defeating him for the Senate became a calling because they refused to allow Johnson to appear with Hughes in joint campaign appearances around the state. Hughes did not object, struggling to balance his candidacy between the Progressive and conservative wings of the party. The absence of Johnson at his rallies sent a signal to Progressives that their leader was not wholly behind Hughes or considered part of the national Republican campaign.[58]

Johnson's outsized ego then blew a simple misunderstanding into a major dispute when Hughes stopped at a Long Beach hotel for the evening. Governor Johnson was also a guest at the hotel, but the two men would never meet. Several reasons have been given for this including their conflicting schedules, Hughes being unaware Johnson was in the hotel; the two men being uncertain of the protocol—whether Hughes should visit Johnson or the governor should call on the presidential candidate. Whatever the reason, the split was widened because the two men would not put aside their differences over a handshake or a cup of coffee. Johnson was also offended by what he perceived as a snub of his wife, who was not allowed on a platform with Hughes during one of his campaign stops. In response, California newspapers associated with Hiram Johnson endorsed the governor for the Senate and Woodrow Wilson for president.[59]

Besides Johnson, other Progressives also looked upon Hughes suspiciously. The candidate tried to placate Roosevelt supporters including the irascible Harold Ickes. The old curmudgeon—the moniker earned during Franklin Roosevelt's administration—was appointed to the campaign staff, but when Ickes offered advice it was ignored, infuriating the tempestuous Progressive. In Wisconsin, Robert La Follette passed on the opportunity to campaign with Hughes while in Pennsylvania the Progressive Amos Pinchot endorsed Wilson. The Republican *Ohio State Journal* endorsed Wilson.[60] Hughes proposed fusion tickets with Progressives in Illinois, Oregon, and Nebraska, but the state parties refused to join with the Republicans. Even more humiliating for Hughes was the refusal of New York's Progressives to join the Republicans and endorse the former governor. Hughes was endorsed by James Garfield Jr. who rallied Ohio Progressives and Indiana Senator Albert Beveridge, the double endorsements giving Hughes some advantage in both swing states.[61]

However, many Progressives embraced Wilson much as they had Roosevelt in 1912, both men appealing to the belief of educated elite in using government to rein in private enterprise. The populist progressivism of William Jennings Bryan was rejected by many east coast intellectuals who sneered at its folksy rural and religious roots. Bryan's populism dismissed elite and bureaucratic rule in favor of more popular control of government and community solutions to problems.

Wilson's academic background and his writings on government heightened his appeal among liberals who wanted to change the Democrats into the intellectual party. The southern tilt of the party was slowly changing as the Midwest, plains, and mountain states moved into Wilson's column in 1912 and 1916. While the Hughes–Wilson campaign offered the two deepest intellects among candidates since Adams and Jefferson in 1800, Progressives overwhelming approved of Wilson's activist presidency versus Hughes's emphasis on limited power and more economic freedom for private enterprise. For the first time, liberal Democrats saw their vision of a Hamiltonian presidency active in legislating and expanding executive power become reality.

The dullness of the campaign and the bickering within the Republican Party did not prevent negative campaigning even as 1916 would be remembered as one of the cleanest presidential elections. On the Republican side, Theodore Roosevelt, who was in perpetual campaign mode, launched broadsides against Wilson, comparing him to Presidents Pierce and Buchanan, the two worse Democrats ever to serve in the White House up to that moment. It was doubtful many voters were familiar with either man's record, and it was a return to the bloody shirt tactics discarded in 1880. Roosevelt embarrassed Hughes with militaristic calls for American involvement in the Great War frightening some voters who worried about his bellicose threats to defeat the Kaiser. Roosevelt criticized Wilson for his lack of war preparation, accusing the president of being "too proud to fight and too proud to prepare."[62]

Wilson's surrogates responded on the foreign policy issue but proved less effective at their task. Attempting to defend American involvement in Mexico, War Secretary Newton Baker offered an odd explanation of Mexican troops' depredations. Baker noted that George Washington's troops broke into churches, stole, and melted down gold religious objects; the same accusations were also leveled against Mexican troops. The continental soldiers also stole supplies from civilians, according to Newton, making them the same as Huerta's Mexican irregulars. The comparison drew howls from Republicans; Baker tried to backpedal, but the damage was done.[63]

The Democrats' main charge leveled against Hughes was his foreign policy inexperience and ties to Roosevelt. Democrat campaign pamphlets accused the justice of meeting with German and Irish groups and making a secret deal in order to win the ethnic vote. Having adopted Bryan's mantra that Wilson had kept the country out of war, Democrats simultaneously tied the justice to the pro-German press and also to the war faction in the Republican Party that wanted to attack Germany. More consistent was their characterizing of Hughes as a tool of Wall Street, a charge that resonated in the Midwest where large banks were considered a worse enemy than the Kaiser.[64]

PREDICTIONS AND POLLS

Polling has become as much a part of American presidential campaigns as speeches, heated rhetoric, and negative advertising. Polling became a widely used tool starting in 1940 with polling companies such as Gallup and Roper offering predictions based on scientific and systematic measures of public opinion. In 1916 those measures were not available with the surveys lacking the scientifically imposed randomness that was necessary for reliable predictions. The mail remained the main method of communication—phones still a luxury in many households—and conducting a survey required an extensive mailing list. Political and news periodicals held such lists and used them to survey their readers. The periodicals also polled newspaper editors and state political leaders who offered insights into how their state and local population would vote. Two publications, the *Nation* and the *Literary Digest*, conducted surveys and published their results to attract readers. By early 1916 the polling revealed a close race as a combined Republican vote exceeded support for Wilson. While the polls were taken before Hughes's nomination, the results revealed the Republican Party enjoyed an advantage over Wilson.

In early 1916, the *Nation* polled its readers for their presidential preference. The poll was nonscientific because *Nation* readers did not represent a cross section of the nation but provided a measure of the elite opinion about Wilson and the Republicans. The surveys included the president along with the three major Republican candidates and several dark-horse candidates. With the split in the Republican vote, it was not surprising that Wilson came out on top with 863 votes, just below his total of 890 in the poll conducted by the *Nation* in the 1912 poll;

Hughes came in a respectable second with 591 votes, outdistancing both Roosevelt (206) and Root (203). However, the Republican vote added with William Howard Taft's 32 votes placed the Republican nominee in the lead if that nominee could corral both conservative votes represented by Root and Taft and also the Progressive Republican votes of Roosevelt in the general election. Wilson faced a more difficult task, having to attract Roosevelt voters from 1912, many of whom leaned toward the Republican Party and would vote for their party if their nominee was seen as sufficiently Progressive.[65]

A month later the *Nation* offered some hope for Wilson with a second survey. In this one Wilson enjoyed a larger lead with 1,557 readers choosing the president and 980 choosing Hughes. Roosevelt with 376 and Root with 355 were far behind. Once again Wilson fell short in a similar survey from 1912 when he garnered 1,644 votes, but was behind the combined 1,711 votes received by the three Republican candidates. The poll was even better news for Hughes, who widened his lead over Roosevelt and Root, strengthening the draft movement on his behalf.[66] The polls showed that Wilson was vulnerable, but that Republicans remained divided along much the same lines as 1912.

The reliable fall campaign indicator, the Maine state elections, predicted a Republican victory as the party swept the gubernatorial and Senate election. A Republican fusion with the Progressives led to a vote victory of 9000–13,000 in statewide races.[67]

PRESIDENT HUGHES?

Election night was a tale of two results. Hughes started the night running up large totals in the northeast and Midwest. Wilson won the solid south and a select few states in the Midwest including Missouri and Ohio, a critical state for every Republican presidential candidate. As election returns were tabulated in states bordering the Mississippi River, Hughes had won 219 of the 266 electoral votes needed for the presidency. He required only 47 of 172 remaining electoral votes in the 23 states in the west. Certain of victory Hughes headed to bed only to awaken to a deadlock, Wilson having swept most of the plains states, the Mountain West, and Pacific West with California holding the key as late returns were counted. Hughes had won only four of 23 states west of the Mississippi and 35 electoral votes. When California was called for Wilson, he became the first Democrat president reelected since Andrew Jackson in 1832.[68]

The final electoral count would be the closest since 1876 with Wilson winning 277 electors and Hughes 254. Wilson's margin of victory is usually attributed to California because its late returns held up the final decision, but other states were critical to Wilson's victory. In Ohio, Wilson won a vote majority of 90,000, his wage law for railroaders earning him their votes while divisions among Ohio Republicans doomed Hughes. Hughes squeaked to victory in two important Midwestern states, winning Minnesota by fewer than 400 votes out of 360,000 votes and winning Indiana by less than 7,000 out of 670,000 votes. Wilson won New Hampshire by 56 votes out of 87,000 and New Mexico by 2,500 votes out of 650,000 votes. His victory in North Dakota by 1,800 out of over 108,000 total votes was part of his near sweep of the west. If Hughes had won North Dakota, New Mexico, and New Hampshire, he would have beaten Wilson by the narrowest of margins—266 electoral votes.[69]

The delay in the California vote count left the country unsure for a day who was the president-elect. The final tally revealed Hughes had lost by less than 4,000 votes while his supposed Republican ally, Hiram Johnson, swept into the Senate by over 296,000 votes. The Progressive conservative split worked against Hughes while Johnson, who decried machine politics, ensured his Progressive political machine did little for Hughes.[70]

Wilson won a popular vote majority of 600,000 though most of his margin was racked up in the Deep South. Hughes won only 1,500 votes in South Carolina giving Wilson a 60,000-vote majority. The Republican received slightly over 4,000 votes in Mississippi and produced a 75,000-vote majority for Wilson, while in Georgia Hughes had only 11,000 votes, producing a Democrat vote majority of 115,000. With the Democrat south suppressing the black vote, Hughes was forced to ring up massive majorities in Republican states to match Wilson's outsized southern majorities.[71]

The Democrats performed more poorly in congressional races as Republicans won 216 House seats. Wilson was able to control the House only when nine Progressives and independents joined the 210 House Democrats to form a narrow three-seat majority. The 20-seat loss was the largest for any reelected president and would have likely hindered Wilson in passing any domestic legislation if war had not broken out. Democrats held onto their 56–40 Senate majority though an erosion of that majority over time and the 1918 midterms would put Republicans in control of Congress. Wilson's congressional loss reflected the continuing Republican majority and how his victory was an upset over the favored Hughes.

Wilson's victory was even more unusual as it was the last narrow incumbent victory of the century. Between Wilson's victory and George W. Bush's 2004 reelection, incumbents who were reelected won by a sizable margin with four incumbents, Roosevelt in 1936, Johnson in 1964, Nixon in 1972, and Reagan in 1984 winning at least 59 percent of the vote. The 2004 election was the narrowest incumbent victory as Bush won with an electoral vote margin of 36, whereas Wilson's 23-vote victory was the smallest in the Electoral College.

AFTERMATH

Narrow presidential contests tend to devastate the loser while making the winner more cautious in his approach to the presidency, but Woodrow Wilson's second term proved as activist as his first term as he sought to redefine American foreign policy and international relations. Declaring war on Germany within six weeks of his second inaugural, Wilson mobilized the country, instituting a massive government bureaucracy including a propaganda bureau within the federal government. After the war, Wilson traveled to Europe where his popularity was at its highest even as his domestic support crumbled with Republicans seizing control of Congress in the 1918 midterms.

Wilson's overreach on the world stage, his messianic and dogmatic rhetoric destroyed the last two years of his term and tarnished his legacy. The country tipped into a depression while Wilson suffered a stroke, and rather than allow a fully functional president to handle the issues of the day, he held tight to the reins of power. Democrats would be punished by Wilson's stubbornness as the 1920 Republican presidential candidate, Warren Harding, won 60 percent of the vote, the highest proportion of the popular vote up to that time.

After the election Charles Evans Hughes returned to practicing law, his six years as a Supreme Court justice making him one of the most sought-after advocates in the country. Four years later he was tapped by Harding as secretary of state and presided over the Washington Naval Conference on reduction of armaments. Resigning in 1925 Hughes served in the private sector for another five years before his appointment as U.S. chief justice. He presided over the Supreme Court for 11 years, the most tumultuous times since John Marshall's first decade as chief. Hughes bested Franklin Roosevelt in the 1937 Court-Packing fight and preserved the independence of the federal judiciary while guiding the Supreme Court away from a controversial economic rights agenda. Hughes provided strong leadership on the Court until his retirement in 1941.

Hughes's success would be compared favorably to the brief life of his rival, Theodore Roosevelt, who lived less than three years after the 1916 election. Considered the front-runner for the 1920 campaign, Roosevelt suffered a crushing loss with the death of his son, Kermit in the Great War and was stiff-armed by the Wilson administration when offering help for the war effort. A combination of malaria and rheumatoid arthritis killed Roosevelt on January 6, 1919.

The Hughes–Wilson contest would be mainly lost to history, the narrow Wilson victory overtaken by the Great War and then economic depression and the Second World War. Wilson's anti-immigrant attacks reflected the biases of his southern base and his messianic vision of his presidency.

The Independent Candidate

TAYLOR VERSUS CASS, 1848

The second greatest presidential upset came only four years after the 1844 upset in which Whig founder Henry Clay was defeated by a virtual unknown. The 1848 election would see the Whigs shake off the effects of 1844 and return to an old formula for election success, the nomination of a popular military hero fresh from the battlefield.

With revolutions in Europe threatening the stability of centuries-old monarchies, the American republic was a model of stability, its populace brimming with confidence for its future. The outgoing Polk administration had set the northern and southern borders of the country ensuring it would never suffer a land invasion. Polk failed to develop a plan for slavery extension and left a party divided by section. Southern Democrats held the key to the party's presidential nominations and demanded that pliable northern Democrats accede to their demands. Northerners saw these "doughface" Democrats as mere puppets of the slave power, a criticism the southerner Polk had avoided.

THE POLK LEGACY

In 1844 James Polk shattered tradition with his nomination and election as a presidential dark horse. Prior to that year, presidential candidates were known quantities either serving in high office including the presidential cabinet or as military heroes who attained the status of icons before their presidency. Polk had been a compromise candidate chosen to break a deadlocked convention. He ran a campaign favoring American expansion and matched his unwavering support for Texas annexation with the memorable slogan of "54 / 40 or fight" as his solution to the controversy over the Oregon territory. Defeating the venerable Henry Clay was a presidential upset for the ages, but Polk's achievements did not end on Election Day. The dark horse constructed a continental nation with a successful war with Mexico and negotiations with the British. The expansion of the country to the Pacific opened vast new lands for settlement and also a dangerous revival of the debate over slavery expansion.

Domestically, Polk was less active. Following Democrat tradition he signed a tariff bill, cutting tax rates from the level created by the Whig's 1842 tariff that had raised taxes. Also following his Democrat predecessors Polk vetoed a Rivers and Harbors Bill, rejecting Henry Clay's American system of internal improvements. Foreswearing a second term meant Polk left others to defend his record. The absence of an incumbent candidate would be the second consecutive election without a sitting president on the ballot and the second of five consecutive elections without an incumbent, a sign of the turmoil that engulfed the government during the era.

Polk's achievements were not universally celebrated. His adding of Texas as a slave state ignited a northern abolitionist movement that became the Free Soil and then the Republican Party. Whig politicians ranging from Henry Clay to the obscure Illinois Congressman Abraham Lincoln denounced the war as a plot to expand slavery to the Pacific. Voters expressed their own displeasure over the war in 1846, with Whigs winning a four-seat House majority and warning Democrats that Polk's Manifest Destiny policies might hurt the party in the 1848 campaign.[1]

Polk's departure from the political scene marked the end of the Jacksonian-dominated party as Andrew Jackson died in 1845 only months after his Tennessee protégé's unlikely victory. None of the Democrat candidates in 1848 could claim the same close relationship with Jackson as enjoyed by Polk or his Democrat predecessor Martin van Buren but could only claim to represent Jackson's ideas and purpose.

WHIG CANDIDATES

The 1848 presidential campaign was a turning point for the Whig party as they struggled to find a leader after Henry Clay's stunning 1844 defeat. Behind Clay was a weak field of hopefuls lacking popular support. The early Whig front-runner was Justice John McLean, a political chameleon who had been respectively a Federalist, a Democrat, an Anti-Masonic, and a Whig. McLean was the highest ranking Whig official in the federal government though he was known best for his presidential bids than his judicial opinions. McLean's support was focused in his home state of Ohio and within the growing nativist movement opposing open immigration. McLean's obsessive campaigning made him an unlikely president, but as the only Whig campaigning he was the front-runner by default.[2]

In Ohio the justice was challenged by Whig Senator Thomas Corwin who saw McLean as a political opportunist who had switched parties after his political rise was blocked by the Democrats and had been using the Whigs out of political convenience.[3] Corwin mounted his own campaign and blocked McLean from controlling the Ohio delegation.

With McLean's candidacy drawing jeers from Whigs, the party searched for alternatives. Relief originated from an unusual source, James Polk. The start of the Mexican War in April 1846 turned the public's attention to the American military and its leadership. During the first 60 years of the republic, generals cultivated military success into political careers with Washington, Jackson, and William Henry Harrison making the transition from military chieftain to civilian leader. The Mexican War would be no different, producing two Whig presidential candidates and one president.

The Whigs had the choice of the voluble Winfield Scott or the unknown Zachary Taylor. Scott was a political general who made impolitic statements exploited by the Democrats. After clashing with Polk at the start of the war, Scott fired off a letter to War Secretary William Marcy complaining he faced "a fire upon my rear, from Washington, and the fire in front, from the Mexicans."[4] Marcy leaked the letter to friendly Democrat papers, and the public was treated to the image of a prima donna general whose comparison of Washington political battles with the actual battlefield formed the image of a man more concerned with personal comfort than his soldiers.

When he was recalled to active service after General Taylor's victory at Buena Vista made him a political threat to the Polk administration, Scott complained the war secretary's summons forced him to "take a hasty plate of soup" rather than his regular dinner. The general's infelicitous phrasing reinforced his image as "old fuss and feathers": the name given him by his soldiers.[5]

However, Scott was the true hero of the war. His march from Veracruz to Mexico City ranked with Sherman's March to the Sea and MacArthur's Inchon landings in terms of military daring and success. His drive is remembered fondly in the Marine Corps hymn with the mention of the Halls of Montezuma. However, Scott's successes were hidden from public views as they occurred deep in the enemy's interior, and he was overshadowed by the nearly unknown Zachary Taylor.

As Scott's presidential aspirations sagged under the weight of his letter writing, his colleague in northern Mexico, Zachary Taylor, saw his stock rise. A Louisiana slave-owner who acquired influence in the Democrat Party from his former son-in-law Jefferson Davis, Taylor became a national figure during the battle of Buena Vista when he utilized his artillery to nearly destroy a much larger Mexican force. The battle added another epigram to military lore as Taylor supposedly told future general Braxton Bragg to "give them a little more grape (shot)" in order to turn back Mexican troops.[6]

In his headquarters on the northern Mexican border, the general dismissed rumors of his candidacy, even rejecting the presidency if running unopposed.[7] However, old Rough and Ready proved too tempting a figure to be ignored by the desperate Whig party. Taylor's status of a professional soldier who served in isolated frontier posts so separated from civilization that he had not voted in his adult life presented political professionals with their perfect candidate. The general's image could be molded: his beliefs were dictated by the demands of the party. His southern roots started with his Virginia birth, whereas his Louisiana plantation appealed to the Whig's southern base of wealthy planters. His status of war hero diluted Whig opposition to the Mexican War, and his status as a slave-owner silenced Democrat attempts to tie the Whigs to the abolitionist movement.

After Taylor's unlikely nomination and election, many in the Whig Party took credit for his sudden rise. Thurlow Weed, the New York political operative who maneuvered William Henry Harrison into the presidency, claimed to have begun the Buena Vista campaign after a chance meeting with Taylor's brother.[8] Senator John Crittenden, Henry Clay's Kentucky ally and 1844 campaign advisor, enjoyed a regular correspondence with his old friend the general. In his letters Crittenden broached the idea of a presidential run and after some persuasion the general agreed.[9]

The Georgia Whig congressman Alexander Stephens contributed to the early draft-Taylor movement when he formed the Young Indians, a group of Whig congressmen who made congressional speeches on Taylor's behalf. The original members of the group included Connecticut's Truman Smith, William Preston and Thomas Flournoy from Virginia, Georgia's Robert Toombs, and Illinois' Abraham Lincoln.[10] Democrats could take some credit or blame as Polk's political manipulation of his generals made Taylor more popular among Whigs. At the start of the war Polk strengthened Taylor's army and removed Scott from active command. Taylor's victory at Buena Vista made him a national figure, and Polk shifted troops and authority back to Scott to undermine the Taylor movement.

In late 1843 Senator Simon Cameron used his position as Pennsylvania boss to endorse Taylor as a Democrat nominee strengthening his later claim of being a bipartisan candidate. Congressional Democrats fueled the fire, diluting a congressional resolution of support for Taylor and burnishing the image of a simple soldier undermined by treacherous politicians. As the campaign progressed Taylor was ridiculed by the Washington establishment which further endeared him to a cynical public.[11]

However, Taylor's candidacy was also sparked by the public. After Buena Vista, Taylor's name, face, and nickname—Rough and Ready—became a commercial sensation. Ice carts, butcher stands, marketplaces and, even cigar boxes sported some variation of the old general's likeness. Without lifting a finger Taylor had become a popular icon loved and respected even by those who opposed the war and Polk. The suggestion of Taylor for president energized popular support and became a public movement born from a population exhausted by war, economic depression, and partisan bickering.[12]

The Taylor bandwagon rolled through the state conventions, the "Buena Vista" movement driving state parties to endorse his candidacy and build his delegate total for the national Whig convention. John Calhoun declared he was "content" with the general, a less than rousing endorsement though it green-lighted his supporters to coalesce around Taylor.[13]

As the excitement of the campaign swept up the public and Whig politicians, Taylor was more annoyed than enthused by the prospect of the presidency. When a letter writer inquired of his interest in the presidency, Taylor claimed he was not seeking the White House with one loophole. According to the general "I will not say I would not serve if the good people were to be imprudent enough as to elect me."[14] The tangled verbiage and the self deprecation endeared Taylor to a public worn from egotistical politicians grasping for office. After the general was criticized by Whigs for one of his letters separating his candidacy from the party, he exploded, "I do not care a fig about the office." He lamented to Crittenden that the presidency was more trouble than it was worth and told the senator to withdraw his name if Crittenden considered it best for the country, stating, "Country first, friendship second."[15]

As the Buena Vista movement swept the country, two veteran Whigs positioned themselves to become Taylor's main challenger. Daniel Webster had run in 1836 as part of a Whig presidential triumvirate, but his tenure as John Tyler's secretary of state damaged his reputation among Whigs. Standing in the footlights was the three-time presidential loser Henry Clay whose candidacy made Whigs' hearts beat faster. Clay had regained his old Senate seat and spent two years denouncing the Mexican War and Polk's expansionist vision. Clay's quarrel with the president went deeper than politics, his son Henry Clay II losing his life at Buena Vista. The suggestion that Clay would run awakened interest as he was favored in the heart of every Whig. Unfortunately for Clay their heads told them the old man could not win, his 1844 defeat proving he was too controversial. By spring 1848 Whigs faced the difficult choice of an unknown candidate versus an unelectable candidate. The party's troubles resembled Democrat struggles as the party also suffered a dearth of candidates.

DEMOCRAT CANDIDATES

When accepting the 1844 nomination Polk promised to serve a single term. While many men claimed they had no interest in the presidency and then leapt to accept the party nomination, Polk's poor health foreclosed a second term. Ill since childhood, Polk had aged rapidly under the demands of the presidency. By 1848 pictures showed a president with hollow eyes and sunken cheeks, resembling a man in his 70s rather than his early 50s. Polk had also accomplished all he had promised by 1848 and could retire peacefully to Tennessee though he would be dead within six months of leaving office.[16]

Polk's administration produced two candidates who could build on his considerable record. Secretary of State James Buchanan had represented Pennsylvania in Congress and headed a Democrat faction in the state, but he was hurt by the Walker Tariff lowering tax rates. Many in Pennsylvania had taken seriously Polk's promise not to cut tariffs and then felt betrayed when he signed the Walker bill; Buchanan's attempts to defend Polk's policies would only damage him in his home state.

Buchanan faced the incumbent vice president, George Dallas, who contributed to Polk's Pennsylvania win in 1844 and wanted to parlay that influence into a promotion. Dallas controlled a different state party faction, and on March 4, 1847, two years to the date of the next presidential inauguration, the two political heavyweights faced off at the state Democrat convention. Buchanan won the first round as delegates nominated his favored candidate for governor. On the more important issue of a presidential endorsement, neither Dallas nor Buchanan convinced the delegates to make the Pennsylvania's favorite son for 1848. Instead, the state party boss, Senator Simon Cameron, rallied the delegates to endorse General Zachary Taylor. Unfortunately for Cameron, Taylor was not an announced candidate and had not declared whether he was a Democrat or Whig. Cameron avoided this by announcing Taylor was a Democrat and would receive the state's delegates at the Democrat convention.[17]

Taylor had become an announced Whig candidate by the time of the 1848 state convention which opened up the Democrats again competing for the state's delegates. The vice president seized a small majority of delegates by narrowly winning control of Philadelphia. This gave Dallas's 47 delegates to the national convention and left Buchanan with 38. The division of the state hurt both candidates and prevented Cameron from wielding the second largest delegate bloc in favor of one candidate.[18]

A third candidate was Justice Levi Woodbury, who led a strange coalition of antislavery New England Democrats and southern proslavery radicals. Woodbury's competition was John Calhoun who was one of the few politicians supporting the Mexican War and opposing the Oregon negotiations because the latter added territory to the North. Calhoun also opposed Polk on personal grounds, having been fired from his position as secretary of state by the president.[19]

Facing his final chance at the presidency Calhoun made a critical error when his name was mentioned as a compromise candidate. Fearing his work on Texas annexation and slavery expansion into the southwest was under threat by the Wilmot Proviso limiting slavery in federal territories, Calhoun launched one of his philosophical and constitutional tirades. The senator declared that territories were the property of all Americans who enjoyed the right to emigrate to the west with their property including slaves. This absolutist vision, similar to what he had expressed in his Pakenham letter of 1844, made Calhoun unacceptable to northern Democrats and moderate southerners who controlled the nomination process.[20]

Another misstep followed after the Washington *Union*, the official administration newspaper, criticized Calhoun in a series of editorials. The South Carolinian's supporters voted to expel the *Union's* reporters from the press gallery. The majority Whigs, eager to sow dissension in Democrat ranks, joined Calhoun in removing the *Union*. The vote reverberated across the country with the press portraying Calhoun as a dictator censoring his critics. Calhoun was also criticized at home as South Carolina governor James Henry Hammond argued that Calhoun's radicalism was harming the slavery cause.[21]

Southern Democrats were not the only ones struggling to find a candidate as New York Democrats failed to offer a favorite son for the convention. Their first choice was former governor Silas Wright until his death in 1847 which left Martin Van Buren's Barnburner faction without a candidate for the state convention. The party was so divided it sent two delegations to the national convention and asked delegates from the other states to settle the party squabbles.[22]

The old northwest states produced the Democrat front-runner, Senator Lewis Cass. The 1848 convention was Cass's second attempt at the Democrat nomination after his 1844 campaign was ignited by Van Buren's collapse after he rejected Texas annexation. Cass had been a minor figure in the Democrat Party prior to 1844, appointed as ambassador to France during the Van Buren administration and continuing into the brief Harrison then Tyler administrations.

Having served as Michigan territorial governor, Cass resigned his ambassadorship because he disapproved of the Webster–Ashburton Treaty setting the American border in the Great Lakes region. Returning to the United States he was one of the candidates who rushed the fill the political vacuum created after Van Buren's collapse. Cass joined with other challengers to deny Van Buren the nomination and created a deadlock that led a rush of delegates to nominate James Knox Polk. Cass was subsequently elected Michigan senator and used the Senate to build his candidacy on the quintessential Jacksonian policy of popular sovereignty.[23]

Among Cass's liabilities was his age as he would be the oldest first-term president just four years after the country had elected Polk—the youngest president. Cass represented the aging Jacksonian ideal, and his personal appearance, a poorly fitting red wig and a mass of facial moles, suggested he was the last of his breed. Yet, his age and physical appearance hid a strong personality and political wits that allowed him to survive a highly partisan period.[24] He would need both to handle the critical issue of the era, the role of slavery in the great western migration.

SLAVERY AND THE WEST

James Polk was elected on the promise of Texas annexation and the implication that the new state would welcome slavery. With the country expanding to the Pacific after the Mexican cession, Polk and the Democrats struggled to solve the problem of extending slavery into the southwest. The 1820 Missouri Compromise line had kept slavery below Missouri's southern border but at the time the American border extended only to eastern Texas. If the Missouri compromise line was drawn to the Pacific, slavery could also extend to the new west coast, a result unacceptable to northern Whigs and Democrats alike. With the Whigs having denounced the Mexican War and the new territories, the Democrats were left to settle the issue. Their plans divided the country through the next four administrations and eventually triggered the Civil War.

The most radical plan originated in Alabama with former Democrat congressman William Yancey. A man of who revered slavery more than the Union, he offered the view that slavery was a constitutionally protected federal regulation of the territories. He demanded passage of a federal slave code as part of Congress' power to regulate territories. Yancey's proposals would go nowhere in the Democrat Party but were partially adopted by the Supreme Court in its 1857 Dred Scott decision striking down the Missouri Compromise and its ban on slavery in northern territories.[25]

The administration offered two proposals. Secretary of State Buchanan suggested extending the Missouri Compromise line to the Pacific. Buchanan's plan was a sop to the south by recognizing the region's claim that slaves could be carried into federal territories. Yet, Buchanan appealed to northern voters in noting the desert southwest was inhospitable to the plantation system. Any extension of slavery would be limited and unlikely to take root in new western states. Polk's vice president, George Dallas, offered a vague proposal territorial settlers to vote on slavery. Dallas's proposal would later become popular sovereignty enacted by Stephen Douglas's 1854 Kansas–Nebraska Act.[26]

Lewis Cass modified Dallas's plan by arguing slavery was a domestic institution and should be left under state regulatory power. Cass rejected any federal limit on slavery imposed by Congress. Cass's convoluted proposal drew scorn from the Charleston *Mercury*, the southern spokesman for the radical wing of the Democrat Party, which editorialized that Cass's plan would destroy slavery because the southwest territories were governed under Mexican law which banned the institution.[27]

At the opposite end of the slavery issue was the Wilmot Proviso. Members of Congress are skillful at adding key changes to bills in the form of amendments that escape the normal committee process. In early August 1846, as the House debated an appropriations bill, Pennsylvania Democrat David Wilmot offered a rider banning the extension of slavery into any newly acquired Mexican territory. The Wilmot Proviso passed the House, its scope not recognized by most congressmen. It failed in the Senate due to a procedural foul-up, but when southern Democrats read and understood the proviso, it became the key issue of 1848.[28]

The proviso tested the sincerity of the Polk administration and Texas annexationists who defended the seizure of Texas and subsequent Mexican War as countering British influence in the region. Blaming the British bogeyman was the favorite tactic of American politicians trying to pass unpopular domestic or foreign policies. Polk rejected the Whig contention that the war was fought to extend the reach of slavery, though John Calhoun linked Texas annexation to the spread of slavery and more slave states. The Proviso would put a lie to that contention for if the southwest territories were seized without slavery in mind, few could object to banning slavery where it was never intended to exist.

Wilmot's proposal proved controversial among Democrats and Whigs alike as none of the major party candidates approved. The slavery question sparked the Free Soil Movement and split northern Democrats—many of whom opposed slavery expansion and had tired of the constant threats emanating from the south.

The different proposals split the party but offered substantive arguments that went unanswered by the Whigs who lacked any plan. However, with issues on their side, Democrats still lacked an inspirational candidate who could run in a simple if misleading slogan like Polk's "54 / 40 or fight." Among the announced candidates Calhoun was too radical; Dallas lacked name recognition and a political base. Buchanan was closely tied to Polk and would take the blame for the president's missteps and a divided Pennsylvania delegation. Cass was the strongest in a weak field, his Michigan roots making him the first presidential candidate to originate in the northwest, the country's most rapidly expanding region. However, Cass's strengths were exceeded by the enemies lurking in the Democrat party. Among them was Van Buren who had not forgotten Cass's role in the setting the two-thirds rule that left the former president tantalizingly close to a third presidential nomination. By 1848 Van Buren lacked the personal drive and political support to mount another campaign, but his New York Barnburner faction was determined to deny Cass the nomination and bar him from the presidency.

Cass began his campaign by publicizing his popular sovereignty proposal in a letter sent to a Tennessee supporter, Alfred Nicholson. Cass presented the plan as a Jacksonian proposal for broadening democracy and promoting westward expansion. Under Cass's proposal, north and south benefitted from popular sovereignty as proslavery and abolitionist views could be vindicated at the polls. The simplicity of the plan, though, hid its weaknesses as slavery proved too volatile an issue to be settled at the ballot box.

Where Cass expected his Nicholson letter to draw appreciation from the northern and southern Democrats alike, it instead drew scorn from the extremes. Proslavery zealots sought constitutional protection of slavery and worried that the institution could be eliminated by popular vote. Antislavery politicians believed the institution was too awful to be granted legitimacy through the ballot box.[29] Their opposition threatened Cass's election because southern extremists would not vote for a party that did not aggressively defend slavery; also, some northern Democrats joined the Free Soilers. Yet, the Nicholson letter made Cass a man with a plan, one acceptable to moderates in both regions.

With his policy positions firmly in place, Cass next went in search of delegate support in state party conventions which chose delegates for the national conventions. Cass swept the delegations in Michigan, Illinois, Indiana, Wisconsin, and Ohio. By the time of the Democrat convention in May 22, 1848, Cass boasted a significant plurality of the delegates and was the undisputed front-runner.[30]

DEMOCRAT CONVENTION

The Democrats met in Baltimore at the Universalist Church, the same location where in 1844 the Whigs nominated Henry Clay, an ominous choice considering Clay's upset loss. Cass entered as the front-runner, benefitting from his hard work and his opponents' ineptitude. Neither James Buchanan nor George Dallas controlled the Pennsylvania delegation as the secretary of state controlled rural delegates and the vice president urban delegates. At the same time, the Democrat boss of Pennsylvania, Simon Cameron, was throwing his support to Taylor and the Whigs. Cameron's split from the Democrats was based on the party's rejection of the protective tariff which Cameron believed was crucial to promoting Pennsylvania's industrial growth. With the Democrat Party dedicated to a lower tariff, Cameron jumped ship and supported Taylor, which helped the Whigs in Pennsylvania. With Cameron using his political influence for the Whigs, and with the state Democrat party split between Dallas and Buchanan, the Democrat candidate would struggle to win the keystone state.[31]

Counting the delegates during the convention's first day, Cass was guaranteed the Midwest while holding most of the moderate slave states including Kentucky, Tennessee, Arkansas, Missouri, and one Deep South state Mississippi. Yet, these delegations were only weakly allied to Cass and willing to jump to a compromise southern candidate such as they had done with Polk in 1844. Buchanan enjoyed support of one Deep South delegation, Louisiana, and several Mid-Atlantic states including Delaware, Maryland, Virginia, and North Carolina.

Justice Woodbury struggled to unite a coalition of Proviso supporters and radical proslavery southerners. William Yancey was the justice's strongest supporter with the South Carolina, Georgia, Alabama, and Florida delegations waiting to jump onto the Woodbury bandwagon. Yet, Yancey's demand for full constitutional recognition and protection of slavery throughout the country was too much for any of the candidates, and the Deep South states would have little influence in the convention. When Woodbury refused to support the Yancey position, his candidacy ended, and a Democrat split seemed inevitable.[32]

The convention wild card was the fractured New York delegation. Establishment Democrats, known as the Hunkers, were pragmatic spoilsmen who "hunkered" after government jobs and cared about a Democrat's electability rather than his policy positions. The Barnburner Democrats were more ideological, seeking to wean the party from its dependence on southern votes and obsession with slavery. Cass's managers demanded each delegation agree to support the Democrat nominee without regard to who it was. When the Barnburners rejected the offer, the Hunkers were recognized as the official delegation, and the convention began.[33]

After the nominating speeches, the first ballot found Cass with 125 out of a total of 251 delegates, nearly a majority but lacking the required two-thirds. Far behind was Buchanan with 55 and Woodbury with 53. While the numbers were worrisome for the two challengers, worse was the loss of their base to Cass, who had taken Mid-Atlantic votes from Buchanan while skimming delegates from the south originally pledged to Woodbury. The next two ballots saw Cass's numbers slowly rise, but with his opponents unable to rally around a single candidate, Cass was nominated on the fourth ballot. After the nomination was approved, Yancey rose to demand a proslavery plank be included in the platform, and when Democrats ignored him, the Alabama delegation stormed from the church.[34] The Barnburners were the next to bolt, heading to upper New York to establish a separate party. The convention adjourned after nominating Kentucky's William Butler as vice president, after which he faded into obscurity.[35]

THE FREE SOILERS

The 1848 campaign marked the coalescing of the antislavery movement into a full-fledged party composed of antislavery Democrats and Conscience Whigs. The original antislavery faction, the Liberty Party, had twice run David Birney for president. In 1844 the Whigs blamed Birney for taking Whig votes from Henry Clay in New York and tilting the state and election to Polk.

In October 1847 the Liberty Party nominated New Hampshire Senator John Hale for president. Hale was a nationally known and controversial figure who won his Senate seat as an antislavery independent, but Hale's nomination was only one step toward creating a broader antislavery movement. Salmon Chase, the antislavery Ohio Democrat, planned a national antislavery campaign which came to fruition after the Barnburners stormed from the Democrat convention. On June 22 in Utica, New York they held a brief convention and nominated Martin Van Buren for president.[36]

The leaders of both the Liberty Party and New York Democrats realized they were competing for the same voters and only by combining their efforts could they affect the result. On August 9 in Buffalo, the Free Soil Party was born during a convention of major antislavery figures. Among them was Charles Sumner, who represented the conscience Whigs, and John Hale. Charles Francis Adams, John Quincy's son and the eldest of the Adams clan, attended, energized by memories of his father's battles with Andrew Jackson and Martin van Buren.[37]

Prior to the convention, the leaders of the new party considered several candidates including John McLean, who declined to resign his Court seat for a quixotic third-party run. The Liberty Party proposed Hale, but his radicalism proved too much for the Free Soilers. When the delegates voted, pro–Wilmot Democrats and Conscience Whigs combined their support to give Van Buren 244 of 427 votes. Hale received 183 votes from Liberty Party supporters and a smattering of Whigs. For vice president the party nominated Charles Francis Adams to appease the conscience Whigs.[38]

The Free Soil convention shifted the political center. The Whig's nomination of Zachary Taylor was expected to hurt the party in New York and the New England states because Whigs would reject a slave-owning candidate; however, with Free Soilers attracting the votes of Wilmot Democrats, New York and its 35 electoral votes was in play. Democrats were not the only ones who were concerned with the Free Soil challenge. Massachusetts Whigs feared Adams inclusion on the Free Soil ticket would drain votes from what was considered a safe Whig state because the Adams name retained considerable popularity. In response the Whigs played up the Adams–Van Buren feud dating back to the Jackson administration. Whigs portrayed him as an aristocrat not befitting the Adams legacy with Congressman Abraham Lincoln lashing out at the Free Soilers during a visit to Massachusetts.[39]

Free Soilers responded to Whig attacks by focusing on Taylor the slave-owner. Charles Sumner denounced the "lords of the lash and the lords of the loom," his words connecting plantation owners producing the cotton with the mill owners who needed the cotton to spin into finished textiles.[40] Sumner's phrasing infuriated both sides, a talent that would see him beaten senseless on the Senate floor a decade later.

Free Soilers appealed to Whigs beyond slavery; they were supporters of river and harbor improvements that were popular in the old northwest region. They also supported homestead settlements, appealing to pro–Wilmot Democrats.[41] Van Buren and Adams had no chance at victory, but they did succeed in halting the westward movement of slaves by turning certain states away from Cass and defeating his popular sovereignty plan.

GOING ROGUE

Letters had proved the undoing of Martin Van Buren and Henry Clay in 1844 after the front-runners for their party nominations published letters opposing Texas annexation. Van Buren's missive resulted in a Democrat revolt, his party rejecting the former president for the nomination. Clay was rejected by the voters, his Raleigh letter against Texas annexation forcing him to publish two more letters parsing his original words, his flip-flops on the issue contributing to his defeat. Mindful of the harm caused by a candidate's public pronouncements, Taylor's managers struggled to control their candidate and his desire to express his opinions to anyone who sought it.

Unlike modern campaigns where a candidate's spoken word is broadcast and analyzed, the 19th-century press relied on the written word as evidence of a candidate's intentions. Even before the campaign began, Taylor angered Whigs and entertained Democrats with his letters on policy, the Whig Party, and his candidacy. While Whigs steamed at Taylor's declarations of his independence from parties, Democrats snickered at the general's poor grammar and spelling, forgetting their hero Andrew Jackson had suffered from the same disabilities in his written skills.

Returning to Louisiana in February, 1848 Taylor answered queries from newspapers and ordinary voters with the assumption his words would remain private. Taylor's letter writing campaign stretched from Cincinnati to Harrisburg, Pennsylvania and Montgomery, Alabama, each new missive damaging his image among the Whig establishment. His decision to accept the nomination of the anti-immigrant Native American Party in September 1847 made Whig politicians blanch.[42] Sneeringly labeled the "Know Nothings' by their opponents, the Native Americans had considerable support in Pennsylvania and in 1844 had fused with the Whigs to win several local and state elections.

The fusion, though, did not help Clay carry the state during the presidential election. Taylor's acceptance of the nomination under the guise of bipartisanship did not arouse the controversy that Clay's dalliances with the Americans had in 1844.

Fearing Taylor's words were alienating Whig delegates, Taylor's chief advisors, Stephens, Toombs, and Crittenden, crafted a letter and sent it to the general for his approval. The old general may have taken the letter in toto or revised it but on April 22, 1848 his letter to John Allison of Alabama calmed the growing Whig concern about their front-runner. The Allison letter spelled out the general's willingness to defer to Congress on economic issues including the tariff, internal improvements, and regulation of the currency, all core Whig issues. At the same time Taylor declared he was a Whig but not an ultra-Whig, a deliberate poke at those demanding ideological purity. Taylor was determined to "act independent of party domination" and made it clear his administration would not serve as an extension of Congress.[43]

Taylor's declarations were more a bow to reality than surrender to the party as he lacked knowledge or clear principles on many domestic issues which forced him to adopt core Whig principles. More helpful was Taylor's rejection of any future wars of "subjugation," an implicit criticism of the Mexican War which had earned him so much fame.[44]

If Taylor had halted his letter writing campaign after the Allison letter, his nomination would have been assured; however, the old general could not be convinced to set down his pen. Angered by some Whigs openly supporting Clay, Taylor responded to this challenge with a letter to the Richmond *Whig*. The old general delivered his most potent political grapeshot to his Whig opponents, declaring he would run for president even if neither the Whig nor the Democrat Party nominated him. The comment had the desired effect, skillfully using Taylor's personal popularity as a club against his critics.[45]

Taylor's image as a nonpartisan candidate could only help him and the minority Whig Party which could only win in November if they appealed to Democrats. The strategy was better suited for the general election when party identification would hurt him in the south and less successful for the nomination battle where he would have to convince Whigs he could represent their party. Once nominated, Taylor used his battles with the Whig establishment to appeal to undecided Democrats. However, the nonpartisan strategy also hurt the party down the ballot. With the general running a seemingly independent campaign, his popularity did not translate into congressional coattails and during his brief presidency Taylor was forced to negotiate with an overwhelmingly Democrat congress.

Taylor's missteps revived interest in Clay. The man who defined the Whig Party had been quietly building support among those who helped him in three presidential campaigns. Clay officially announced his candidacy at a speech in Lexington, Kentucky on April 10, 1848. His words revealed a beaten man, one going through the motions of running for the presidency to stop Zachary Taylor rather than mounting a candidacy of ideas. In his announcement Clay spoke vaguely of acceding to the decision of the Whig convention as if the senator expected to be drafted. He avoided controversial subjects, either too tired or wiser from his 1844 letter writing campaign on slavery and territorial expansion. His decision to run was not greeted with the delirious joy of his 1844 candidacy, even his old friend Crittenden refusing to support a fourth campaign, preferring to stay with his other old friend, Zachary Taylor.[46]

The Clay boom reflected panic within the Whig establishment that feared Taylor could not win the general election, and even if he did he would be too independent to follow the lead of party leaders. The rush toward a Taylor coronation suddenly became a traditional nomination battle with the old general forced to rely on men like Stephens and Toombs who knew how to maneuver within the state convention system.

The leaders of the Young Indians convinced southern state conventions in all but three major slave states—Kentucky, Missouri, and Virginia—to send pro-Taylor delegations to the national convention. Once again Clay was rejected by his slaveholding brethren, an ominous reminder of his inability to carry the south in the 1844 election and Clay was left with northeastern delegates.[47]

The question for Whig delegates was which candidate could best expand the Whig voting bloc. Solidly Whig New England was unlikely to vote Democrat even with Taylor at the top of the ticket, but the south had demonstrated a strong aversion to Clay. Taylor was the strongest national candidate, able to take votes in the northeast, Mid-Atlantic, and Deep South states. His tendency to irritate the Whig establishment with ill-timed letters was less dangerous than Clay's ability to alienate voters with his letters. As Clay became the favorite among some Whigs for a fourth nomination, the question of electability dogged his campaign.

However, the general was losing allies by spring 1848. Thurlow Weed had retreated from his early support of the Taylor, having sensed his western New York voter base was uneasy with a slave-owner heading the Whig ballot. Weed went in search of other candidates, but unfortunately for the publisher the alternative in New York was the hated Henry Clay. New York was the scene of the strongest anti-Taylor movement and sensing his party was tumbling toward a fourth doomed Clay nomination, Weed joined former Congressman Millard Fillmore in working covertly for Taylor, trying to slow the Kentuckian's momentum while hoping a third candidate would arise.[48] Another Whig who doubted the wisdom of a Taylor nomination was Horace Greeley, publisher of the New York *Tribune*. Greeley was a virulent abolitionist who cringed at the possibility of his party electing a slave-owner and supported Clay as a stopgap measure though he failed to generate much enthusiasm in calling for nominating a three-time loser.[49]

Other alternatives rose and fell. Justice John McLean and Senator Corwin battled for the status of Ohio favorite son, but Ohio Whigs were too divided to endorse either man.[50] Weed and Greeley eventually latched onto the Winfield Scott, whose Mexican War successes made him as successful as Taylor. However, old doubts about Scott resurfaced; Greeley accused him of nativism for opposing immigration, and the anti–Buena Vista movement lost momentum.[51]

Taylor's candidacy widened the split between the Whig old guard and a new cadre of leaders who wanted to move the party beyond its narrow policy ideas. Henry Clay represented the party's old guard which had built it on support for a national bank, a protective tariff, and a weak executive. The old guard with Clay in the lead attacked the Mexican War in terms of the expansion of presidential power. Clay feared Polk had reinvented the Jacksonian presidency, his veto of the Rivers and Harbors Bill contravening the central principle of acompliant president signing congressional legislation. However, such ideas proved unpopular in a presidential campaign as voters expected their president to use rather than foreswear his powers.

Representing the new Whig party was the Stephens–Toombs alliance joined by John Crittenden. The trio judged the war as an opportunity to revive the party, particularly in the south, and hoped to rekindle the spark of the 1840 campaign, when a popular general and Whig candidate swept the Democrats from the White House and Congress. They believed Zachary Taylor represented the best chance for

the Whigs to win the White House, whereas Clay worried he was in-
sufficiently supportive of basic Whig principles.

The younger Whig faction realized Taylor offered a southern heritage that evaded the Kentuckian Clay, whose four decades in Washington isolated him from his region. The Young Indians were willing to
exploit the slavery issue, much as John Tyler and James Polk had done
in 1844, using Taylor's status as Louisiana planter to soothe the worries of southern Whigs that the northern branch of the party was secretly abolitionist. Stephens and Toombs skillfully used Taylor's status
as a relative unknown to construct a favorable biography unmarred by
scandal or past controversy.

However, as his challengers fell away, Taylor further ignited concern about his dedication to the Whig Party. In a letter published in
the *Charleston News*, Taylor reiterated he would not be a president
of a party, a deliberate appeal to southern Democrats. The old general's acceptance of the nomination of the Charleston Democrat Party
strengthened his claim of bipartisanship and was more than mere
campaign rhetoric. Whig politicians were less understanding, a growing fear that Taylor was a political "free agent" using the party for personal glory serving as the strongest argument for Clay at the national
convention.[52]

WHIG CONVENTION

The Whigs met on June 7 with Taylor firmly in the lead, but Clay
was gaining momentum and capitalizing on growing Whig concern
over the general's mistakes. The Whig convention had a different
rhythm than past meetings. Most 19th-century conventions began
with speeches nominating candidates and floor battles over rules followed by a roll call of states. The convention's first ballot offered guidance as to the general feeling of the delegates, and few candidates were
nominated on the first ballot. Subsequent ballots had candidates maneuvering for support with vote trading and promises of administration jobs bandied about. In the 1848 convention, though, the first ballot
proved critical because Clay supporters had raised expectations of his
candidacy and convinced many Whigs that he would lead the first
ballot. Reality would be much different.

Instead of the first ballot starting Clay's drive to the nomination, it
represented the high point of his candidacy. The general earned 111

delegates and Clay only 97 with 140 as the majority. Clay's numbers dwindled in subsequent ballots, dropping to 86 while Taylor's crept up to 118. As the ballots progressed, the general picked up individual delegates: his total higher for each ballot while Clay continued to decline with the totals for Winfield Scott and Daniel Webster remaining stagnant.[53]

Without a clear victor in sight, the convention adjourned to the next day with the general in the lead and his opponents squabbling over which candidate could mount a final challenge to Taylor. Clay supporters refused to surrender the possibility of a fourth nomination, whereas Scott and Webster supporters faced the cold reality that their candidates could not win. If the delegates threw their support behind Clay, he would be nominated but they could not escape the fear of another crushing defeat. Supporting Taylor represented a leap in the dark as the unknown general bungled his way to the nomination and possibly another general election defeat. However, even with his mistakes the old general was aided by his superior organization, the work of the Young Indians, and the disarray of his opponents who could not agree on a single candidate to oppose him. Relying upon almost unanimous support of southern Whigs, the general held his vote steady, and he was nominated on the fifth ballot.

Northern Whigs despaired at the nomination of a slave-owner because they worried that conscience Whigs in the northeast and New York would abandon the party. Whigs in New England grumbled about southern domination and the choice of an unqualified candidate based on military heroism and region. The response was a regional balance on the ticket with two New York candidates for the vice-presidential slot: Congressman Millard Fillmore and William Seward. Because Weed's preferred candidate Seward was distrusted in the south, Fillmore used his tenure as chairman of the House Ways and Means Committee to promote himself as a moderate Whig. With Fillmore's nomination confirmed after a brief fight, the Whig enjoyed a home state advantage in targeting New York's electoral votes.[54]

However, Fillmore's nomination proved problematical in the south after a letter was uncovered suggesting his opposition to slavery extension and support for abolition in the nation's capital. Fillmore's letter was a response to an inquiry from a local New York antislavery group, and the congressman's flippant response was a simple agreement with every aspect of the group's platform. Democrats used the missive to pin the abolitionist label on Fillmore, but as in most presidential elections, voters focus on the name at the top of the ticket rather than the vice- presidential candidate.[55]

Taylor's close call at the Whig national convention did not curb his enthusiasm for letter writing. A candidate's nomination acceptance letter was used to propose policies and appeal to both the party base and those independents who leaned toward one party or the other. However, Taylor's letter was delayed by one of the more curious events in election history.

As a national icon, Taylor was deluged by letters from all over the country. Under postal regulations the postage for those letters would be paid by the recipient. Unwilling to pay the costs of receiving mail, Taylor had dozens of letters kept at the local post office's dead letter file. Among these was the official announcement of his nomination to the presidency. Only after the letter was delivered did Taylor respond though the general's long silence further frayed Whig nerves.

Concerned about what Taylor might write in accepting the nomination, Thurlow Weed offered the general a letter composed by William Seward intended to soothe Whig concerns. However, Taylor rejected Weed's blatant attempt to handle him and produced a bare-bones acceptance. The diminished letter would have aroused little criticism except that Taylor had spent July and August separating from the Whig Party. In a letter to a Philadelphian correspondent George Lippard, Taylor announced he was not a party candidate. To prove his claim Taylor accepted the endorsement of Democrats from Charleston, South Carolina who produced a ticket of the old general for president and Cass's running mate, William Butler, for vice president.[56]

The weak acceptance letter and his seeming bipartisan campaign sparked a near revolt by the Whig establishment. To calm them Taylor published his second Allison letter on September 4, declaring his fealty to the Whigs and his belief in party principles while accepting any Democrat support he could manage. Taylor declared himself the peoples' candidate rather than a representative of narrow interests. The letter seemed a reiteration of the general's disdain for parties but Crittenden, Stephens, and Weed were quick to spin the letter as Taylor's formal embracing of the party.[57]

As the campaign progressed, Whig leaders accepted that Taylor was not a full-fledged Whig but were desperate enough for office to ignore his pandering to Democrats and his threats to remain independent. The only state to reject Taylor's sincerity was South Carolina, its leaders interpreting the second Allison letter as rejecting the state's purist principles on slavery. This moved many radicals back to the Democrats and Cass, whose squatter sovereignty was more acceptable.

STATE ELECTIONS

Whigs and Democrats hoped victory in congressional, gubernatorial, and state legislative contests would provide momentum for the November election. Unlike previous elections in 1800 and 1824, by 1848, electors were chosen almost exclusively by the voters. Standing alone among the states, South Carolina was the only state that continued the practice of its state legislature choosing presidential electors. The legislative elections in October offered insight into how traditionally Democrat southern states might vote. If Taylor did better than expected, it could mean a Whig landslide in the region as South Carolina was an overwhelmingly Democrat state. However, South Carolina voters chose a pro-Cass majority ensuring the state's electoral votes would be cast for the Democrat. Other states also held state and congressional elections with mixed results.

Whigs elected John Crittenden as Kentucky governor though the small margin for the longtime senator and Clay ally suggested trouble for the party. Kentucky was considered a safe Whig state in the presidential election, but Taylor's Deep South roots and his weak attachment to the party hurt him in Clay's home state. Georgia was a Deep South state considered a toss-up. With Alexander Stephens and Robert Toombs using their congressional districts to increase the Whig vote in Georgia, Whigs hoped to steal the normally Democrat voting state. Their efforts bore fruit in the state legislative races as Whigs picked up seats, a warning to Democrats to redouble their efforts in a state they had swept easily in 1844.

Clay and the Whigs narrowly carried Ohio in 1844, but with Taylor heading the ticket the state was targeted by Democrats. In October elections Whigs won the governorship by a mere 350 votes, much reduced from the large majorities enjoyed in past elections. The results offered the party little momentum in a state Taylor would have to win. Democrats won Pennsylvania in 1844, but the Walker tariff made it a potential Taylor pickup. In early elections Whigs elected a governor, but Democrats swept congressional races. The congressional defeats were partly the result of Taylor's separating himself from the party.

The old general seemed satisfied to attract Democrat voters while those same voters elected Democrats to the Congress.[58]

Without a clear winner in the October state elections, the two parties struggled to implement their campaign plans. The Whig strategy of focusing on parts of the south while retaining or expanding on northern states won by Clay suffered a setback with some of the southern state elections. Democrats saw their own vote totals decline in states as disparate as Georgia and Pennsylvania, Cass's candidacy not energizing Democrat voters to go to the polls.

THE CAMPAIGN

The 1844 election had been the first to make slavery a wedge issue in a presidential campaign. Democrats took advantage of James Knox Polk's support for Texas annexation and slavery expansion to appeal to slaveholders, whereas the Whigs were forced to run on Henry Clay's anti- annexationist platform. However, in 1848 it was the Democrats who struggled with slavery as Cass tried to straddle the issue by appealing to voters from both regions on the issue of slavery in the newly acquired territories. With Zachary Taylor on the ticket, Whigs competed in the south, able to show their dedication to the maintenance of slavery without making a public pronouncement on the issue. The 1848 election would be the last in over a century in which both parties had a realistic chance to win multiple states in all regions of the country. Not including the Reconstruction years, it was not until 1928 that a Republican won more than one southern state in what became a solid Democrat south.

The Whigs and Democrats adjusted their messages according to the region and the audience, a typical political approach but with the Whig refusing to issue a platform in 1848, the Democrats were left punching the air while Whigs ran on Taylor's personality and heroism. In the north Whigs denounced Cass for his squatter sovereignty and the potential for slavery expansion into northern territories. The party tied Cass to the Mexican War, highly unpopular with northern Whigs and antislavery Democrats.

These same voters mistrusted Taylor who had carried out Polk's war policy and was believed to share his proslavery views. Northern Democrats and antislavery conscience Whigs had their own litmus test for Taylor by demanding his support for the Wilmot Proviso. Whigs dodged a direct answer by reminding voters that Cass's popular sovereignty granted citizens the authority to decide whether to allow slavery in their territory. As Cass explicitly rejected the Wilmot Proviso, antislavery voters were left with the choice of Taylor the slaveholder or the third-party Free Soilers. To attract antislavery voters, Whigs offered their boilerplate philosophy on presidential power which denied Taylor had an opinion on the Wilmot Proviso. The proviso was a congressional initiative and therefore according to Whig doctrine, Taylor could not veto the proviso without ignoring his party's basic beliefs.[59]

While the Whigs wisely avoided the issue, their explanation convinced few voters who understood the sectional divisions within the Congress. The Wilmot Proviso was unlikely to pass even a Whig Congress, and a Democrat Congress would never allow a limitation on slavery to reach the president. Taylor's opinion on the Wilmot Proviso was irrelevant as he would have little control over the issue.

Whigs changed their tactics when introducing Taylor to southerners. Instead of emphasizing his dedication to Whig principles, southern Whigs such as Stephens and Toombs, downplayed the possibility of the Proviso passing and making Taylor an irrelevant player on the issue. The implication was that Taylor, the slave-owning president, would never agree to any restrictions on slavery extension in the territories. The argument attracted Whig voters back to the party but failed to influence many Democrats or proslavery radicals such as Yancey.[60]

Democrats' rhetoric tried to soothe southern concerns about a northern candidate. In the north they associated Cass with western aspirations of growth and cheap land. His squatter sovereignty expanded on the Jacksonian dedication to greater democracy in the slavery debate by allowing territorial voters decide the issue. The narrative appealed to pro and antislavery voters who could interpret vague statements as reflecting their values.

In the north, Democrats exploited Taylor's slaveholding and his attachment to southern values. Cass appealed to pro–Wilmot Democrats by suggesting the slave-owner would never approve any limitations on slavery in the territories. Democrats portrayed the old general as a doddering novice lacking political knowledge and ability. Once in office, Democrats warned, Taylor would be influenced by a cabal of southern slave-owners led by Stephens and Toombs who promoted his candidacy with the hope they could attain national power.

In the south, the two parties not unexpectedly portrayed Cass on starkly different terms. Whigs exploited his northern roots, tying him to the Free Soil Movement and harboring a plan to impose the Wilmot

Proviso on the region. The Whig narrative compared Cass to Van Buren who was hated in the south because of his opposition to Texas annexation. Whigs went further to present an image of southern partisans, adopting Calhoun's criticism of Polk's Oregon treaty with Britain as it opened up vast northern territories free of slavery.[61]

For the first time southern Democrats were on the defensive. The region had been the base of Jeffersonian Republicans and their successors, the Jacksonian Democrat. Taylor's candidacy opened up the region and forced Democrats to commit resources on their political base. Cass's squatter sovereignty proved a weak gruel for southerners even as it was considered a better option than the hated and feared Wilmot Proviso. Cass, though, would not bend to the growing demands of southerners for legal recognition of slave rights throughout federal territories. With the southern slaveholder Taylor offering regional loyalty and military heroism to southern voters, Democrats offered the existence of the Free Soil Party as proof that Cass did not harbor secret abolitionist tendencies.

With the slavery issue turned against them, Democrats focused on Taylor's inexperience and the hypocrisy of the Whig Party offering an unknown general as their candidate after having built the party on opposition to Andrew Jackson and his activist presidency.[62]

ELECTION

Voters in all the states would go to the polls on the same day for the first time in general election history. The 1845 federal election law set the date as the first Tuesday after the first Monday in November, the odd arrangement based partly on the demands of rural folk to attend church on Sunday and finish their business on Monday. The first Tuesday after the first Monday also ensured Election Day would never fall on the first day of November, celebrated by Catholics as All Saints Day. The single day was seen by some as a dangerous attempt by the federal government to regiment individual behavior and dilute state power over their elections.

The election results would vex Democrats and surprise Whigs. The Whig's southern strategy proved a success with Taylor splitting the region's vote with Cass. Stephens and Toombs delivered Georgia and its ten electors to the Whigs, neighboring Florida with three electors, and North Carolina with 11 votes. Louisiana not unexpectedly voted for its favorite son. Taylor took the Whig strongholds of Tennessee and Kentucky and therefore carrying over a third of the slave states. His southern strength extended to states he did not win, losing the strongly Democrat state of Alabama by a mere 900 votes, losing Virginia by 1,200 votes, and losing by 600 votes in Mississippi.[63]

Taylor was more than a southern candidate, holding onto the Whig northeastern strongholds of Massachusetts, Connecticut, Vermont, and Rhode Island. Cass was strongest in the old northwest sweeping Illinois, Indiana, Wisconsin, and Michigan, his home state, though his vote totals were below Polk's numbers in 1844. He also took Ohio, which Clay had won in 1844.

The slavery issue, represented in the north by the Wilmot Proviso and the breakaway Free Soil Party affected both candidates. Free Soil influence extended beyond its New York base and hurt Whigs in two key states. In Illinois the Free Soil Party polled 15,000 votes while Taylor lost the state by 3,300 votes. Many Illinois Free Soil votes were likely Conscience Whigs who would not support a slaveholder president. In Maine the Free Soil candidates polled 12,000 votes while Taylor lost by fewer than 5,000. However, the most dramatic shift came in New York where Van Buren and his Barnburner Democrat faction knocked Cass into a third-place finish. Taylor won 48 percent of the vote in the three-way race, but took all 35 electoral votes which proved to be his margin of victory. The Whigs also took the Polk state of Pennsylvania and its 26 electoral votes as Democrats were forced to defend the unpopular Walker Tariff and the Whig promise to enact a protective tariff tilted the state to Taylor.[64]

Overall Taylor took just over 47 percent of the national vote and 163 electoral votes to Cass's 42 percent of the vote and 127 electoral votes. While New York was identified as the key state, if Cass had carried three southern states won by Polk, North Carolina, Georgia, and Florida, the additional 24 electoral votes would have put him over the top. Pennsylvania's 26 votes which had been taken by Polk in 1844 with the help of George Dallas would also have put Cass over the top.[65]

AFTERMATH

The 1848 election proved to be the Whig Party's last gasp. Taylor's candidacy revealed the party's weaknesses. In 1844 Whigs finally accepted the difficult truth that their founder, Henry Clay, could not win the presidency running a campaign purely on Whig principles. Borrowing from 1840 when the party chose a personally popular candidate, Whigs used Taylor's war celebrity to win an unlikely victory. Unlike 1840 when economic depression and an unpopular incumbent had been convenient campaign targets, the 1848 campaign was conducted against a popular party and a candidate who lacked personal appeal but sported a record of accomplishment. Moreover, like in 1840 when John Tyler succeeded William Henry Harrison and adopted policies that ran counter to Whig principles, President Taylor proved as independent-minded in office as he had during the campaign. Rejecting many Whig regulars for the cabinet Taylor struggled to impose control over his party during the debate over the 1850 Compromise.[66] As Henry Clay maneuvered a compromise bill through Congress he faced another disastrous clash with his party's president until fate intervened. After a Fourth of July celebration, Taylor was struck by cholera and succumbed. His presidency went unmourned, and the old soldier has been rated among the worst presidents. The Whig Party would die four years later after a crushing loss in the 1852 election.

Lewis Cass enjoyed a longer and more eventful career after his defeat. Cass's squatter sovereignty proposals would be enacted into law in the Kansas–Nebraska Act. In 1857 President James Buchanan appointed Cass as secretary of state though he served as a placeholder with the former secretary of state Buchanan running his own foreign policy. Cass shined during the secession crisis, arguing for Buchanan to take action against South Carolina. When the president refused, Cass resigned: a clear statement of disgust for his party's weakness. Cass would live to see the end of war, never admitting the trigger that popular sovereignty served in igniting the civil war.[67]

12

The Greatest Upset

THE WAR HORSE VERSUS THE DARK HORSE, 1844

Americans in the 1840s lived through tumultuous times as they faced economic depression, the death of a president, a major war, and five presidential administrations. Political failure became the norm as did sectional division that drove the country to the edge of civil war. Amidst this turmoil were two dramatic presidential elections in 1844 and 1848 featuring the two greatest upsets in presidential history as the first dark-horse candidate, James Polk, and the only novice presidential candidate, Zachary Taylor, defeated more experienced opponents. The 1844 presidential election outranks others based on the disparity between the two opponents. Henry Clay was an iconic figure during his lifetime and likely more recognized by modern readers than the man who defeated him, President James Knox Polk. Though the 1844 election is overshadowed by modern political upsets in 1948 and 1960, the shock of Clay's third presidential defeat by a relative unknown during a time of Whig ascendancy places it as the greatest presidential upset.

TYLER ADMINISTRATION

The Whig and Democrat parties in 1844 faced an election where neither controlled the issues that would decide the election. Instead, President John Tyler, former Democrat and Whig, manipulated the political agenda for his own benefit and outmaneuvered two of the most powerful politicians of the era. Tyler was dismissed as a radical—a common political slur tossed about American campaigns with little thought to its meaning. Republics and their political leaders tend toward the middle and the maintenance of the status quo except in times of great distress. Some of the most prominent American presidents including Jackson, Lincoln, Franklin D. Roosevelt, and Reagan were denounced as radicals before or during their administrations, and each would have a political era bearing their name.

Tyler was one of the office's most rigid ideologues who exacerbated sectional divisions and started the process that led to the Civil War. As a senator from Virginia, Tyler abandoned the Democrats for the Whig Party over disagreement with Andrew Jackson's bank policy. In 1840 Tyler was picked to run as vice president with William Henry Harrison under the slogan "Tippecanoe and Tyler Too" which defeated President Martin Van Buren in a landslide.

Tyler became president after Harrison's sudden death. His administration was engulfed in controversy as Congress debated whether he was a mere "acting" president. The Whig leader Henry Clay controlled Congress, passing legislation to reestablish the Bank of the United States which Tyler vetoed. The angry Clay accused Tyler of overstepping his prerogatives as Whig presidents were expected to bend to the will of Congress and use their veto power only in rare case of an unconstitutional law. Clay crafted a second bank bill which Tyler also vetoed, triggering a political crisis as the president found himself at odds with his adopted party.

The two vetoes isolated Tyler from the Whigs, and on September 11, 1841 most of Harrison's cabinet resigned, leaving only Secretary of State Daniel Webster.[1] The mass resignation triggered a period of administrative chaos as Tyler employed three secretaries of state, four treasury secretaries, four war secretaries, three attorneys general, and five Navy secretaries in rapid succession. The rapid turnover had cabinet members serving in more than one department with his Secretary of State Abel Upshur running the state department while also serving as war secretary. Earlier Attorney General Hugh Legare ran the justice and state departments. In early 1844 Upshur and Navy Secretary John Gilmer died in the explosion of the Navy ship *Princeton*, further complicating governance.[2] They were replaced by proslavery ideologues John Calhoun and John Mason who later promoted radical views on government. Calhoun's theory of interposition was the predecessor to secession while Mason was responsible for the 1854 Ostend Manifesto calling for U.S. annexation of Cuba.

In addition to his official cabinet Tyler utilized a kitchen cabinet of informal advisors, the most prominent being Beverley Tucker. The

University of Virginia law professor's radical ideas on slavery included authoring an 1836 dystopian novel, *The Partisan Leader* predicting secession and civil war if Martin van Buren was elected. This combination of kitchen and official cabinet led Tyler down an ideological path that would split the country along sectional lines.[3]

By 1844 Tyler was determined to win a second term and saw the annexation of Texas as a wedge issue that would win him reelection. His first appointed Secretary of State, Abel Upshur, defended Texas annexation on geopolitical grounds, warning Texas could become a British ally and endanger the country's southwestern border. Upshur's successor, Calhoun, rejected geopolitics in favor of domestic politics. Composing a letter to Richard Pakenham, the British minister in Washington, Calhoun made Texas annexation an issue of slavery expansion and defended the institution as a moral and economic necessity. When the letter was made public Texas annexation became a sectional issue with southerners generally in support and northerners generally in opposition. By spring 1844 the Whig and Democrat front-runners faced a political scene dominated by the Texas question.[4]

The 1844 campaign promised a battle between political heavy-weights. Former president Martin van Buren, known as the little magician for his political abilities, represented the Democrats, whereas the two-time presidential loser Clay was the Whig front-runner. The Van Buren–Clay battle would have matched the two greatest politicians of an era for the first time since the 1800 presidential election between John Adams and Thomas Jefferson, but the political forces unleashed by Tyler and Calhoun in their quest for Texas statehood stopped the battle before it could begin.

THE LITTLE MAGICIAN

Though known as a loyal Jacksonian, Martin Van Buren had not always supported the old general. A dedicated Republican in 1824, Van Buren had supported William Crawford, the one true Jeffersonian in a crowded four-candidate field. Leader of New York's Regency faction, Van Buren worked for Crawford's election but failed miserably as he angered allies with his political manipulations, leading to John Quincy Adams and Henry Clay dividing up most of the state's electors.

Though Crawford was one of the three candidates to reach the House of Representatives, Van Buren failed to deliver the New York

House delegation for him, and the state provided the deciding vote for John Quincy Adams. After his defeat, Van Buren shifted his support to Andrew Jackson who rewarded him with appointment as secretary of state. In 1832 Jackson chose him to replace John Calhoun as vice president and then four years later endorsed Van Buren for president. Disaster followed when Jackson's economic policies caused a bank panic and depression that engulfed Van Buren's administration.

After four years of battling economic depression and congressional Whigs, Van Buren in 1840 faced a pitch-perfect presidential campaign that utilized favored slogans and songs while ignoring policy arguments to win a landslide victory. His defeat was followed by four years in New York exile where the little magician yearned for a return to the White House. Considered Jackson's heir, Van Buren prepared to win his third Democrat nomination and take on Henry Clay.

However, Van Buren had lost touch with the political culture. John Tyler's igniting of southern nationalism made Texas annexation a litmus test among Democrats. No candidate could win the Democrat nomination without support of the party's southern wing, but Van Buren ignored that reality, hubris and ideology clouding his usual clear political instincts as he came to believe he could overcome all obstacles.

Van Buren's first mistake was assuming that he enjoyed Andrew Jackson's support. While Jackson was the creator of the doctrine of manifest destiny, Van Buren expected the old general to automatically oppose any policy offered by his two rivals: Tyler and Calhoun. Tyler had voted against rescinding the Senate's censure of Jackson while John Calhoun defied the president during the South Carolina secession crisis of 1832. However, Jackson was unpredictable, and he put aside personal feelings in favor of his country.

As Tyler and Calhoun moved closer to a formal annexation treaty with Texas, the administration's congressional allies promoted the issue. In a letter in February 1844 Mississippi Democrat Senator Robert Walker offered the Jeffersonian argument that spreading slavery among the states and territories benefitted the entire country and not just the slave-owning south. Walker pressed Van Buren to publicly support annexation, and if he refused Walker warned that southern Democrats would find another candidate.[5]

Van Buren's response came in a letter to another Mississippi Democrat: Congressman William Hammet. The so called Hammet letter was a 72-page argument against Texas annexation. Van Buren began by defending his Texas policy as secretary of state and president, noting he had supported buying the territory from the Mexicans. However,

Van Buren worried that the plans of Tyler and Calhoun would lead to war with Mexico over Texas' southern border. The letter dismissed the claim that Great Britain would gain influence in Texas if the United States did not act. Van Buren proposed delaying any treaty with Texas until the republic had worked out its border disputes with Mexico, therefore ensuring the United States would not be dragged into war.[6]

Van Buren's letter roiled the Democrat president race, and Andrew Jackson called on his former protégé to withdraw from the nomination race. With Van Buren in disfavor, Jackson's endorsement was available to the other potential Democrat candidates with the only requirement being a wholehearted support of Manifest Destiny. The Hammet letter complicated the Whigs' election strategy with Henry Clay convinced that he would face Van Buren who shared his doubts about the wisdom of Texas annexation.[7]

THE WHIGS

Van Buren's Whig opponent was to the most successful American politician never to reach the White House. Henry Clay had swept into power in 1810 along with a faction of young Turks known as the War Hawks. Elected speaker of the House in his first term, Clay transformed the office into a powerful position, using his control over committee assignments to exert near absolute control over the chamber. Two presidential runs followed, and his 1824 "corrupt bargain" with John Quincy Adams earned him the undying enmity of Andrew Jackson. A second presidential run in 1832 under the banner of the new Whig Party also ended in defeat. In 1836 he declined nomination, and the Whigs embarked on a peculiar three-candidate campaign that elected a Democrat president. Four years later with Van Buren staggering toward near certain defeat, Clay was denied nomination, rejected for the popular general William Henry Harrison.

Harrison's election swept in a Whig Congress and offered Clay an opportunity to enact his American system of internal improvements and a protective tariff. Clay planned to guide the Whig agenda through Congress and have the pliable general sign it, making the senator the de facto prime minister. Whether the old general would have agreed with the senator's arrangement is an unsolved mystery: Harrison's death a month into his administration and his replacement by John Tyler upset all of Clay's plans. Tyler's veto of two bank bills created a split in the party with Clay accusing the president of creating a "corporal's guard" of advisors and defying the Whig Party that elected him. Stymied in his plans and approaching 65 years of age, Clay resigned his Senate seat in March 1842, needing a respite from Washington political battles to gird for his third and likely final presidential campaign. Clay, though, left Washington with more enemies than friends with prominent Democrats and independents such as Tyler, James Buchanan, and John Calhoun working against him.[8]

Even out of office, Clay influenced the Whigs as he engineered a purge of the party to eliminate all of Tyler's followers. Over the next three years Whigs who accepted Tyler's patronage or voted with the president faced Whig challengers for the party nomination. The effort to cleanse the party ran into a considerable obstacle in Massachusetts where Daniel Webster remained in Tyler's cabinet and worked hard to settle Canadian boundary disputes with the British. When Massachusetts' Whigs loyal to Clay tried to seize control of the state party, Webster fought them off. The internal Whig battle split the party and hindered Clay's efforts to unite the party for 1844.[9]

The 1842 midterm elections placed Whigs in a political predicament not faced by most parties. Midterms are usually marked by steep losses suffered by the party controlling the White House. In 1842 Tyler was recognized by the public as a Whig even after his party abandoned him. With the country entering the seventh year of an economic depression, congressional Whigs would be punished as much as the Democrats suffered in 1838 and 1840. Clay's unwise purge further divided the party as some Whig congressmen were rejected by the party and replaced with weaker candidates. In addition, congressional gains by the party in 1838 and 1840 elected many Whigs in traditional Democrat districts, further damaging their reelection prospects.

The midterms produced dramatic drops in Whig voter turnout in state and congressional elections. A Whig House majority of 43 was eliminated with the party winning only 79 seats to 142 seats for Democrats. The promised Whig revolution of 1840 instead produced larger Democrat congressional majorities, but the Whig setback proved only temporary. Between 1842 and 1844 Whigs recovered some of their losses at the state legislative level. In 1842 Democrats controlled both houses in 14 state legislatures, whereas the Whigs controlled only five legislatures. By 1844 Whig-controlled legislatures had increased to nine while Democrat- controlled legislatures also numbered nine.[10] In Georgia, Whigs seized control of the state legislature and put the state into play for 1844. Another southern Whig victory came in Andrew

Jackson's Tennessee as former House speaker and governor, James Knox Polk, was defeated in his third run for governor. Tennessee became a swing state, further convincing Clay he could win in the state if Van Buren was the Democrat nominee.[11]

With their sudden change in fortune, the Whig defeat in 1842 was less predictive of the 1844 presidential election than most midterms. The confused politics of the time with an independent president appealing to Democrats also scrambled predictions for 1844. Even while losing the House Whigs maintained their Senate majority, and by 1844 after they were fully separated from the unpopular Tyler, their midterm losses seemed less important.

With the 1844 election approaching, Tyler made plans for reelection. He manipulated patronage, appointing supporters including Democrats to government positions with some of his appointees influencing the Democrat presidential nomination. Webster's resignation in 1843 solidified Whig opposition to Tyler and eliminated the president as a viable candidate in the northeast and northwest. Tyler's candidacy, though, would dramatically affect Democrats as the president appealed to pro-Texas southerners which were the base of the Democrat Party. Tyler's presence in the race would only benefit his old enemy, Henry Clay, and possibly help the Whigs steal some southern states from the Democrats.

In May 1842 Martin Van Buren visited Clay's Ashfield plantation and during a five-day visit the two men engaged in friendly reminiscences, reliving past battles and discussing personal affairs. It was rare during the era for presidential candidates to meet: access to the candidates carefully managed by their advisors who feared they might misspeak. Later, the meeting would spark conspiracy theories after both men published letters within three days of each other denouncing the Texas annexation and refusing to make it an issue for the fall campaign.[12]

After Van Buren's visit, Clay began a slow-motion campaign for the presidency while state Whig conventions endorsed him. During a massive barbecue in the summer of 1842 Clay attacked Tyler and Jackson in the same breath, appealing to the Whig base and trying to tie the unpopular Tyler to the Democrat party.

In December 1843 he launched a southern tour intended to strengthen his appeal among the region's Democrats and exploiting Van Buren's New York origins. As in 1824 and 1832 Clay miscalculated; his belief in his political abilities led him to take his base for granted and reach out to voters who were unlikely to change their vote no matter where the Democrat nominee lived. Successful candidates use their early campaign days to solidify their base, which for Clay and the Whigs was the old northwest stretching from Missouri to Ohio and Pennsylvania. The voters in these states were susceptible to proposals for a higher tariff and greater spending on internal improvements. However, Clay believed Van Buren's expected nomination would make the south, particularly Tennessee, Louisiana, and Georgia, susceptible to a Whig appeal. When the little magician's magic failed him for the last time at the Democrat convention, Clay's strategy also failed.

His travels presented the image of a "new" Clay who appealed to southerners. Starting in New Orleans then continuing along the Gulf Coast, the senator enjoyed large and enthusiastic crowds. However, instead of conducting a listening tour in which he gauged voters' interest, Clay tried to mold public opinion with a series of speeches on the tariff and national bank even as Texas was on the lips of most southerners who were exhausted with unending Washington economic debates and eager to enjoy the fruits of new territory. Clay ignored this sentiment: a strategic error that has never been explained. It is possible that he had discussed Texas with Van Buren during his Kentucky visit and had been convinced to oppose annexation and remove it as a campaign issue. Possibly Clay's hatred of Tyler clouded the senator's judgment as he sought to hand the president a loss. Clay had surrendered his Senate seat in frustration with Tyler, and reversing course on Texas policy may have felt like one more defeat. While Clay basked in the jubilant celebrations of his visits, he ignored the advice offered by his southern hosts on the Texas question.[13]

During his Georgia visit Clay pandered to the memory of Georgia native William Crawford and revealed that he supported the treasury secretary for the presidency in 1824 until Crawford was struck by illness. His words had little effect as few recalled a man dead for a decade, but his mention of 1824 dredged up memories of a corrupt bargain and Clay's reputation for slick dealings. A trip to Charleston, South Carolina was followed by a stop in Raleigh, North Carolina where Clay destroyed his campaign, composing a letter rejecting questions on Texas annexation. According to legend, Clay drew up his "Raleigh" letter on April 17 under the leaves of an oak tree. Clay's words eviscerated the good feelings created during his four months journey.[14]

Clay began with a dig at John Quincy Adams, blaming the former secretary of state for signing the Adams–Onis Treaty foreswearing Texas annexation. After settling a score, Clay warned that Tyler's plan for Texas annexation would destabilize the country's regional balance. Clay also mentioned debt: a subject tackled by Van Buren in his Hammet letter and raising suspicions of collusion. The debt issue was irrelevant to southern expansionists who saw Texas as an opportunity rather than a burden. Clay mailed the letter to Washington and had it published in major Whig newspapers just as he ended his southern tour.[15]

Van Buren's Hammet letter was published three days later, and the joint publication raised suspicions that the two political manipulators were trying to remove a divisive issue from the campaign. Clay's Raleigh letter likely had less to do with Van Buren and the November election than with Tyler's negotiations with Texas Governor Sam Houston on an annexation treaty and its presentation to the Senate for approval. With publication of the Raleigh letter, Whig policy counseled rejection of the annexation treaty: a measure of revenge for Clay against the man who had twice vetoed his national bank. The letter's publication was the action of a man beyond reason as Clay forbade all his advisors, including fellow Kentucky Whig John Crittenden, from changing a single word or debating the wisdom of rejecting annexation. The sheer recklessness of stating his views and allowing his enemies to control the debate was not the actions of a calculating politician but rather of a man seeking revenge from a rival who had dashed his plans.

On June 8, the Senate rejected the Texas annexation treaty as 24 of 25 Whig senators rejected it and handed Tyler and Calhoun an embarrassing defeat. Clay had his revenge, but the rejection strengthened the hand of the pro-annexation party because Texas remained an election issue, and Tyler continued his plans to run under a third-party label.[16]

In forcing the Texas question, Tyler aroused the latent abolitionism building in the North. Calhoun's extreme defense of slavery in his Pakenham letter convinced many that the federal government had been seized by radical southerners bent on expanding slavery through annexation and war. Tyler's strategy that included forming a third party based on states' rights and making slavery a sectional issue had disastrous effects beyond 1844.

DEMOCRATS FOR PRESIDENT

While Clay campaigned through the south in 1844, Martin Van Buren struggled to fend off Democrat rivals. During the winter and spring

12 of 18 Democrat state conventions endorsed the former president. By the time of the Democrat convention in May, Van Buren had a majority of pledged delegates, making him the party front-runner. Van Buren's support masked weakness in his campaign as he struggled with Tyler, his own political record, and other Democrats who challenged his nomination.[17]

Van Buren's past was tied to Jacksonian economic doctrine which many voters associated with failed bank policies and 1837 depression. If Clay and the Whigs were trapped by stale economic theories such as the national bank and the tariff, Van Buren and the Democrats clung to their controversial subtreasury plan, passed after three years of congressional infighting and then repealed with a stroke of Tyler's pen. Without a successful record to run on, Van Buren was a decided underdog to Clay—the Whigs reminding voters why they turned out the little magician only four short years earlier.

Van Buren faced a weaker challenge from his own party, the Democrats fielding a weak bench of candidates who would try to upend the former president. Former Michigan territorial governor and ambassador to France Lewis Cass mounted a late campaign for the nomination. Returning to the United States in 1843 after his overseas posting, Cass was unburdened by the failed Van Buren and Tyler administrations which offered him the advantage of running as an outsider who was uninvolved in the pitched political battles of the era.

With Jacksonian economics discredited by the 1837 Depression, Cass took a Jeffersonian approach, opposing tariffs and internal improvements, but did not mention the depression, its causes, or how to end it. Cass's caution earned him the reputation as an unreliable Democrat: his sparse political record and lack of elective office made the Democrat establishment wary. Cass's campaign began in December 1843 and gained little traction even as he presented his Jacksonian credentials in the form of a letter of July 1843 from Andrew Jackson praising Cass's "discretion and talents" for opposing Webster–Ashburton. The ambassador distributed the letter to friendly newspapers as proof of his Jacksonian and Democrat roots. However, Cass's late start left him with a handful of delegates facing Van Buren's majority of pledged delegates. His only hope was a stumble by Van Buren, the Hammet letter suddenly making the Michigander a viable challenger.[18]

When Van Buren declared his opposition to annexation, Cass came out in support. While the decision may have seemed easy, it offered its own dangers. The Texas issue had revived antislavery opinion in the north, and Van Buren's barnburner faction in New York was suspicious of southern motives in promoting southwest expansion. Many northern Democrats opposed allowing slavery to move into the southwest, and Cass's approval of the Tyler effort threatened to lose him northern votes.[19]

Cass's challenge for northern Democrat votes was matched by two southern candidates: former vice president under Van Buren, Richard Johnson, and former House speaker, James Knox Polk. Both men competed for votes in the region considered the Van Buren's weakest.

A former soldier, Johnson was plagued by controversy including a disputed claim of killing the Indian leader Tecumseh and his several children with his former common-law wife, a slave. In 1836 Johnson was elected vice president by the Senate because several Van Buren electors rejected him and denied Johnson an Electoral College majority. In 1840 the Democrat convention rejected a second term for Johnson, but Van Buren remained loyal, allowing him to run on the ticket.[20] After his defeat Johnson planned a comeback, and the 1844 convention offered him the chance for the presidency or the vice presidency. However, Johnson's control of the Kentucky and Arkansas delegations doomed Van Buren even as Johnson never rose above 38 votes at the convention. His main competitor among southerners was another Jackson protégé.

James Knox Polk experienced a childhood rivaling that of Andrew Jackson in difficulty and danger. While Jackson fought in the Revolution at age 13 and received a scar on his head from a British sword, Polk was born and raised in North Carolina near Charlotte after the revolution. He was a sickly youth and at age 17 underwent a dangerous gallbladder surgery without the benefit of anesthesia. The operation proved a success, and Polk's health was temporarily restored.[21]

During the 1824 presidential election he was elected to the House of Representatives but because he was not seated until March 1825, he did not have the opportunity to vote for the man who would become his political hero and patron. For the next 14 years he was a loyal Jacksonian, serving four years as House speaker and guiding through such critical bills as the 1837 Judiciary Act which allowed Jackson to pack the Supreme Court. In 1835 Polk was caught in the middle of the slavery debate after South Carolina Congressman James Henry Hammond demanded that antislavery petitions presented to the House be rejected without debate. From December 16, 1835 through February 8, 1836, the House was engulfed in debate over the so called gag rule which would have banned any discussion of the petitions. Polk eventually found a compromise, sending the slavery petitions to a special committee where they died without comment. This early test of his leadership exposed Polk to the intense feelings over slavery and taught him how to balance sectional interests, a talent that served him well in 1844.[22]

As the Van Buren administration ground to a halt over its subtreasury plan that Polk could not pass, the Speaker left the House and in 1839 was elected Tennessee governor, drawing him closer to the retired Jackson and making him a potential presidential candidate. However, presiding over the state government was not enough action for a politician who helped Jackson battle the Bank of the United States and struggled to remake the country's financial system during the depression. In 1840 he launched his campaign to remove Vice President Richard Johnson from the Democrat ticket.[23] The controversial Johnson was an easy target, but Polk's defeat at the 1840 presidential convention began a downward spiral in his political career. Polk was defeated for reelection in 1841 and then lost his comeback attempt for the same office in 1843. By the spring of election year his political career was at a standstill: his one hope was another quixotic run for the vice presidency. Van Buren's expected nomination as the Democrat candidate made Polk a perfect fit because a southern Jacksonian would help the New Yorker in the slave states.

Polk's vice-presidential quest began in Tennessee where he maintained tight control of the state party. At the state's December 1843 convention Polk was nominated for vice president: one of the first state endorsements of any candidate. Unlike many states that would nominate Martin Van Buren or a favorite son candidate, Tennessee left its presidential nomination vacant, implicitly tying the state's convention delegation to Polk and his vice-presidential candidacy. Tennessee Democrats then chose Gideon Pillow as its convention chair. Pillow exploited the relationship between Polk and Massachusetts' George Bancroft, who had led the 1840 effort to replace Richard Johnson with Polk. Bancroft's control of the Massachusetts and New Hampshire delegations proved the key to Polk's convention strategy as the two states started the Polk bandwagon and showed that the Tennessean could attract New England as well as southern Democrats.[24]

Polk's campaign for the vice presidency was an effective front for his secret presidential campaign. As Polk sought Van Buren's support for the vice presidency, the little magician may have suspected that Polk was trying to defeat him. Polk's managers were scooping up delegates for vice president though pledges for the second slot could be transformed into votes for the top slot at the first sign of a deadlock.

Youth was Polk's greatest handicap. Not yet 50, Polk could remain a national candidate through two or three election cycles while his main opponents had a shorter political future. Van Buren could not run for reelection in 1848, and as vice president Polk could follow Van Buren's example in 1836 and collect delegates for an 1848 run. His two rivals for 1848 were Thomas Hart Benton and James Buchanan, both older than Polk, while Lewis Cass would be too old to run for president in 1852, the last year of a two-term Polk presidency.

DEMOCRAT CONVENTION

The 1844 Democrat convention began on May 27 and immediately descended into chaos. A North Carolina delegate Romulus Saunders seized the rostrum at the convention's opening minutes and pushed through the appointment of Pennsylvanian Hendrick Wright as convention chair. Wright was a close ally of Congressman James Buchanan and approved of Texas annexation. Saunders then sought to push through the two-thirds voting rule for the nomination. Under the rule a Democrat candidate would have to receive two-thirds rather than a simple majority of delegate votes. The two-thirds vote had first been instituted at the 1832 Democrat convention and used for Van Buren's vice-presidential nomination. The same rule was used in 1836 but then waived at the 1840 convention. Saunders's thrust was parried because delegates rejected such a critical vote before the convention's invocation and while delegates were settling into their seats.[25]

Saunders's bold attempt was a sign of disarray in Van Buren's campaign. Instead of taking control of the convention, Van Buren's manager, former attorney general Benjamin Butler, allowed the proceedings to be dominated by Van Buren opponents. Butler appeared unprepared for the battle over the two-thirds rule as his candidate was endorsed by a majority of Democrat delegates. Butler could wield that majority to strike down the rule as all rules changes required only a bare majority. Instead, Butler allowed Van Buren's opponents to rally these delegates to their cause, reminding Democrats they were pledged to vote for Van Buren for president but not pledged to vote against the rule. This oversight was even more indefensible as prominent Democrats warned Van Buren of the plan to impose the two- thirds rule majority. Among these was George Bancroft who wrote the New Yorker on May 23, predicting Van Buren would receive 154 first ballot votes, two short of his actual number, but warning that southerners would push for a two-thirds rather than majority rule. Van Buren and Butler ignored the warning.[26]

In the dying hours of the convention's first day, Butler was pressed into a debate over the rule with Mississippi Senator Robert Walker. Having helped provoke the split between northern and southern Democrats over annexation, Walker convinced the Mississippi delegation not to vote for Van Buren, noting that while the state party endorsed the New Yorker the state legislature endorsed Texas annexation, and the latter should guide Mississippi Democrats.[27]

The importance of Wright's choice as convention chair became apparent during the two- thirds debate. Walker offered the argument for a super majority, noting a bare majority vote at the convention might not represent all Democrats and that only by listening to the desires of the minority could the party win in November. Butler followed with his counterargument, noting the party had not always used the two-thirds vote and warning of a deadlock if the rule was imposed. Butler's arguments were so convincing that Democrats appeared on the verge of defeating the two- thirds rule, but Wright adjourned the convention and allowed anti–Van Buren Democrats to lobby the delegates overnight.[28]

The decision on the two-thirds rule came on the second day with the key votes coming from Pennsylvania and Tennessee. The Pennsylvania delegation split with 13 against and 12 for the rule while all 13 Tennessee delegates voted for the rule. Van Buren lost the vote 148–118, but the 25 votes from the two delegations would have given Van Buren a 143–123 win.[29] Van Buren watched as the state delegations of Alabama, Louisiana, Michigan, and Illinois voted for his candidacy after approving the two- thirds rule preventing him from winning the nomination.[30] The beneficiary of the turmoil was the Polk campaign as Gideon Pillow allowed Cass and Johnson to take the lead on the rule. By remaining in the background, the Polk campaign could plausibly deny they led the stop–Van Buren movement. Polk escaped blame for Van Buren's loss while Cass and Johnson bore the brunt of the little magician's anger at being denied his third nomination.[31]

With the rules set, the convention began the long process of counting votes. The first ballot saw Van Buren collect 146 votes: a majority but short of the 177 votes required for a two- thirds majority. Much of

Van Buren's deficit could have been made up with Richard Johnson's votes potentially placing the former president within shouting distance of the nomination. Cass was far behind with 83 and in the next five ballots the New Yorker's totals eroded while Cass's totals crept up.[32] The first ballot failure was another sign of Ben Butler's incompetence. Candidates and their managers usually held back votes from the first to the second ballot, wanting to show an increase in support as the voting progressed. The momentum was used to attract wavering delegates and create a flood of votes leading to nomination. With a majority of delegates in his pocket, Butler expected Van Buren to win on the first ballot but with the change to a two-thirds majority requirement, Butler lacked an alternative and struggled to scrape together additional votes on the second ballot. The result was a slow and inexorable decline in Van Buren's delegate totals.

By the sixth ballot, Van Buren had lost 40 votes, and Cass was the leader but far from the two-thirds majority. When Cass passed Van Buren the frustration of the little magician's delegates spilled over onto the convention floor. Some openly cursed John Tyler, blaming the president for provoking the Texas crisis and destroying Van Buren's chances. Angry words provoked fistfights and then challenges to duels—chaos threatening the party and the nomination.

At that moment the Polk campaign stepped forward. Polk had yet to receive a convention vote, his campaign maintaining the fiction he was purely a vice-presidential candidate. Gideon Pillow met with the New Yorkers and offered Polk as their vice-presidential candidate. With Van Buren unable to win, the Barnburners offered an alternative, Silas Wright: the little magician's protégé and a reliable spokesman for his wing of the party. When Wright refused to offer his name in nomination, a Polk–Wright ticket was proposed, and the Tennessean's presidential campaign was formally launched.[33]

Pillow's offer of Polk as an alternative was accepted by the Van Buren camp as they had focused on Cass rather than Polk as the prime mover for the two-thirds rule. Pillow needed the New York vote which would guide the other die-hard Van Buren delegates at the convention; nonetheless, first Polk would have to demonstrate he was acceptable to other regions of the Democrat Party.

Returning to the convention floor on the third day of the meeting, the delegates were greeted with a sudden change. The New England delegates, firmly in Van Buren's camp, proposed Polk to replace him. As Maine, New Hampshire, and Massachusetts fell into the dark-horse's column, pandemonium erupted. As states changed their votes, the New York delegates left to consider their options. Virginia then moved to Polk and started the southern shift to the Tennessean. The wave broke when New York returned, officially pulling Van Buren's name from the convention and voting for Polk. By the time it was over, Cass was left with Michigan's votes, just as surprised and defeated as Van Buren.[34] In an effort to calm angry Van Buren supporters, the convention offered the vice presidency to Silas Wright but he rejected it, remaining loyal to the man who had helped build his career. After two ballots, Pennsylvania's George Dallas was nominated.[35]

Polk's stunning nomination left the Democrats sharply divided. Van Buren supporters were furious at their defeat on a technicality and primarily blamed Cass, but the choice of a pro- annexation, southern slave-owner was certain to alienate antislavery and anti–Texas Democrats. More worrisome for the party was Tyler's independent campaign: the president nominated by his followers also in Baltimore as the Democrats struggled to nominate Polk. Tyler used the tactics of 1843 and 1844—packing the federal government with his supporters. He was most aggressive in the New York Customs House with hundreds of lucrative patronage jobs filled with men loyal to the president. In Pennsylvania, Tyler partisans competed for local, state, and congressional offices, threatening to split the Democrat vote in the important state. With Polk and Tyler competing for the same votes in the south, it seemed in spring 1844 that the Whigs had an inside track to the presidency.[36]

THE WHIGS AND CLAY

Prior to the Democrat meeting, the Whig convention opened in Washington on May 1 with little suspense. The Whigs had one of the shortest conventions in party history as Clay became the only nonincumbent candidate to be unanimously nominated by acclamation: his influence over the Whigs so complete no figure dare challenge him. The Whig platform was astonishingly brief considering the rabid national debate over Texas, the tariff, and slavery. The party wobbled on the tariff question, refusing to call for a full protectionist tariff. The Whigs had also learned their lesson from the uproar created by Clay's Raleigh letter and skipped over the Texas issue. The party committed one error in choosing a vice-presidential candidate. The nomination of Theodore Frelinghuysen drew howls from Democrats. Frelinghuysen was a leading religious figure: the president of the American Tract Society and vice president of the Sunday School Union. Frelinghuysen's presence on the ticket drew an unfavorable moral comparison to Clay, who was known for his gambling, drinking, and womanizing. The Whig ticket was sneeringly referred to as bane and antidote—the moralist vice president and the rascally Clay. Frelinghuysen brought little to the ticket in comparison with the Democrat candidate George Dallas, who helped swing Pennsylvania to Polk.[37]

With Clay at the top of the ticket, Whigs had the best candidate they could offer and could claim a hand in the economic recovery that took hold in the summer of 1843. The 1842 tariff raised taxes on imports, cutting back on the flow of gold from the country and slowly returning banks to solvency. Running in 1844 Clay could claim credit that his tariff policies had ended the depression after only a single year, whereas the Democrats had failed to revive the economy during Van Buren's entire presidential term.

However, Whig confidence ignored the anomaly that was the 1840 campaign. William Henry Harrison, the Whig candidate, lacked Clay's political baggage, and Harrison had less grandiose view of his own abilities. Harrison had allowed Thurlow Weed and Horace Greeley to run an issueless campaign free from the candidate's ill-timed letters as Harrison maintained a dignified silence. In 1844 Clay would serve as his own campaign manager, ignoring the advice of old friends and colleagues including Kentucky's John Crittenden, considered Clay's closest Senate ally. He would commit the ultimate sin of refighting past elections while not solidifying his base support in certain states—a recipe for an unexpected defeat.

Winning the Whig nomination was the high point of the campaign for Clay even as his party was confident that their man could defeat the Democrats. That confidence was based on the 1840 election, but that year Whigs faced a depression-hobbled Martin Van Buren whose economic record proved an easy target for the Whits. With Clay as candidate, the advantage was reversed as Democrats had 30 years of Clay speeches, actions, and legislation to grease their attack machine. Clay's record included the 1824 corrupt bargain, his previous ties to the unpopular second National bank, and his association with the growing Nativist movement. His personal peccadilloes became fodder because Clay was accused of gambling, excess drinking, irreligiosity, and womanizing. The stories were well known and retold, and Clay could offer little in defense. The usual Whig economic arguments had fallen flat; the tariff was popular in some states and highly unpopular in others. Without issues there was little for Clay to use as a reason for electing him. There would be no repeat of "Tippecanoe and Tyler Too," as Clay and Frelinghuysen lacked the same poetry.

With the Texas annexation issue putting him on the defensive in southern states, Clay struggled to rebuild a southern coalition and steal states from Polk. The obstacle to this approach was his Raleigh letter and its seemingly absolute rejection of annexation. However, just as the Texas annexation issue appeared on the verge of swallowing Clay's campaign, he enjoyed a turn of luck. The Senate rejection of the Texas treaty offered some hope the issue would die down while allowing Clay to push his own moderate plan for Texas statehood after settling issues with Mexico. However, Tyler was not finished wreaking havoc on Clay.

THE 1844 CAMPAIGN

The United States of 1844 was a country on the move. Only three states, Missouri, Arkansas, and Louisiana, sat on territory west of the Mississippi, but their isolation was tempered by vastly expanding populations. Voters of the era, much like voters of every era, sought federal benefits but true to the limited government credo of the time, the government could only provide land: the spoils of Jefferson's Louisiana Purchase. Jacksonian doctrine favored land acquisition to galvanize economic growth and personal liberty, and Polk's campaign reflected those frontier values. Texas annexation offered that land with the presumption that slavery would not take hold as deeply as in the black belt of the southeast.

However, Polk did not campaign purely on territorial acquisition in the south. His "45/40 or fight" slogan challenged an old enemy, Britain, for control of the Pacific Northwest. With "Tippecanoe and Tyler Too" or "Log Cabin and Hard Cider" still ringing in their ears from 1840, Democrats earned a measure of revenge over Whigs as Polk provided the one memorable phrase of the campaign—striking a nationalistic chord and stirring voters to the Democrats. Instead of the manipulative Van Buren with the disastrous record or the untrustworthy, dictatorial, and amoral Clay, Polk offered an unreserved view of the major issue of the day. He settled his base, eliminating the need for an independent

Tyler campaign and placing his name beside the still popular Andrew Jackson.

His first duty was to draw together the disparate factions of the Democrat party. He reached out to his major rivals, recognizing their desire for the White House. In his acceptance letter, Polk foreswore a second term even though he would be the first American president under the age of 50.[38] For other Democrats a Polk win would not mean an eight-year hiatus from presidential politics but rather a four-year breathing space as they could run on Polk's record in 1848 while making it politically profitable to support his candidacy. Each of his rivals—Cass, Buchanan, and Van Buren—held out some hope for the 1848 nomination and would work hard in three important states, Michigan, Pennsylvania, and New York respectively: all states going to Polk.[39]

Polk proved a better strategist than Clay, carefully picking his positions and using his few letters to bolster support in swing states. With Buchanan's help, Polk targeted the swing state of Pennsylvania, where Clay's support of a protective tariff was popular among workers and business in the industrializing state. Democrats had been tagged as free traders by the Whigs, and Polk was forced to separate himself from the Jackson and Van Buren legacy of low tariffs. Senator Robert Walker, who would author the 1846 Walker tariff cutting rates, offered Polk advice on how to handle the issue. He suggested spinning the tariff question by mentioning "incidental protection" and allowing pro-tariff voters to interpret it in their favor. Polk offered his tariff position in a letter to Democrat supporter John Kane in which he followed Walker's formula for smoothing over the tariff question, appealing to industrial workers who feared foreign competition, while he left open the question on the type of tariff he would support or if the tax rates would simply raise revenue or advance the economic goal of creating a domestic market. With his letter, Polk appealed to northern voters without alienating southerners, who were focused on Texas rather than import taxes[40]

Before his nomination, Polk publicly endorsed Texas statehood. A group of Ohioans opposed to Texas annexation and led by nominal Democrat Salmon Chase wrote a letter seeking his views on the issue. In his letter Polk declared absolute support for Texas joining the union. His arguments focused on the threat of British interference in the southwest and ignored the slavery issue. The letter proved effective at two levels. In writing to an anti-Texas group Polk was answering his opponents and could not be accused of offering a political response intended to please its readers. His letter was also certain to receive wide distribution by Chase's group which wanted to use it to undermine his campaign. His honest response would be favorably compared to Clay's mixed responses to the issue.[41]

Polk's greatest advantage was his status as a dark-horse candidate. Though serving as House speaker during Jackson's second term, Polk was unknown to most Americans. Unlike Clay, who suffered from the fact that most voters either loved or hated him and everyone held a firm opinion, Polk was able to slide through the election generating little criticism of his record or positions. His response to the tariff question was just as deceptive and vague as Clay's letters on Texas, but most voters interpreted Clay's effort as the act of a desperate politician trying to avoid the issue or a craven attempt to appeal to all sides.

Polk's nomination further helped Democrats as they benefitted from the advantage of surprise. The Whigs and Clay expected Van Buren's nomination, having collected a considerable dossier of attacks on the Democrat including economic depression, failed economic policy, and a supposed extravagant White House lifestyle. A Van Buren candidacy would have placed many southern states in play as Clay could appeal to the region while still enjoying New England as a solid base of support.

The vice-presidential candidates had their individual appeal though the Whig choice created more problems for Clay than the Democrat candidate did for Polk. Frelinghuysen's association with the temperance movement angered Irish and German voters who saw the movement's focus on alcohol as attacking their personal behavior. Though from New Jersey, Frelinghuysen was nominated with overwhelming support of southern Whigs: the wing of the party most suspicious of immigrants and supportive of what would become the Know Nothing or American Party. Pennsylvania was crucial to the anti-immigrant movement. The Whigs were weakest among Irish Catholic immigrants, their protestant base making Catholics suspicious of the party's motives and support for immigration. An anti-Catholic riot in Philadelphia in May pushed Whigs to denounce the American Party, but political expediency forced Whigs into an alliance with the party, and fused parties routed Democrats in early Pennsylvania state elections. The Pennsylvania results coincided with positive Whig showings in state elections all over the country. Yet, the enthusiasm shown for Whigs proved to be local in nature, and the fervor died down when presidential voting began. Democrats seized on the issue, tying the Whigs to a general nativism, driving up the Catholic and Irish votes in the cities targeted by the Whigs.[42]

The Jacksonians of the 1830s and the Whigs of 1840 used mass rallies to stimulate supporters and undecided voters. Both parties held rallies in Nashville in August 1844, trying to appeal to southern and moderate voters in the state and region. The Democrats' meeting had initially been called as a pro-Texas rally. Southern radicals threatened secession if Texas did not join the union. South Carolina Democrats had not sent a delegation to the national convention in protest of Van Buren's expected nomination. Robert Barnwell Rhett, the South Carolina politician who was a leader of the fire eaters or proslavery radicals, issued bloodcurdling threats. He counseled southerners to "shake off oppression if you can and if you cannot, die like a man." He offered a battle cry of "Disunion, the only remedy," and endorsed the southern Democrat meeting as a means to further his goal of secession.[43]

The mere murmur of secession frightened Democrats, and they feared radicals would alienate unionists in the north and south if their threats were associated with Polk. The August 15 meeting became a celebration of the union with a pro-annexation candidate putting down any talk of civil war or separation from the national government.

Whigs saw the Democrat meeting as an opportunity, and six days after the Democrat meeting the party held a Nashville rally: a daring invasion of the home turf of Polk and Andrew Jackson that also served to draw a distinction between patriotic Whigs and Democrats bent on destroying the Union. Long on pageantry and spectacle, the meeting was part of the strategy to appeal to southern moderates in states where the Whigs could win. Clay targeted Tennessee, North Carolina, and Louisiana, all three southern states sporting a lively Whig Party and offering a chance to break the solid Democrat south.[44]

While Texas and the tariff are identified as the seminal issues in the 1844 campaign, mudslinging was also a part of the campaign. Democrats were quick to remind voters of Henry Clay's personal foibles while Whigs struggled to undermine Polk's image as a strong leader—his relative obscurity forcing them to turn to past rumors. Polk was simultaneously accused of fighting duels and of being a coward when he refused to accept a challenge to fight a duel. Whigs exploited his slave-ownership—forgetting that Clay also was a slave-owner—to attack him among northern voters. They revived the Roorsback story that had Polk branding his slaves with his initials—J.K.P—to assert his ownership. Whigs pointed to this as a sign of the Democrat's cruelty, a story that had been repeated but never proven in the past. Whigs then dug back to revolutionary times, claiming Polk's grandfather had been a British sympathizer. Democrats responded with a pamphlet defending the Polk family as loyal patriots.[45]

With negative attacks against Polk failing, Clay and the Whigs may have perceived his weaknesses in the industrializing northeast and sought alliances with local and state leaders known more for corruption than dedication to the Whig cause but who could turn out votes in critical states. At times these local leaders treated their own electoral prospects more seriously than the presidential contest, but the Whigs could do little except abide by their allies' plans.

Hovering over the election was John Tyler with his Texas annexation plans and independent candidacy. The defeat of the Texas treaty hurt Whigs more than expected as it kept the issue open for discussion. If the treaty had been ratified, the annexation question would have dimmed in importance as the next president would be presented with a fait accompli of an additional state. Much like the Whigs would learn in 1848 with the end of the Mexican War and the acquisition of territory, when the subject turned to slavery expansion they enjoyed an advantage with their northern supporters.

However, under the prodding of Henry Clay, Whig senators defeated Texas and forced the senator to try and wriggle free from his Raleigh letter's denunciation of the plan. The letter had put him on the defensive in the south, but his subsequent adjustments to the letter—known to House members as revising and extending his remarks—hurt him in the north while doing little to strengthen support in the south. For a politician of Clay's abilities and experience, his letter writing campaign in July 1844 seemed more the actions of a desperate novice candidate.

His first letter was sent to an Alabama supporter and parsed the Raleigh letter, noting "Personally I have no objection to the annexation of Texas but I certainly would be unwilling to see the existing Union dissolve . . . for the sake of acquiring Texas." He also took a shot at South Carolina politicians like Rhett who threatened secession and noted that Deep South states would suffer much less than border state Kentucky in any conflict with the north.[46]

The first "Alabama" letter was interpreted by northern and conscience Whigs as a retreat from the Raleigh letter's firm rejection of annexation. Southerners were offended by his equating their desire for territorial expansion with supporting disunion. With his first Alabama letter not providing a surge in his campaign, Clay composed a second letter at the end of the month. He retreated further from the Raleigh missive noting "far from having any personal objection to the annexation of Texas, I should be glad to see it." Clay then listed the requirements for his support including settlement of border issues between Texas and Mexico and an American consensus for annexation.[47]

The second letter was no more helpful, Clay having missed his opportunity with the Raleigh letter. In the spring he could have focused on the requirements for annexation, conditionally supporting it when his requirements were met. This approach would have turned the conversation away from the correctness of annexation to what Texas government would have to do. However, Clay was too confident in his own instincts and believed opposing Texas was a winning issue.

As Clay struggled to deliver the right message on Texas, his path to victory was made that much more difficult as John Tyler disappeared from the scene. The Whigs' best hope for victory was Tyler's independent campaign pulling enough annexationist votes from Polk to allow Clay to win some southern states. Among these tossups were North Carolina, Georgia, Tennessee, and Louisiana, all of which had voted for Harrison in 1840 and had Whig congressmen and senators.

Tyler had remained a candidate through the summer, holding out a diminishing hope for a second full term. With his campaign the only trump card he enjoyed in any negotiations with Polk and the Democrats, Tyler held onto the possibility of continuing into November and potentially undermining the Polk candidacy. As a former Democrat who led former Democrats, Tyler wanted to return to his old party with his supporters eligible for offices in the Polk administration.

The independent campaign ended only after Tyler received a letter from Jackson, who reached out to the president, appealing to his dedication to the cause of Texas. Jackson complimented Tyler for his strength of personality and while not asking the president to withdraw or promising jobs in a future administration made clear that the apostate and his followers would be accepted back into the fold as soon as they halted the independent campaign. On August 20, Tyler pulled out of the race and joined his secretary of state John Calhoun in endorsing Polk.

With the challenge to the Democrats over, the Whigs suddenly worried about the challenge of the antislavery Liberty Party. Conscience Whigs who opposed slavery extension also opposed Texas annexation and, whereas Clay's Raleigh letter appealed to some, most abolition-ists categorically refused to vote for a slave-owner—no matter what his views. Polk ignored his segment of voters, most of them in states far beyond the grasp of Democrats, especially a southern Democrat.

EARLY ELECTIONS AND PREDICTIONS

State and congressional elections were held in September and October and offered insight into the presidential election. If, as 19th-century political observers noted, the country followed Maine, then Clay and the Whigs were doomed as Democrats swept the state legislative elec-tions. Whigs did win the governorship of Maine and Vermont, but saw their majorities diminished by Liberty Party voters.

In Ohio a narrow win for the Whig gubernatorial candidate calmed some of the fears while in Pennsylvania, state elections showed the ef-fectiveness of the Whig–American fusion, the combined vote of the two parties overwhelming the Democrat vote and making it a swing state.[48]

Whigs showed unexpected strength in Louisiana as they seized control of the state legislature and won a congressional seat. Louisi-ana's proximity to Texas and its strong pro- annexationist movement had not doomed the Whigs, leaving the state viable for Clay. More Whig victories in Kentucky— one of the strongest Whig parties in the South—and Missouri offered more, though weaker evidence of a growing Whig vote.

This was countered by Democrat victory in Illinois and mixed re-sults in Indiana, both key states to Whigs. With swing states like Penn-sylvania and New York in the balance, Democrats steadied Polk's campaign by choosing popular candidates for governor in both states. Martin Van Buren's ally, Silas Wright, replaced the sitting Democrat governor on the New York ballot because Wright was considered the best candidate and able to appeal to the Barnburner faction. Without a solid New England bloc, Clay would have to sweep the large northern states and peel off southern states from Polk.

RIGHT BUT NOT PRESIDENT

Voters went to the polls in November 1844 facing a clear difference in policies and chose the Democrats and westward expansion. They also unwittingly chose war because Polk's policies would lead to conflict with Mexico within two years of his inauguration. Nearly 2.7 million people voted as Polk squeezed out a bare majority—just over 50 percent of the vote with Clay at 48 percent: some 38,000 fewer than the Democrat.

Clay's southern strategy netted him Polk's home state of Tennessee by a 113-vote plurality out of 120,000 votes—the only time a president elect had lost his home state—along with North Carolina and his home state of Kentucky. Clay pulled in some of the old northwest winning Ohio but losing the key states of Michigan and Indiana. The Tennessean proved more popular in the north than expected, stunning the Whigs with wins in New Hampshire and Maine while losing New Jersey by fewer than 1,000 votes. Polk's Kane letter propelled him to a 6,000- vote win in Pennsylvania. In New York the antislavery Liberty party earned 15,000 votes while Clay lost the state by just over 5,000 votes. Polk's 170–105 Electoral College victory would have been a 141–134 Clay victory if the Whig had won New York.[49]

AFTERMATH

Clay's defeat broke the Whig Party. No longer able to run on a platform of higher taxes and no expansion of cheap land, the final two Whig candidates would be generals. The Democrat sweep of the Deep South heightened panic among southern Whigs and began the turn toward a one- party region that would not break until a century and a half later. Clay would spend his last years struggling to effect compromises on slavery, his mantle of Senate leadership passing to lesser men such as Stephen Douglas. John Tyler would sink into the failed category of presidents. Tyler's Texas machinations changed the tone of future elections with slavery or civil rights dominating presidential campaigns for 40 years.

The 1844 election would recede in popular memory, the television age requiring every campaign to be suspenseful. The 1948 and 1960 election captured popular interest though the victories of Truman and Kennedy were much less unexpected than that of Polk: neither Dewey nor Nixon holding sway over the popular imagination like Henry Clay.

Martin van Buren saw his political comeback crushed by his convention defeat though he would have his revenge, running on the Free Soil Party ticket and taking enough votes from his old rival Lewis Cass in 1848 to allow Zachary Taylor to win New York and the election.

With his national hopes dashed and the New York regency no longer under his control, Van Buren retired from politics, dying in 1862 just as the Civil War entered its bloodiest phase.

The victor, James Knox Polk, suffered through a tumultuous four years—his health was wrecked by the Mexican War, but he fulfilled his massive agenda. Generally seen as the greatest one-term president in history, Polk established the United States as a continental country, establishing much of the Mexican border and drawing the Pacific border with Canada. His Manifest Destiny policies established the United States as the dominant power in the western hemisphere but also triggered a decade-long debate over slavery expansion in the Mexican cession. Suffering from ill health, Polk kept his convention promise and retired after a single term, though his Tennessee retirement was brief. A visit to New Orleans after his presidency led to cholera and his death a few months after leaving office in 1849.

13

Presidential Upsets

PAST, PRESENT, AND FUTURE

Presidential upsets provide a different insight into the presidential electoral system. Predicting a presidential winner is a difficult task when considering the seemingly unending variables that can affect an election outcome. The 11 upsets that were featured were decided by foreign affairs, mismanaged campaigns, "October surprises," local officials, and candidates' missed opportunities. With such variables in effect, predicting whether an election such as 2012 will be an upset comes with many problems.

While observing presidential upsets from the safe and comfortable position of the historian, it is easy to criticize the campaign decisions made by the candidate who allowed victory to slip away. Observing a presidential election and potential upset contemporaneously eliminates that margin of safety.

The 2012 election could well be considered an upset no matter which candidate won. President Obama suffers from the twin maladies of bad policy—his unpopular health care bill and a poor economy—while Republican Mitt Romney is distrusted by conservatives—creating a potential split in the party—and a lack of charisma that makes him a less than exciting choice. While public opinion polls in early summer showed a dead heat, the tenor of the campaign suggests that Obama is not favored for reelection as his campaign has begun to resemble that of two other incumbent presidents, Woodrow Wilson and Harry Truman, who faced tough reelection battles.

Wilson ran a negative campaign: his attacks on hyphenism and attempts to tie Charles Evans Hughes to the German government represented wedge issues intended to stir public opinion on an emotional rather than policy level. The Truman campaign was profoundly negative in using an attack strategy devised by Democrat operatives Clark Clifford and James Rowe. The Obama campaign seems to have adopted Truman's strategy of a full-bore negative campaign. The attacks by Truman were diversionary, blaming the Republican Congress for the very economic maladies that are usually blamed on an incumbent president.

The 2012 election resembles that of 1948 with Republicans winning big in the midterm elections of 2010 and 1946. With inflation, high unemployment, slow growth, and a burgeoning debt, Obama faces the difficult task of convincing voters that a continuation of his administration is a better choice than a Romney administration. The attempts to label Romney as a bigot for opposing gay marriage, as a misogynist for opposing free birth control for women, and as an unfeeling businessman because of his tenure as chairman of a private equity firm have fallen flat. However, the barrage of negative information is a far cry from the strategy of a successful incumbent president running a retrospective campaign. With Americans downcast about the country's direction, an Obama victory in 2012 would be construed as a presidential upset.

Beyond 2012 election observers can apply lessons learned from past upsets to identify and predict when an underdog candidate could win a surprise victory. Beyond the basic economic and campaign issues that are part of presidential upsets, certain candidate characteristics are prevalent. In several upsets, 1876, 1880, 1916, and 1948, the losing candidate was ineffective in countering charges against him and tended to be passive in the face of his opponent's attacks. This bodes poorly for Obama in 2012 as the Romney campaign has demonstrated the ability to respond to attacks quickly and effectively.

In other upset elections, 1844, 1848, 1916, and 2000, the winning candidate in the election was able to appeal beyond the party base and take states that were expected to be won by his opponent. In 1844, Polk won Pennsylvania and New York, and in 1848 the southerner Taylor took the same two states. In 1916, Wilson appealed to western voters and farmers which had usually voted Republican. In 2000, George W. Bush won Tennessee and Arkansas, which were the home states of the Al Gore and Bill Clinton and expected to go Democrat once again. These unexpected victories demonstrated that the winning candidate could appeal beyond the base toward independents and weak followers of the opposition party. The 2012 Obama campaign seems focused on a direct appeal to the party base with the president approving of gay marriage, focusing on contraception, and attacking the wealthy, all issues popular with the left wing of the Democrat party but of little consequence to independents or weak Republican voters.

Obama faces another difficulty as the country has become more Republican over the past two decades. Since 1994, Republicans have controlled Congress for more years than Democrats for the first time since the beginning of the 20th century. The resilience of the Republican Party in taking control of the branch with which they had enjoyed little success for half a century suggests that voters are more comfortable voting for the GOP. Yet, that congressional success has come at the price of less presidential success as Democrats have controlled the White House for 12 of the past 20 years, whereas Republicans had controlled the White House for 20 of the 24 years between 1968 and 1992. An Obama victory would turn back that Republican tide, whereas a Romney victory might represent that rarest of events—the partisan-realigning election.

Notes

Chapter 1

1. Pace, Eric, "Louis H. Bean, 98, Analyst best known for 1948 prediction," *New York Times*, August 8, 1994.
2. Bean, Louis, *How to Predict Elections* (Westport, CT: Greenwood Press Reprints, 1972).
3. Lewis-Beck, Michael, and Tom Rice, "Forecasting Presidential Elections: A Comparison of Naïve Models," *Political Behavior* 6 (1984): 9–21.
4. Silver, Nate, "Which Economic Indicators best predict Presidential Elections?" *New York Times*, November 18, 2011.
5. Lewis-Beck, Michael, and Charles Tien, "The Future of Forecasting: Prospective Presidential Models," *American Politics Quarterly* 24 (1996): 468–91.
6. Lichtman, Allen, *The Keys to the White House* (Lanham, MD: Madison Books, 1996), 3.

Chapter 2

1. Ambrose, Stephen, *Eisenhower the President* (New York: Simon and Schuster, 1984), 620–21.
2. Montgomery, Gayle, and James Johnson, *One Step from the White House* (Berkeley, CA: University of California Press, 1998), 243–45.
3. Farrell, John, *Tip O'Neill and the Democratic Century* (Boston, MA: Little, Brown, 2001), 171–72.
4. Morris, Roger, *Richard Milhous Nixon* (New York: Henry Holt, 1990), 325–26.
5. Ibid., 827–32.
6. Caro, Robert, *Master of the Senate* (New York: Vintage, 2003), 982.
7. Ambrose, Stephen, *Eisenhower the President* (New York: Simon and Schuster, 1984), 326–30.

8. Perret, Geoffrey, *Eisenhower* (New York: Random House, 1999), 596–97.

9. Newton, Jim, *Eisenhower* (New York: Doubleday, 2011), 324.

10. Carty, Thomas, *A Catholic in the White House* (New York: Palgrave-Macmillan, 2004), 64–65.

11. White, Theodore, *The Making of the President 1960* (New York: Atheneum Publishers, 1988), 69–70.

12. Ibid., 72–74.

13. *Newsweek*, April 25, 1960, 29.

14. *Newsweek*, June 6, 1960, 33–34.

15. Rorabaugh, W., *The Real Making of the President* (Lawrence, KS: University Press of Kansas, 2009), 104–5.

16. White, *The Making of the President 1960*, 186–87.

17. Rorabaugh, W., *The Real Making of the President*, 109–11.

18. Ibid., 112–14.

19. Gifford, Laura Jane, "South Carolina Republicans and the Election of 1960," *Journal of Policy History* 19 (2007): 213.

20. O'Neill, Thomas, and William Novak, *Man of the House* (New York: Random House, 1987), 181.

21. Rorabaugh, W., *The Real Making of the President*, 113–14.

22. Walsh was discovered at a male brothel operated by a German spy ring: an inappropriate location for the chairman of the Senate Naval Committee.

23. Rorabaugh, W., *The Real Making of the President*, 115–16.

24. Caro, Robert, *The Passage of Power*, 155.

25. Ibid., 144–45.

26. Caro, Robert, *Master of the Senate*, 446–48.

27. *Newsweek*, April 4, 1960, 32.

28. Reeves, Thomas, *A Question of Character* (New York: Free Press, 1991), 142.

29. Carty, Thomas, *A Catholic in the White*, 7.

30. Rorabaugh, W., *The Real Making of the President*, 47.

31. Ibid.,51.

32. *Newsweek*, April 18, 1960, 31.

33. Fleming Jr., Dan B., *Kennedy v. Humphrey, West Virginia, 1960* (Jefferson, NC: McFarland, 1992), 25–26.

34. *Newsweek*, April 18, 1960, 39.

35. *Newsweek*, April 18, 1960, 34; Fleming, *Kennedy v. Humphrey, West Virginia, 1960*, 108–109.

36. Fleming, *Kennedy v. Humphrey, West Virginia, 1960*, 50–51.

37. Ibid., 61.

38. Dallek, Robert, *Lone Star Rising* (New York: Oxford University Press, 1992), 572.

39. Davis, Kenneth, *The Politics of Honor* (New York: GP Putnam & Sons, 1967), 432–37.

40. Rorabaugh, W., *The Real Making of the President*, 70–71.

41. Ibid., 70–71.

42. Ibid., 75.

43. Dallek, Robert, *Lone Star Rising*, 574.

44. Caro, Robert, *The Passage of Power*, 136–37.

45. Ibid., 114–15.

46. Rorabaugh, W., *The Real Making of the President*, 86–88.

47. Ibid., 90.

48. Ibid., 126–27.

49. Novotny, Patrick, "John F. Kennedy, the 1960 Election and Georgia's Unpledged Electors in the Electoral College," *Georgia Historical Quarterly* 88 (2004): 382.

50. Rorabaugh, W., *The Real Making of the President* 127.

51. "Nobody's Winning," *Newsweek*, August 22, 1960, 17–18.

52. "Nobody's Winning," *Newsweek*, August 22, 1960, 18.

53. Aitken, Jonathan, *Nixon: A Life* (London: Wiedenfield and Nicolson, 1993), 276.

54. Rorabaugh, W., *The Real Making of the President*, 147.

55. Ibid., 132.

56. Robertson, David, *Sly and Able* (New York: W.W. Norton, 1994), 91.

57. Rorabaugh, W., *The Real Making of the President*, 152.

58. Aitken, Jonathan, *Nixon: A Life*, 277–78.

59. Ibid., 278.

60. Schroeder, Alan, *Presidential Debates* (New York: Columbia University Press, 2000), 4, 16.

61. Aitken, Jonathan, *Nixon: A Life*, 278.

62. Jamieson, Kathleen Jamieson, *Packaging the Presidency* (New York: Oxford University Press, 1984), 152.

63. Krause, Sidney, *Televised Presidential Debates and Public Policy* (Mahwah, NJ: Lawrence Erlbaum Associates Publishers, 2000), 35.

64. Kallina Jr., Edmund, *Kennedy v. Nixon* (Gainesville, FL: University of Florida Press, 2010), 126–27.

65. Ibid., 127–29.

66. "What's happening in the South?" *Newsweek*, September 5, 1960, 15–16.

67. Gifford, Laura Jane, "Dixie is no Longer in the Bag," *The Journal of Policy History* 9 (2007): 207, 213.

68. Ibid., 208.

69. Ibid., 225.

70. Rorabaugh, W., *The Real Making of the President* (Lawrence, KS: University Press of Kansas, 2009), 167–70.

71. Robertson, David, *Sly and Able* (New York: W.W. Norton, 1994), 28–29.

72. Carty, Thomas, *A Catholic in the White House* (New York: Palgrave-Macmillan, 2004), 55.

73. Ibid., 54–55.

74. Frady, Marshall, *Billy Graham* (Boston, MA: Little, Brown, 1979), 443; Though Sam Rayburn was House Speaker in 1960, age and declining health likely meant John McCormack of Massachusetts would take over the reins. In the Senate, Lyndon Johnson's number two man, Mike Mansfield of Montana, would become majority leader. Both were Catholics.

75. Kallina Jr., Edmund, *Kennedy v. Nixon* (Gainesville, FL: University of Florida Press, 2010), 170–71.

76. Frady, Marshall, *Billy Graham* (Boston, MA: Little, Brown, 1979), 442–43.

77. Carty, Thomas, *A Catholic in the White House* (New York: Palgrave-Macmillan, 2004), 56, 59.

78. Ibid., 59–60.

79. "Hot and getting Hotter," Newsweek, September 19, 1960, 37–38; Carty, Thomas, *A Catholic in the White House* (New York: Palgrave-Macmillan, 2004), 63–64.

80. Casey, Shawn, *The Making of a Catholic President* (London: Oxford University Press, 2004), 23–24.

81. Ibid., 49–50.

82. Carty, Thomas, *A Catholic in the White House*, 69.

83. Ibid., 73–74.

84. Casey, Shawn, *The Making of a Catholic President*, 102.

85. Ibid., 103.

86. Ibid., 157–58.

87. Carty, Thomas, *A Catholic in the White House*, 61–62.

88. Casey, Shawn, *The Making of a Catholic President*, 166.

89. Fleming Jr., Dan B., *Kennedy v. Humphrey, West Virginia, 1960*, 137.

90. Ibid., 136.

91. Jenkins, Philip, *The New Anti Catholicism* (London: Oxford University Press, 2003), 45.

92. White, Theodore, *The Making of the President 1960*, 317.

93. Sorenson, Theodore, "Election of 1960," in *History of American Presidential Elections*, Vol. 4, eds. Fred Israel and Arthur Schlesinger Jr. (New York: Chelsea House Publishers, 1971), 3562.

94. Ibid., 3562.

95. Ibid., 3562.

96. Caro, Robert, *The Passage of Power*, 150–51.

97. Ibid., 152–53.

98. Kallina, Edward, *Courthouse over the White House* (Orlando, FL: University of Central Florida Press, 1988), 114–16.

99. "The Challenges," Newsweek, December 5, 1960, 28.

Chapter 3

1. The 1860 Republican convention included not only Abraham Lincoln but also the following strong contenders: a future secretary of state, William Seward; a future treasury secretary and U.S. chief justice, Salmon Chase; and a future war secretary, Simon Cameron. In 1980, the contenders for the Republican nomination were the following: two presidents, Ronald Reagan and George H.W. Bush; two future Senate majority leaders, Howard Baker and Robert Dole; and a former treasury secretary John Connally. This may have been strongest field to ever run for any party's nomination.

2. Current, Richard Nelson, *Those Terrible Carpetbaggers* (New York: Oxford University Press, 1988), 77.

3. Taylor, Joe Gray, *Louisiana Reconstructed* (Baton Rouge, LA: Louisiana State University Press, 1974), 142.

4. Jordan, David, *Winfield Scott Hancock* (Bloomington, IN: Indiana University Press, 1988), 206.

5. Mitchell, Stewart, *Horatio Seymour of New York* (Cambridge, MA: Harvard University Press, 1938), 425–29.

6. Jordan, David, *Winfield Scott Hancock*, 229–30.

7. Flick, Alexander, *Samuel Jones Tilden* (Westport, CT: Greenwood Press, 1973), 446–47.

8. Ibid., 448–49.

9. Ibid., 459.

10. Tansill, Charles, *The Congressional Career of Thomas Bayard* (Washington, DC: Georgetown University Press, 1946), 275.

11. Flick, Alexander, *Samuel Jones Tilden*, 456–57.

12. Tansill, Charles, *The Congressional Career of Thomas Bayard*, 242.

13. Ibid., 249.

14. Swisher, Carl Brent, *Stephen Field* (Washington, DC: Brookings Institution, 1930), 289–92.

15. Tansill, Charles, The Congressional Career of Thomas Bayard, 280–81.

16. Clancy, Herbert, *The Presidential Election of 1880* (Chicago: Loyola University Press, 1958), 139.

17. Jordan, David, *Winfield Scott Hancock*, 277–78.

18. Smith, Jean, *Edward Grant* (New York: Simon and Schuster, 2001), 614–15.

19. Jordan, David, *Roscoe Conkling of New York* (Ithaca, NY: Cornell University Press, 1971), 322–23.

20. Jordan, David, Roscoe Conkling (New York: Cornell University Press, 1971), 233.

21. Jordan, David, *Winfield Scott Hancock*, 253–54.

22. Flick, Alexander, *Samuel Jones Tilden*, 171.

23. Peskin, Allan, *Garfield* (Kent, OH: Kent State University Press, 1999), 211–13.

24. Lamers, William, *The Edge of Glory* (Baton Rouge, LA: Louisiana State University Press, 1999), 354–56.

25. Leech, Margaret, and Harry Brown, *The Garfield Orbit* (New York: Harper and Row, 1978), 185–86.

26. Jordan, David, *Winfield Scott Hancock*, 285–88.

27. Peskin, Allan, *Garfield* (Kent, OH: Kent State University Press, 1999), 456–58.

28. Flick, Alexander, *Samuel Jones Tilden*, 173.

29. Reeves, Thomas, *Gentleman Boss* (New York: Alfred Knopf, 1975), 179–81.

30. Clancy, Herbert, The Presidential Election of 1880 (Chicago: Loyola University Press, 1958), 169–70.

31. Muzzey, David, *James G. Blaine* (New York: Dodd, Mead, 1935), 173.

32. Clancy, Herbert *The Presidential Election of 1880* (Chicago: Loyola University Press 1958), 190–91.

33. Jordan, David, *Winfield Scott Hancock*, 285–86.

34. Clancy, Herbert *The Presidential Election of 1880* (Chicago: Loyola University Press 1958), 173–75.

35. Jordan, David, *Winfield Scott Hancock*, 289–90.

36. Clancy, Herbert, *The Presidential Election of 1880* (Chicago: Loyola University Press, 1958), 176–77.

37. "Election," *Nation,* September 23, 1880, 211.

38. *Nation*, September 23, 1880, 215.

39. *Nation*, September 30, 1880, 229.

40. Clancy, Herbert, *The Presidential Election of 1880* (Chicago: Loyola University Press, 1958), 195.

41. Ibid., 220–21.

42. Smith, Willard, *Schuyler Colfax* (Indianapolis, IN: Indiana Historical Bureau, 1957), 369–72.

43. Crawford, J. B., *The Credit Mobilier of America, its Origins and History* (Boston, MA: C. W. Calkins, 1880), 133–34.

44. Ackerman, Kenneth, *Dark Horse* (New York: Carroll and Graf, 2005), 220

45. Dinnerstein, Leonard, "Election of 1880," in *The History of American Presidential Elections,* eds. Arthur Schlesinger and Fred Israel (New York: Chelsea House Publishers, 1971), 1558.

46. Dinnerstein, Leonard. "Election of 1880," in *The History of American Presidential Elections,* eds. Arthur Schlesinger and Fred Israel (New York: Chelsea House Publishers, 1971) 1558

47. Dinnerstein, Leonard. "Election of 1880," in *The History of American Presidential Elections,* eds. Arthur Schlesinger and Fred Israel (New York: Chelsea House Publishers, 1971) 1558

48. Ibid., 1558.

Chapter 4

1. Herrnson, Paul S., "The Congressional Elections," in *The Election of 2000,* ed. Gerald Pomper (New York: Chatham House Publishing, 2000), 153.

2. Burns, James McGregor, and Georgia Sorsenson, *Dead Center* (New York: Scribner, 2001), 233–34.

3. Garvey, Gerald, "False Promises: The NPR in Historical Perspective," in *Inside the Reinvention,* eds. John DiIulio and Donald Kettl (Washington, DC: The Brookings Institution Press, 1995), 101; Defenders of bureaucratic rules had their defenders. In an episode of the *West Wing,* the same destruction of the ashtray would be performed by an ensign played by Christian Slater who would break a $400 glass ashtray and then explain that the regulation was military-based because a glass ashtray that broke into hundreds of pieces posed a danger in a combat zone.

4. Caesar, James, and Andrew Bush, *The Perfect Tie* (Lanham, MD: Rowman & Littlefield Publishers, 2001), 73.

5. Rose, Ted, "Is Tony Coelho a Crook?" *Slate,* April 7, 2000.

6. Duffy, Michael, and Karen Tumulty, "Gore's Secret Guru," *Time,* November 8, 1999, 38.

7. White, Theodore, *The Making of the President 1972* (New York: Atheneum Publishers, 1973), 29–34.

8. Forbes launched a multimillion dollar assault on Dole in Arizona. The endless attacking advertisements destroyed Dole in the state and for the first time since 1948, the state voted for the Democrat presidential candidate. Woodward, Bob, *The Choice* (New York: Touchstone Books, 1997), 358.

9. Bush, George W., *Decision Points* (New York: Crown Publishers, 2010), 33–34.

10. Germond, Jack, and Jules Witcover, *Whose Broad Stripes and Bright Stars?* (New York: Warner Books, 1989), 352.

11. Bush, George W., *Decision Points*, 55–56.

12. In the midst of the Clinton impeachment debate, House Speaker Newt Gingrich had resigned his seat after losing seats in the 1998 midterm. His replacement, Louisiana Congressman Robert Livingston, was also forced to resign because of personal peccadilloes that Republicans were using against Clinton.

13. Saletan, William, "The Gary Bauer Scandal," *Slate,* October 1, 1999; Edsall, Thomas B., and Hanna Rosin, "Bauer Says He Did not Have Affair," in *Washington Post,* September 30, 1999, A14. The Edsall and Rosin article included the fact that Nevada Senate candidate John Ensign refused to be in a car alone with a women out of concern with potential rumors of infidelity. Ensign would be forced to resign from the Senate in 2011 for infidelity and allegedly misappropriating campaign funds to cover up his affair.

14. Carney, Jay, "Playing the POW Card," *Time,* September 9, 1999, 44. Carney would later become President Obama's press secretary, casting doubts on his neutrality during the 2000 campaign.

15. During the economic crisis of fall 2008, McCain made an angry and hysterical speech denouncing the SEC Chairman Christopher Cox and demanded his resignation because he presided over the collapse of the financial system.

16. Ratesnar, Remesh, "Where McCain hits Bush the Hardest," *Time,* December 13, 1999, 48–49.

17. Pooley, Eric, "A Sense of Where You're not," *Time,* January 1, 2000, 30–33.

18. Ibid., 33.

19. Lopez, Steve, "Meet Forbes the great Romancer," *Time,* January 24, 2000, 28.

20. Caesar, James, and Andrew Bush, *The Perfect Tie,* 79–80.

21. Caesar, James, and Andrew Busch, *The Perfect Tie* (Lanham, MD: Rowman & Littlefield Publishers, 2001), 80.

22. The same would occur eight years later as a downtrodden McCain campaign hemorrhaging money swept the New Hampshire primary, coming from behind in an upset victory. Unlike 2000, McCain faced a divided conservative movement, and he squeaked through the South Carolina primary, winning only 34 percent of the vote and then winning the nomination, frequently with victories below 50 percent.

23. Pooley, Eric, "Giving McCain the Boot," *Time,* February 2, 2000, 30.

24. Gibbs, Nancy, "McCain's Moment," *Time,* February 14, 2000, 32.

25. Pooley, Eric, "Who is the Real Reformer?" *Time,* February 21, 2000, 28–31.

26. Gibbs, Nancy, "McCain's Moment," *Time,* February 14, 2000, 34.

27. Gibbs, Nancy, "Fire and Brimstone," *Time,* March 13, 2000, 30–34.

28. Beeme, David Van, "Catholic Bashing," *Time*, March 6, 2000, 52.

29. Gibbs, Nancy, "Fire and Brimstone," *Time*, March 13, 2000, 32.

30. Ibid., 33.

31. Germond, Jack, and Jules Witcover, *Whose Broad Stripes and Bright Stars?* (New York: Warner Books, 1989), 312–14.

32. Campbell, James E., "The Curious and Close Presidential Campaign of 2000," in *America's Choice*, ed. William Crotty (Boulder, CO: Westview Press, 2001), 110.

33. Quirk, Paul, and Sean Matheson, "The Presidency: The Election and the Prospects for Leadership," in *The Elections of 2000*, ed. Michael Nelson (Washington, DC: Congressional Quarterly Press, 2001), 168.

34. Ibid., 127.

35. Freidenberg, Robert, "The 2000 Presidential Debates," in *The 2000 Presidential Campaign*, ed. Robert Denton Jr. (Boulder, CO: Praeger, 2002), 137.

36. Ibid., 137.

37. Ibid., 139–40.

38. Ibid., 146–47.

39. Ibid., 152–55.

40. Francovic, Kathleen, and Monika McDermott, "Public Opinion in the 2000 Election," in *The Election of 2000*, ed. Gerald Pomper (New York: Chatham House Publishing, 2000), 85.

41. Freidenberg, Robert, "The 2000 Presidential Debates," in *The 2000 Presidential Campaign*, ed. Robert Denton Jr. (Boulder, CO: Praeger, 2002), 157–58.

42. Francovic, Kathleen, and Monika McDermott, "Public Opinion in the 2000 Election," in *The Election of 2000*, ed. Gerald Pomper (New York: Chatham House Publishing, 2000), 85.

43. Ibid., 85.

44. Shaw, Daron, *The Race to 270* (Chicago, IL: University of Chicago Press, 2006), 159–60.

45. Shepard, Alicia, "A Late Breaking Campaign Skeleton," *American Journalism Review*, December, 2000.

46. Dover, E. D., *Missed Opportunity*, 157.

47. Shaw, Daron, *The Race to 270* (Chicago, IL: University of Chicago Press, 2006), 126.

48. Dover, E. D., *Missed Opportunity*, 157.

49. Tseng, Margaret, "The Clinton Effect," in *The Election of the Century*, eds. Stephen J. Wayne and Clyde Wilcox (Armonk, NY: M.E. Sharpe, 2002), 201.

50. Ibid., 207.

51. Ibid., 202.

52. Dover, E. D., *Missed Opportunity*, 165–66.

53. Quirk, Paul, and Sean Matheson, "The Presidency: The Election and the Prospects for Leadership," in *The Elections of 2000*, ed. Michael Nelson (Washington, DC: Congressional Quarterly Press, 2001), 169.

54. Campbell, James E., "The Curious and Close Presidential Campaign of 2000," in *America's Choice*, ed. William Crotty (Boulder, CO: Westview Press, 2001), 133.

55. Ibid., 133.

56. Brodsky, David, and Robert Swanbrough, "Tennessee: A Native Son Scorned" in *The 2000 Presidential Elections in the South*, eds. Robert Steed and Laurence Moreland (Westport, CT: Praeger, 2002), 182–83.

57. Ibid., 185–88.

58. Barth, Jay, Janine Parry, and Todd Shields, "Arkansas: Non-stop Action in Post-Clinton Arkansas," in *The 2000 Presidential Election in the South*, eds. Robert Steed and Laurence Moreland (Westport, CT: Praeger, 2002), 137.

59. Ibid., 140.

60. Dover, E. D., *Missed Opportunity*, 153.

61. Merzer, Martin, *The Miami Herald Report* (New York: St. Martin's Press, 2001), 36–38.

62. Ibid., 42–43.

63. Harris was criticized for not extending the deadline though her constitutional and legal duty was to execute the state court ruling. Her rejection of partial recount infuriated some though the purpose of a recount was to count all ballots, not just enough to overturn an election result.

64. Weisberg, Jacob, "The Heresies of Pat Buchanan," The New Republic, October 22, 1990, 28.

65. *Bush v. Palm Beach County Canvassing Board*, 531 U.S. 70 (2000).

66. Merzer, Martin, *The Miami Herald Report* (New York: St. Martin's Press, 2001), 165–66.

67. Gillman, Howard, *The Votes that Counted* (Chicago, IL: University of Chicago Press, 2001), 100–101.

68. Posner, Richard, *Breaking the Deadlock* (Princeton, NJ: Princeton University Press, 2001).

69. *Bush v. Palm Beach County Canvassing Board*, 531 U.S. 1046–47 (2000).

70. Gillman, Howard, *The Votes that Counted* (Chicago, IL: University of Chicago Press, 2001), 130–31.

71. Ibid., 135–36.

72. *Bush v. Gore*, 531 U.S. 98 at 105–7 (2000).

73. With Florida a total of 538 electoral votes would have to be tabulated with 270 as the majority. Without Florida's 25 electoral votes, only 513 electoral votes would be sent to Congress, with 257 votes representing a majority. Al Gore had 267 electoral votes without Florida; George Bush had 246. If the 257 majority had been accepted, then Al Gore would have been elected president: an outcome certain to have provoked a constitutional challenge and another Supreme Court case.

74. *Bush v. Gore*, 531 U.S. 98 at 129.

75. *Bush v. Gore*, 531 U.S. 98 at 116–18.

76. *Bush v. Gore*, 531 U.S. 98 at 110–11.

77. "Senator's son arrested in New Mexico," *ABC News*, September 27, 2000.

Chapter 5

1. States could set the election date and decide whether state voters were allowed to vote their presidential preference.

2. Smith, Richard Norton, *Patriarch* (New York: Houghton Mifflin, 1993), 170–73.

3. Rossiter, Clinton, *The Federalist Papers* (New York: Penguin Books, 1961), Xiii–XV.

4. Beard, Charles, *The Economic Origins of the Constitution* (New York: The Macmillan, 1935).

5. Smith, Page, "The Election of 1796," in *The History of American Presidential Elections,* ed. Schlesinger (New York: Chelsea House Publishers, 1971), 71–72.

6. After his crushing defeat in the 1872 election, Greeley died causing his electors to divvy up their votes among five men—Greeley, Thomas Hendricks, Gratz Brown, David Davis, and Charles Jenkins. Gillette, William, "Election of 1872," in *The History of American Presidential Elections,* ed. Schlesinger (New York: Chelsea House Publishers, 1971), 1375.

7. Smith, Page, "The Election of 1796," in *The History of American Presidential Elections,* ed. Schlesinger (New York: Chelsea House Publishers, 1971), 98.

8. Ferling, John, *John Adams* (New York: Henry Holt, 1996), 353–54.

9. Weisberger, Bernard, *America Afire* (New York: William Morrow, 2000), 192.

10. Ibid., 191–93.

11. The 1902 British Parliament election was fought over the Boer War: a minor conflict that the ruling Tories used to bash the liberal party and win an overwhelming 134-seat majority. Massie, Robert K., *Dreadnought* (New York: Ballantine Books, 1991), 289.

12. Sharp, James Roger, *The Deadlocked Election of 1800* (Lawrence, KS: University Press of Kansas, 2010), 70–71.

13. Miller, John, *Crisis in Freedom: the Alien and Sedition Acts* (Boston, MA: Little, Brown, 1951), 213.

14. Watkins, William, *Reclaiming the American Revolution* (New York: Palgrave Macmillan, 2004), 67–69.

15. Ferling, John, *John Adams* (New York: Henry Holt, 1996), 394–95.

16. Hendrickson, 4–6.

17. Hendrickson, 22–23.

18. Chernow, Ron, *Alexander Hamilton* (New York: Penguin Press, 2004), 98–99.

19. Hendrickson, 336.

20. Chernow, Ron, *Alexander Hamilton*, 101–3.

21. Ibid., 231–33.

22. Schachner, Nathan, *Aaron Burr* (New York: A. S. Barnes, 1971), 99–101.

23. Chernow, Ron, *Alexander Hamilton*, 471–72.

24. Malone, Dumas, *Jefferson and the Ordeal of Liberty* (Boston, MA: Little, Brown, 1962), 473.

25. Smith, Page, "Election of 1796," in *History of American Presidential Elections,* Vol. 1, eds. Arthur Schlesinger Jr. and Fred Israel (New York: Chelsea House Publishers, 1971), 98.

26. Isenberg, Nancy, *Fallen Founder* (New York: Viking Adult, 2007), 197–98.

27. Larson, Orville, *American Infidel* (New York: The Citadel Press, 1962), 100; Isenberg, Nancy, *Fallen Founder* (New York: Viking Adult, 2007) 198;

Livingston would be recognized for his New York efforts and rewarded by Jefferson with a Supreme Court seat.

28. Sharp, James Roger, *The Deadlocked Election of 1800* (Lawrence, KS: University Press of Kansas, 2010), 85.

29. The other six would be the following: Clay and Jackson in 1824 and 1832; John Quincy Adams and Andrew Jackson in 1824 and 1828; William Henry Harrison and Martin van Buren in 1836 and 1840; Benjamin Harrison and Grover Cleveland in 1888 and 1892; William McKinley and William Jennings Bryan in 1896 and 1900; and Dwight Eisenhower and Adlai Stevenson in 1952 and 1956.

30. Zahriser, Marvin, *Charles Cotesworth Pinckney* (Chapel Hill, NC: The University of North Carolina Press, 1967), 216.

31. Larson, Orville, *American Infidel* (New York: The Citadel Press, 1962), 120–121; Sharp, James Roger, *The Deadlocked Election of 1800* (Lawrence, KS: University Press of Kansas, 2010), 90–92.

32. Isenberg, Nancy, *Fallen Founder* (New York: Viking Adult, 2007), 202–203.

33. Sharp, James Roger, *The Deadlocked Election of 1800* (Lawrence, KS: University Press of Kansas, 2010), 105.

34. Malone, Dumas, *Jefferson and the Ordeal of Liberty* (Boston, MA: Little, Brown, 1962), 468–70.

35. Sharp, James Roger, *The Deadlocked Election of 1800* (Lawrence, KS: University Press of Kansas, 2010), 106–7.

36. Ferling, John, *John Adams* (New York: Henry Holt, 1996), 150–51.

37. Peterson, Merrill, *Thomas Jefferson and the New Nation* (New York: Oxford University Press, 1970) 570–72.

38. Ferling, John, *John Adams* (New York: Henry Holt, 1996), 152–54; Larson, Orville, *American Infidel* (New York: The Citadel Press, 1962), 172.

39. Larson, Orville, *American Infidel* (New York: The Citadel Press, 1962), 173–74.

40. Sharp, James Roger, *The Deadlocked Election of 1800* (Lawrence, KS: University Press of Kansas, 2010), 111–12.

41. Larson, Orville, *American Infidel* (New York: The Citadel Press, 1962), 186.

42. Sharp, James Roger, *The Deadlocked Election of 1800* (Lawrence, KS: University Press of Kansas, 2010), 108.

43. Ibid., 103–4.

44. Zahriser, Marvin, *Charles Cotesworth Pinckney* (Chapel Hill, NC: The University of North Carolina Press, 1967), 223–25.

45. Chernow, Ron, *Alexander Hamilton* (New York: Penguin Press, 2004), 622–23.

46. Cunningham, Noble, "Election of 1800," in *History of American Presidential Elections*, Vol. 1, eds. Arthur Schlesinger Jr. and Fred Israel (New York: Chelsea House Publishers, 1971), 105.

47. Malone, Dumas, *Jefferson and the Ordeal of Liberty* (Boston, MA: Little, Brown, 1962), 460–61.

48. Sharp, James Roger, *The Deadlocked Election of 1800* (Lawrence, KS: University Press of Kansas, 2010), 156–57.

49. Malone, Dumas, *Jefferson and the Ordeal of Liberty*, 463–64.

50. Van Der Linden, Frank, *The Turning Point* (Washington, DC: Robert Luce, 1962), 228–30.

51. Sharp, James Roger, *The Deadlocked Election of 1800* (Lawrence, KS: University Press of Kansas, 2010), 193, Appendix C.

52. Ibid., 193, Appendix C.

53. Broussard, James, *The Southern Federalists* (Baton Rouge, LA: Louisiana State University Press, 1948), 31.

54. Freneau to Jefferson on December 2, 1800, "South Carolina in the Presidential Election of 1800," *American Historical Review* IV (October 1898): 128.

55. Bayard to Hamilton on January 7, 1801, *The Papers of Alexander Hamilton July 1800–April 1802*, ed. Harold Syrett (New York: Columbia University Press, 1977), 300–301.

56. Sedgwick to Hamilton on January 10, 1801, *The Papers of Alexander Hamilton July 1800–April 1802*, ed. Harold Syrett (New York: Columbia University Press, 1977), 311–12.

57. Rutledge to Hamilton on January 10, 1801, *The Papers of Alexander Hamilton July 1800–April 1802*, ed. Harold Syrett (New York: Columbia University Press, 1977), 308–9.

58. Hamilton to Sedgwick on December 22, 1800, *The Papers of Alexander Hamilton July 1800–April 1802*, ed. Harold Syrett (New York: Columbia University Press, 1977), 269–70.

59. Hamilton to Bayard on December 17, 1800, *The Papers of Alexander Hamilton July 1800–April 1802*, ed. Harold Syrett (New York: Columbia University Press, 1977), 276–77.

60. Hamilton to Wolcot on December 1800, *The Papers of Alexander Hamilton July 1800–April 1802*, ed. Harold Syrett (New York: Columbia University Press, 1977), 287.

61. Ferling, John, *John Adams* (New York: Henry Holt, 1996), 181.

62. Ibid., 178.

63. Ibid., 180.

64. Cunningham, Noble, "Election of 1800," in *History of American Presidential Elections,* Vol. 1, eds. Arthur Schlesinger Jr. and Fred Israel (New York: Chelsea House Publishers, 1971), 129.

65. Sharp, James Roger, *The Deadlocked Election of 1800* (Lawrence, KS: University Press of Kansas, 2010), 155.

66. Borden, Morten, *The Federalism of James Bayard* (New York: Columbia University Press, 1955), 89–91.

67. Ferling, John, *John Adams* (New York: Henry Holt, 1996), 191–93.

68. Ellis, Richard, *The Jeffersonian Crisis* (New York: Oxford University Press, 1971), 41–43.

Chapter 6

1. Jeffers, H. Paul, *An Honest President* (New York: Perennial, 2000), 40, 171.

2. Ibid., 49.

3. Ibid., 54.

4. 71 U.S. 333 (1866).

5. Muzzey, David, *James G. Blaine* (New York: Dodd, Mead, 1935), 362.

6. Welch Jr., Richard, *The Presidencies of Grover Cleveland* (Lawrence, KS: University of Kansas Press, 1988), 83.

7. Muzzey, David, *James G. Blaine*, 362–63.

8. Brodsky Alyn, *Grover Cleveland* (New York: St. Martin's Press, 2000), 182–83.

9. Spitzer, Robert, *The Presidential Veto* (Albany, NY: SUNY Press, 1988), 61–62.

10. Jackson, Carlton, *Presidential Vetoes* (Athens, GA: University of Georgia Press, 1945), 115.

11. Spitzer, Robert, *The Presidential Veto*, 61–62.

12. Calhoun, Charles, *Minority Victory* (Lawrence, KS: University Press of Kansas, 2008), 150.

13. Brodsky Alyn, *Grover Cleveland*, 185.

14. Calhoun, Charles, *Minority Victory*, 153–55.

15. Ibid., 150–51.

16. McConnell, Stewart, *Glorious Contentment* (Chapel Hill, NC: The University of North Carolina Press, 1992), 150–51.

17. Bailey, Thomas, *A Diplomatic History of the American People* (New York: Appleton-Century-Croft, 1964), 403–4.

18. 118 U.S. 356 (1886); 12 F Cas 252 (1879).

19. Calhoun, Charles, *Minority Victory*, 158–59.

20. Blaine authored *Twenty Years in Congress: From Lincoln to Garfield* published in 1886. It was a campaign document for a potential presidential run but also an in-depth if partisan look at Congress through five Republican administrations.

21. Muzzey, David, *James G. Blaine*, 365–66.

22. Ibid., 368–70.

23. Hirshson, Stanley, *The White Tecumseh* (New York: John Wiley and Sons, 1997), 346.

24. Kehl, James, *Boss Rule in the Gilded Age* (Pittsburgh, PA: University of Pittsburgh Press, 1981), 87.

25. Croly, Herbert, *Marcus Alonzo Hanna* (New York: Macmillan, 1912), 132.

26. Gage, Leland, *William Boyd Allison* (Iowa City, IA: State Historical Society of Iowa, 1956), 321.

27. Gresham, Matilda, *Life of Walter Quentin Gresham,* Vol. 2 (Chicago, IL: Rand McNally, 1919), 557–59.

28. Ibid., 565–66.

29. Calhoun, Charles, *Minority Victory*, 95–96.

30. Sievers, Harry J., *Benjamin Harrison, Hoosier Statesman* (Newtown, CT: American Political Biography, 1997), 9–10.

31. Ibid., 44–45.

32. Ibid. 122–23.

33. Ibid., 242–43.

34. Stewart III, Charles, "Lessons from the Post Civil War Era," in *The Politics of Divided Government,* eds. Gary Cox and Samuel Kernell (Boulder, CO: Westview Press, 1991), 218.

35. Bass, Herbert, *I am a Democrat* (Syracuse, NY: Syracuse University Press, 1961), 79–80.

36. Wesser, Robert, "Election of 1888," in *History of American Presidential Elections*, eds. Fred Israel and Arthur Schlesinger Jr. (New York: Chelsea House Publishers, 1971), 1623.

37. Ibid., 1623–24.

38. Nevins, Allen, *A Study in Courage* (New York: Dodd, Mead, 1938), 434.

39. Calhoun, Charles, *Minority Victory*, 60–61.

40. Muzzey, David, *James G. Blaine*, 372–74.

41. Gresham, Matilda, *Life of Walter Quentin Gresham*, 574, 594.

42. Croly, Herbert, *Marcus Alonzo Hanna*, 136–37.

43. Henry A. Wallace and Henry C. Wallace were father and son who served as agriculture secretaries: the eldest with Harding and Coolidge and the younger with Franklin Roosevelt.

44. Kehl, James, *Boss Rule in the Gilded Age*, 63–64.

45. Ibid., 86–87.

46. Sievers, Harry J., *Benjamin Harrison, Hoosier Statesman*, 319–20.

47. Ibid., 337.

48. Ibid., 344–45.

49. Gage, Leland, *William Boyd Allison*, 222–23.

50. Muzzey, David, *James G. Blaine* (New York: Dodd, Mead, 1935), 377–78.

51. Gage, Leland, *William Boyd Allison* (Iowa City, IA: State Historical Society of Iowa, 1956), 224–26; Sievers, Harry J., *Benjamin Harrison, Hoosier Statesman* (Newtown, CT: American Political Biography, 1997), 349–52.

52. Nevins, Allen, *A Study in Courage*, 415.

53. Ibid., 415–17.

54. Ibid., 172.

55. Calhoun, Charles, *Minority Victory*, 10–11.

56. Nevins, Allen, *A Study in Courage*, 420–21.

57. Merrill, Horace, *Bourbon Leader* (Boston, MA: Little, Brown, 1957), 129.

58. Nevins, Allen, *A Study in Courage*, 433.

59. Ibid., 434.

60. *Nation*, July 5, 1888, 1.

61. *Nation*, November 8, 1888, 366.

62. *Nation*, October 27, 1888, 345.

63. *Nation*, October 25, 1888, 324.

64. *Nation*, November 1, 1888, 346.

65. Nation, July 27, 1888, 24.

66. *Nation*, August 9, 1888, 101.

67. Merrill, Horace, *Bourbon Leader*, 130–31.

68. Bass, Herbert, *I am a Democrat*, 114.

69. Calhoun, Charles, *Minority Victory* 165–67.

70. Bass, Herbert, *I am a Democrat*, 97–98.

71. Ibid., 94–95.

72. Wesser, Robert, "Election of 1888," in *History of American Presidential Elections*, eds. Fred Israel and Arthur Schlesinger Jr. (New York: Chelsea House Publishers, 1971), 1646–47.

73. Tansill, Charles, *The Foreign Policy of Thomas Bayard* (Fordham, NY: Fordham University Press, 1940), 326–27.

74. Ibid., 332, 339.

75. Nevins, Allen, *A Study in Courage* (New York: Dodd, Mead, 1938), 431.

76. Sievers, Harry J., *Benjamin Harrison, Hoosier Statesman* (Newtown, CT: American Political Biography, 1997), 404–5.

77. *Nation*, August 16, 1888, 127; *Nation*, August 23, 1888, 141.

78. Kehl, James, *Boss Rule in the Gilded Age* (Pittsburgh, PA: University of Pittsburgh Press, 1981), 97.

79. Ibid., 104–5.

80. *Nation*, November 8, 1888, 365–66.

81. *Nation*, November 8, 1888, 365–66.

82. Gresham, Matilda, *Life of Walter Quentin Gresham*, Vol. 2 (Chicago, IL: Rand McNally, 1919), 603–5.

83. Ibid., 605.

84. Wesser, Robert. "Election of 1888," in *History of American Presidential Elections*, eds. Fred Israel and Arthur Schlesinger Jr. (New York: Chelsea House Publishers, 1971) 1700.

85. Wesser, Robert, "Election of 1888," in *History of American Presidential Elections*, eds. Fred Israel and Arthur Schlesinger Jr. (New York: Chelsea House Publishers, 1971), 1700.

86. Ibid., 1646.

87. *Nation*, November 15, 1888, 385.

Chapter 7

1. Lightner, Otto, *A History of Business Depressions* (New York: Benjamin Franklin, 1970), 113–15.

2. Dangerfield, George, *The Era of Good Feeling* (New York: Harcourt Brace, 1952), 98–100.

3. Ibid., 310–11.

4. Klein, Philip, and Ari Hoogenboom, *A History of Pennsylvania* (University Park, PA: The Penn State University Press, 1973), 135.

5. Wiltse, Charles M., *John C. Calhoun; 1782–1828* (New York: Russell and Russell, 1944), 200–202.

6. Ibid., 254–55.

7. Mooney, Chase, *William H. Crawford* (Lexington, KY: University Press of Kentucky, 1974), 242–45.

8. Wiltse, Charles M., *John C. Calhoun; 1782–1828*, 254–55, 258.

9. Ammon, Henry, *James Monroe* (Charlottesville VA: University Press of Virginia, 1990), 500–501.

10. Remini, Robert, *Henry Clay* (New York: W.W. Norton, 1993), 113–17.

11. Nagel, Paul, *John Quincy Adams* (Cambridge, MA: Harvard University Press, 1993), 250.

12. Remini, Robert, *Henry Clay*, 173–75.

13. Mooney, Chase, *William H. Crawford*, 20–23.

14. Niven, John, *Martin Van Buren* (New York: Oxford University Press, 1983), 51–52.

15. Mooney, Chase, *William H. Crawford*, 222–23.

16. Ibid., 218–20.

17. Niven, John, *Martin Van Buren*, 146–47.

18. Ammon, Henry, *James Monroe* (Charlottesville VA: University Press of Virginia, 1990), 494–95.

19. Mooney, Chase, *William H. Crawford*, 235.

20. Ibid., 241–42.

21. Dangerfield, George, *The Era of Good Feeling*, 310–11.

22. Nagel, Paul, *John Quincy Adams*, 175–77.

23. Livermore Jr., Shaw, *The Twilight of Federalism* (Princeton, NJ: Princeton University Press, 1962), 139–40.

24. Nagel, Paul, *John Quincy Adams*, 249–51.

25. Wiltse, Charles M., *John C. Calhoun; 1782–1828*, 138–40.

26. Klein, Philip, and Ari Hoogenboom, *A History of Pennsylvania* (University Park: Pennsylvania State University Press, 1980),135.

27. Belohlavek, John, *George Mifflin Dallas* (University Park, PA: The Pennsylvania State University Press, 1977), 20–21.

28. Klein and Hoogenboom, *A History of Pennsylvania*, 135.

29. Newsome, Albert Ray, *The Presidential Election of 1824* (Chapel Hill: University of North Carolina Press 1939), 138–39.

30. Belohlavek, John, *George Mifflin Dallas*, 21.

31. Wiltse, Charles M., *John C. Calhoun; 1782–1828*, 282–84.

32. Dangerfield, George, *The Era of Good Feeling*, 237–39.

33. Remini, Robert V., *Andrew Jackson*, Vol. 3 (Baltimore, MD: The Johns Hopkins University Press, 1984), 479.

34. Dangerfield, George, *The Era of Good Feeling*, 132–36.

35. Smith, Elbert, *Magnificent Missourian* (Philadelphia, PA: J. B. Lippincott, 1958), 93–94.

36. Newsome, Albert Ray, *The Presidential Election of 1824*, 131–33.

37. Livermore Jr., Shaw, *The Twilight of Federalism*, 143–45.

38. "Jackson to James Monroe October 23, 1816" in *The Papers of Andrew Jackson*, Vol. 25, eds. Harold Moser, David Hoth, and George Hoemann (Knoxville, TN: The University of Tennessee Press, 1994), 69–70.

39. "Jackson to James Monroe November 12, 1816" in *The Papers of Andrew Jackson*, Vol. 25, eds. Harold Moser, David Hoth and George Hoemann (Knoxville, TN: The University of Tennessee Press, 1994), 75.

40. "Jackson to James Monroe January 6, 1817" in *The Papers of Andrew Jackson*, Vol. 25, eds. Harold Moser, David Hoth, and George Hoemann (Knoxville, TN: The University of Tennessee Press, 1994), 81.

41. "Jackson to James Monroe January 6, 1817," 81.

42. "Jackson to James Monroe January 6, 1817," 81.

43. Newsome, Albert Ray, *The Presidential Election of 1824* (Chapel Hill, NC: University of North Carolina Press 1939), 70–71.

44. Ibid., 87–90.

45. Sibley, Joel, *Martin van Buren* (Lanham, MD: Rowman & Littlefield, 2002), 39–41.

46. Kolodny, Robin, "The Several Elections of 1824," *Congress and the Presidency Fall 1996*, Vol. 23, 139, 143–44.

47. Newsome, Albert Ray, *The Presidential Election of 1824*, 105–6.

48. Walters Jr., Raymond, *Albert Gallatin* (Pittsburgh, PA: University of Pittsburgh Press, 1969), 59–63.

49. Dungan, Nicholas, *Gallatin* (New York: New York University Press, 2010), 137–38.

50. Remini, Robert, *Andrew Jackson*, Vol. 2 (Baltimore, MD: The Johns Hopkins University Press, 1981), 82.

51. Kolodny, Robin, "The Several Elections of 1824," *Congress and the Presidency Fall 1996*, Vol. 23, 151.

52. Ibid., 164.

53. Ibid., 150–51.

54. Remini, Robert, *Andrew Jackson*, Vol. 2 (Baltimore, MD: The Johns Hopkins University Press, 1981), 83.

55. Remini, Robert, *Martin van Buren* (New York: Columbia University Press, 1951), 75.

56. Remini, Robert, *Martin van Buren*, 76–77.

57. Ibid., 77–80.

58. Remini, Robert, *Henry Clay* (New York: W.W. Norton, 1993), 249.

59. Remini, Robert, *Henry Clay* (New York: W.W. Norton, 1991), 263-265

60. Nagel, Paul, *John Quincy Adams* (Cambridge, MA: Harvard University Press, 1993), 297.

61. Livermore Jr., Shaw, *The Twilight of Federalism* (Princeton, NJ: Princeton University Press, 1962), 107–9.

62. Remini, Robert, *Henry Clay* 266–67.

63. Ibid., 251.

Chapter 8

1. Holt, Michael, *The Disputed Presidential Election of 1876* (Lawrence, KS: University of Kansas Press, 2008), 23.

2. Simpson, Brooks, *The Political Education of Henry Adams* (Columbia, SC.: University of South Carolina Press, 1996), 85.

3. Webb, Ross, *Benjamin Helm Bristow* (Lexington, KY: University of Kentucky Press, 1969), 226–30.

4. Trefousse, Hans, *Carl Schurz* (Knoxville, TN: University of Tennessee Press, 1982), 94–95.

5. Hamburger, Philip, *Separation of Church and State* (Cambridge, MA: Harvard University Press, 2002), 297.

6. Ibid., 322–23.

7. Ibid., 325–26.

8. Holt, Michael, *The Disputed Presidential Election of 1876* (Lawrence, KS: University of Kansas Press, 2008), 101.

9. Ibid., 104.

10. Flick, Alexander, *Samuel Jones Tilden* (Westport, CT: Greenwood Press, 1973), 82–85.

11. Ibid., 267–68.

12. Holt, Michael, *The Disputed Presidential Election of 1876* (Lawrence, KS: University of Kansas Press, 2008), 115.

13. Ibid., 105–6.

14. Flick, Alexander, *Samuel Jones Tilden* (Westport, CT: Greenwood Press, 1973), 283–84.

15. Holt, Michael, *The Disputed Presidential Election of 1876* (Lawrence, KS: University of Kansas Press, 2008), 111.

16. Flick, Alexander, *Samuel Jones Tilden* (Westport, CT: Greenwood Press, 1973), 286–90.

17. Holt, Michael, *The Disputed Presidential Election of 1876* (Lawrence, KS: University of Kansas Press, 2008), 131–32.

18. "This Week," *Nation*, July 6, 1876, 1.

19. "The Week," *Nation*, July 6, 1876, 4.

20. "The Week," *Nation*, July 6, 1876, 1.

21. "The Week," *Nation*, July 6, 1876, 5.

22. Muzzey, David Saville, *James Blaine* (New York: Dodd, Mead, 1935), 100–101.

23. Ibid., 77–79.

24. Ibid., 81.

25. Foulke, William Dudley, *The Life of Oliver P. Morton* (Indianapolis, IN: Bowen-Merrill, 1898), 388.

26. Ibid., 389–90.

27. Ibid., 398–99.

28. Holt, Michael, *The Disputed Presidential Election of 1876* (Lawrence, KS: University of Kansas Press, 2008) 82–83.

29. Hoogenboom, Ari, *Rutherford Hayes* (Lawrence, KS: University Press of Kansas, 1995), 211–13.

30. Ibid., 226–27.

31. Ibid., 258–60.

32. Holt, Michael, *The Disputed Presidential Election of 1876* (Lawrence, KS: University of Kansas Press, 2008), 84–85.

33. Larson, Orville, *American Infidel* (New York: The Citadel Press, 1962), 119–20.

34. Foulke, William Dudley, *The Life of Oliver P. Morton* (Indianapolis, IN: Bowen-Merrill, 1898), 400.

35. Pomerantz, Sidney "Election of 1876" in History of American Presidential Elections eds, Arthur Schlesinger and Fred Israel (New York: Chelsea House, 1971), 1398.

36. Bradley, Erwin, *Simon Cameron* (Philadelphia, PA: University of Pennsylvania Press, 1966), 371–73.

37. Muzzey, David Saville, *James Blaine* (New York: Dodd, Mead, 1935), 111–12.

38. Muzzey, David Saville, *James Blaine* (New York: Dodd, Mead, 1935), 111; Holt, Michael, *The Disputed Presidential Election of 1876* (Lawrence, KS: University of Kansas Press, 2008), 93–94.

39. Simpson, Brooks *The Political Education of Henry Adams* (Columbia: University of South Carolina Press, 1996), 98-99

40. George, Mary Karl, *Zachariah Chandler* (Lansing, MI: Michigan State University Press, 1969), 241–43.

41. "The Week," *Nation*, August 3, 1876, 81.

42. George, Mary Karl, *Zachariah Chandler* (Lansing, MI: Michigan State University Press), 253.

43. Holt, Michael, *The Disputed Presidential Election of 1876* (Lawrence, KS: University of Kansas Press, 2008), 123–24.

44. "The Week," *Nation*, July 20, 1876, 33.

45. Holt, Michael, *The Disputed Presidential Election of 1876*, 135–37.

46. Ibid., 139–41.

47. Ibid., 142–43.

48. Ibid., 144–45.

49. Larson, Orville, *American Infidel* (New York: The Citadel Press, 1962), 121–22.

50. Flick, Alexander, *Samuel Jones Tilden* (Westport, CT: Greenwood Press, 1973), 276–77.

51. Holt, Michael, *The Disputed Presidential Election of 1876* (Lawrence, KS: University of Kansas Press, 2008), 145–46.

52. "This Week," *Nation*, October 12, 1875, 220.

53. George, Mary Karl, *Zachariah Chandler* (Lansing, MI: Michigan State University Press), 251.

54. Larson, Orville, *American Infidel* (New York: The Citadel Press, 1962), 120–21.

55. Hamburger, Philip, *Separation of Church and State* (Cambridge, MA: Harvard University Press, 2002), 129–30.

56. "This Week," *Nation*, July 20, 1876, 34–35.

57. Holt, Michael, *The Disputed Presidential Election of 1876* (Lawrence, KS: University of Kansas Press, 2008), 153.

58. Flick, Alexander, *Samuel Jones Tilden* (Westport, CT: Greenwood Press, 1973), 317.

59. Holt, Michael, *The Disputed Presidential Election of 1876* (Lawrence, KS: University of Kansas Press, 2008), 160.

60. Ibid., 162.

61. Keneally, Thomas, *American Scoundrel* (New York: Doubleday 2009), 287–89.

62. See, Keneally, and Thomas Reeves, *Gentleman Boss* (New York: American Political Biography Press, 1991).

63. Polakoff, Keith Ian, *The Politics of Inertia* (Baton Rouge, LA: Louisiana State University Press, 1973), 201–3.

64. West, Jerry, *The Bloody South Carolina Election of 1876* (Jefferson, NC: McFarland Press, 2011), 78–79.

65. "This Week," *Nation*, October 12, 1876, 220–21.

66. Rubin III, Hyman, *South Carolina Scalawags* (Columbia, SC: University of South Carolina Press, 2066),

67. West, Jerry, *The Bloody South Carolina Election of 1876* (Jefferson, NC: McFarland Press, 2011), 112–13.

68. Rubin III, Hyman, *South Carolina Scalawags* (Columbia, SC: University of South Carolina Press, 2066), 108–9.

69. West, Jerry, *The Bloody South Carolina Election of 1876* (Jefferson, NC: McFarland Press, 2011), 115–16.

70. "This Week," *Nation*, November 30, 1876, 319–20.

71. Zuczek, Richard, *State of Rebellion* (Columbia, SC: University of South Carolina Press, 2009), 194–96.

72. West, Jerry, *The Bloody South Carolina Election of 1876* (Jefferson, NC: McFarland Press, 2011), 130–31.

73. "This Week," *Nation*, December 21, 1876, 361.

74. Murphy, James, *Lucius Lamar Pragmatic Patriot* (Baton Rouge, LA: Louisiana State Press, 1973), 164–65.

75. Andrew Jr., Rod, *Wade Hampton* (Chapel Hill, NC: University of North Carolina Press, 2008), 417.

76. West, Jerry, *The Bloody South Carolina Election of 1876* (Jefferson, NC: McFarland Press, 2011), 143.

77. Morris Jr., Roy, *Fraud of the Century* (New York: Simon and Schuster, 2004), 146–48.

78. Polakoff, Keith Ian, *The Politics of Inertia* (Baton Rouge, LA: Louisiana State University Press, 1973), 217.

79. Shofner, Jerrell, *Nor is it over Yet* (Gainesville, FL: University of Florida Press, 1974), 320–21.

80. Ibid., 320–21.

81. Polakoff, Keith Ian, *The Politics of Inertia* (Baton Rouge, LA: Louisiana State University Press, 1973), 216–17.

82. Rehnquist, William, *Centennial Crisis* (New York: Vintage, 2005), 104–5.

83. Tunnell, Ted, *Edge of the Sword* (Baton Rouge: Louisiana State University Press, 2001), 95–97.

84. Taylor, Joe Gray, *Louisiana Reconstructed 1863–1877* (Baton Rouge, LA: LSU Press, 1974), 247–48; Twitchell, Marshall Harvey, *Carpetbagger from Vermont* (Baton Rouge, LA: LSU Press, 1989), 170–72.

85. Taylor, Joe Gray, *Louisiana Reconstructed 1863–1877* (Baton Rouge, LA: LSU Press, 1974) 239–40.

86. Ibid., 287–91.

87. Ibid., 491.

88. Flick, Alexander, *Samuel Jones Tilden* (Westport, CT: Greenwood Press, 1973), 340–41.

89. Taylor, Joe Gray, *Louisiana Reconstructed 1863–1877* (Baton Rouge, LA: LSU Press, 1974), 492.

90. Morris Jr., Roy, *Fraud of the Century* (New York: Simon and Schuster, 2004), 190–92.

91. Holt, Michael, *The Disputed Presidential Election of 1876* (Lawrence, KS: University of Kansas Press, 2008), 27–28.

92. Flick, Alexander, *Samuel Jones Tilden* (Westport, CT: Greenwood Press, 1973), 349.

93. Ibid., 347.

94. Ibid., 353–56.

95. Holt, Michael, *The Disputed Presidential Election of 1876* (Lawrence, KS: University of Kansas Press, 2008), 207–8.

96. Ibid., 208.

97. As the crisis expanded, some southerners threatened a rebellion, but under the baleful eye of General Sherman, much of the south understood the deadly consequences of taking up arms and rejected the option.

98. Holt, Michael, *The Disputed Presidential Election of 1876* (Lawrence, KS: University of Kansas Press, 2008), 223.

99. King, Willard, *David Davis* (Cambridge, MA: Harvard University Press, 1960), 292–93.

100. *United States v. Cruikshank* 92 U.S. 542 (1876).

101. Rehnquist, William, *Centennial Crisis* (New York: Vintage, 2005), 163–65.

102. Holt, Michael, *The Disputed Presidential Election of 1876* (Lawrence, KS: University of Kansas Press, 2008), 225–26.

103. Ibid., 227–28.

104. Barrows, Chester *William* Evarts (Chapel Hill: The University of North Carolina Press, 1941), 303–4.

105. Rehnquist, William, *Centennial Crisis* (New York: Vintage, 2005) 168–80.

106. Ibid., 170–72.

107. Ibid., 172–74.

108. Holt, Michael, *The Disputed Presidential Election of 1876* (Lawrence, KS: University of Kansas Press, 2008), 232–33.

109. Ibid., 203–5.

110. Flick, Alexander, *Samuel Jones Tilden* (Westport, CT: Greenwood Press, 1973), 360–61.

111. Holt, Michael, *The Disputed Presidential Election of 1876* (Lawrence, KS: University of Kansas Press, 2008), 235.

112. Woodward, Bob, *The Choice* (New York: Touchstone Books, 1997), 138–40, 150.

113. Ibid., 120, 148.

114. Jordan, David, *Roscoe Conkling of New York* (Ithaca, NY: Cornell University Press, 1971), 262–63.

115. Woodward, Bob, *The Choice* (New York: Touchstone Books, 1997), 184–85.

116. Ibid., 184–85.

117. Holt, Michael, *The Disputed Presidential Election of 1876* (Lawrence, KS: University of Kansas Press, 2008), 229–31.

118. Eckenrode, H. J, *Rutherford B. Hayes* (Port Washington, NY: Kennikat Press, 1963), 154–55.

119. Eckenrode, 105–7.

Chapter 9

1. McCullough, David, *Truman* (New York: Simon and Schuster, 1992), 244.

2. Fleming, Thomas, *The New Dealers' War* (New York: Basic Books, 2001), 399–400.

3. McCullough, David, *Truman* (New York: Simon and Schuster, 1992), 493.

4. Smith, Richard Norton, *Thomas E. Dewey and his Times* (New York: Simon and Schuster, 1982), 206.

5. Evans, Hugh, *The Hidden Campaign* (Armonk, NY: M. E. Sharpe, 2002), 76.

6. Smith, Richard Norton, *Thomas E. Dewey and his Times* (New York: Simon and Schuster, 1982), 427–29.

7. Patterson, James, *Mr. Republican* (Boston, MA: Houghton Mifflin, 1972), 438.

8. Ibid., 292–93.

9. Ibid., 385–86.

10. Smith, Richard Norton, *Thomas E. Dewey and his Times* (New York: Simon and Schuster, 1982), 408.

11. Tanenhaus, Sam, *Whittaker Chambers* (New York: Random House, 1997), 314–15.

12. Hechler, Ken, "Truman laid the Foundation for the Civil Rights Movement," in *The Civil Rights Legacy of Harry S. Truman*, ed. Raymond Geselbracht (Kirksville, MO: Truman State University Press, 2007), 55.

13. Acacia, John, *Clark Clifford* (Lexington, KY: University of Kentucky Press, 2009), 126–27.

14. Ibid., 142–44.

15. Farr, Finis, *Fair Enough* (New Rochelle, NY: Arlington House Publishers, 1975), 180.

16. Gullan, Harold, *The Upset that Wasn't* (Chicago, IL: Ivan R. Dee, 1998), 84–87.

17. Lowitt, Richard *The New Deal and the West* (Norman, OK: University of Oklahoma Press, 1984), 56–57.

18. Fleming, Thomas, *The New Dealers' War* (New York: Basic Books, 2001), 217–20.

19. Ibid., 390–92.

20. McCullough, David, *Truman* (New York: Simon and Schuster, 1992), 514–17.

21. "Third Parties," *Time*, August 9, 1948, 17.

22. White, Graham, and John Maze, *Henry A. Wallace* (Chapel Hill, NC: The University of North Carolina Press, 1995), 258–60; "The Pink Façade," *Time*, August 2, 1948 12–13.

23. Stout, David, "Leo Isacson, 86, Upset Winner of Bronx Congressional Seat," *New York Times*, September 26, 1996.

24. White, Graham, and John Maze, *Henry A. Wallace* (Chapel Hill, NC: The University of North Carolina Press, 1995), 261–62.

25. Peterson, F. Ross, *Prophet without Honor* (Lexington, KY: The University Press of Kentucky, 1974), 112–15.

26. Farr, Finis, *Fair Enough* (New Rochelle, NY: Arlington House Publishers, 1975), 188–90.

27. "Love that Man," *Time*, September 20, 1948, 27.

28. White, Graham, and John Maze, *Henry A. Wallace* (Chapel Hill, NC: The University of North Carolina Press, 1995), 278–80.

29. Ibid., 263. Stalin responded to Wallace's letter declaring he made "an open and honest attempt" at peace.

30. *Time*, August 23, 1948, 19.

31. Caro, Robert, *Master of the Senate* (New York: Alfred A. Knopf, 2003), 471–73.

32. Donaldson, Gary, *Dewey Defeats Truman* (Lexington, KY: The University Press of Kentucky, 2000), 120–21.

33. Mann, Robert, *The Walls of Jericho* (New York: Harcourt Brace, 1996), 14.

34. Ibid., 17–19.

35. Kirkendall, Richard, "Election of 1948," in *History of American Presidential Elections*, Vol. 4, eds. Arthur Schlesinger Jr. and Fred Israel (New York; Chelsea House Publishers, 1971), 3118.

36. "Tumult in Dixie," *Time*, July 26, 1948, 15–16.

37. Cohodas, Nadine, *Strom Thurmond* (New York: Simon and Schuster, 1993), 175–76.

38. Ibid., 82–83.

39. Ibid., 122–23.

40. Fredrickson, George, *A Nation Divided* (Minneapolis: Burgess Publishing, 1975), 154.

41. Cohodas, Nadine, *Strom Thurmond* (New York: Simon and Schuster, 1993), 185–86.

42. "The Pot Boils," *Time*, October 4, 1948, 22.

43. In 2010, sitting Senator Lisa Murkowski of Alaska won a write in reelection after her defeat in the Republican primary.

44. Patterson, James, *Mr. Republican* (Boston, MA: Houghton Mifflin, 1972), 406–7.

45. Smith, Richard Norton, *Thomas E. Dewey and his Times* (New York: Simon and Schuster, 1982), 491.

46. Ibid., 493.

47. Berger, Meyer "Convention Hall is Rechristened as 'the Steamboated Iron Lung.'" *New York Times*, June 25, 1948, 3.

48. Smith, Richard Norton, *Thomas E. Dewey and his Times* (New York: Simon and Schuster, 1982), 480.

49. Karabell, Zachary, *The Last Campaign* (New York: Alfred A. Knopf, 2000), 152–53.

50. Ibid., 159–60.

51. Donaldson, Gary, *Dewey Defeats Truman* (Lexington, KY: The University Press of Kentucky, 2000), 167–70.

52. Karabell, Zachary, *The Last Campaign* (New York: Alfred A. Knopf, 2000), 187–88.

53. Ibid., 186.

54.

55. "Pitched High," *Time*, September 27, 1948, 23.

56. "Line Squall," *Time*, July 26, 1948, 14.

57. "Mowing 'em Down," *Time*, September 27, 1947, 23–24.

58. "They'll Tear you Apart," *Time*, October 4, 1948, 19–20.

59. "Dogi Clegin and the West," *Time*, October 4, 1948, 21.

60. "The Real Fight," *Time*, October 25, 1948, 21.

61. "The Good Tempered Candidate," *Time*, September 27, 1948, 22.

62. Gullan, Harold *The Upset that Wasn't* (Chicago: Ivan R. Dee, 1998), 64.

63. Rosenstone, Steven, Roy Behr, and Edward Lazarus, *Third Parties in America* (Princeton, NJ: Princeton University Press, 1984), 37–43.

64. Fredrickson, George, *A Nation Divided* (Minneapolis: Burgess Publishing, 1975) 157.

65. Ibid., 159–61.

66. Ibid., 163–64.

67. Ibid., 154–55.

68. Kirkendall, Richard, "Election of 1948," in *History of American Presidential Elections*, Vol. 4, eds. Arthur Schlesinger Jr. and Fred Israel (New York: Chelsea House Publishers, 1971), 3211.

69. Ibid., 3211.

70. Karabell, Zachary, *The Last Campaign* (New York: Alfred A. Knopf, 2000), 261–62.

Chapter 10

1. The first Congress passed the 1789 Judiciary Act creating the federal court system, the federal post office, the major cabinet departments including state, treasury, war and navy, and also ratified 12 constitutional amendments—10 of which would become the Bill of Rights. The Republican Congress passed the 1862 Judiciary Act reorganizing the federal judiciary, the transcontinental railway act, the Morrill Land Grant Act, and the Homestead Act while organizing, funding, and arming the largest army in the nation's history up to that time.

2. Fleming, Thomas, The Illusion of Victory (New York: Basic Books, 2003) 9–10.

3. Ibid., 69–70.

4. Brands, H. W., *T. R: The Last Romantic* (New York: Basic Books, 1997), 751–52.

5. Gilderhus, Mark, *Diplomacy and Revolution* (Tuscon, AZ: University of Arizona Press, 1977), 2–13.

6. Link, Arthur, *The New Freedom* (Princeton, NJ: Princeton University Press, 1958), 238–41.

7. Link, Arthur, *The Struggle for Neutrality* (Princeton, NJ: Princeton University Press, 1960), 197–98.

8. Leopold, Richard, *Elihu Root and the Conservative Tradition* (Boston, MA: Little, Brown, 1954), 107.

9. Jessup, Philip, *Elihu Root* (New York: Dodd, Mead, 1938), 335.

10. Leopold, Richard, *Elihu Root and the Conservative Tradition* (Boston, MA: Little, Brown, 1954), 108–10; Jessup, Philip, *Elihu Root* (New York: Dodd, Mead, 1938), 339.

11. Jessup, Philip, *Elihu Root* (New York: Dodd, Mead, 1938), 340–41.

12. Doenecke, Justus, *Nothing Less than War* (Lexington, KY: University Press of Kentucky, 2011), 201.

13. Jessup, Philip, *Elihu Root* (New York: Dodd, Mead, 1938), 335.

14. Leopold, Richard, *Elihu Root and the Conservative Tradition* (Boston, MA: Little, Brown, 1954), 110–11.

15. Jessup, Philip, *Elihu Root* (New York: Dodd, Mead, 1938), 344–46.

16. Brands, H. W., *T. R: The Last Romantic* (New York: Basic Books, 1997), 489–95.

17. Milkis, Sidney, *Theodore Roosevelt, the Progressive Party and the Transformation of American Democracy* (Lawrence, KS: University Press of Kansas, 2009) 260–61.

18. Stratton, David, *Tempest over Teapot Dome* (Norman, OK: University of Oklahoma Press, 1998), 132–33.

19. Lovell, S. D., *The Presidential Election of 1916* (Carbondale, IL: Southern Illinois University Press, 1980), 14–15.

20. Ibid., 16–17.

21. Ibid., 20.

22. 234 U.S. 342 (1914).

23. 219 U.S. 291 (1911).

24. Bickel, Alexander, and Benno Schmidt, *The Judiciary and Responsible Government 1910–1921* (New York: Macmillan, 1985), 399.

25. Pusey, Merlo, *Charles Evans Hughes* (New York: Macmillan, 1951), 316–17.

26. Ickes, Harold, The Autobiography of a *Curmudgeon* (New York: Regnal and Hitchcock, 1943)*316.*

27. Pusey, Merlo, *Charles Evans Hughes* (New York: Macmillan, 1951), 318–19.

28. Lovell, S. D., *The Presidential Election of 1916* (Carbondale, IL: Southern Illinois University Press, 1980), 155–56.

29. Levine, Laurence, *Defender of the Faith* (Cambridge, MA: Harvard University Press, 1987), 115–16; Sixty years later another convention observer, Republican Ronald Reagan, would be called down to the podium during his party's 1976 convention. His speech galvanized party faithful and viewers but was derided by the political class and media as a swan song because of Reagan's age. Unlike Bryan who disappeared from electoral politics, Reagan used the speech to win the 1980 nomination and the presidency.

30. Ashley, LeRoy, *William Jennings Bryan* (New York: Twayne Publishing, 1987), 166–67.

31. Leinwald, Gerald, *William Jennings Bryan* (Lanham, MD: Rowman & Littlefield, 2007), 117–18.

32. Coletta, Paolo, *William Jennings Bryan Political Puritan* (Lincoln, NE: University of Nebraska Press, 1969), 40.

33. Ashley, LeRoy, *William Jennings Bryan* (New York: Twayne Publishing, 1987), 167.

34. Link, Arthur, *The Struggle for Neutrality* (Princeton, NJ: Princeton University Press, 1960), 235–37.

35. Ibid., 226–27.

36. Cooper Jr., John Milton, *Pivotal Decades* (New York: Norton, 1990), 250.

37. Pusey, Merlo, *Eugene Meyer* (New York: Alfred A. Knopf, 1974), 126–27.

38. Davis, Kenneth, *The Politics of Honor* (New York: GP Putnam & Sons, 1967), 44–45.

39. "The Week," *Nation*, January 20, 1916, 66–67.

40. Lovell, S. D., *The Presidential Election of 1916* (Carbondale, IL: Southern Illinois University Press, 1980), 48–50.

41. Pusey, Merlo, *Eugene Meyer* (New York: Alfred A. Knopf, 1974), 330.

42. Lovell, S. D., *The Presidential Election of 1916* (Carbondale, IL: Southern Illinois University Press, 1980), 130.

43. "The Disappointing Candidates," *Nation*, October 19, 1916, 367.

44. Lovell, S. D., *The Presidential Election of 1916* (Carbondale, IL: Southern Illinois University Press, 1980), 93.

45. Ibid., 100–102.

46. Tolzman, Don Heinrich, *The German-American Experience* (Amherst, NY: Humanity Books, 2000), 272–73.

47. Keller, Phyllis, *States of Belonging* (Cambridge, MA: Harvard University Press, 1979), 169.

48. Ibid., 153.

49. Lovell, S. D., *The Presidential Election of 1916* (Carbondale, IL: Southern Illinois University Press, 1980), 62–63.

50. Link, Arthur, *The Struggle for Neutrality* (Princeton, NJ: Princeton University Press, 1960), 247.

51. Pusey, Merlo, *Eugene Meyer* (New York: Alfred A. Knopf, 1974), 357.

52. "The Week," *Nation*, October 19, 1916, 368.

53. Lovell, S. D., *The Presidential Election of 1916* (Carbondale, IL: Southern Illinois University Press, 1980), 77–78.

54. Ibid., 82.

55. "The Issue of Character," *Nation*, September 14, 1916, 251.

56. Giglio, James, *H.M. Daugherty and the Politics of Expedience* (Kent, OH: Kent State University, 1978), 78–80.

57. Lower, Richard, *A Bloc of One* (Stanford, CA: Stanford University Press, 1993), 75.

58. Ibid., 81.

59. Weatherson, Michael, and Hal Bochin, *Hiram Johnson* (Lanham, MD: University Press of America, 1995), 76–77; Lower, Richard, *A Bloc of One* (Stanford, CA: Stanford University Press, 1993), 81.

60. "The Week," *Nation*, September 21, 1916, 267.

61. Lovell, S. D., *The Presidential Election of 1916* (Carbondale, IL: Southern Illinois University Press, 1980), 126–29.

62. Ibid., 150.

63. Ibid., 113–14.

64. Pusey, Merlo, *Eugene Meyer* (New York: Alfred A. Knopf, 1974), 355.

65. *Nation*, March 23, 1916, 326; Oddly enough 12 *Nation* readers spent the time and suffered expenses to send back a survey announcing they were undecided.

66. *Nation*, April 6, 1916, 375.

67. "The Result in Maine," *Nation* September 21, 1916, 271.

68. Grover Cleveland won a second presidential term in 1892 but as a challenger to the incumbent Benjamin Harrison.

69. Link, Arthur S., and William Leary. "Election of 1916." In *History of American Presidential Elections*, edited by Arthur Schlesinger Jr. and Fred Israel. Vol. 3 (New York: Chelsea House Publishers, 1971), 2345.

70. Link, Arthur S., and William, Leary, "Election of 1916," in *History of American Presidential Elections,* Vol. 3, eds. Arthur Schlesinger Jr. and Fred Israel (New York: Chelsea House Publishers, 1971), 2345; Lower, Richard, *A Bloc of One* (Stanford, CA: Stanford University Press, 1993), 86.

71. Link, Arthur S., and William Leary. "Election of 1916." In *History of American Presidential Elections,* edited by Arthur Schlesinger Jr. and Fred Israel. Vol. 3 (New York: Chelsea House Publishers, 1971), 2345.

Chapter 11

1. Holman, Hamilton, "The Election of 1848," in *The History of American Presidential Elections,* eds. Arthur Schlesinger and Fred Israel (New York: Chelsea House Publishers, 1969), 874.

2. Rayback, Joseph, *Free Soil: The Election of 1848* (Lexington, KY: University of Kentucky Press, 1970), 36.

3. Ibid., 9–10.

4. Johnson, Timothy, *Winfield Scott* (Lawrence, KS: University Press of Kansas, 1998), 154.

5. Ibid., 155–56.

6. Bauer, K. Jack, *Zachary Taylor* (Baton Rouge, LA: Louisiana State University Press, 1985), 204–5.

7. Rayback, Joseph, *Free Soil: The Election of 1848* (Lexington, KY: University of Kentucky Press, 1970), 36.

8. Bauer, K. Jack, *Zachary Taylor* (Baton Rouge, LA: Louisiana State University Press, 1985), 215–16.

9. Kirwan, Albert, *John J. Crittenden* (Lexington, KY: University of Kentucky Press, 1962), 204–5.

10. Thompson, William, *Robert Toombs* (Baton Rouge, LA: Louisiana State University Press, 1966), 46.

11. Bauer, K. Jack, *Zachary Taylor* (Baton Rouge, LA: Louisiana State University Press, 1985), 220.

12. Dyer, Brainerd, *Zachary Taylor* (New York: Barnes and Noble, 1967), 269.

13. Rayback, Joseph, *Free Soil: The Election of 1848* (Lexington, KY: University of Kentucky Press, 1970), 43–45.

14. Dyer, Brainerd, *Zachary Taylor* (New York: Barnes and Noble, 1967), 267.

15. Ibid., 272–74.

16. Rayback, Joseph, *Free Soil: The Election of 1848* (Lexington, KY: University of Kentucky Press, 1970), 11–12.

17. Klein, Philip, *President James Buchanan* (University Park, PA: The Pennsylvania State University Press, 1962), 196.

18. Ibid., 198–99.

19. Rayback, Joseph, *Free Soil: The Election of 1848* (Lexington, KY: University of Kentucky Press, 1970), 19–21.

20. Bauer, K. Jack, *Zachary Taylor* (Baton Rouge, LA: Louisiana State University Press, 1985), 221.

21. Rayback, Joseph, *Free Soil: The Election of 1848* (Lexington, KY: University of Kentucky Press, 1970), 31–33.

22. Ibid., 14.

23. Ibid., 16–18.

24. Klunder, William, *Lewis Cass and the Politics of Moderation* (Kent, OH: Kent State University Press, 1996), 177–78.

25. Walther, Eric, *William Loundes Yancey* (Chapel Hill, NC: University of North Carolina Press, 2006), 102.

26. Sibley, Joel, *Party over Section* (Lawrence, KS: University of Kansas Press, 2009), 50–53.

27. Rayback, Joseph, *Free Soil: The Election of 1848* (Lexington, KY: University of Kentucky Press, 1970), 120.

28. Freehling, William *The Road to Disunion* (New York: Oxford University Press, 1990), 458.

29. Klunder, William, *Lewis Cass and the Politics of Moderation* (Kent, OH: Kent State University Press, 1996), 179–80.

30. Rayback, Joseph, *Free Soil: The Election of 1848* (Lexington, KY: University of Kentucky Press, 1970), 135–36.

31. Ibid., 131–33.

32. Ibid., 139–41.

33. Sibley, Joel, *Party over Section* (Lawrence, KS: University of Kansas Press, 2009), 62; Klunder, William, *Lewis Cass and the Politics of Moderation* (Kent, OH: Kent State University Press, 1996), 188–89.

34. Klunder, William, *Lewis Cass and the Politics of Moderation* (Kent, OH: Kent State University Press, 1996), 186.

35. Rayback, Joseph, *Free Soil: The Election of 1848* (Lexington, KY: University of Kentucky Press, 1970), 191.

36. Johnson, Reinhard, *The Liberty Party* (Baton Rouge, LA: Louisiana State University Press, 2009), 80–81, 84–85.

37. Blue, Frederick, *The Free Soilers* (Champaign, IL: University of Illinois Press, 1973), 67.

38. Ibid., 76–77.

39. Ibid., 115–16.

40. Donald, David Herbert, *Charles Sumner and the Coming of the Civil War* (New York: Sourcebooks, 2009), 140.

41. Blue, Frederick, *The Free Soilers* (Champaign, IL: University of Illinois Press, 1973), 127–28.

42. Holt, Michael *The Rise and Fall of the American Whig Party* (London: Oxford University Press, 1999), 302–3.

43. Ibid., 309–10.

44. Rayback, Joseph, *Free Soil: The Election of 1848* (Lexington, KY: University of Kentucky Press, 1970), 155.

45. Remini, Robert, *Henry Clay* (New York: W.W. Norton, 1993), 704.

46. Ibid., 703.

47. Rayback, Joseph, *Free Soil: The Election of 1848* (Lexington, KY: University of Kentucky Press, 1970), 158.

48. Klunder, William, *Lewis Cass and the Politics of Moderation* (Kent, OH: Kent State University Press, 1996), 272–74.

49. Rayback, Joseph, *Free Soil: The Election of 1848* (Lexington, KY: University of Kentucky Press, 1970), 162–63.

50. Holt, Michael *The Rise and Fall of the American Whig Party* (London: Oxford University Press, 1999), 316.

51. Ibid., 318.

52. Klunder, William, *Lewis Cass and the Politics of Moderation* (Kent, OH: Kent State University Press, 1996), 270–71.

53. Holt, Michael *The Rise and Fall of the American Whig Party* (London: Oxford University Press, 1999), 324–25.

54. Ibid.328–29.

55. Rayback, Joseph, *Free Soil: The Election of 1848* (Lexington, KY: University of Kentucky Press, 1970), 258–59.

56. Holt, Michael *The Rise and Fall of the American Whig Party* (London: Oxford University Press, 1999), 351–52.

57. Ibid., 361.

58. Klunder, William, *Lewis Cass and the Politics of Moderation* (Kent, OH: Kent State University Press, 1996), 277.

59. Holt, Michael *The Rise and Fall of the American Whig Party* (London: Oxford University Press, 1999), 238–39; Rayback, Joseph, *Free Soil: The Election of 1848* (Lexington, KY: University of Kentucky Press, 1970), 239.

60. Holt, 239; Rayback, 242.

61. Sibley, Joel, *Party over Section* (Lawrence, KS: University of Kansas Press, 2009), 111–12; Rayback, Joseph, *Free Soil: The Election of 1848* (Lexington, KY: University of Kentucky Press, 1970), 241.

62. Holt, Michael *The Rise and Fall of the American Whig Party* (London: Oxford University Press, 1999), 243–44.

63. Holman, Hamilton, "The Election of 1848," in *The History of American Presidential Elections*, eds. Arthur Schlesinger and Fred Israel (New York: Chelsea House Publishers, 1969), 918.

64. Ibid., 918.

65. Ibid., 918.

66. Holt, Michael *The Rise and Fall of the American Whig Party* (London: Oxford University Press, 1999), 473–77.

67. Klunder, William, *Lewis Cass and the Politics of Moderation* (Kent, OH: Kent State University Press, 1996), 304–5.

Chapter 12

1. Peterson, Norma Lois, *The Presidencies of William Henry Harrison and John Tyler* (Lawrence, KS: University of Kansas Press, 1989), 86.

2. Hall, Claude, *Abel Upshur* (Madison, WI: The State Historical Society of Wisconsin, 1964), 207–11.

3. Brugger, Robert, *Beverley Tucker* (Baltimore, MD: The Johns Hopkins University Press, 1978), 123–24.

4. Monroe, Dan, *The Republican Vision of John Tyler* (College Station, TX: Texas A&M University Press, 2003), 174.

5. Shenton, James, *Robert John Walker* (New York: Columbia University Press, 1961), 38–39.

6. "Martin Van Buren letter on Texas Annexation," in *Historic Documents on Presidential Elections 1787–1989,* ed. Michael Nelson (Washington, DC: Congressional Quarterly Press, 1991), 183–87.

7. Remini, Robert, *Andrew Jackson,* Vol. 3 (Baltimore, MD: The Johns Hopkins Press, 1984), 498–99.

8. Peterson, Norma Lois, *The Presidencies of William Henry Harrison and John Tyler* (Lawrence, KS: University of Kansas Press, 1989), 238–39.

9. Remini, Robert, *Henry Clay* (New York: W.W. Norton, 1991), 610.

10. Holt, Michael, *The Rise and Fall of the American Whig Party* (London: Oxford University Press, 1999), 154.

11. Ibid., 160–61.

12. Remini, Robert, *Henry Clay* (New York: W.W. Norton, 1993), 612–13.

13. Ibid., 640.

14. Ibid., 638–39.

15. Clay to editors of the *Washington Daily National Intelligencer* April 17, 1844 in *The Papers of Henry Clay,* Vol. 10, ed. Melba Porter Hayes (Lexington, KY: University of Kentucky Press, 1991), 42.

16. Holt, Michael, *The Rise and Fall of the American Whig Party* (London: Oxford University Press, 1999), 173.

17. Ibid., 164–65.

18. Klunder, William, *Lewis Cass and the Politics of Moderation* (Kent, OH: Kent State University Press, 1996), 132.

19. Ibid., 136.

20. Wilson, Major, *The Presidency of Martin Van Buren* (Lawrence, KS: University Press of Kansas, 1984), 201.

21. Sellers, Charles, *James K. Polk: Jacksonian 1795–1843* (Princeton, NJ: Princeton University Press, 1957), 39–40.

22. Ibid., 312–13.

23. Wilson, Major, *The Presidency of Martin Van Buren* (Lawrence, KS: University Press of Kansas, 1984), 202.

24. Hughes, Jr., Nathaniel Chears, and Ray Stansifer Jr., *The Life and Wars of Gideon Pillow* (Chapel Hill, NC: University of North Carolina Press 1993), 21–24.

25. Shenton, James, *Robert John Walker* (New York: Columbia University Press, 1961), 44.

26. Howe, DeWolfe, ed., *The Life and Letters of George Bancroft* (New York: De Capo Press, 1970), 249–51.

27. Shenton, James, *Robert John Walker* (New York: Columbia University Press, 1961), 42–45.

28. Ibid., 44–45.

29. Meyer, Leland Winfield, *Colonel Richard M. Johnson of Kentucky* (New York: Columbia University Press, 1932), 468.

30. Garraty, John Arthur, *Silas Wright* (New York: Columbia University Press, 1949), 270–71.

31. Sellers, Charles, *James K. Polk: Jacksonian 1795–1843* (Princeton, NJ: Princeton University Press, 1957), 114–15.

32. Borneman, Walter, *Polk* (New York: Random House, 2008), 100; Hughes, Jr., Nathaniel Chears, and Ray Stansifer Jr., *The Life and Wars of Gideon Pillow* (Chapel Hill, NC: University of North Carolina Press 1993), 33.

33. Garraty, John Arthur, *Silas Wright* (New York: Columbia University Press, 1949), 273.

34. Borneman, Walter, *Polk* (New York: Random House, 2008), 105.

35. Meyer, Leland Winfield, *Colonel Richard M. Johnson of Kentucky* (New York: Columbia University Press, 1932), 470.

36. Sellers, Charles, *James K. Polk: Jacksonian 1795–1843* (Princeton, NJ: Princeton University Press, 1957), 136–37.

37. Borneman, Walter, *Polk* (New York: Random House, 2008), 96–97.

38. McCormac, Eugene, *James K. Polk* (Berkeley, CA: University of California Press, 1922), 253–54.

39. Ibid., 237–38; Kane would be rewarded for his brief appearance in the campaign when Polk appointed him as a federal district judge.

40. McCormac, Eugene, *James K. Polk*, 260.

41. Ibid., 226–27.

42. Holt, Michael, *The Rise and Fall of the American Whig Party* (London: Oxford University Press, 1999), 191–92.

43. Sellers, Charles, *James K. Polk: Jacksonian 1795–1843* (Princeton, NJ: Princeton University Press, 1957), 124.

44. McCormac, Eugene, *James K. Polk* (Berkeley, CA: University of California Press, 1922), 274–75; Sellers, Charles, *James K. Polk: Jacksonian 1795–1843* (Princeton, NJ: Princeton University Press, 1957), 112.

45. McCormac, 273; Sellers, 149.

46. Clay to Stephen Miller in *The Papers of Henry Clay*, ed. Melba Porter Hay (Lexington, KY: University of Kentucky Press 1991), 79.

47. Clay to Thomas Peters and John Jackson, July 27, 1844 in *The Papers of Henry Clay*, 91.

48. Holt, Michael, *The Rise and Fall of the American Whig Party* (London: Oxford University Press, 1999), 186–87.

49. Sellers, Charles, "Election of 1844" in *History of American Presidential Elections*, eds. Fred Israel and Arthur Schlesinger Jr. (New York: Chelsea House Publishers, 1971) 861.

Bibliography

Acacia, John, *Clark Clifford* (Lexington, KY: University of Kentucky Press, 2009).

Aitken, Jonathan, *Nixon: A Life* (London: Weidenfeld and Nicolson, 1993).

Ambrose, Stephen, *Eisenhower the President* (New York: Simon and Schuster, 1984).

Ashley, LeRoy, *William Jennings Bryan* (New York: Twayne Publishing, 1987).

Bailey, Thomas A., *Diplomatic History of the American People* (New York: Appleton-Century-Croft, 1964).

Barth, Jay, Janine Parry, and Todd Shields. "Arkansas: Non-stop Action in Post-Clinton Arkansas," in *The 2000 Presidential Election in the South*, eds. Robert Steed and Laurence Moreland (Westport, CT: Praeger, 2002).

Bass, Herbert, *I am a Democrat* (Syracuse, NY: Syracuse University Press, 1961).

Bauer, K. Jack, *Zachary Taylor* (Baton Rouge, LA: Louisiana State University Press, 1985).

Belohlavek, John, *George Mifflin Dallas* (University Park, PA: The Pennsylvania State University Press, 1977).

Bickel, Alexander, and Benno Schmidt, *The Judiciary and Responsible Government 1910–1921* (New York: MacMillan, 1985).

Blue, Frederick, *The Free Soilers* (Champaign, IL: University of Illinois Press, 1973).

Borden, Morten, *The Federalism of James Bayard* (New York: Columbia University Press, 1955).

Borneman, Walter, *Polk* (New York: Random House, 2008).

Brands, H. W., *T. R.: The Last Romantic* (New York: Basic Books, 1997).

Brodsky, Alyn, *Grover Cleveland* (New York: St. Martin's Press, 2000).

Brodsky, David, and Robert Swanbrough. "Tennessee: A Native Son Scorned," in *The 2000 Presidential Elections in the South*, eds. Robert Steed and Laurence Moreland (Westport, CT: Praeger, 2002).

Broussard, James, *The Southern Federalists* (Baton Rouge, LA: Louisiana State University Press, 1948).

Brugger, Robert, *Beverley Tucker* (Baltimore, MD: Johns Hopkins University Press, 1978).

Burns, James McGregor, and Georgia Sorsenson, *Dead Center* (New York: Scribner, 2001).

Bush, George W., *Decision Points* (New York: Crown Publishers, 2010).

Caesar, James, and Andrew Busch, *The Perfect Tie* (Lanham, MD: Rowman & Littlefield Publishers, 2001).

Calhoun, Charles, *Minority Victory* (Lawrence, KS: University Press of Kansas, 2008).

Campbell, James E. "The Curious and Close Presidential Campaign of 2000," in *America's Choice,* ed. William Crotty (Boulder, CO: Westview Press, 2001).

Caro, Robert, *Master of the Senate* (New York: Vintage, 2003).

Caro, Robert, *The Passage of Power* (New York: Knopf, 2012).

Carty, Thomas, *A Catholic in the White House* (New York: Palgrave- Macmillan, 2004).

Casey, Shawn, *The Making of a Catholic President* (London: Oxford University Press, 2004).

Clay, Henry. The Papers of Henry Clay, edited by Melba Porter Hayes. Vol. 10 (Lexington, KY: University of Kentucky Press, 1991).

Cohodas, Nadine, *Strom Thurmond* (New York: Simon and Schuster, 1993).

Coletta, Paolo, *William Jennings Bryan Political Puritan* (Lincoln, NE: University of Nebraska Press, 1969).

Crawford, J. B., *The Credit Mobilier of America, its Origins and History* (Boston, MA: C. W. Calkins, 1880).

Croly, Herbert, *Marcus Alonzo Hanna* (New York: Macmillan, 1912).

Cunningham, Noble. "Election of 1800." In *History of American Presidential Elections,* edited by Arthur Schlesinger Jr. and Fred Israel. Vol. 1 (New York: Chelsea House Publishers, 1971).

Dallek, Robert, *Lone Star Rising* (New York: Oxford University Press, 1992).

Dangerfield, George, *The Era of Good Feeling* (New York: Harcourt Brace, 1952).

Davis, Kenneth, *The Politics of Honor* (New York: GP Putnam & Sons, 1967).

Dinnerstein, Leonard. "Election of 1880," in *The History of American Presidential Elections,* eds. Arthur Schlesinger and Fred Israel (New York: Chelsea House Publishers, 1971).

Doenecke, Justus, *Nothing Less than War* (Lexington, KY: University Press of Kentucky, 2011).

Donaldson, Gary, *Dewey Defeats Truman* (Lexington KY: The University Press of Kentucky, 2000).

Dover, E. D., *Missed Opportunity* (Westport, CT: Praeger, 2002).

Dungan, Nicholas, *Gallatin* (New York: New York University Press, 2010).

Dyer, Brainerd, *Zachary Taylor* (New York: Barnes and Noble, 1967).

Ellis, Richard, *The Jeffersonian Crisis* (New York: Oxford University Press, 1971).

Evans, Hugh, *The Hidden Campaign* (Armonk, NY: M. E. Sharpe, 2002).

Farr, Finis, *Fair Enough* (New Rochelle, NY: Arlington House Publishers, 1975).

Farrell, John, *Tip O'Neill and the Democratic Century* (Boston, MA: Little, Brown, 2001).

Fleming Jr., Dan B., *Kennedy v. Humphrey, West Virginia, 1960* (Jefferson, NC: McFarland, 1992).

Fleming, Thomas, *The Illusion of Victory* (New York: Basic Books, 2003).

Fleming, Thomas, *The New Dealers' War* (New York: Basic Books, 2001).

Flick, Alexander, *Samuel Jones Tilden* (Westport, CT: Greenwood Press, 1973).

Frady, Marshall, *Billy Graham* (Boston, MA: Little, Brown, 1979).

Francovic, Kathleen, and Monika McDermott. "Public Opinion in the 2000 Election," in *The Election of 2000,* ed. Gerald Pomper (New York: Chatham House Publishing, 2000).

Freehling, William, *The Road to Disunion* (New York: Oxford University Press, 1990).

Freidenberg, Robert. "The 2000 Presidential Debates," in *The 2000 Presidential Campaign,* ed. Robert Denton Jr. (Boulder, CO: Praeger, 2002).

Gage, Leland, *William Boyd Allison* (Iowa City, IA: State Historical Society of Iowa, 1956).

Garraty, John Arthur, *Silas Wright* (New York: Columbia University Press, 1949).

Garvey, Gerald. "False Promises: The NPR in Historical Perspective," in *Inside the Reinvention,* eds. John DiIulio and Donald Kettl (Washington, DC: Brookings Institution Press, 1995).

Germond, Jack, and Jules Witcover, *Whose Broad Stripes and Bright Stars?* (New York: Warner Books, 1989).

Gifford, Laura Jane, "Dixie is no Longer in the Bag," *The Journal of Policy History* 19 (2007) 208.

Giglio, James, *H. M. Daugherty and the Politics of Expedience* (Kent, OH: Kent State University, 1978).

Gilderhus, Mark, *Diplomacy and Revolution* (Tuscon, AZ: University of Arizona Press, 1977).

Gillman, Howard, *The Votes that Counted* (Chicago, IL: University of Chicago Press, 2001).

Gresham, Matilda, *Life of Walter Quentin Gresham,* Vol. 2 (Chicago, IL: Rand McNally, 1919).

Gullan, Harold, *The Upset that Wasn't* (Chicago, IL: Ivan R. Dee, 1998).

Hall, Claude, *Abel Upshur* (Madison, WI: The State Historical Society of Wisconsin, 1964).

Hechler, Ken. "Truman laid the Foundation for the Civil Rights Movement," in *The Civil Rights Legacy of Harry S. Truman,* ed. Raymond Geselbracht (Kirksville, MO: Truman State University Press, 2007).

Herrnson, Paul S. "The Congressional Elections," in *The Election of 2000,* ed. Gerald Pomper (New York: Chatham House Publishing, 2000).

Hirshson, Stanley, *The White Tecumseh* (New York: John Wiley and Sons, 1997).

Holman, Hamilton. "The Election of 1848," in *The History of American Presidential Elections,* eds. Arthur Schlesinger and Fred Israel (New York: Chelsea House Publishers, 1969).

Holt, Michael, *The Rise and Fall of the American Whig Party* (London: Oxford University Press, 1999).

Howe, DeWolfe, ed., *The Life and Letters of George Bancroft* (New York: De Capo Press, 1970).

Isenberg, Nancy, *Fallen Founder* (New York: Viking Adult, 2007).

Jackson, Carlton, *Presidential Vetoes* (Athens, GA: University of Georgia Press, 1945).

"Jackson to James Monroe October 23, 1816." In *The Papers of Andrew Jackson,* edited by Harold Moser, David Hoth, and George Hoemann. Vol. 25 (Knoxville, TN: The University of Tennessee Press, 1994).

Jamieson, Kathleen Jamieson, *Packaging the Presidency* (New York: Oxford University Press, 1984).

Jeffers, H. Paul, *An Honest President* (New York: Perennial, 2000).

Jenkins, Philip, *The New Anti Catholicism* (London: Oxford University Press, 2003).

Jessup, Philip, *Elihu Root* (New York: Dodd, Mead, 1938).

Johnson, Reinhard, *The Liberty Party* (Baton Rouge, LA: Louisiana State University Press, 2009).

Jordan, David, *Roscoe Conkling of New York* (Ithaca, NY: Cornell University Press, 1971).

Jordan, David, *Winfield Scott Hancock* (Bloomington, IN: Indiana University Press, 1988).

Johnson, Timothy, *Winfield Scott* (Lawrence, KS: University Press of Kansas, 1998).

Kallina, Edward, *Courthouse over the White House* (Orlando, FL: University of Central Florida Press, 1988).

Kallina Jr., Edmund, *Kennedy v. Nixon* (Gainesville, FL: University of Florida Press, 2010).

Karabell, Zachary, *The Last Campaign* (New York: Alfred A. Knopf, 2000).

Kehl, James, *Boss Rule in the Gilded Age* (Pittsburgh, PA: University of Pittsburgh Press, 1981).

Keller, Phyllis, *States of Belonging* (Cambridge, MA: Harvard University Press, 1979).

Kirkendall, Richard. "Election of 1948." In *History of American Presidential Elections,* edited by Arthur Schlesinger Jr. and Fred Israel. Vol. 4 (New York: Chelsea House Publishers, 1971).

Kirwan, Albert, *John J. Crittenden* (Lexington, KY: University of Kentucky Press, 1962).

Klein, Philip, *President James Buchanan* (University Park, PA: The Pennsylvania State University Press, 1962).

Klein, Philip, and Ari Hoogenboom, *A History of Pennsylvania* (University Park, PA: The Penn State University Press, 1973).

Klunder, William, *Lewis Cass and the Politics of Moderation* (Kent, OH: Kent State University Press, 1996).

Kolodny, Robin, "The Several Elections of 1824," in *Congress and the Presidency.* Vol. 23, 139. Fall 1996.

Krause, Sidney, *Televised Presidential Debates and Public Policy* (Mahweh, NJ: Lawrence Erlbaum Associates Publishers, 2000).

Lamers, William, *The Edge of Glory* (Baton Rouge, LA: Louisiana State University Press, 1999).

Leinwald, Gerald, *William Jennings Bryan* (Lanham, MD: Rowman & Littlefield, 2007).

Leopold, Richard, *Elihu Root and the Conservative Tradition* (Boston, MA: Little, Brown, 1954).

Levine, Laurence, *Defender of the Faith* (Cambridge, MA: Harvard University Press, 1987).

Lightner, Otto, *A History of Business Depressions* (New York: Benjamin Franklin Press, 1970).

Link, Arthur, *The New Freedom* (Princeton, NJ: Princeton University Press, 1958).

Link, Arthur, *The Struggle for Neutrality* (Princeton, NJ: Princeton University Press, 1960).

Link, Arthur S., and William Leary. "Election of 1916." In *History of American Presidential Elections*, edited by Arthur Schlesinger Jr. and Fred Israel. Vol. 3 (New York: Chelsea House Publishers, 1971).

Livermore Jr., Shaw, *The Twilight of Federalism* (Princeton, NJ: Princeton University Press, 1962).

Lovell, S. D., *The Presidential Election of 1916* (Carbondale, IL: Southern Illinois University Press, 1980).

Lower, Richard, *A Bloc of One* (Stanford, CA: Stanford University Press, 1993).

Lowitt, Richard, The New Deal and the West (Norman, OK: University of Oklahoma Press, 1984).

Malone, Dumas, *Jefferson and the Ordeal of Liberty* (Boston, MA: Little, Brown, 1962).

Mann, Robert, *The Walls of Jericho* (New York: Harcourt Brace, 1996).

"Martin Van Buren letter on Texas annexation," in *Historic Documents on Presidential Elections 1787–1989*, ed. Michael Nelson (Washington, DC: Congressional Quarterly Press, 1991).

Massie, Robert K., *Dreadnought* (New York: Ballantine Books, 1991).

McConnell, Stewart, *Glorious Contentment* (Chapel Hill, NC: The University of North Carolina Press, 1992).

McCormac, Eugene, *James K. Polk* (Berkeley, CA: University of California Press, 1922).

McCullough, David, *Truman* (New York: Simon and Schuster, 1992).

Merrill, Horace, *Bourbon Leader* (Boston, MA: Little, Brown, 1957).

Merzer, Martin, *The Miami Herald Report* (New York: St. Martin's Press, 2001).

Meyer, Leland Winfield, *Colonel Richard M. Johnson of Kentucky* (New York: Columbia University Press, 1932).

Milkis, Sidney, *Theodore Roosevelt, the Progressive Party and the Transformation of American Democracy* (Lawrence, KS: University Press of Kansas, 2009).

Miller, John, *Crisis in Freedom: the Alien and Sedition Acts* (Boston, MA: Little, Brown, 1951).

Mitchell, Stewart, *Horatio Seymour of New York* (Cambridge, MA: Harvard University Press, 1938).

Mooney, Chase, *William H. Crawford* (Lexington, KY: University Press of Kentucky, 1974).

Monroe, Dan, *The Republican Vision of John Tyler* (College Station, TX: Texas A&M University Press, 2003).

Morris, Roger, *Richard Milhous Nixon* (New York: Henry Holt, 1990).

Muzzey, David, *James G. Blaine* (New York: Dodd, Mead, 1935).

Nagel, Paul, *John Quincy Adams* (Cambridge, MA: Harvard University Press, 1993).

Nevins, Allen, *A Study in Courage* (New York: Dodd, Mead, 1938).

Newsome, Albert Ray, *The Presidential Election of 1824* (Chapel Hill, NC: University of North Carolina Press, 1939).

Newton, Jim, *Eisenhower* (New York: Doubleday, 2011).

Niven, John, *Martin Van Buren* (New York: Oxford University Press, 1983).

Novotny, Patrick, "John F. Kennedy, the 1960 Election and Georgia's Unpledged Electors in the Electoral College," in *Georgia Historical Quarterly* 88 (Fall, 2004).

O'Neill, Thomas, and William Novak, *Man of the House* (New York: Random House, 1987).

Patterson, James, *Mr. Republican* (Boston, MA: Houghton Mifflin, 1972).

Perret, Geoffrey, *Eisenhower* (New York: Random House, 1999).

Peskin, Allan, *Garfield* (Kent, OH: Kent State University Press, 1999).

Peterson, F. Ross, *Prophet without Honor* (Lexington, KY: The University Press of Kentucky, 1974).

Peterson, Merrill, *Thomas Jefferson and the New Nation* (New York: Oxford University Press, 1970).

Peterson, Norma Lois, *The Presidencies of William Henry Harrison and John Tyler* (Lawrence, KS: University of Kansas Press, 1989).

Posner, Richard, *Breaking the Deadlock* (Princeton, NJ: Princeton University Press, 2001).

Pusey, Merlo, *Eugene Meyer* (New York: Alfred A. Knopf, 1974).

Rayback, Joseph, *Free Soil: The Election of 1848* (Lexington, KY: University of Kentucky Press, 1970).

Reeves, Thomas, *A Question of Character* (New York: Free Press, 1991).

Reeves, Thomas, *Gentleman Boss* (New York: Alfred Knopf, 1975).

Remini, Robert, *Andrew Jackson*, Vol. 2 (Baltimore, MD: The Johns Hopkins University Press, 1981).

Remini, Robert, *Andrew Jackson*, Vol. 3 (Baltimore, MD: The Johns Hopkins Press, 1984).

Remini, Robert, *Henry Clay* (New York: W.W. Norton, 1991).

Remini, Robert, *Martin van Buren* (New York: Columbia University Press, 1951).

Robertson, David, *Sly and Able* (New York: W.W. Norton, 1994).

Rorabaugh, W., *The Real Making of the President* (Lawrence, KS: University Press of Kansas, 2009).

Rosenstone, Steven, Roy Behr, and Edward Lazarus, *Third Parties in America* (Princeton, NJ: Princeton University Press, 1984).

Saletan, William, "The Gary Bauer Scandal," *Slate* (October 1, 1999).

Schachner, Nathan, *Aaron Burr* (New York: A. S. Barnes, 1971).

Schroeder, Alan, *Presidential Debates* (New York: Columbia University Press, 2000).

Shaw, Daron, *The Race to 270* (Chicago, IL: University of Chicago Press, 2006).

Sellers, Charles, *James K. Polk: Jacksonian 1795–1843* (Princeton, NJ: Princeton University Press, 1957).

Sharp, James Roger, *The Deadlocked Election of 1800* (Lawrence, KS: University Press of Kansas, 2010).

Shenton, James, *Robert John Walker* (New York: Columbia University Press, 1961).

Shepard, Alicia, "A Late Breaking Campaign Skeleton," *American Journalism Review* (December 2000).

Sibley, Joel, *Martin van Buren* (Lanham, MD: Rowman & Littlefield, 2002).

Sibley, Joel, *Party over Section* (Lawrence, KS: University of Kansas Press, 2009).

Sievers, Harry J., *Benjamin Harrison, Hoosier Statesman* (Newtown, CT: American Political Biography, 1997).

Smith, Elbert, *Magnificent Missourian* (Philadelphia, PA: J. B. Lippincott, 1958).

Smith, Hedrick, *The Power Game* (New York: Ballantine, 1988).

Smith, Jean, *Edward Grant* (New York: Simon and Schuster, 2001).

Smith, Richard Norton, *Thomas E. Dewey and his Times* (New York: Simon and Schuster, 1982).

Smith, Willard, *Schuyler Colfax* (Indianapolis, IN: Indiana Historical Bureau, 1957).

Sorenson, Theodore. "Election of 1960." In *History of American Presidential Elections*, edited by Fred Israel and Arthur Schlesinger Jr. Vol. 4 (New York: Chelsea House Publishers, 1971).

"South Carolina in the Presidential Election of 1800," *American Historical Review* IV (October 1898).

Spitzer, Robert, *The Presidential Veto* (Albany, NY: SUNY Press, 1988).

Stewart III, Charles. "Lessons from the Post Civil War Era," in *The Politics of Divided Government*, eds. Gary Cox and Samuel Kernell (Boulder, CO: Westview Press, 1991).

Stratton, David, *Tempest over Teapot Dome* (Norman, OK: University of Oklahoma Press, 1998).

Swisher, Carl Brent, *Stephen Field* (Washington, DC: Brookings Institution, 1930).

Syrett, Harold, ed., *The Papers of Alexander Hamilton: July 1800-April 1802* (New York: Columbia University Press, 1977).

Tanenhaus, Sam, *Whittaker Chambers* (New York: Random House, 1997).

Tansill, Charles, *The Congressional Career of Thomas Bayard* (Washington, DC: Georgetown University Press, 1946).

Tansill, Charles, *The Foreign Policy of Thomas Bayard* (Fordham, NY: Fordham University Press, 1940).

Taylor, Joe Gray, *Louisiana Reconstructed* (Baton Rouge, LA: Louisiana State University Press, 1974).

Thompson, William, *Robert Toombs* (Baton Rouge, LA: Louisiana State University Press, 1966).

Tolzman, Don Heinrich, *The German-American Experience* (Amherst, NY: Humanity Books, 2000).

Van Der Linden, Frank, *The Turning Point* (Washington, DC: Robert Luce, 1962).

Walters Jr., Raymond, *Albert Gallatin* (Pittsburgh, PA: University of Pittsburgh Press, 1969).

Walther, Eric, *William Loundes Yancey* (Chapel Hill, NC: University of North Carolina Press, 2006).

Watkins, William, *Reclaiming the American Revolution* (New York: Palgrave Macmillan, 2004).

Weatherson, Michael, and Hal Bochin, *Hiram Johnson* (Lanham, MD: University Press of America, 1995).

Weisberg, Jacob, "The Heresies of Pat Buchanan," *The New Republic* 203 (October 22, 1990).

Weisberger, Bernard, *America Afire* (New York: William Morrow, 2000).

Welch Jr., Richard, *The Presidencies of Grover Cleveland* (Lawrence, KS: University of Kansas Press, 1988).

Wesser, Robert. "Election of 1888," in *History of American Presidential Elections,* eds. Fred Israel and Arthur Schlesinger Jr. (New York: Chelsea House Publishers, 1971).

White, Graham, and John Maze, *Henry A. Wallace* (Chapel Hill, NC: The University of North Carolina Press, 1995).

White, Theodore, *The Making of the President 1960* (New York: Atheneum Publishers, 1988).

White, Theodore, The Making of the President 1972 (New York: Atheneum Publishers, 1973).

Wilson, Major, *The Presidency of Martin Van Buren* (Lawrence, KS: University Press of Kansas, 1984).

Wiltse, Charles M., *John C. Calhoun: 1782–1828* (New York: Russell and Russell, 1944).

Woodward, Bob, *The Choice* (New York: Touchstone books, 1997).

Zahriser, Marvin, *Charles Cotesworth Pinckney* (Chapel Hill, NC: The University of North Carolina Press, 1967).

Index

About the Author

DOUGLAS CLOUATRE, PhD, is a political science and history instructor who writes on the Supreme Court and the American presidency. His published works include *Presidents and Their Justices* and contributions to *The Leviathan's Choice: Capital Punishment in the 21st Century.*